LEARNING TO KNEEL

Modernist Latitudes

Modernist Latitudes
Jessica Berman and Paul Saint-Amour, Editors

Modernist Latitudes aims to capture the energy and ferment of modernist studies by continuing to open up the range of forms, locations, temporalities, and theoretical approaches encompassed by the field. The series celebrates the growing latitude ("scope for freedom of action or thought") that this broadening affords scholars of modernism, whether they are investigating little-known works or revisiting canonical ones. Modernist Latitudes will pay particular attention to the texts and contexts of those latitudes (Africa, Latin America, Australia, Asia, Southern Europe, and even the rural United States) that have long been misrecognized as ancillary to the canonical modernisms of the global North.

COLUMBIA UNIVERSITY PRESS   New York

CARRIE J. PRESTON

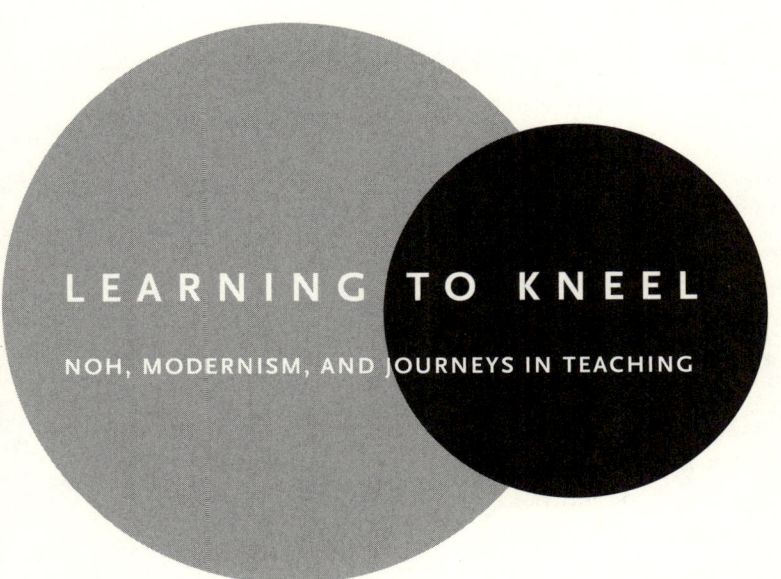

LEARNING TO KNEEL

NOH, MODERNISM, AND JOURNEYS IN TEACHING

COLUMBIA UNIVERSITY PRESS

PUBLISHERS SINCE 1893

NEW YORK   CHICHESTER, WEST SUSSEX

CUP.COLUMBIA.EDU

Copyright © 2016 Columbia University Press

Library of Congress Cataloging-in-Publication Data
Names: Preston, Carrie J., author.
Title: Learning to kneel : noh, modernism, and journeys in teaching / Carrie J. Preston.
Description: New York : Columbia University Press, 2016. | Series: Modernist latitudes |
    Includes bibliographical references and index.
Identifiers: LCCN 2015050685 | ISBN 9780231166508 (cloth : alk. paper)
Subjects: LCSH: Nåo—History. | Nåo plays—Appreciation—Europe. | European
    literature—20th century—History and criticism. | European literature—Japanese
    influences. | Modernism (Literature) | Acting—Study and teaching—Japan. |
    Nåo—Influence.
Classification: LCC PN2924.5.N6 P84 2016 | DDC 792.0952—dc23
LC record available at http://lccn.loc.gov/2015050685

c 10 9 8 7 6 5 4 3 2 1

COVER IMAGE: DANCER MICHIO ITO AS "THE HAWK" IN W. B. YEATS'S PLAY, "AT THE HAWK'S
WELL," 1916. MAKER: ALVIN LANGDON COBURN © GEORGE EASTMAN HOUSE,
INTERNATIONAL MUSEUM OF PHOTOGRAPHY AND FILM (DIGITAL POSITIVE FROM
NITRATE ROLLFILM NEGATIVE)
COVER DESIGN: DEREK THORNTON/FACEOUT STUDIOS

CONTENTS

6. Trouble with Titles and Directors:
   Benjamin Britten and William Plomer's *Curlew River*
   and Samuel Beckett's *Footfalls/Pas* 203

   Coda 243

PREFACE

Learning to Kneel tells the story of the fascination that Japanese noh drama held for European and American artists of the early twentieth century—and for me studying noh precisely a century after it was introduced to the artistic movement called "modernism." As I took lessons in noh chant, dance, and drumming; began writing plays based on noh models; and choreographed dances with gestures toward noh movement, I realized I was replicating many of the stories typically told about how modernist artists learned about noh. These stories usually include a pedagogical scene in which "Western" students of noh, like me, become captivated by the ancient form of theater and by their teachers and collaborators in the transnational lesson. We train, study, translate, adapt, perform, and ultimately teach something we call noh, usually with some recognition that we are failing our teachers. We misunderstand aspects of the noh theater and its history or find ourselves using noh to teach aesthetic or political lessons other than those we intend. We sometimes exaggerate our knowledge, determine we hate studying noh, decide we miss it too much, and return more or less humbly for more training. Scholars of cultures call the experience "orientalism" and point to variations of my fascinations, lessons, misunderstandings, and misrepresentations in nearly all of the "West's" engagements with the "East."[1] Orientalism so persistently influences our thought and language that even though I have tried to abandon the terms "West" and "East" (and I will drop the scare quotes now), I have found no accurate replacements.

The repetition of a story is built into the conventional structure of many noh plays: First an elderly couple (*Nishikigi, Takasago*), grieving mother (*Sumidagawa*), student (*Tanikō*), or another average person relates the story of an interesting place to a traveler, often a monk on a religious journey. This first teller, called the *shite*, mysteriously disappears. In the interlude, the *ai* actor tells the story again in the style of *kyōgen* speech and performance, a more comedic and colloquial theater, at least by the standards of Japan in the Muromachi period (1392–1573). Finally, the *shite* returns to the stage in the second act as the ghost of the story's protagonist and reenacts the events.

In keeping with noh's practice of retelling stories in different styles and tenses, this book draws from several different writing conventions. I tell the story of my experience taking noh lessons in a style that might range from the ethnographic field note to the memoir. I describe what I learned about noh's pedagogical practices and how the experience of training in noh affected my work as a professor of modernism, transnational performance, and gender and sexuality studies. The stories of my cast of noh modernists—Ezra Pound, W. B. Yeats, Itō Michio, Bertolt Brecht, Benjamin Britten, and Samuel Beckett—are told using biographical and historical research, literary-critical approaches, and performance studies. My engagement with theories of gender, sexuality, and postcolonialism are occasionally placed in that other scholarly genre, the note, in order to maintain the book's focus on its central methodology: pedagogy, or the journeys of learning and teaching.

I use these various styles and approaches in an attempt to reach several audiences, in the same way that noh's combination of music, dance, ritual, and comedy was designed for wide appeal, just as its most famous actor and theorist Zeami Motokiyo (ca. 1363–ca. 1443) strategized in *Performance Notes*.[2] My hope is that this book will be of some use to scholars of modernism, noh, gender and sexuality, and Japanese studies, as well as to readers with a general interest in these topics and to performers, poets, dancers, and teachers. Some readers will be most engaged by the personal stories. Scholars might find the (many) notes detailing research and sources to be most useful. Japan

specialists might be concerned that I do not use the scholarship on noh written in Japanese, which I did not because I cannot read the language. I learned
enough spoken Japanese to enable me to take noh lessons, follow dance choreography, and conduct interviews with some assistance, as well as stumble
through daily life in Tokyo. But I did not learn to read scholarly literature and
thus had to rely on translations and my teachers' generosity. I try—but fail—
to console myself with the excuse that at least I was able to learn the dances,
chants, and drum patterns and thus can discuss them from the perspective of
someone who sweated over them. Clips of my own performances of dances
discussed in this book (marked in the text as [Clip]) can be found at http://
sites.bu.edu/learningtokneel/, along with sound files and other supplementary material.[3]

Failure, but really our shallow conception of failure and success, is a major topic of Learning to Kneel. Many accounts of noh and modernism focus on
Euro-American artists' failures to fully understand noh and other elements of
Japanese culture: Ezra Pound's knowledge of Japanese was probably as limited as mine when he published his influential and often beautiful translations of noh plays and classical poetry; William Butler Yeats failed to use his
noh-inspired plays to unambiguously reject British colonial rule and build a
certain kind of Irish nation; Itō Michio failed to merge his notion of Eastern
and Western arts into an aesthetic that could promote peace; Bertolt Brecht
revised his play based on noh at least three times but still could not manage to
create a production that would teach student-actors the values of a proletarian revolution; Benjamin Britten and his librettist, William Plomer, scrapped
titles and settings in their attempts to find the right relation to their noh
source and the right form for a serious drag Christian parable; and Samuel
Beckett failed to conceal the influence of Japanese theater and to remain the
ghostly director of his plays forever. In focusing on these failures, we seem to
imply that we can know our own cultures and art forms, an assumption that
is based on a very narrow definition of knowing and equally thin definitions
of failure and success.

"We learn best from our failures" is one of those clichés that is all the
more infuriating for its practicality. Nonetheless, I will not learn to perform
Hagoromo's kiri dance perfectly by failing and trying again. Zeami's famous
pedagogical notes have taught me that I needed to train in noh for a lifetime
before writing this book. My best noh teachers learned from teachers who
trained their entire lives but still claim not to understand noh completely. The
emphasis on learning and training in noh pedagogy and my own humbling

experience as a noh student challenged my assumptions about failure, success, and mastery. As I knelt and bowed in front of my teacher, I addressed him with the honorific "sensei" (teacher), and I began to question my interest in subversive art (noh did not strike me as that) and the emphasis on subversion in popular and scholarly ideas of what it means to be a person. We often assume that to be an interesting, un-duped, or whole human being is to reject convention and rejoice in uniqueness: Be yourself. Think outside the box. Just say noh. (I promise not to use that bad pun again in this book.) These slogans are powerful, as are the gender and postcolonial theories that emphasize forms of agency based on the subversion of the many misogynistic, racist, homophobic, and ethnocentric laws and practices of imperialist and neoimperialist states. But noh lessons led me to reconsider my assumptions about *subversion* and *submission*. The similarity of popular clichés and critical theories suggests that celebrations of subversion can be twisted into advertisements for buying our unique style.

Noh lessons also taught me that I tend to ignore the importance of authority and expertise in teaching and learning and to devalue seemingly conservative traditions from around the world. Few of us manage to live primarily in the realm of subversion. There are pleasures in submission—dangerous pleasures, to be sure—as my story of modernist noh's entanglement with fascism emphasizes. But that story also reveals the danger of ignoring the appeal of submission. Gender theory warns that my focus on submission will seem retrograde and conservative. Postcolonial theory points out that orientalism clouds my perspective on a cross-cultural pedagogical scene that inevitably serves empire. By focusing on the collaborative work of teaching and learning noh, I hope to avoid the critical habits that lock me into common assumptions about failure versus success, submission versus subversion, cultural appropriation versus multiculturalism, and others.

With my tremendous gratitude, this book is for the teachers I could never quite honor enough.

ACKNOWLEDGMENTS

FOREMOST AMONG THE BELOVED TEACHERS AND COLLABORATORS who made this book possible are those who gave me noh lessons and taught me to kneel: Furukawa Mitsuru, David Crandall, Elizabeth Dowd, Richard Emmert, and Jubilith Moore. *Fukaku kansha shite orimasu.* I would also like to thank the other students and Theatre Nohgaku members who worked with me at the Noh Training Project in Bloomsburg, Pennsylvania, and Tokyo. David Surtasky generously provided photographs as well as encouragement for the project.

I am grateful to Yamanaka Reiko, director of the Nogami Memorial Noh Theatre Research Institute of Hōsei University and the other professors and staff members who sponsored me as a visiting researcher. Among them, Takeuchi Akiko helped me at crucial points in my research. I also honor and miss my partner in lessons, the late Jon Brokering.

The students and family of Itō Michio generously shared his legacy and taught me his technique and repertory. Ryutani Kyōko and Komine Kumiko welcomed me into their studio and gave me private lessons, followed by Itō technique and repertory classes with the Repertory Dance Theatre, directed by Linda C. Smith. Itō's granddaughter, Michele, shared her indispensable archives, answered numerous questions, and arranged a helpful interview with her mother, the dancer Hanayagi Wakana. Mizuki Waka and Mizuki Makito invited me into their school of nihon buyō (Japanese dance) in Tokyo. Itō scholars Takeishi Midori, Mary-Jean Cowell, and Kevin Riordan shared research and resources. Maki Kato, director of the 2007 NHK documentary Itō Michio, granted an informative interview. I received an excellent lesson in eurhythmics from Lisa Parker.

I am grateful to Martin Puchner, whose formerly blind review years ago transformed this project and gave me permission to write Learning to Kneel in a more accessible and personal style. Martin's careful readings and fruitful discussions have been invaluable to me from the initial book proposal to the final title trimming. My editor at Columbia University Press, Philip Leventhal, patiently guided this project, believed in its potential, and served as a crucial advocate. The series editors of Modernist Latitudes, Paul Saint-Amour and Jessica Berman, encouraged every unusual aspect of the book and have become mentors in the profession more generally.

Gayle Rogers generously read rough drafts and offered his wisdom at many crucial moments, including those when the book just needed to "simmer." Kevin Salfen commented on a draft of the Benjamin Britten sections and significantly shaped their final version. David Crandall offered a whirlwind final read-through of the entire manuscript that caught those last few errors and made it possible for me to finish revising.

My colleagues at Boston University have supported my work in countless ways, and I am particularly grateful for the mentorship of John T. Matthews throughout this project and career phase. J. Keith Vincent and Sarah Frederick helped me find my way into the field of Japanese studies, and Anna Zielinska-Elliott gave me expert and patient language classes. The influence of the Faculty Gender & Sexuality Studies Group is evident throughout the book, and I am particularly grateful to Catherine Connell, Jennifer Knust, Erin Murphy, and Karen Warkentin for invaluable discussions. For guidance and support, I would also like to thank Robert Chodat, Bonnie Costello, William C. Carroll, Gene Andrew Jarrett, Maurice Lee, Elizabeth Loizeaux, Anita Patterson, Leland Monk, John Paul Riquelme, and Virginia Sapiro. The WGS program coordinator, Jaho King, assisted with photographic touchups and beautiful design ideas, as well as a generous supply of treats on tough days.

My students have always been my teachers as well. I offer my thanks to those in two semesters of Modernist Exoticisms for learning about noh with me and deepening my understanding of pedagogy. I am also grateful for two seminars at the Mellon School of Theater and Performance Research at Harvard, and thank its director, Martin Puchner, and its executive director, Rebecca Kastleman.

A Peter Paul Career Development Professorship provided crucial resources to launch into international research and spend the necessary time taking noh lessons and studying languages. A few postcards from the travel that Peter Paul enabled were small recompense for his generosity, personal kindness, and general cheerleading—not to mention several cases of Peter Paul wines! My research was supported by grants from the Japan Society for the Promotion of Science, Hōsei University, and the Boston University Center for the Humanities. The Boston University Center for the Humanities also provided a Publication Production Award to offset production costs. Librarians and archivists at the New York Public Library for the Performing Arts, Beinecke Rare Book and Manuscript Library at Yale University, Harvard Theatre Collection, and Howard Gotlieb Archival Research Center at Boston University were tremendously helpful.

My research benefited particularly from presentations and conversations at the Modernist Studies Association's annual meetings, as well as lectures and talks with the Modernism Seminar at Harvard University, Interdisciplinary Performance Studies at Yale University, Harvard University's Drama Colloquium, University of Georgia's Modernism Seminar, American Conference for Irish Studies, Dramanet at Freie Universität Berlin, Modern Language Association, and Mellon School for Theater and Performance Research.

The last phases of writing and manuscript preparation were supported by my amazingly organized and persistent research assistant, Nicole Rizzo, and by Boston University's Undergraduate Research Opportunities Program. Nicole's abilities to root out academic jargon and third-party permissions were invaluable.

My dear family has endured and supported the conferences, residencies abroad, noh lessons, and unfamiliar performances. Callan, Derek, Cindy, Chuck, Ian, Ilona, and Leroy, I hope you might be able to read this one. Regardless, thank you!

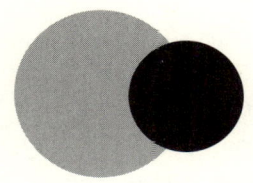

ABBREVIATIONS

AHW Manu	W. B. Yeats, "At the Hawk's Well" and "The Cat and the Moon": Manuscript Materials, ed. Andrew Parkin (Ithaca, N.Y.: Cornell University Press, 2010).
BCDW	Samuel Beckett, The Complete Dramatic Works (London: Faber & Faber, 1989).
BCP	Bertolt Brecht, Collected Plays, vol. 3, part 2, "The Mother" and Six Lehrstücke, ed. John Willett (London: Methuen, 1997).
BOT	Bertolt Brecht, Brecht on Theatre: The Development of an Aesthetic, ed. and trans. John Willett (New York: Hill & Wang, 1964).
BPFAL	Britten–Pears Foundation Archives and Library, The Red House, Aldeburgh, England.
CR	William Plomer, Curlew River: A Parable for Church Performance Set to Music by Benjamin Britten (London: Faber & Faber, 1964).
CR Score	Benjamin Britten, Curlew River: A Parable for Church Performance (London: Faber & Faber, 1964).

IAuto   Ian Carruthers, "A Translation of Fifteen Pages of Ito Michio's Autobiography 'Utsukushiku naru kyoshitsu,' " *Canadian Journal of Irish Studies* 2, no. 1 (1976): 32–43.

JND   Royall Tyler, trans and ed., *Japanese Nō Dramas* (London: Penguin, 1992).

NYPLPA   New York Public Library for the Performing Arts.

PC   W. B. Yeats, *Plays and Controversies* (New York: Macmillan, 1924).

PCMI   Personal Collection of Michelle Ito.

PFNoh   Ezra Pound and Ernest Fenollosa, *The Classic Noh Theater of Japan* (1917; repr., New York: New Directions, 1959).

VP   W. B. Yeats, *The Variorum Edition of the Plays of W. B. Yeats*, ed. Russell K. Alspach and Catherine C. Alspach (New York: Macmillan, 1966).

YPNLI   Yeats Papers, National Library of Ireland, Dublin.

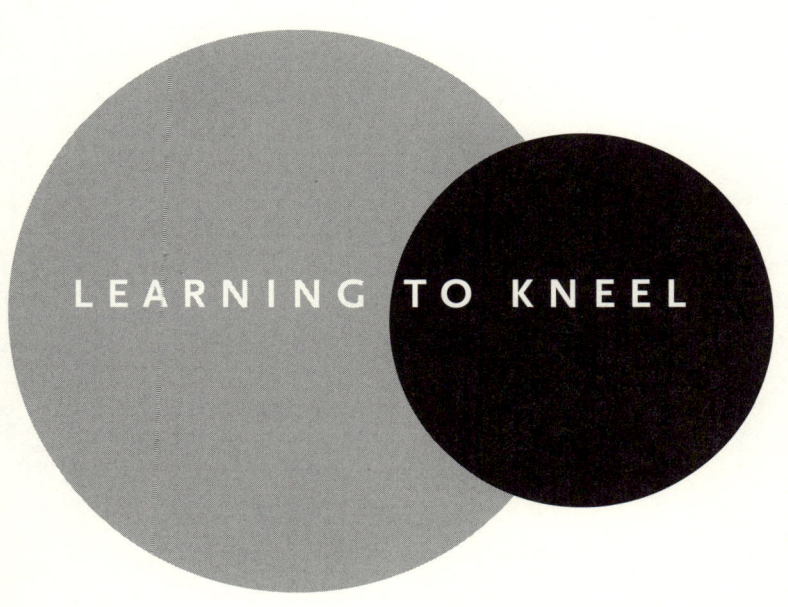

LEARNING TO KNEEL

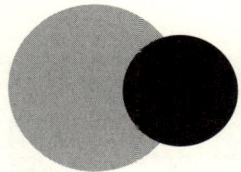

INTRODUCTION TO NOH LESSONS

THE FIRST THING I LEARNED ABOUT NOH PERFORMANCE technique was how much it hurt to kneel in *seiza*, with my legs folded beneath my body and my buns resting on my heels (figure I.1). Having taken a quarter century of ballet and modern dance classes and endured the torture of pointe shoes and a few minor injuries, I was shocked to discover that *being still* was the most challenging aspect of noh lessons. Maybe *seiza* was not painful for professional noh actors, who kneel while practicing, teaching, and perform-ing? I asked my teacher in Tokyo, Furukawa Mitsuru, about the position after attending several lessons and watching him kneel in the chorus (*jiutai*) for more than an hour during his group's production of *Kamo* (figure I.2). He told me that *seiza* is painful for everyone but worse for beginners and foreigners, like me. He seemed sympathetic when, after kneeling before him to practice noh chant (*utai*) for fifteen minutes, I would slowly uncurl my legs to stand. "Stop, stop," he said once, resorting to English in his worry that I might in-jure myself by trying to walk on numb feet. But I needed to move in the next

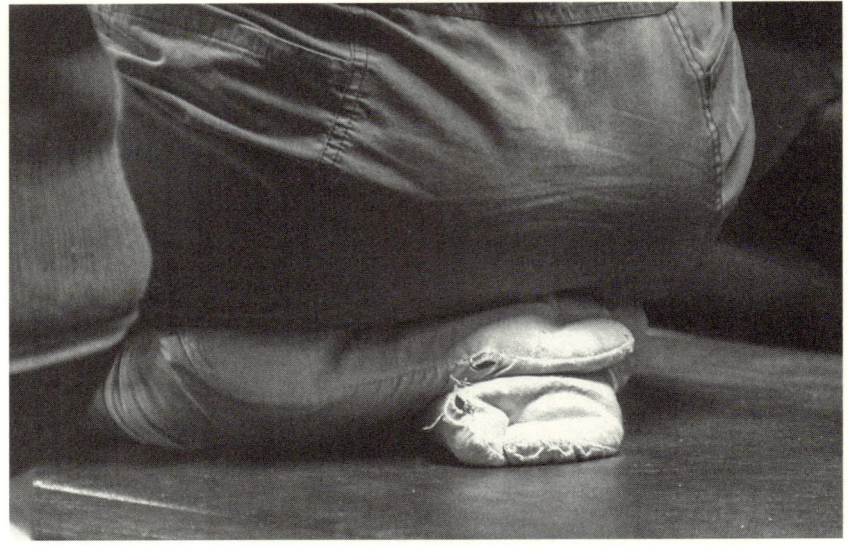

FIGURE I.I Learning to kneel. (Courtesy of David Surtasky)

phase of the lesson to practice the dance (*shimai*) that I was learning from the closing section (*kiri*) in *Hagoromo* (*The Feather Mantle*) (clip 1).[1] At the end, I was on my knees again, as a noh lesson opens and closes with the student in *seiza*, bowing to the teacher, forehead almost touching the floor. With the first bow, I would say, *Yoroshiku onegaishimasu*, an almost untranslatable ritual phrase that, in this context, means something like "Thank you (for your help and guidance now and in the future)." I would end the lesson with a formal expression of gratitude, *Arigatō gozaimashita* (Thank you very much).[2]

I began taking noh lessons and studying the Japanese language to better understand why many Europeans and Americans associated with the early-twentieth-century artistic movements known as "modernism" became fascinated with a form of dance-drama that developed in Japan in the Muromachi period (1392–1573).[3] The pain of learning to kneel in *seiza* was not my only surprise. I also was startled by my own fascination with noh and the ways that my lessons changed the emphasis of my research. I began to focus on the complicated nature of learning and teaching, particularly when the lessons crossed cultural, racial, or gendered boundaries. It is tempting to imagine transnational (we also use the terms "intercultural" or "global") learning and performance as a dance across such divisions, something we breezily celebrate as the "college study abroad experience." Noh lessons taught me

FIGURE I.2 The author's teacher, Furukawa Mitsuru, in the noh play *Atsumori*.
(Courtesy of Carrie Preston)

that transnational learning is, and ought to be, uncomfortable, as it forces us to confront deeply ingrained assumptions about how to be good students or teachers. Noh training exposed my tendency to value an egalitarian pedagogy over one that is explicitly hierarchical, innovation over convention, casual as opposed to formal relationships, and, especially, subversion rather than submission.

My response to noh lessons replicated that of the European and American students of noh whom I discuss in this book. One of the first students to influence modernism was Ernest Fenollosa, an American-born scholar of Japanese art who studied noh chanting (or singing, *utai*) in Tokyo briefly in 1883 and regularly from 1896 to 1901.[4] After he died, the draft translations of noh plays that he produced with a former student, Hirata Kiichi, were passed to the American poet Ezra Pound, who "finished" and began publishing them while living with the Irish poet-playwright W. B. Yeats. Pound placed his first noh play, *Nishikigi*, in the magazine *Poetry* in May 1914, and then four translations appeared in *Certain Noble Plays of Japan* in 1916 with Yeats's now famous introduction.[5] When Pound and Yeats began using noh as a model for their own drama and poetry, they also studied with Japanese artists, including Itō Michio, who choreographed and performed in the first of Yeats's noh-inspired "plays for dancers," *At the Hawk's Well* (1916). Itō took Yeats's play on a little-known world tour with stops in London, New York, Los Angeles, Mexico City, and Tokyo. The Yeats-Pound-Itō collaboration initiated a transnational circuit of noh-inspired performance, which later influenced the German playwright Bertolt Brecht, particularly his *Lehrstücke* (learning plays); the famous British composer Benjamin Britten and the parables for church performance he created with the South African writer/librettist William Plomer; and the spare dramaturgy of Irish-French writer Samuel Beckett. As this list indicates, modernist artists do not fit easily into studies based on national categories.[6] Accordingly, it's ironic that one of the reasons that Itō's contributions to modernist noh, modern theater, dance, and film have been overlooked is that he was not an "authentically trained Japanese Noh dancer," that is, not sufficiently rooted in national traditions—which also is true of the other modernists on the list who are more canonical.[7]

The authenticity expected of Itō, but not to the same degree of Euro-American modernists, is not so different from the authentic experience of another culture that every travel guide promises the tourist. Nor is it so different from my own desire to travel to Japan (with my *Lonely Planet* guidebook) to take a "real" noh lesson, as if there were one correct technique and tradition of noh and only one place to learn it. Of course, I know that every art form responds to different audience desires, aesthetic standards, and political regimes, and this is particularly true of noh, which has been closely associated with the height of Japanese aesthetic and political achievement. I also know that the noh repertory has changed over the centuries and is even interpreted and performed quite differently by various *ryū* (schools).[8] I appreciate the "invention" and instability of traditions in the other performance forms I've studied, from the almost as ancient ballet to the comparatively young modern dance. Yet I do not long for an authentic ballet class. Noh lessons disturb my critical and physical balance, provoke unsteady fantasies, and risk leading me to write an overly enchanted memoir.

THE PEDAGOGY OF NOH

My sensei (teacher) and I usually knelt together to drink green tea with a *wagashi* (Japanese sweet) before the lesson, but no, it is all part of the lesson. After bowing, we remained kneeling in *seiza* facing each other to practice chanting. He sang a line from one of the approximately two hundred plays in the noh repertory, and then I imitated him, attempting to replicate his pitch, rhythm, pronunciation, and even his breathing patterns in a method aptly called "parrot-like repetition" (*ōmugaeshi*) (clip 2).[9] In the *shimai* (noh dance) part of the lesson, my sensei performed the movement sequences called *kata* from a play while I followed behind, mimicking his posture, steps, gestures, and physical effort. Students practice noh technique while learning a repertory that is directly transmitted from teacher to student within a hierarchical, pseudofamilial organization. That is, students memorize dances from canonical plays rather than rehearsing a basic movement vocabulary, such as in a ballet barre routine. Lessons emphasize conformity to the teacher's style, which is determined primarily by the teacher-performer's membership in one of five noh schools (*ryū*) led by a family head (*iemoto*), who traces his ancestry back centuries to a founding patriarch. The largest school, Kanze, was begun by Kannami (ca. 1333–1384), father of the most celebrated playwright, performer, and theorist, Zeami Motokiyo (ca. 1363–1443). The current head, Kanze Kiyokazu (b. 1959), is the twenty-sixth descendant of Kannami to become an *iemoto*.[10] Three of the other schools also claim a (contested) relation to Zeami, but these patrilineal "bloodlines" were invented largely to garner the support of the ruling Tokugawa shogunate in the Edo (or Tokugawa) period (1600–1867).[11] The *iemoto* still controls the repertory, performance style, and "certification" of professionals and teachers. Many of the roughly 2,500 actors, including my sensei, were not born into noh families but are included in the "fictional family," as are amateurs who support the school with their tuition.[12]

In my lessons with Furukawa sensei, I tried to embrace the *ōmugaeshi* method and "parrot" his phrases and movements, suppressing my desire to add an original style or flair that would have been prized in my ballet and modern dance training. I recognized my tendency to value innovation and individual interpretation over performance traditions, especially when, as in noh, the tradition does not adhere to my political commitment to gender equality. Women have performed noh since the fourteenth century as amateurs but could not become professionals until 1948, and they continue to be marginalized today. During the militarization of the Taishō period (1912–1926), noh was regarded as a leisure pursuit that would help women establish a "Japanese body and mind" and prepare them for "giving birth and educating strong and healthy Japanese nationals."[13] Prohibitions against women performing in public were tested when Tsumura Kimiko (1902–1974) performed *Hagoromo* in 1921 in Japan-occupied Korea. She was expelled from the Kanze school. Women were finally admitted, with much controversy, into the Nihon nōgakukai (Japanese Noh Society) in 2004, but their performing opportunities remain limited.[14] They are prohibited from participating in the *shikisanban* (three rites), plays that are thought to be particularly sacred and traditionally require performers to engage in a period of "purification," which includes avoiding contact with women who might "'transfer' impurities."[15] In this case, my rejection of gender-based exclusion is in tension with my respect for artistic tradition and cultural difference.

I had expected to feel constrained by the mimicry and humiliated by the gestures of deference scripted into noh lessons, but I performed them in order to take an "authentic" lesson. Contrary to my presumptions, these aspects of noh pedagogy separated my lessons from the mundane world and offered me access to a space of distinction. The rituals of submission also encouraged a unique intimacy with my teacher. Performing reverence for the sensei seems to produce that feeling: even professional actors who have many students of their own return periodically to their own teacher for lessons. Noh emphasizes lifelong study and positions the pedagogical experience at the center of artistic achievement. The student's bond to the teacher is also fostered by the *ōmugaeshi* (parrot-like repetition) method and the celebration of person-to-person transmission of the repertory. Mimicking the teacher is obviously necessary for students, like me, who cannot read noh texts. Although books for chanting, utaibon, are available, some use old forms of characters, which do not match the modern pronunciation, and might even contain obsolete symbols.[16] The diagrams of dances (katazuke) are challenging to decipher without the guidance of a teacher familiar with the repertory. Of course, movement is difficult to notate in all dance forms, even when using modern scripts like labanotation, and noh's model of direct transmission of movement is similar to practices in other dance arts.[17] Still, noh texts are rarely revised to be more helpful to students or even to conform to current performance practices, and in this way, they document respect for noh traditions and the central role of the teacher within them.

The structure of noh lessons encourages students to develop forms of diligence and discipline that will help them meet the demands of performance. Students need their teachers in order to learn the repertory so completely that a group of professionals and even serious amateurs can gather and perform a play with minimal rehearsal. This is particularly remarkable given that noh never has a conductor, and the music alternates between metered and nonmetered passages and between songs that are matched and unmatched to the drums. In the most common of noh's rhythmic structures, hiranori, the (usually) twelve syllables of poetry are distributed over an eight-beat rhythmic pattern in one of two ways, mitsuji utai or tsuzuke utai. The pattern chosen by the drummers determines the singing, so actors must listen for how the drumbeats fall in relation to the first syllable of the poetic line to determine which rhythm to chant. Actors, chorus, and musicians must attend very carefully to slight variations made by fellow performers and adapt immediately.[18] This ability to listen is developed through the ōmugaeshi method and the student's submission to the teacher. Both help the actor achieve a strong stage presence that does not rely on the individuality or flair that I was encouraged to express in other forms of performance training. The mask covering the face, tension in the throat and oral cavity required by the vocal production, and formulaic blocking and choreography all discourage the presentation of a realistic human individual—and produce a formal stylization that contributed to noh's appeal to modernist artists who were interested in theater that did not follow the conventions of stage realism.

The unfamiliar vocal techniques, movements, and even seiza pain I experienced in noh lessons challenged my deeply ingrained bodily and mental habits. My previous dance training interfered with the execution of seemingly simple gestures, movements, and postures, as my muscles strained against unusual positions. When I practiced the walking technique of *suriashi*, literally "sliding foot," I realized that the pedestrian heel-to-toe walk in Euro-American realist theater is merely a convention so ubiquitous it seems "normal" for actors to pretend they are not walking on a stage in front of an audience. In Japan, it is more "real" to acknowledge the fact of the performance using a stage step like *suriashi*, which is common in noh, *kyōgen*, kabuki, and other Japanese performance forms.

Parallel to my bodily habits were the mental ruts that produced assumptions about agency, pedagogy, and culture that clashed with those I encountered in noh lessons. I used to call my pedagogy for classes on modernism and gender at Boston University "democratic" and "feminist," assuming that my style of teaching was obviously superior to a formal, hierarchical relationship between teacher and student, like that in noh. The intellectual habits I brought to this study were largely derived from feminist, postcolonial, and queer theories, all of which celebrate the subversion of tradition and authority. These theories have generated crucial insights, but the tendency to celebrate particular forms of agency rooted in subversion can also deepen Eurocentric biases. To learn all I could from noh, I had to set my theories aside or below, as in a footnote, and let the confusing, often painful, and always collaborative lesson itself be front and center. And I seek to keep the pedagogical scene central throughout this book.

MODERNIST NOH

> I have studied noh for most of my life. I still have no idea what it is.
> Hajime Sano

Hajime Sano, a renowned *shite* actor of the Hōshō school who performed noh professionally until his death at eighty-one, studied noh much longer than I've studied modernism (figure I.3). I am not brave enough to claim that I have no idea what modernism and noh are, but I do not intend to offer limiting definitions of either in this book. Rather, I will tell the story of the global circulation of noh-inspired performances and the ways they affected the arts of the twentieth century, mainly drama, poetry, modern dance, film, and popular entertainment. If this book began as a study of noh's influence on modernism, it now has turned into something much more ambiguous and ambivalent. I believe that modernist noh has a good deal to teach us about

FIGURE I.3 The noh master Hajime Sano choreographing David Crandall's *The Linden Tree*, 1986. (Photo by Tim Macmillan, 1986; courtesy of Tim Macmillan)

the complexity of art's place in the infamously shrinking globe, and about our lives too. But these lessons are not the commonly celebrated ones about how art can subvert the new world order or how our appreciation of art, especially foreign art, can contribute to our liberation in any quantifiable, definable way. Instead, *Learning to Kneel* is about submitting to discomfort, confusion, boredom, conformity, and the authority of the teacher as a crucial but undervalued way of learning, particularly in cross-cultural contexts. This way of learning is not amenable to standardized assessments and may not directly contribute to that supposedly universal human goal of liberation.

This section title, "Modernist Noh," seems like an oxymoron in that it brings together a set of aesthetic movements associated with innovation and an art form frequently advertised as the oldest continuously performed theater in the world. Even contemporary Japanese artists interested in adapting noh describe it as a "museum piece, performed for too long without change."[19] Ezra Pound's "Make it new" has become the most famous slogan of modernism among later critics, so frequently quoted out of context that it is worth reminding ourselves that he generated it in *Canto LIII* from a phrase steeped in Chinese mythology and associated with Cheng Tang (Pound's

Tching Tang), emperor of China from 1766 to 1753 B.C.E.[20] "Make it new" emerged from the same interest in Asia and the past that produced Pound's fascination with noh.

If modernism is not quite as new as certain slogans suggest, some elements of noh are not so old. Modernist artists idealized many features of noh that date not to the fifteenth century but to their own raucous time period. The challenges that noh institutions faced during the modernization of the Meiji Restoration, beginning in 1868, led them to assert that, as Pound echoed, "the tradition of Noh is unbroken" (PFNoh, 9, 12).[21] Yet noh and modernism, like all traditions, are continuously subject to reinvention, and recent shifts have changed the relationship between the two. When modernism was understood as a refined drive for formal experiments, especially in literature of the first half of the twentieth century, it seemed to be confined to Euro-American urban centers: London, Paris, New York, Los Angeles, and Berlin, to name some of the cities that appear in this book. Empire, that machine of cultural contact, got little attention, even in studies that claimed to take an international perspective.[22] Recent books tend to focus on modernism's relation to global conflict and conquest, but the corrective can swing too far, resulting in caricatures of modernism as the aesthetic ammunition for colonial and fascist atrocities. Some critics refer to Yeats's noh adaptations as "another form of cultural colonization" and bemoan "the wounds that Noh suffered in the process of its transplantation to Western soil."[23] Well-intended accusations of "cultural colonization" can exaggerate the power of one Western artist to injure a rather resilient dramatic form that is always changing in response to foreign contact.

Cultural contact is inevitable in modernity, but few models of artistic exchange do not focus on appropriation, irony, and fear.[24] To focus only on Western appropriation is to presume that all instances of international contact always confirm the power asymmetries we already know, as we keep our attention fixed on the Euro-American artists already considered central.[25] Accusations of appropriation begin from a desire for cultural sensitivity, but they can unintentionally reinforce the notion of an unbridgeable divide between East and West when they efface the unique circumstances of each exchange. The circumstances of Japan do not fit easily into the standard histories of the Western conquest of the East and related cultural thefts. Noh was not stolen for modernism from a colonized people because even though Japan certainly experienced coercion from Western governments, it was not a colony in the early twentieth century. Partially to stave off the colonization in China and elsewhere, Japan began building an empire based on (and in competition with) Europe, adopting European orientalist justifications for "civilizing" other parts of Asia to build a Pan-Asian power. Japan annexed Taiwan in 1895 and Korea in 1910 and was expanding into Manchuria and China when Pound and Yeats became interested in noh.

Yeats does not fit the common mold of a cultural colonizer because he used noh to envision "a certain possibility of the Irish dramatic movement" that would battle British imperialism (PFNoh, 151). He chose to "go to Asia for a stage-convention" in part to avoid theatrical models derived from England (PFNoh, 155). Itō Michio, like many Japanese artists in the late Meiji period (1868–1912), went to Europe for his stage conventions, assuming that nothing "good" came from Japan.[26] His autobiography claims that his work with Pound and Yeats convinced him of the value of noh for modern performance, a belief he carried back to Japan after he was imprisoned by the United States as an enemy spy during World War II and then repatriated. While Pound was broadcasting the pro-Mussolini speeches on Rome Radio that would get him arrested for treason, Japan was gripped by its own fascist militarization. The supposedly "unbroken" tradition of noh in Japan was adapted to the goals of wartime propaganda with *new* war plays and benefit performances (*kenkin nō*).[27] In the postwar period, Euro-American noh adaptations inspired innovation in the Japanese theater in a fertile circuit of adaptation rather than unilateral appropriation. Yokomichi Mario reconfigured Yeats's At the Hawk's Well for the noh stage as Taka no izumi (1949) and then as the even more experimental Takahime (1967). Other versions of the play have continued to be staged into the twenty-first century.[28]

In discussing modernist noh as a complex transnational circuit, I call attention to how cultural forms cross borders to reveal affiliations that transcend national identities; I also acknowledge the ways that nationalisms, even fascist nationalisms, encourage creativity and fulfill human (not demon) desires.[29] The transnational tour of modernist noh was propelled by many of the atrocities of the last century, troubling our tendencies to assume bad orientalism and appropriation, as opposed to *good* multiculturalism and hybridity, or *bad* Western colonizers oppressing innocent colonial subjects struggling to save their cultures.[30] Without ignoring important historical patterns of suffering, I note overgeneralized histories and moralities. I do not intend to provoke shame for our struggles to approach global cultures or to propose a new *good*; instead, I encourage us to recognize that cultural exchange is problematic and inevitable, shaped by both misunderstanding and remarkable creativity.

THE TROUBLE WITH TEACHERS: PEDAGOGY/PERFORMANCE

> The confident use that teachers make of the university idiom is no more fortuitous than students' tolerance of semantic fog . . . magisterial language derives its full significance from the situation in which the relation of pedagogic communication is accomplished, with its social space, its ritual, its temporal rhythms; in short, the whole system of visible or invisible constraints which constitute pedagogic action as the action of imposing and inculcating a legitimate culture.
>
> Pierre Bourdieu and Jean Claude Passeron, *Reproduction in Education, Society, and Culture*

Bourdieu and Passeron suggest that university teachers use their "foggy language" to construct cultural rules; train students to believe that these are the "natural" and "legitimate" rules; punish the rebellious, often violently; and conceal evidence of that violence. Claims that pedagogical institutions brainwash (to put it un-magisterially) students are made mostly by either employees of colleges and universities (like Bourdieu, Passeron, and myself) or conservative critics who accuse these institutions of being "bastions of radical ideas."[31] I'm concerned that both university professors and their right-wing critics demonize teachers, albeit from different perspectives. Noh is a didactic dramatic form that employs "ritual," "magisterial" poetry, and "temporal rhythms"—to borrow some of Bourdieu and Passeron's own magisterial language (which admittedly is very difficult to avoid). Noh pedagogy probably seems far more authoritarian and conservative than what goes on in European and American college classrooms. Nonetheless, my noh lessons were filled with collaboration, productive failures, and unexpected pleasures, as well as power relations. The cultural identities of teachers and students can be disciplined in noh lessons, but they also are shared and revised.

In noh, pedagogy and performance are deeply intertwined. The noh lesson is ritualized and theatrical, and if an actor or a musician makes a mistake during a play, the *koken* (stage assistants kneeling at the back of the stage) will correct or, if necessary, even replace the performer. During a performance

I attended at the National Noh Theater in Tokyo, the koken began chanting to correct the shite, who had started singing the wrong scene. It is hard to imagine one of my dance teachers or directors correcting me in the middle of the show. Those steeped in noh traditions might find it difficult to imagine how the show could continue if the error were not corrected, given that actors, musician, and chorus parts are all interconnected. But Western theater tends to find some way to hide the errors (the show must go on!), and Western theorists of culture tend to set pedagogy in opposition to performance. The pedagogical realm is associated with Bourdieu and Passeron's "magisterial language" and "visible or invisible constraints" based on historical authority and archaic traditions.[32] Performance is imagined as unpredictable, changeable, and often subversive of the status quo—hardly a space in which a teacher interrupts and corrects a soloist. Anyone who has sweated through a ballet barre, practiced musical scales or drum patterns, or memorized the lines of a script can speak to the tedium of learning to perform, as well as the important role of his or her teachers and directors.

The presumption that performance is subversive is present in many analogies between stage performances and "performativity" in everyday life—or the ways we perform roles in social contexts, sometimes with the help of clothing that functions like a costume.[33] A brief departure into the famous controversies over the practice of veiling by Muslim women is a useful example. In French-occupied Algeria, colonial officials focused on "teaching" Algerian women to throw off their veils as a way of suppressing the Arab culture and faith.[34] For the French, the veil was a symbol of women's oppression, and they used the liberation of women to justify conquest (as was echoed in some justifications for the United States–led invasions of Iraq and Afghanistan).[35] Some revolutionary women unveiled in a performance fulfilling French desires so they could more easily carry weapons and messages for the resistance against foreign rule. Once the French military realized that women who appeared to be "Westernized" were actually more likely to be nationalists, revolutionaries resumed wearing their veils and hid their weapons in the swathes of cloth. Critics of empire thus have celebrated the strategic use of Western and traditional dress as a subversive "camouflage."[36] Feminists have pointed out that the veil took on very different meanings again after Algerian independence in 1962 when patriarchal institutions renewed their hold on the country and women were forced to wear their veils again.[37] Veiling remains contentious in France, where a 2004 law prohibiting headscarves and other religious symbols in public schools was extended by a 2010 ban on burqas and niqabs in all public places, a law that was upheld by the European Court of Human Rights in 2014.[38] The veil that served as a costume and "symbol of resistance" when it concealed bombs and Algerian opposition to the French Empire is also understood as a danger to public security and European secular values. From the perspective of the unnamed Muslim woman who brought the case against the French ban, as well as her supporters, the veil remains subversive of France's attempts to suppress religious faith and enforce secular uniformity.

Depending on the perspective, the veil seems capable of reflecting many different interests and desires. In noh, it's like a mask that can be tipped down slightly to convey sadness and tipped up into the light for joy.[39] For Western commentators, the possibility that religious belief or respect for national tradition motivate women to veil is not nearly so desirable as a revolutionary aspiration, and according to the European Court of Human Rights, veiling for faith is not a freedom or self-expression to be protected. But these were part of the explanations that contemporary women in the Egyptian mosque movement gave to Saba Mahmood for veiling and other practices they understood as important to cultivating personal piety.[40] Mahmood argues that feminists fail to understand women's participation in Islam or other nonliberal movements owing to a common assumption that agency is "the capacity to realize one's own interests against the weight of custom, tradition, transcendental will, or other obstacles."[41] This definition often leads to the conclusion that adherence to religious or cultural traditions is a kind of false consciousness or that women have internalized misogynistic teachings and fail to recognize their own interests against the pedagogues. Feminists who acknowledge the secular-liberal bias in this perspective—and the condescension—focus instead on the "practical resources" that religion might offer or on how women can "recode" norms to serve their own agendas. But the presumed link between agency and subversion is rarely examined. According to Mahmood, contemporary feminist theory has created a "normative political subject . . . whose agency is conceptualized on the binary model of subordination and subversion."[42]

I do not wish to underestimate the importance of subversive forms of agency or ignore their impact on my academic and personal life. But my studies of noh reminded me that most of my daily acts (say, of learning and kneeling), the roles I choose to occupy (student, teacher), and my institutional commitments (to universities or noh schools) are not motivated by subversion. And they are often no less central to my self-definition for having other purposes. For all the wariness I have been taught by my very specialized education before noh, I cannot attribute my submissive choices to cultural indoctrination in norms, traditions, and other regulative forces. My noh lessons forced me to confront my own assumptions about agency, subversion, and submission to tradition. In that pedagogical space, I chose to obediently repeat parrot-like after my sensei, fully believing I could have refused and often wishing I could be a more "normal" participant in a community of noh learners that I could never fully join.

LEARNING PAINS AND PLEASURES

Learning to Kneel, coupled with my emphasis on the pain of *seiza* and the gestures of submission in noh lessons, called up sadomasochism (S/M) for several of my early readers, much to my initial discomfort. Theorists and practitioners of S/M, however, offer alternative perspectives on individual agency. S/M and the erotic aspects of learning are not frequently addressed outside queer theory, although the tense relationship of pain, pleasure, and pedagogy is explored in such classic texts as Plato's *Symposium* (ca. 385 B.C.E.); Jean-Jacques Rousseau's *Émile* (1762); the Marquis de Sade's *Philosophy in the Bedroom* (*Philosophie dans le boudoir*) (1795); *Venus in Furs* (*Venus im Pelz*) (1870) by Leopold von Sacher-Masoch, which is alluded to in James Joyce's *Ulysses* (1922);. and of course, nobody can ignore E. L. James's best-selling book *Fifty Shades of Grey* (2011) and its major motion picture (2015), even if we wouldn't classify it with the other books on the list.[43] I will not enter here into the decades-old debates about whether S/M's dramas of dominance and submission are an extreme version of misogyny or a challenge to oppressive sexual norms.[44] Instead, I want to point out that the two prevailing definitions of sadomasochism—*perversion* and *subversion*—both assume the value of individual freedom but instead locate the expression of that freedom in different sexual practices. Those who define S/M as an individual's *perversion* tend to argue that other individuals must be protected from his or her crimes.[45] Those who argue that S/M is subversive suggest that an individual's sexual practice has the power to disrupt the rules that regulate sexuality; in seeming contradiction, they tend to locate S/M in a private sphere in which individual choices should be protected.[46] Both positions rely on ideas of individual agency and freedom, and both need to account for the historical and cultural factors that influence these ideas, along with sexual practices and desires.

Consensual S/M has been presented as a practice of strategically stressing the body to cultivate ideas of personhood based not on agency and subversion but on "submission" and "transcendence," terms that also are relevant to noh pedagogy.[47] David Halperin compared S/M's disciplined, voluntary labor on the self with ancient Greek ethics and forms of homoeroticism in which the "rigorous and austere adherence to the norms of ancient morality was also an exceptional practice that, far from achieving for its practitioners a greater degree of normality, surrounded them with a brilliant and extraordinary distinction."[48] Halperin's description could apply to the austere lifelong training regimen in noh performance technique and repertory that, as described by Zeami Motokiyo's treatises (written between about 1402 and 1433), should have been accompanied by a striving for moral purity. Noh lessons, like S/M, use bodily stress to help students cultivate and perform what I call an "impersonal self." In drawing this comparison, I do not wish to ignore the specificity of the sex act but to acknowledge that learning has erotic and bodily aspects. The uncomfortable posture of seiza, as practitioners of meditation and yoga have long recognized, can cultivate a focused concentration and unique experience of the relation between mind and body. The power differential between noh teachers and students is marked by bowing and other gestures of submission that establish a "self-stylization" associated with "beauty." The lesson in which students imitate their teacher to learn the repertory also encourages them to give up an individual style and develop an impersonal self that will help them achieve the performance aesthetics of noh.

Noh is a theater of teaching and learning, and the didactic and ethical topics of most plays are drawn from Buddhism, noh's religious and philosophical core. The Buddhist warning against "wrongful clinging" to worldly objects, relationships, and even selfhood—or one particular incarnation of self—is part of most plays in the noh repertory. Eve Sedgwick uses Buddhism, which she describes as "radically self-defined in pedagogical terms," to help her imagine a pedagogy that incorporates failure, the diverse ways and erotic aspects of learning, and the conundrum of learning not to be.[49] Buddhism's central "negational" urge is evident in the idea that "the happiest fate is not to be born (or reborn)."[50] In Western philosophical traditions, "to find a motive in nonbeing was thought, for some reason, to fall outside the definitional bounds of the human"—and far outside standard definitions of agency.[51] These definitions rely on a "pseudodichotomy between repression and liberation" while "dramatizing only the extremes of compulsion and voluntarity" and ignoring "the middle ranges of agency," in which most of us live and learn.[52]

Noh lessons encouraged me to experience "the middle ranges of agency" in my shifting roles as a student, migrant, and privileged American interloper. As a woman attempting to play the celestial maiden of *Hagoromo* with a deep guttural chant and a movement style that felt heavy with centuries of men performing ideal/divine femininity, I found myself in a complicated drag performance (figure I.4). During a public presentation at Hōsei University, my teacher claimed that he felt "jealous" because it seemed so easy for me to be "girlish and innocent" while dancing as a character who remembers playing with her deceitful lover when they both were children.[53] He did not feel he could draw on my source of girlish innocence when he performed the role. Complex gendered, erotic, and ageist relations or identifications are evident here and in many interactions between teachers and students. Acknowledging them is uncomfortable because it might call up the origins of the word "pedagogy" in the ancient Greek *paidagōgos*, the servant or slave who led the boy to school, and even "the stereotypical image of the pederast fondling boys on the way to school."[54] Sedgwick describes the common, although frequently ignored, "pederastic/pedagogical" story in which a "seduction with the unmerged but unrepudiated 'inner' child" seems essential to self-knowledge or "interiority."[55] The theme appears in noh dramas when a young warrior haunts his killer (*Atsumori*) and both are saved in the confrontation; a thief describes and honors the boy who killed him (*Kumasaka*); and a teacher helps throw his student off a mountain and facilitates his resurrection (*Tanikō*).

The dead boys haunting noh plays—and modernist interpretations of them—point to pedagogical and erotic traditions in Japan, particularly *shudō*, or "the way of (loving) youths." *Shudō* should not to be misunderstood as a sexual identity; gay, straight, bisexual, or queer identities would have meant nothing to those who practiced it.[56] Rather, *shudō* played a role in noh's historical development and pedagogy and as a "staple theme" in noh plays.[57] Zeami was an eleven-year-old child actor when he found favor and patronage with the ruling shogun, Ashikaga Yoshimitsu (1358–1408). The shogun oversaw Zeami's study of classical Japanese and Chinese poetry, Confucian philosophy, Shinto myth, and Buddhism, all of which contributed to Zeami's aesthetic theories and dramatic practice. The relationship was probably characterized by both artistic submission and sexual intimacy.[58] Yoshimitsu's affection for Zeami was troubling to some, including the aristocrat Go'oshikōji

FIGURE 1.4 The author dancing the closing section (*kiri*) from the noh play *Hagoromo*. (Courtesy of David Surtasky and Carrie Preston)

Kintada, but not because of Zeami's gender or youth. The aristocrat instead complained in 1378 that Yoshimitsu should not associate with Zeami because noh was "the occupation of beggars (kotsujiki)."[59]

For those who practiced shudō, the beautiful, young male body was a locus of aesthetic, sensual, and spiritual attractions that could promote the personal growth of both student and teacher. Yūgen, an ancient aesthetic ideal associated with noh and usually defined as a profound, mysterious, and elegant beauty, was linked to the attractions of youthful male students for Zeami.[60] His second use of the term in the earliest surviving treatise (ca. 1400–1418) is part of his description of the actor's first stage of training at the age of twelve or thirteen, when "since he is a child, anything he does will entail yūgen. . . . A pretty little boy with a good voice who is talented besides can hardly go wrong. All the same, such a flower is not the true flower."[61] Zeami demanded that adult performers preserve the yūgen of the boy and cultivate the mind of a "beginner," even in old age.[62] In what may be Zeami's last treatise, "The Flower in . . . Yet Doubling Back" (1433), he claims that "the effect of doubling back" (kyakurai) cannot be taught to anyone under the age of forty and can be used only "once in a lifetime" as an enlightened return to the "flower" of the young boy's yūgen.[63]

The connection between yūgen and youthful male beauty has faded over the centuries, but noh plays frequently feature the forms of shudō practiced by Buddhist priests with their adolescent acolytes (chigo) and by samurai with their apprentices (wakashu). The literary form called chigo monogatari (tales of acolytes) emphasized the sacred dynamic of the priest's infatuation with the chigo while teaching him religious and moral virtue; the youth provided companionship but also spiritual revelation.[64] The stories are of a beautiful young novice whose death reveals him to be the embodiment of a bodhisattva, one who serves the pedagogical function of helping another reach enlightenment.[65] The death of the chigo teaches the priest to renounce earthly attachments. This spiritual function of the chigo contrasts with Buddhist presumptions of the corrupting influence of sex with women, who were assumed to be morally inferior.[66] The relationship between the older samurai nenja and his apprentice wakashu similarly helped transmit codes of honor (giri) through instruction in the warrior arts (budō) and the associated "mental attitude (kokorogake)."[67] The nenja and wakashu engaged in strenuous physical training to achieve the standards of elite masculinity, and the bond was physical, spiritual, and long lasting, although the sexual partnership was supposed to end once the boy reached adulthood.[68]

Noh plays that adapted popular stories about *chigo* and *wakashu* satisfied the taste for both ethical and homoerotic performances during the period.[69] In *Tanikō* (*The Valley-Hurling*), a *chigo*-like student goes on a pilgrimage with his sensei to pray for his sick mother. The boy falls ill while climbing a mountain and, according to the rules of the Buddhist sect, must be thrown into the valley so as not to pollute the journey. The boy accepts his sacrifice, but his master's grief moves the other pilgrims to prayer, and the boy is resurrected to teach the pilgrims (and audience) of Buddha's miraculous power. Arthur Waley's famous translation, *The Nō Plays of Japan* (1922), represents *Tanikō* as a play about "the ruthless exactions of religion" and describes the resurrection in a brief footnote rather than providing a substantial translation of the second half of the play.[70] Waley knew something about *shudō*, particularly as pursued by samurai, since his close friend Edward Carpenter wrote an entire chapter about "their Ideal" in *Intermediate Types Among Primitive Folk* (1914).[71] Carpenter's argument against British homophobia claimed that "where the homosexual tendency was of the robuster and more manly sort," it produced great warriors like the samurai, but when it "was of a more effeminate and passive sort" it led to religious devotion, like that of the Buddhist priests.[72] This text that encouraged modernist interests in Japan may have encouraged Waley's preference for the virility of noh's warrior plays over the "exactions of religion" that Carpenter associated with femininity.

The mixed erotic and pedagogical elements of noh texts influenced twentieth-century adaptations, generally contributing to modernist noh's tendency to explore submission to authorities and forces outside oneself. When Bertolt Brecht adapted Waley's version of *Tanikō* (using Elizabeth Hauptmann's German translation) as *Der Jasager* (*He Said Yes*, 1930), he ignored the footnote and erased the miracle altogether. He kept the student dead, ostensibly as a lesson in self-sacrifice for the socialist revolution Brecht supported. In response to the children who protested and the Nazis and religious groups who applauded the boy's death, Brecht brought the student back to life in *Der Neinsager* (*He Said No*). But without the fascinating score that Kurt Weill provided for *Der Jasager*, the second play is rarely performed. Five of the noh translations that Pound published while serving as a kind of secretary-apprentice to Yeats during their winters together at Stone Cottage (1913–1916) tell the stories of beautiful young men using the *chigo* or *wakashu* trope. Among them, *Kumasaka* (by Zenchiku) features Ushiwaka, a character memorialized in epic poetry as a beautiful *chigo* and flutist and in noh as a *wakashu* with supernatural abilities in swordplay.[73] In Pound's version, Ushiwaka is a sixteen-year-old *wakashu* who slaughtered Kumasaka and thirteen bandits to prevent them from robbing his master (PFNoh 39). Three decades later, Pound recalled Kumasaka's tribute to his murderer, presenting it in The *Pisan Cantos* as a counterpoint to "Greek rascality" and "vulgarity."[74] Benjamin Britten and William Plomer resurrected the potential of the "beautiful boy" when they used noh and the play *Sumidagawa* (by Zeami's son Motomasa) as the basis for a didactic Christian theater that would allow for drag performance without humorous cross-dressing. The dead boy of *Sumidagawa*, whose graveside appearance fails to comfort his grieving mother, is reformed in *Curlew River* (1964) as the *chigo*-like inspiration for a spiritual transformation in the mother and other travelers.

Noh's stories of *chigo* and *wakashu* celebrate an attachment and devotion between student and teacher that endures beyond death. The pedagogical form of the noh lesson still encourages an intimacy between student and teacher, one that invited me to reconsider my assumption that submission to an authority and tradition would always be dehumanizing and oppressive. In the twentieth century, noh was adapted to teach values that opposed the semicolonial forced Westernization of the Meiji period and then those that supported Japan's march toward militaristic nationalism and World War II. Noh also circulated across national borders to encourage artistic collaborations and confrontations with cultural difference that taught modernism very different lessons. In this book, I want to take the "pedagogical" from its vexed place in the grand narratives of cultural theory and reposition it in the lessons, classrooms, studios, and stages where daily teaching and learning takes place. In these spaces, students submit to the authority of the teacher and to the pedagogical practices of any discipline, whether literary studies, piano lessons, or ballet. But that submission does not prevent students from having forms of agency, particularly the crucial "middle ranges." It might enable feelings of transcendent self-discovery or ascetic self-discipline, moments in which the self seems to explode or be created. Particularly when the pedagogical system is unfamiliar, it may expose our assumptions about selfhood, subversion, and submission.

The part I play in the pages that follow is a little like noh's *waki* (watcher or witness) role. The *waki* is usually a traveler on a mission to see and learn about a sacred place, and he serves as the onstage audience while a ghost appears to recount a love story or the tale of a battle from the Genpei war (1180–1185)— many of which have contributed to myths about the "essence" of Japan. My resemblance to the *waki* ends before his priestly act of praying for the ghost to help him or her to find peace by letting go of the Buddhist sin of "wrongful clinging." But like the *waki*, I remain persistently and self-consciously kneeling at the side of the stage, aware of my complicated position as a Westerner, woman, and scholar who, like the noh modernists I study, went looking for noh lessons.

In the first chapter, I discuss Pound and Yeats's collaboration with Itō and how noh influenced Pound's imagism and translation theory before helping him launch *The Cantos*, the long poem that celebrates authoritarian politics, among other somewhat distasteful themes that make it a challenging text to teach. The second chapter begins the story of the long international journey of *At the Hawk's Well*, discussing how the play figured in Yeats's ambitions for the Irish theater and ambivalent nationalism. My third chapter focuses on Itō Michio's career staging versions of *Hawk's Well*, noh-esque theater, and *japonistic* modern dance in the United States before being imprisoned as an enemy spy shortly after the Japanese attack on Pearl Harbor. I take a "pedagogical intermission" after considering the Pound-Yeats-Itō collaboration to write a lesson plan about a pedagogical exercise, and I describe a trick I have used to teach Brecht's revisions on his noh-inspired *Lehrstücke*, *Der Jasager* and *Der Neinsager*. I then consider how modernist noh influenced noh scholarship and performance in Japan, with a look at how the films of Ozu Yasujirō adapted the so-called traditional performance to modernist cinema. Finally, I examine Britten and Plomer's Christian drag "parable for church performance," *Curlew River*, and Beckett's eerie *Footfalls/Pas* as noh-influenced late modernist dramas.

Although I offer just one official pedagogical intermission, I intersperse my analysis of modernist noh with stories of learning and teaching this material, including noh lessons, dance technique classes, conference presentations, and classroom exercises. I am part of my own messy circuit of collaboration, learning, teaching, and misunderstanding that has regularly reminded me of the first thing I learned about taking noh lessons: it hurts. But the meditative, formal, and respectful position of *seiza* also helped me confront my assumptions about art, teaching, and performing. In some situations, it might be right to encounter cultures and art forms on our knees, having informed ourselves of the rituals of submission and decorous phrases in their pedagogies—that is, if we hope to learn.

1. EZRA POUND AS NOH STUDENT

[A] celestial maiden of the moon-laurel tree . . . present here briefly: for so the world learned the East Country's Suruga Dance!
Royall Tyler, *Japanese Nō Dramas*

HAGOROMO (THE FEATHER MANTLE) IS ONE OF THE MOST POPULAR and frequently performed plays in the noh repertory and often the first studied by amateur students like myself.[1] An angel (*tennin*) from the palace of the moon teaches a sacred dance to a fisherman after he steals and returns the feather garment that allows her to fly home. The unknown author of the play draws partly from the myth of a dance lesson given by a "heavenly maiden," which Zeami references as a divine influence on the development of noh.[2] Ezra Pound and W. B. Yeats studied *Hagoromo*, or an impression of the play, in 1914 with Itō Michio and several of the Japanese dancer's friends. Itō, who had not trained in noh performance technique (not even as an amateur), staged the first version of *Hagoromo* in the United States in 1923. He used the English translation first published in 1914 by Ezra Pound, who had not studied Japanese. Yeats then relied on Itō and *Hagoromo* when he developed his own bird-maiden for *At the Hawk's Well* (1916), the first and most influential of his dance plays modeled on noh. Judgmental accounts of the network claim that Yeats appropriated the noh form from Pound's error-ridden translations and Itō's unreliable teachings. *Hagoromo* opens with the theft of a sacred object and ends with a dance class that also teaches humility, a lesson that might apply to the difficulty of differentiating cultural robbery from collaborative teaching and learning.

Pound, Yeats, and even Itō certainly misunderstood aspects of noh and exhibited orientalist assumptions about the East as spiritual, traditional, mysterious, and essentially different from the West. But this might be the least interesting thing to say about a collaboration and series of lessons that influenced some of the most fascinating artworks of the twentieth century. Pound's so-called "mis"-representations and "mis"-translations point to the errors and creativity that are present in any translation. Cultural exchange always provokes uncertainties about who should be authorized to represent or teach a culture, why and how students should learn it, and even if there is a "real" or "true" culture that can be taught.[3] My goal here is not to "correct" the errors that I consider inevitable; to do so would imply that I claim the authority to represent a "true" Japan and knowledge of some "essence of noh," a claim that would fall into the orientalist trap of imagined, essential differences between the East and West. In the spirit of the fisherman who learns noh from a moon angel, I engage Pound's modernist noh collaborations with a focus on the pedagogical practices, desires, and erotics that shape the transmission of any cultural form. Like all performance genres, noh is a learned technique, and a focus on pedagogy is particularly appropriate to the emphasis on training in the noh tradition, the didactic elements in plays like *Hagoromo*, and the lessons that disseminated noh in modernism.

In this chapter, I use the play *Hagoromo* to introduce noh drama and its Buddhist-inflected ideas of personhood or subjectivity that are not defined by oppositions between subversion and submission. Noh's representations of subjectivity influenced Pound's construction of a multilayered or (what he might have called) "ideogrammic" poetic speaker as well as his rejection of common Western and liberal definitions of the person. Pound's putative failures as a noh student and teacher had a generative function that is evident in his performances, theories of imagism, and *The Pisan Cantos* (1948). Composed when he was imprisoned by the U.S. military for treason and controversially awarded the Bollingen Prize while he was incarcerated at St. Elizabeths Hospital (formerly the Government Hospital for the Insane), *The Pisan Cantos* presents anti-Semitic and pro-fascist ideas along with many ghosts from noh plays and the collaborators who helped him translate them. Although Pound was not the only modernist artist to use foreign art to promote distasteful politics and bigotry, he did so more loudly than many others. Considering Pound as a translator, collaborator, and noh student provides a different foundation from which to read the controversial works that exerted such a profound influence on modernism and still have much to teach us about the atrocities of the twentieth century.

THE LESSONS OF HAGOROMO

At the opening of Hagoromo, stage assistants place a small pine tree with a robe in its branches at center stage to suggest the setting at Miho Bay's pine groves (Miho no matsubara). The only scenery for noh plays are stage properties called tsukurimono (literally, "built things"), like this pine or the bare frame of a boat, usually made of bamboo wrapped in white cloth with little effort to make it look like a real thing (figure 1.1). A large pine tree called the oi matsu (old pine) is painted on the back wall of the theater as, according to Fenollosa, "a congratulatory symbol of unchanging green and strength" (PFNoh, 36). The stage is constructed of polished Japanese cypress to form a square with pillars (hashira) at the four corners (figure 1.2).[4] A bridgeway (hashigakari) extends approximately twenty-five feet from stage right and is flanked by three pine trees of decreasing size to create an impression of distance (figure 1.3). The orchestra (hayashi) includes a shoulder drum (kotsuzumi), hip drum (ōtsuzumi), flute (nōkan), and, in Hagoromo and slightly more than half of the 250 other plays in the noh repertory, a stick drum (taiko).[5] Stage assistants (koken) kneel in seiza behind the musicians at the back of the stage, and eight to ten performers in the chorus (jiutai) kneel stage left.

With the stage set, the waki (witness character) and several companions (wakizure) enter down the hashigakari. They sing of the fishermen at Mio in a verse pattern (shōdan) known as issei, an ornate section sung in a rhythm that does not match the beat of the drums.[6] In most plays, the shite soloist chants the issei, and by disrupting this convention, Hagoromo presents the waki as exceptional. He introduces himself in the second section, a naming verse (nanori), as "a fisherman named Hakuryō" (JND, 101). Hakuryō means "White Dragon" and refers to a Chinese story about a dragon that left heaven, turned himself into a fish, and was injured by a fisherman (JND, 99). The King of Heaven refused to condemn the fisherman because humans are permitted to kill fish. The author of Hagoromo, reading the Chinese myth as would an

FIGURE 1.1 A *tsukurimono* (built thing): the frame of a boat bound to the wall. (Courtesy of David Surtasky)

FIGURE 1.2 A noh stage. (Courtesy of David Surtasky)

FIGURE 1.3 The *hashigakari* (bridgeway) leading to the noh stage. (Courtesy of David Surtasky)

early modern Buddhist, uses Hakuryō to invoke the multilayered nature of humanity and the accretion of reincarnated lives. Hakuryō contains within himself the injured dragon, fallen from divinity and reborn through karma as the object of his hatred, as well as a human fisherman at risk of descending farther into hell.

Hakuryō's encounter with the feather mantle is a test, and his failure would result in his further fall from enlightenment. Early in the play, he celebrates in poetic language the pleasures of spring, indicating that it is possible for him to be uplifted by a "beauty to transport the heart with keen delight!" (JND, 101). The "wave washes the shore" and the "moon / loiters in the plains of Heaven," lines that bring together distinct, even oppositional substances (water, moon, and earth) and suggest that they could merge like the dragon and fisherman (JND, 101). As the *waki*, Hakuryō's function is to enable and witness the appearance of the *shite*, the *tennin* (angel) from the palace of the moon. He takes the feather mantle from the pine, and the angel calls out in protest from offstage.[7] The angel walks slowly down the bridgeway in the *suri-ashi* (sliding-foot walk) dressed in a sumptuous costume, elaborate headdress, and, usually, the *zō-onna* mask for young women and divinities (figure 1.4).

Hakuryō initially refuses to return the mantle, for high-minded familial and nationalistic reasons; he will "show it to the elders" and "make it a treasure of the realm" (JND, 102). Several other passages celebrate Japan's emperors as "gods' offspring" who "still rule / the moon-illumined land, source of the sun" (JND, 106). The play also quotes from a poem that was adapted for the modern Japanese national anthem, a passage suggesting the nation will endure for as long as it takes an angel's mantle to wear away the rock it brushes. These references to Japan's longevity as a sacred nation made *Hago-romo* an obvious choice for performance at the coronation of the Taishō emperor in 1915.[8] The play sets earthly values, politics, and beauty next to the heavenly, asking, "Heaven and earth, why, are they not one?" (JND, 105). If they were, the angel would not need her feathered mantle to return to her home on the moon. The play suggests that oppositional, divisive thought is one source of the separation. Hakuryō's challenge is to find the divine dragon within his fallen human state, not by an assertion of power, but through a deep sympathy that closes the gap between self and other, fisherman and *tennin*, waves and shore.

Hakuryō's lesson in sympathy begins as the angel pleads with him to return the robe in language that is emotionally elevated by a shift from prose to poetry (*mondō* to *kakeai*).[9] Hakuryō acknowledges his own unkindness, just as

FIGURE 1.4 *Hagoromo*: "It is as if the whole dance lives in the sleeves of the feather robe, performing the way of the Palace of the Moon." (Photograph © Toshiro Morita, provided by website http://www.the-noh.com)

the angel laments "her desperate plight" (JND, 103). The connection between the characters is emphasized when Hakuryō takes lines that might have been sung by the angel or a narrator:

ANGEL: What then shall I do? in distress she cries,
HAKURYŌ: and when Hakuryō still withholds the mantle,
ANGEL: helpless,
HAKURYŌ: hopeless. (JND, 103)

The chorus (jiutai) breaks in at this moment to describe the "five signs of an angel's decline" that signal her approaching death (JND, 103). The noh chorus sometimes chants lines that represent the speech of the shite or waki and sometimes describes the stage action as would a narrator, a variation that seems to break down the distinctions between characters.

Noh language in English translation feels not only poetic but also "unrealistic," in part because Japanese pronouns do not specify subjects. The translator faces difficult choices with pronouns because English speakers rarely refer to themselves in the third person, and Hakuryō's reference to himself by name is not particularly unusual in Japanese but is unusual in English. Other unrealistic features in noh performance include the chant-like vocal delivery, masks, ornate and bulky costumes, slow suriashi walk, forward-leaning posture (kamae), musicians, chorus, and stage attendants, that is, nearly every aspect of noh performance. Pound and other modernists appreciated these features as part of noh's demand for "acting that is not mimetic" (PFNoh, 5). Noh is not mimetic in that it does not imitate Western ideas of "reality" or comply with the conventions of Euro-American realist performance, even though convention is precisely what makes an acting style seem like a realistic representation of life. Euro-American audiences expect actors to ignore their presence in a theater, but another performance tradition might assume that a realistic, truthful performance would acknowledge the audience. The common claim that noh is "antitheatrical" or "not dramatic" ignores the definitions of theatricality operating in Japanese performing arts. The conventionally theatrical suriashi walk and kamae posture are shared by kabuki, Japanese dancing (nihon buyō), the puppet theater (bunraku), and martial arts, among others.

The characteristics of noh that Pound and others understood as "not mimetic" contribute to the pedagogical goals of noh, particularly its teachings about what it means to be human. These techniques maintain a distance between the actor and the character, a distance that Western realistic or "method acting" seeks to eliminate.[10] Noh performance technique does not encourage audience members to suspend their disbelief that an actor is not actually the character. When playing the angel or another feminine character, noh actors (still usually men but even women) chant in a deep chest voice, never attempting to sound feminine. The delicate masks do not completely cover the actors' faces. Noh presents dramatic characters not as personal subjects but as stage "objects" like the tsukurimono constructions of pines, boats, or graves. The illusion of becoming a character might be considered an arrogant pretension when playing the angel of Hagoromo or a figure of historical or religious importance. A noh actor's humble relationship to character is evident in the practice of having a child actor (kokata) play an emperor or highly ranked official so as to eliminate any pretension toward "realistic" impersonation. Humility is reinforced by noh pedagogy's demand that students submit to the authority of the teacher and the "parrot-like repetition" (ōmugaeshi) method that emphasizes memorizing the repertory and performance technique rather than interpreting the play.

For students like me who fail to restrain their impulse toward textual analysis, Hagoromo might be interpreted as both an originary noh dance class and a lesson in humility in which the surrender of a personal self allows for an approach to the heavenly sphere. As the angel and Hakuryō trade lines and her divinity fades, he begins to sympathize with her plight. Hakuryō says he will return the feather mantle if she agrees to perform her "angel dance" (JND, 104). Although she would "gladly" leave a dance for "this sad, lower world," she needs her mantle to perform it (JND, 104). Hakuryō initially refuses, believing she might fly off if he gives it to her before the dance lesson, but she shames him: "No, no, suspicion is only for humans. / In Heaven, falsehood is quite unknown" (JND, 104). Hakuryō finally returns the mantle, which is presented quite literally as a costume when the stage assistants dress the angel in the garment onstage in view of the audience. Hakuryō's theft misattributed value to a costume, failing to recognize that its sacredness was achieved only through its use in performance.

The angel, like Hakuryō, has her own "role" that she must "faithfully serve": the teaching of the dance performed by "fifteen angel maidens," who, "robed in white or black," produce the moon phases (JND, 105). She submits to that performance and also to the one in which she was "divided in two, / and present here briefly: for so the world learned / the East Country's Suruga Dance!" (JND, 105). These lines suggest that the angel was magically divided to appear on earth while never leaving the heavens, "like the moon reflected below" (JND, 105). The reflection of the moon in water is present "below," although the moon never falls from the sky, and like the reflection, the angel is present on the stage for a short time to teach Hakuryō and the audience a lesson. If she also is a representative of the "almighty Seishi, source of the Lord of the Moon," as her prayer to the divinity implies, she could have easily wrested the mantle away from the lowly fisherman (JND, 106). Yet she appeared before him as a vulnerable girl and even allowed herself to begin to suffer an angel's death in order to teach Hakuryō compassion and bring him closer to enlightenment.

We tend to teach theater as if conflict were necessary, but noh suggests that this may be a "curious European—Christian and then bourgeois individualist—fixation on adversariness."[11] The protagonist's battle against an antagonist is less important to noh than are "revelation" and "celebration."[12] The conflict-driven individualism in Euro-American drama is part of a wider culture that suggests we all should be unique. "Being ourselves" often implies struggling against an opponent and subverting the norms and traditions that would diminish our individuality. In contrast, Hakuryō's agency or uniqueness is not of great interest in *Hagoromo*. His last lines are chanted halfway through the play and simply describe the sleeves of the "celestial mantle" as they "sway and flutter" (JND, 104). He watches silently, mirroring the audience for the rest of the play, which features the angel's dance and poetry celebrating her "loveliness" as "the moon's own" and the full moon as "the face of accomplished truths" before she "fades into the heavens, / lost for ever to view" (JND, 106–7). Fulfillment and beauty are linked to loss at the end of *Hagoromo*, and the submission to the loss of the angel is also part of the lesson.

The angel's appearance, suffering, and departure guide Hakuryō toward enlightenment and also enable the world to learn the Suruga Dance. A divine dance lesson was invoked as well in Zeami's discussion of the "Dance of the Heavenly Maiden" as "the basis" for all noh.[13] He wrote that the dance was part of his family's teachings and that direct transmission was more important than skill: "We should assign the authentic effect to reside only where there has been an oral transmission through a proper lineage."[14] Direct transmission from teacher to student within the hierarchical organization of the noh schools (ryū) is still celebrated. Ernest Fenollosa learned this principle from his teacher, Umewaka Minoru, claiming, "In Noh everything comes down by tradition from early Tokugawa days and cannot be judged by any living man, but can only be followed faithfully." Pound added a footnote: "This is not so stupid as it seems; we might be fairly grateful if some private or chartered company had preserved the exact Elizabethan tradition for acting Shakespeare" (PFNoh, 29).

Noh's emphasis on tradition, submission, and celebration rightfully worries critics like Darko Suvin, who asked, "Is that compatible with the heritage (which I do not wish to lose) of the Marxist lesson of class-struggle, or with Nietzsche's and Freud's lessons of hypocrisy and repression as the inevitable basis of all ruling-class pieties?"[15] I do not wish to lose these lessons or other critiques of gender oppression, empire, and bigoted nationalisms, but I also worry about the pieties these "heritages" can produce. Suvin concluded, "I find revelation and/or celebration simply too important to be conceded (as the Left has often most misguidedly done) to the rulers."[16] The "revelation" and "celebration" that many art forms offer are not always less beautiful or instructive for having been patronized by the ruling classes, whether the Tokugawa *bakufu*, Medici family, or Solomon R. Guggenheim. We submit to many different heritages and to the teachers, dissertation directors, and reviewers who help us learn them. If we study performance, we submit to the labor of attempting to recover Shakespeare, noh, and other theatrical traditions and to our inevitable failure to realize them on stages or describe them in our writing. That is, we submit to a good deal, as we live mostly in "the middle ranges of agency" rather than the extremes we tend to emphasize.[17]

POUND AS HAKURYŌ IN COLLABORATION

TENNIN: Learn then this dance that can turn the palace of the moon. . . .
> But give me my mantle, I cannot do the dance rightly without it.
HAKURYŌ: Not yet, for if you should get it, how do I know you'll not be off
> to your palace without even beginning your dance, not even a measure?
TENNIN: Doubt is of mortals; with us there is no deceit.
HAKURYŌ: I am again ashamed. I give you your mantle.
> Ezra Pound and Ernest Fenollosa, *The Classic Noh Theater of Japan*

Pound treated noh the way that *Hagoromo's* fisherman Hakuryō stole the mantle of an angel and traded it for a sacred dance, or so it would seem from the two charges leveled against his noh translations: They are (1) riddled with errors or full of "deceit" and (2) are among the "thefts" that inspired modernist aesthetic experiments. The deceit and theft paradigms imply that non-Western texts and cultural traditions in the early twentieth century would have been stable and healthy if they had not been attacked by Western imperialism. The

production, publication, and dissemination of texts and traditions are collaborative acts, often carried out through pedagogical networks of exchange.
Definitive noh texts have never existed because the five different schools and
even groups in the same school perform different versions.[18] Plays like *Hagoromo* were created anonymously in the fourteenth and fifteenth centuries by
actors with little interest in publication, and textual records are considered
subordinate to direct transmission in lessons. Presenting a source text as if it
were a pure document of a culture and evaluating a translation by some rigid
standard of "fidelity" ignore the complex relationship between texts and the
heterogeneous cultures of their collective producers. I offer a more sympathetic model of Pound's intercultural teaching and collaboration to supplement the deceit and theft paradigms. Cross-cultural lessons often nurture
intimate relations between teacher and student, and every pedagogical scene
presents messy erotics and a risk of failure. These features of Pound's noh
lessons fostered his identification with the fisherman Hakuryō, who doubts
the angel-teacher and his ability to learn her dance.

The spoils of global conquest appear everywhere in modernism: Pablo
Picasso famously invented cubism and began collecting "African art" after a
1907 visit to Paris's Trocadéro Museum, which featured works taken by the
French during the colonization of Africa.[19] Ernest Fenollosa collected Japanese art that was undervalued during the Westernization of the Meiji period
(1868–1912), and his collection eventually went to the Boston Museum of Fine
Arts, where he served as curator of the department of "Oriental art" from
1890 to 1895. His manuscripts containing draft translations of Chinese poetry and noh plays went to Pound, who acted as Fenollosa's literary executor.
The Mexican poet and Nobel Prize laureate Octavio Paz observed that Pound
treated texts like a "Roman conqueror": "Appropriating a foreign god and
making off with the text of an alien people are magic rites whose meaning
is the same."[20] Nonetheless, Pound's translation and circulation of "foreign"
texts were part of his commitment to challenging "Provincialism the Enemy,"
and he did this work as part of a series of collaborations that provoke questions about who owns a text, who can teach a "rite" or a dance, and how the
preferred answers to those questions have changed over time.[21]

Far from presenting himself as a "conqueror" in relation to noh, Pound
generally emphasized a Hakuryō-like humility. A fisherman associated with
Hagoromo is the first poetic persona in Pound's initial drafts of *The Cantos* published in *Poetry* in 1917, just after his most intense work on noh translations:
"Say that I dump my catch, shiny and silvery / As fresh sardines flapping and

slipping on the marginal cobbles?"[22] This Hakuryō has stolen and donned the mantle of artistic inspiration but doesn't know what to do with it: "Whom shall I hang my shimmering garment on; / Who wear my feathery mantle, hagoromo; / Whom set to dazzle the serious future ages?"[23] Searching for a "new form" ("semi-dramatic, semi-epic") and speaker for the massive poem that he would write for the rest of his life, Pound invoked figures from the past and suggested that each is a version of himself: "Is't worth the evasion, what were the use / Of setting figures up and breathing life upon them / Were't not our life . . ."[24] Pound presented himself in the racial, gendered, and "temporal drag" of the Japanese fisherman who wonders how to "dazzle" readers.[25] This version of drag questions the progress of the "future ages" as it reanimates the dead without hiding the actor "breathing life" into the ghostly mask.

Pound's noh translations were the product of a series of intercultural, homosocial, and often homoerotic collaborations in which Pound frequently positioned himself as the receptive student.[26] By focusing on the erotic aspects of Pound's collaborations but refusing to define the sexual identities of the players, I risk seeming to make too much of suggestive details. But artistic collaborations often create an erotic potential that exceeds the confines of identity labels (like gay/straight). In Pound's noh work, this potential is heightened by the confusions and misunderstandings produced by his interest in what he considered "exotic" and ancient arts and his lack of familiarity with the languages and cultures of his collaborators. When Mary Fenollosa asked Pound to be her late husband's literary executor, she encouraged his interest in Hagoromo and (albeit unintentionally) in beautiful noh students. Her letter of November 25, 1913, claimed, "Hagoromo is perhaps the favorite of all, with the average Japanese Nōh lover, and is a legend strangely like the old Celtic one of the mermaid who had her magic sea-garments stolen by a mortal."[27] If she had decided to edit the book herself, she would have begun with an anecdote about Umewaka Minoru's "two beautiful sons . . . whether real or adopted I am not sure, but that doesn't matter in Japan. The son who is adopted for reasons of fitness, talent, and capability of carrying on an artistic tradition is considered more real than a son who is merely of the flesh. All the great artists of old times adopted successors this way."[28] She invoked the practice of formally adopting students into the noh schools (ryū) and families to establish a kinship of "talent" rather than "flesh," also an indication of the intimate bonds developed by teachers and students. She was probably not aware of the historical connections between the noh aesthetic of yūgen and youthful male beauty, but she dwells on the appearance of the sons and compares Indian and Japanese styles of exoticism: "Both were beautiful . . . the younger, our teacher in the singing of Nōh, was more like a soulful and very handsome East Indian poet than a Japanese."[29]

In his publication of the noh translations, Pound described Ernest Fenollosa's career as "the romance par excellence of modern scholarship" and celebrated Fenollosa's "wonderful" progress as a student of Umewaka Minoru and sons (PFNoh, 3).[30] Pound exaggerated Fenollosa's efforts to save Japan's so-called native art and claimed that after he died in London in 1908, "the Japanese government sent a warship for his body, and the priests buried him within the sacred enclosure at Miidera" (PFNoh, 3).[31] Fenollosa's ashes were, in fact, interned at the Miidera temple near Kyoto overlooking Lake Biwa, but they were carried to Japan on the Siberian railroad. If the apocryphal warship story did not fulfill persistent exotic longings, New Directions Publishing Corporation might not have continued to reprint it on the dust jacket (leading to my own humbling error in a conference presentation). While Pound embellished the response to Fenollosa's teaching that Japan must "stop the aping of Europe," he suppressed another pedagogical relationship crucial to the transmission of the noh texts (PFNoh, 3). Mary Fenollosa's 1913 letter about the "beautiful sons" also described, albeit with much less enthusiasm, "little Mr. Hirata, a pupil of my husband's" who "did" the translations, although she did not "think much of his literary style."[32] Hirata Kiichi (1873–1943) was Fenollosa's colleague, not student, at the Higher Normal School. He was not a student of noh, but he became a renowned scholar of English literature under the pen name of Tokuboku.[33] He accompanied Fenollosa to lessons and produced literal translations of plays before they attended, for example, a production of *Hagoromo* on January 15, 1899.[34] Hirata appears twice without explanation in the publication of what should be called the Fenollosa-Hirata-Pound translations (PFNoh, 27, 115). Pound celebrated Fenollosa's lessons with the noh master Umewaka but avoided discussing his more complex and fluid collaboration with Hirata.

Pound positioned himself in the assistant role, explaining in his "Note" to the translations, "The vision and the plan are Fenollosa's. In the prose I have had but the part of literary executor; in the plays my work has been that of translator who has found all the heavy work done for him and who has had but the pleasure of arranging beauty into the words" (PFNoh). Pound thereby confessed his "own ignorance" in a rhetorical gesture that made him the student of a ghostly or supernatural teacher, like many noh characters. His work with noh was dramatically shaped by a series of live collaborations centered

on Itō Michio. Pound met Itō in May 1915 at the Café Royal, a haunt of ex-
patriate artists, and asked for his assistance in editing the Fenollosa-Hirata
draft translations. Itō claimed in his autobiography that he told Pound that
he had seen noh as a child, "but as far as I'm concerned there's nothing more
boring. Besides I couldn't presume to assist you."[35] Pound persisted, and
Itō contacted Kōri Torahiko and the painter Kume Tamijurō (Pound's Tami
Koumé) to help him give a demonstration for Pound and Yeats in June or July
1915; Kōri and Kume probably chanted utai while Itō danced an impression of
a noh shimai (dance).[36] Kume had studied noh performance with Fenollosa's
teacher, Umewaka, and Pound claimed in a 1939 article for the Japan Times and
Mail, "Study of Noh Continues in the West," that Kume performed Hagoromo
at the recital: "Tami Koumé had danced the Hagoromo before the Emperor,
taking the tennin part when he was, as I remember, six years old. At twenty
he still remembered the part and movements of the tennin's wings, which as
she returns to the upper heavens, are the most beautiful movements I have
seen on or off any stage."[37]

    Although it is extremely unlikely that a child actor would ever play the an-
gel in Hagoromo (much less in a full play before an emperor), Kume probably studied the play with Umewaka. Pound's retelling of the anecdote almost
twenty-five years after the performance indicated the significance of Hagoromo in his thinking about noh, stage movement, and beautiful collaborators. Pound celebrated Kume's study of noh technique as preferable to the
knowledge of a "mere philologist" but claimed that Kume could not answer
questions about "metaphysics" and other concerns Pound believed to be "essential to the meaning." Pound suggested this was due to the "poetic values"
and "vague" qualities of the noh plays: "a haze over the almond blossoms."[38]
Still, Pound appreciated Kume's assistance with the translations in a mourn-
ful letter of 1936: "But since Tami Koumé was killed in that earth quake [Sep-
tember 1, 1923] I have had no one to explain the obscure passages or fill up
the enormous gaps of my IGNORANCE."[39]

    The seventeen surviving letters from Kume to Pound show that they had
a warm friendship with erotic undertones. When Pound was "sick in bed,"
Kume wrote that he was "so anxious" and had planned to visit but was "temp-
tated" to "study some play" with Itō and Edmund Dulac [sic].[40] The pedagogical network had clearly expanded to include smaller study groups initiated
by Itō as well as Pound. When Kume left London the following year, he declared his "sentimentalism" and asked for "nice poems," which Pound seems
to have sent.[41] Kume "admired" a photograph of Pound given to him by Alvin

Langdon Coburn, sent drawings, and addressed Pound as "MY DEAREST
FRIEND ON THE EARTH."[42] In 1921, Kume sent a letter consisting entirely
of a poem that ended with a stanza referencing Oscar Wilde's novel, *The Picture of Dorian Gray* (1891), which was famously used as evidence in his trial for
homosexual acts:

> What you call the soul
> Is!
> Hearing the inaudible voice
> From the picture of Dorian Grey.[43]

Pound sponsored an exhibition of Kume's paintings in 1922 in Paris, includ-
ing a large painting that Pound entitled "Tami's dream" and later hung in the
Venice house of his lover Olga Rudge. It was among the treasures of the "hidden nest" destroyed during the war that Pound mourns in *The Pisan Cantos*.[44]
Just before his death, Kume wrote to Pound about his marriage engagement:
"I am sure you will like her, as you do like me, after you shall know her a little
more."[45] Pound's responses were most likely lost in the earthquake that killed
Kume, but the surviving letters sketch out the transnational homosocial col-
laborations that contributed to Pound's understanding of noh.

The most famous of Pound's collaborations, as well as one of modernism's
favorite stories of poetic inspiration, took place at Stone Cottage in Sussex,
England, in the winters of 1913 to 1916, where Pound served as a "secretary"
for the older Irish poet and playwright, W. B. Yeats.[46] Stone Cottage is easily exaggerated as a domestic hideaway where two great poets helped each
other transform their careers and determined the course of modernist poetics. The cottage near the Five Hundred Acre Wood (inspiration for A. A.
Milne's Winnie-the-Pooh stories) was also the setting for much of the translation of noh, the instigation of Pound's *Cantos*, and Yeats's renewed efforts to
write plays. Pound read his noh drafts and other (mostly "esoteric") literature
aloud to Yeats, whose eyesight was failing; Pound also famously taught Yeats
to fence.[47] They engaged in "verbal fencing matches" as well, with Yeats com-
menting on the galley proofs of *Certain Noble Plays of Japan* (1916), a book of
four noh translations that Yeats had convinced his sisters to publish at their
Cuala Press. In the account of the night battle between Kumasaka and the
"young boy" Ushiwaka, with the erotic description of Kumasaka "holding
his long spear against his side" and lifting it until "the two weapons were
twisted together," Pound's translation relates: "Slowly the wound— / seemed

to pierce" (PFNoh, 44–45). Yeats responded, "This raises an incorrect mental picture. A weapon not a wound 'pierces.'"[48] Pound ignored this and most of his mentor's corrections, but he did not forget *Kumasaka*, referring to the play in "Ur-Canto II" and *The Pisan Cantos* and discussing the battle repeatedly in his comments on noh. He was particularly interested in the ghost of the robber who "makes reparation for his brigandage by protecting the country" and returns "to praise the bravery of the young man who had killed him in single combat" (PFNoh, 39).

Pound's collaborations with Yeats, Itō, and Kume, along with his work on the Fenollosa-Hirata manuscripts, encouraged me to present the intimacy of translation as an alternative to moralistic evaluations of fidelity or deceit.[49] Pound's own theories of translation emphasized various forms of intimacy, often homosocial and misogynistic forms. He recommended collaborative translation in his famous dictum "Literature belongs to no one man, and translations of great works ought perhaps to be made by a committee."[50] In 1935, he described looking back on a translation he had done eighteen years earlier, during the time of his noh work, and finding a lack of intimacy: "I did not see Guido [Cavalcanti] at all."[51] For Pound, *seeing* Guido would have meant capturing a desirable "*robustezza*, a masculinity" that his translation had missed.[52] His struggle to achieve intimacy with Guido was not stymied by the Italian language that he was attempting to translate, but by "the crust of dead English, the sediment present in my own available vocabulary. . . . I hadn't in 1910 made a language."[53] To extricate himself from the bog of normal English, Pound did not invent a new language but turned back to an earlier moment in the history of his language and chose an archaic "pre-Elizabethan English" for Guido's thirteenth-century Italian. Translating the poem in an anachronistic language, he believed, was actually more "faithful" because it preserved the "masculinity," the feeling of "antiquity," and the "fervor of the original."[54] His one caveat, that "the translator is in all probability impotent to do all the work for the linguistically lazy reader," indicates that Pound imagined the scene of translation as an erotic triangle requiring readers, writers, and translators to labor in an intimate embrace.[55]

Pound's imagined scene of translation and actual collaborations produced an intimacy inflected with masculinist *robustezza*. This form of intimacy mirrors the plots of noh plays like *Hagoromo* and *Kumasaka*, as they perform ideal bonds among even former opponents in battle as occasions for translation between humans and spirits. Such relations among enemies, living humans, and ghosts did not usually disrupt codes of masculinity or femininity in

Japan—or the norms of nation, race, class, ethnicity, and the like. But noh did offer nonliberal, nondualistic, often submissive, and erotic forms of being, which influenced modernism through creative translations that were never imagined as aspiring to common standards of fidelity or accuracy. I do not claim that Pound produced what might be called "queer translations" because I do not want to suppose a threshold of queerness that would ultimately depend on the submission/subversion bind. (For example, is this translation *subversive* enough to be queer?)[56] Instead, I want to present the intimacy and eroticisms of collaborative translation as an example of cross-cultural teaching and learning in which misunderstanding can be fertile and creative.

Teaching "Unity of Image" and Other Creative Translations

> [A] Japanese emperor whose name I have forgotten and whose name you needn't remember, found that there were TOO MANY NOH PLAYS, he picked out 450 and the Noh stage LASTED from 1400 or whenever right down till the day the American navy intruded, and that didn't stop it. Umewaka Minoru started again as soon as the revolution wore off.
>
> Ezra Pound, ABC of Reading

Pound began this particular noh lesson by forgetting the name of the emperor that limited the canon, which ensured the survival of noh from an uncertain date ("1400 or whenever") until an invasion that failed to "stop it" and a revolution that also "wore off."[57] From the discarded plays to failed revolutions, the passage emphasizes failure and the difficulty of transmitting knowledge across cultures. The Fenollosa-Hirata-Pound translations have occasionally inspired critics to produce a "balance sheet" of "errors" blamed on Pound.[58] Others have defended them not as translations but as original contributions to English literature, again crediting Pound.[59] Set against the collaborative nature of the translations, both the blame and the praise for Pound indicate an investment in models of individual agency and authorship. The Fenollosa-Hirata-Pound plays contributed to Euro-American modernism largely through the *creativity* of the translation. If I occasionally point out productive errors, it is not because I believe that it is possible for anyone to transmit a perfect or "real" noh.[60] Even expert noh actors in the same school perform and understand their work differently. Pound used creative translations to invent a version of noh and imagism that influenced Euro-American and Japanese modernisms and even—by another skewed translation—the partially invented and contested noh tradition in Japan (a story I tell in chapter 5). Creative learning might take place when teaching appears to fail, a useful lesson at a time when teachers must defend their relevance against digital networks of information and produce measurable learning outcomes, standardized assessments, and *U.S. News & World Report* rankings.

Pound published the first translation of *Hagoromo* in October 1914 before the play was performed on December 8, 1915, to celebrate the coronation of Emperor Taishō, an event indicating that the ancient arts could influence modern nationalisms.[61] Pound's introduction to the play emphasized noh's role in the court and the actors' "pride of descent, pride in having served dynasties now extinct" (PFNoh, 6). Pound framed *Hagoromo* as evidence of "the relation of the early Noh to the God-dance," following Fenollosa's claim that the "most certainly Japanese element of the drama was the sacred dance in the Shinto temples," which "repeated the action of a local god on his first appearance to men" (PFNoh, 98, 63). The Fenollosa-Hirata-Pound *Hagoromo* is quite similar to the widely accepted translations by Royall Tyler and Kenneth Yasuda, although Pound made the English sound more foreign with unusual syntax, unfamiliar names, and stereotypical images of Japan:

Windy road of the waves by Miwo,
Swift with ships, loud over steersmen's voices.
Hakuryō taker of fish, head of his house, dwells upon the barren pine-
waste of Miwo. (PFNoh, 98)

The relation between subjects and adjectives is ambiguous: Is the road "windy," or are the waves following a metaphorical "windy road"? Are the ships "swift," or do the waves or road seem swift because of the ships sailing there? Hakuryō seems more foreign when described as a "taker of fish" rather than a fisherman.

Pound also inserted modern European interests into the text by creating an angel who teaches lessons on imagism and modernist aesthetics in addition to the divine dance. Pound claimed that "the Noh has its unity in emotion. It has also what we may call Unity of Image. At least, the better plays are all built into the intensification of a single Image: . . . the mantle of feathers in the play of that name, Hagoromo" (PFNoh, 27). Pound never explained how this "Unity of Image" is achieved, but he referred to the feathered mantle throughout his version of the play to establish related clusters of images. Hakuryō and his companions sing of spring's beauty, and the angel appears to be a vernal spirit whose flowers begin "drooping and fading" after Hakuryō steals her mantle (PFNoh, 100). Images of her celebratory dance unite her flowing robe with the season's blossoms and storms: "The sleeves of flowers are being wet with the rain" (PFNoh, 102). "The rustling of the flowers, the putting on of the feathery sleeve; they bend in the air with the dancing" (PFNoh, 104). The chorus sings of the "plumage of heaven," "feathery skirt of the stars," and "robe of mist" (PFNoh, 103–4). As these related images create a structural unity for the play, Pound's Hakuryō realizes that nature, humanity, and the spirit world "are doing one step," and he learns to dance in "unity" as well (PFNoh, 102). The "Unity of Image" that Pound celebrated matches the play's theme of connecting heaven and earth or the divine dragon and the fisherman.

Literary scholars have long recognized that Pound adapted principles from Japanese art and poetry for imagist aesthetics, but they tend to focus on haiku and ukiyo-e woodblock prints or group noh or include noh as part of a generalized fascination with Japan (japonisme) rather than attend to its specific aesthetics.[62] Pound's work on noh contributed to the shift from his first modernist poetic school, imagism (or "les Imagistes"), to his next, more interdisciplinary aesthetic movement, vorticism (ca. 1914). But noh's impact on his evolving theories is usually ranked below factors like his battle with Amy Lowell over the leadership of "les Imagistes."[63] The dating of Pound's statements on imagism and noh help clarify the major influences on the development of his poetic ideas. Pound published his iconic "In a Station of the Metro" in Poetry, April 1913, and T.P.'s Weekly of June 6 gave his first description of how, inspired by the Japanese haiku, he had compressed a thirty-line draft about his "sudden emotion" in Paris's La Concorde Metro station into the famous two-liner.[64] Pound retold the story of "Metro" fifteen months later in his famous "Vorticism" essay published in Fortnightly Review, but with an important difference derived from his work on noh. He added a footnote to his passage from the Paris Metro to the haiku of a Japanese naval officer (with stops in Kandinsky's Germany and Picasso's Spain): "I am often asked whether there can be a long imagiste or vorticist poem. The Japanese, who evolved the hokku, evolved also the Noh plays. In the best 'Noh' the whole play may consist of one image. I mean it is gathered about one image. Its unity consists in one image, enforced by movement and music. I see nothing against a long vorticist poem."[65]

At this point, Pound had finished his work on Hagoromo, which appeared in the October edition of the Quarterly Review with Kinuta and a version of Fenollosa's 1903 lecture on noh.[66] He had also finished *Nishikigi* (*The Brocade Tree*) and sent it, instead of his own work, to Harriet Monroe for *Poetry* magazine, saying that it "will give us some reason for existing."[67] Mary Fenollosa had encouraged Pound to translate *Hagoromo*, *Kinuta*, and *Nishikigi* first, which proved to be important to Pound's thinking about noh and the possibility of a "long imagiste or vorticist poem."[68] When he restated his footnote from "Vorticism" about noh's "unity of image" in the book-length *"Noh," or Accomplishment* (1917), Pound provided the examples of *Nishikigi*'s "red maple leaves and the snow flurry," "the pines" in *Takasago*," *Suma Genji*'s "wave pattern," and *Hagoromo*'s "mantle of feathers" (PFNoh, 27). *Hagoromo*'s mantle recurs as a trope gathering images of spring and dance to teach a lesson about the unity of nature, humanity, and the spiritual world. This unity seemed to offer a model for expanding modernist poetics from the haiku-like brevity of the "Metro" poem. Pound enthusiastically generalized the idea of unity of image to all noh, thereby leading him to misread or mistranslate other plays.[69]

Pound's approach to *Nishikigi* and its influence on both modernism and Japanese noh scholarship is a particularly interesting case study in creative misunderstanding. The Fenollosa-Hirata-Pound translations usually cut parts of their source text (for example, they translated just 20 percent of *Sotoba Komachi*), but their *Nishikigi* is actually longer.[70] Belonging to the fourth category of dream plays (*mugen nō*), *Nishikigi* is more typical than *Hagoromo*: A traveling monk journeys to the fictitious town of Kefu where he meets an old man and woman who attempt to sell him the famous products of the region, nishikigi (brocade trees), decorated sticks used as love charms, and hosonuno, a woven cloth so narrow that it came to symbolize unrequited love.[71] They tell the story of a man who set nishikigi outside the gate of the woman he had loved for three years. She went on weaving her narrow hosonuno and never took the charms inside to signal her acceptance and love. He died in despair, and she died soon after hearing of his pain. They were buried together. The old couple guide the monk to the grave mound, represented onstage as a tsukurimono and then seem to disappear inside. The monk says a prayer for them before falling asleep, and in the second act, he dreams that they return as the ghosts of the suffering lovers. They reenact their story in song and dance, and the monk's prayer helps them reconcile before dawn ends the dream.

Pound's *Nishikigi* includes these basic features of the story, but he appears to have added "unity" to the play by inventing additional images of maple leaves and snow flurries. Each has a limited presence in Japanese versions of the play, but Pound misread or creatively reinterpreted the Fenollosa-Hirata drafts. "Leaf" first appears in Pound's version in a line describing a storm: "trees giving up their leaf" (PFNoh, 81). Pound developed the image from Fenollosa's gloss or paraphrase of two Chinese characters that are read together as "cold gusts" or "storm winds."[72] Among Fenollosa's manuscripts was the essay "The Chinese Written Character as a Medium for Poetry," which celebrated and overemphasized the "images" or "ideograms" in Chinese characters by calling them "shorthand pictures of actions and processes in nature," like "trees giving up their leaf" rather than adjectives and nouns like "cold gusts."[73] Although Pound had not yet published the essay when he was working on the noh drafts, he began using Fenollosa's creative interpretation of the Chinese language to develop an ideogrammic method for the translation and interpretation of noh. He associated falling leaves with the play's references to autumn and with the charm sticks when he described the scarlet lacquered nishikigi as "dyed like the maple leaf" (PFNoh, 81).[74] Although images of leaves do not appear again in the Japanese text or Fenollosa's draft, Pound's later references to nishikigi recalled the colors of autumn leaves: "Until the year's end is red with autumn, / Red like these love-wands" (PFNoh, 86). Pound gathered maple leaves, autumn trees, and scarlet nishikigi into a unified image reinforcing the play's message of the brevity of life and the need for reconciliation, even after death.[75]

Pound derived his second unity, the image of snow, in a similarly creative process, since the word appears just once in his source text in a conventional phrase describing the dancers' "sleeves fluttering like snowflakes" or, as Pound wrote, "like snow-whirls."[76] He gave his ghost-woman other snow images: "Our hearts have been in the dark of the falling snow, / We have been astray in the flurry" (PFNoh, 83). According to Takeuchi Akiko, the phrase is usually translated as "I've been wandering in the darkness of a tormented heart" (kakikurasu kokorono yamini madoiniki). But Fenollosa wrote a comment in the draft translation suggesting that the word kakikurasu (tormented/darkened) was "used when snow falls" and "had [a] meaning of struggling and so feeling one's self going out."[77] Takeuchi pointed out that there is only a weak suggestion of snow in kakikurasu, and we do not know if perhaps Hirata revealed that to Fenollosa or if one of them particularly liked snow imagery. In any event, Pound chose the image of a winter flurry to capture the psychological suffering and cold feeling that Fenollosa's notes implied.[78] Pound's monk replies by asking the ghosts, "Only show me the old times over-past and snowed under" (PFNoh, 83). In the Japanese text, he simply requests, "Please reenact the past." Takeuchi indicated that Pound inserted "snowed

under" because he misread the word "show" in Fenollosa's handwritten manuscript, but it is also possible that he was following the snowy trope he had
established.

My intention in comparing translations is not to expose Pound's failure
by reasserting the usual standards of fidelity.[79] Instead, I propose that Pound
received the noh texts when he was seeking a method for expanding his imagist aesthetics. He found evidence of recurring images in the first plays he edited, particularly *Hagoromo*, and then creatively translated other plays so they
supported his generalized theory of noh's unity: "The spirit is invoked and
appears," he wrote in his foreword to *Tsunemasa* (PFNoh, 54). Pound invoked
a spirit of unity that helped him solve the problems he was facing in his own
poetic writing, and it appeared for him in other plays. He passed on the idea
of noh's unity to Euro-American poets, especially Yeats and T. S. Eliot, and it
is now a commonplace that modernist and contemporary poetry, in the absence of classical form, regular meter, and rhyme, is organized by recurring
images that build on one another until the trope resolves itself in a revelation
or unified impression.[80] Yeats's introduction to the Fenollosa-Hirata-Pound
translations provides a detailed analysis of *Nishikigi*'s pattern of images:

> I wonder am I fanciful in discovering in the plays themselves . . . a play-
> ing upon a single metaphor, as deliberate as the echoing rhythm of line in
> Chinese and Japanese painting. In the "Nishikigi" the ghost of the girl-lover
> carries the cloth she went on weaving out of grass when she should have
> opened the chamber door to her lover, and woven grass returns again and
> again in metaphor and incident. The lovers, now that in an aery body they
> must sorrow for unconsummated love, are "tangled up as the grass pat-
> terns are tangled." Again they are like an unfinished cloth: "these bodies,
> having no weft, even now are not come together . . ." (PFNoh, 160–61)

Yeats's discussion of the cloth and grass trope draws together the woman's
weaving of *hosonuno* with the entanglement of the troubled spirits of the lovers.

Pound, Yeats, and Eliot all used unified imagery in their poetry, and
they also hoped the recurring images might structure a new form of poetic
drama. Yeats was interested in noh primarily as theater rather than poetry
and claimed that "with the help of these plays. . . . I have invented a form
of drama, distinguished, indirect and symbolic" (PFNoh, 151). The most famous of the plays that resulted, *At the Hawk's Well*, also was an occasion for the
three to meet. Pound took Eliot to the first performance in 1916, and thirty

years later, Eliot recalled Itō, the "celebrated Japanese dancer," and claimed that the play made him think differently of Yeats, "rather as a more eminent contemporary than as an elder from whom one could learn."[81] Eliot's first comment on "The Noh and the Image," published a year after he saw *At the Hawk's Well*, quoted Pound's reference to "unity" but emphasized theatricality: "The peculiarity of the Noh is that the focus of interest, and centre of construction, is the scene *on the stage*."[82] In *Hamlet* and *Macbeth*, scenes are imagined "as they would be in reality," but noh provides a folded red kimono to symbolize the sick woman in the noh play *Aoi no ue*, or a robe hung on a tiny imitation pine tree to represent an angel's feather mantle. Eliot claimed, "The English stage is merely a substitute for the reality we imagine; but the red kimono is not a substitute in this sense; it is itself important."[83] He praised the "symbolist" and "dreamlike" quality of noh in which "it is only ghosts that are actual" and "enacted," while human "passions" are seen in "retrospect."[84] Pound's and Yeats's interpretations of noh introduced Eliot to new performance techniques as well as new structuring devices for poetic drama. In a letter describing his vision of *Sweeney Agonistes*, Eliot called for masked actors and an accompaniment of "light drum taps," claiming that "the action should be stylized as in the Noh drama—see Ezra Pound's book and Yeats' preface and notes to *The Hawk's Well*."[85]

Pound's work on noh not only encouraged a shift in his poetic theories but also inspired him to participate in performance experiments that attempted to combine poetry, music, and dance as in noh. Pound's "Vorticism" essay added an emphasis on movement and energy as well as the footnote on noh as a long "imagiste" poem: "THE IMAGE IS NOT an idea . . . it is what I can, and must perforce, call a VORTEX, from which, and through which, and into which, ideas are constantly rushing."[86] Two decades later, Pound's *ABC of Reading* (1934) insisted that the "diluters" of imagism disregarded the "moving image" and failed to realize that poetry would "atrophy" if it departed from "music," which in turn would "atrophy" if it departed from "dance."[87] Pound's interest in dance, music, and poetry was undoubtedly shaped by his overlooked 1915 collaboration with Itō Michio. In the summer of 1915, after his second winter with Yeats at Stone Cottage, Pound was back in London, where Itō may have lived with him for a time and helped him edit Fenollosa's manuscripts.[88] In the fall, they organized three dance recitals called "Sword-Dance and Spear-Dance," mostly attended by artists, at a small theater-studio in Kensington on October 28, November 2, and November 9, 1915.[89] Itō danced to five Japanese poems, which Pound translated with the help of "notes by

Utchiyama Masirni" and published in *Future* (1916).[90] For Pound, the collaboration with Itō revealed how a sequence of imagist poems might function in a performance combined with dance and chant.[91]

"Sword-Dance and Spear-Dance" grew out of Pound's collaborative translation of noh plays, set the stage for the later project of At the Hawk's Well (1916), and initiated the "long imagiste poem" that he would write for the rest of his life. Itō, like *Hagoromo*'s angel, taught Pound about dance and movement, the value of combining the arts into an intense dance poem, and even how to use the past in modern poetry. Pound published an anecdote about riding in an "omnibus" with Itō, who provided "material for an hokku" when he described dressing in his samurai grandfather's armor as a child while his grandmother wept at the resemblance. The story taught Pound that "poetry does touch modern life."[92] The concentrated drama of the sword-dance poems and noh plays helped Pound imagine a way of building on the resemblance of past and present and relating historical events from different cultures. Pound tried to write plays modeled on noh, including *Tristan* (1916), which brought the lovers of *Nishikigi* to the myth of Tristan and Iseult. Another foray into noh-inspired drama was supposed to appear with Yeats's At the Hawk's Well in Lady Emerald Cunard's drawing room. The double bill would have included what Pound called a "brief skit," probably the one-act unfinished satire *Consolations of Matrimony*. The skit may have been conceived as a *kyōgen*, a comedic form that functions as an interlude between noh plays and parodies their serious, austere style.[93] Although Pound's work was cut from the program, he remained fascinated by the idea that a sequence of noh plays or dance poems could provide a "complete diagram of life and recurrence" (PFNoh, 11–12). When Pound received the Fenollosa-Hirata noh drafts and began his collaboration with Itō, he already was searching for the "diagram" of a new dramatic poetry. These collaborations were crucial to his efforts to move beyond his initial conception of imagism and begin the long form of *The Cantos*. The earliest extant draft of "Canto IV," which supplied the material for his first finished canto, is on the back of four flyers advertising Itō's "Sword-Dance and Spear-Dance."[94]

NOMAN: IDEOGRAMMIC SPEAKERS IN THE PISAN CANTOS

The draft of "Canto IV" that Pound typed on the back of announcements for Itō's dance recitals indicates that he had started *The Cantos* as early as 1915 while he was also *backing* Itō. I am tempted to look for other correspondences between dance flyer and poem, front and back. The canto draft most likely is referring to Itō or possibly Kume as a "man" who "talked" with "Sen-sei Pere Henri Jacques" who "Talks with *sennin*" (Japanese spirits or sages).[95] Revealing Pound's ambivalence regarding all that "talking" and posturing about the "orient" at events like Itō's recitals, a later typescript adds an ironic description of "manufactured, 'well-taught' orientals, / talking of Emerson and Hoffmansthal." Pound discarded this along with most of the material in the "Three Ur-Cantos" he was drafting at the same time, including the fisherman speaker joining Hakuryō and Odysseus. Still, the final draft of "Canto IV" contained the first reference to noh in *The Cantos*: "The pine at Takasago / grows with the pine of Isé" (4.74–75). Pound's version of Zeami's noh play *Takasago*, lost for almost eighty years, offers insight into Pound's compositional methods. It also clarifies his fusion of poetry and politics, creative individualism, and submission to totalitarian rule, which led to his imprisonment in 1945 near Pisa. There, in a cage visited by the angel of *Hagoromo*, the spirits of Yeats, Itō, Kume, and other collaborators, and the warrior-ghosts of *Kumasaka* and *Kagekiyo*, he composed *The Pisan Cantos*. After considering *Takasago*, I will examine *The Pisan Cantos*, Pound's famous long poem in which noh's ghosts helped him construct an ideogrammic poetic speaker and notion of personhood or subjectivity as Noman, a composite, negatively defined "no" man.

The allusion to *Takasago* in "Canto IV" has provoked much speculation, bolstered by Pound's comment to Harriet Monroe that the "theme" of *The Cantos* "is roughly the theme of 'Takasago,' which story I hope to incorporate more explicitly in a later part of the poem."[96] Hugh Kenner claimed that Pound "never got round to the *Takasago*," and Daniel Albright argued that "Canto IV" suggests "the Cantos could aspire, not simply to include pretty elements of Japanese theatre, but to *be* a kind of Noh play."[97] Pound actually got to *Takasago* quite early in his work on noh, as references to the play printed in 1915 indicate, but it is also a stretch to claim that *The Cantos* "aspired" to be noh.[98] His *Takasago* was never published because he sent the manuscript to Alice Corbin Henderson on July 7, 1915, for inclusion in *Poetry*, but it was "mislaid" until Ira Nadel found it among Henderson's letters and published it in 1993.[99] Pound's version of *Takasago* helps clarify his poetic method and "theme" and reveals an understanding of noh's formal construction that is evident nowhere else in his writing.

Pound correctly identified *Takasago* as a "congratulatory" play (*shūgen*), a category "used at the beginning and end of the full Noh programme, and this very ending on the opening note is a sort of symbol of perpetuity."[100] A song from *Takasago* is still frequently sung at the end of a noh performance, as well as at weddings and other celebratory events. *Takasago* enjoys this status partially because Zeami explicitly connected *shūgen* with the pine tree, the "unified image" of the play: "[The pine's] color is constant, appearing unchanged for a thousand autumns. . . . The music of *shūgen* closely resembles the pine as the mode evoking the joys of peace on earth."[101] *Takasago* is also understood to be "perfect in its construction," Pound claimed, because the "various parts . . . are by various authorities held to be each in its proper position."[102] He indicates a familiarity with noh's composition by "parts" (*shōdan*), conventional musical forms, dance patterns, and poetic devices.[103] Pound refers to several *shōdan* in the order they appear in *Takasago*: "the speech telling the names" (*nanori*) and "the speech saying: we have arrived" (*tsukizerifu*). He gives the Japanese name of another *shōdan*, the *issei*, which he defines as "the hero's voice raised for the first time."[104] An *issei* is a common entrance song for the *shite* and companions (*tsure*), like the old man and woman in *Takasago*. It is followed, Pound notes, by a "*sashi koye*" (*sashi-koe*), which he defines as a "flow-along tune," a fairly accurate description of a type of *sashi* that usually features a lyrical poem sung in a smooth or flowing manner.[105]

This list of noh terminology may be baffling to nonspecialists, but it underscores that Pound had a surprising knowledge of the formulaic composition of *Takasago* and the continuities of *shōdan* across the plays he studied. And Pound's familiarity with noh structure should clarify that he was not attempting to construct the *Cantos* as a noh play.[106] It would be just as inaccurate to suggest the *Pisan* sequence is commedia dell'arte because it is set in Italy and mentions a dog named for the commedia character "Arlechino" (77.197). *Takasago* influenced primarily Pound's approach to representing history, art, and politics. The play tells the story of two pine trees understood to be "paired" (*aioi*), despite growing nearly sixty miles apart along the shores of the Inland Sea and Osaka Bay. The spirits of the Takasago and Sumiyoshi pines visit each other and appear to the priest (*waki*) as an old woman and an old man insisting, in Pound's rendering, that they are "near in the ways of love," regardless of any distance.[107] Pound's introduction gives the "clue, first to the 'sense of past time in the present', second, to the symbolism of Takasago (the past age) and Sumiyoshi (the present)."[108] He is interested in spiritual continuities across historical and geographical space represented by two pine trees, separated by miles, that are somehow bound at the roots.

Takasago was inspired by and quotes a passage from the *Kokinshū* (ca. 905), the first Japanese anthology of poetry commissioned by an emperor. Pound references "the preface of the Kokin," which reads, 'It seems the pine trees of Takasago and Suminoye grow together."[109] Their union (*aioi*) is "a sign of the happier reign." The Old Woman (companion, *tsure*) in Pound's version states, "Takasago means the old age of the emperor Manyoshu," but the Man'yōshū is actually the very oldest collection of Japanese poetry, compiled privately in the eighth century. *Takasago* connects that volume with the Kokinshū and the "present" of the play. The older Man'yōshū is represented by the Takasago pine, and the Kokinshū is linked to Sumiyoshi; pines and poetry grow together and are paired (*aioi*). Pound's mistaken replacement of a poetry anthology with an emperor actually highlights one of *Takasago*'s central goals: to unite poetry with the good sovereign, whose power and artistic inspiration extend over the realm even though he is rooted in the capital. Pine needles are figured as the "inexhaustible words" of poetry because they are eternally green. The chorus sings of the poet "Chaio" (Chōnō) who wrote that "all things" have "voices," from water to wind to crickets, but the pine is "over them all" because it was decreed "noble" by the "emperor Shiko."[110] The chorus calls, "Come near to the Shikishima," which Pound connects to the "island of verses," or Japan (JND, 285). Pound's version ends before the *ai-kyōgen* interlude, after which the priest sails to the Sumiyoshi Shrine where the pine-god performs a sacred dance (*kagura*) as a manifestation of the perfect sovereign. But Pound had managed to link the past and present through the idea that nature has a poetic voice, literary tradition is continuous, and poetry both celebrates and is preserved by great governments and leaders.

Pound's half translation of *Takasago* never reached Sumiyoshi or publication in *Poetry*. He mistook the name of a ruler for the title of a poetry anthology and then misquoted the play in "Canto IV" when he wrote, "The pine at Takasago / grows with the pine of Isé" rather than Sumiyoshi (4.74–75).[111] The Fenollosa-Hirata-Pound draft of *Takasago* does not mention Ise, so the reference in "Canto IV" may be an error, or Pound may have been suggesting a third link between Takasago and the sacred shrines of Sumiyoshi and Ise.[112] Either way, Pound used *Takasago* to establish continuities between poetry and politics in a way that seems to foreshadow the bungled journey that would land Pound in a six-by-six-foot open "death cell" at the U.S. Army's Disciplinary Training Center north of Pisa: He supported the wrong ruler (Mussolini) with an anthology (of more than 120 pieces) of pro-fascist, anti-Semitic broadcasts on Rome Radio, believing "Il Duce" would nurture poetry and create a Shikishima, or "city of Dioce" (74.11).[113] *Translation—at least Pound's* collaborative, intimate, and creative translation—subtly joins *treason*, a crime that requires transnational engagement.[114]

While *The Pisan Cantos* is not a noh play, its tale of Pound's incarceration would make a fantastic subject for a noh cycle: The warrior-poet is exhausted by a round of imaginary fencing in his cage under the blazing Italian sun and blinding prison floodlight.[115] He falls asleep and, in the first-category *god play*, dreams of the *tennin*: "the nymph of Hagoromo came to me, / as a corona of angels" (74.180–81).[116] In the *warrior play*, the ghost of Itō appears in a Japanese "damio" costume, with samurai sword and "overcoat" as an example of "sincerity, the precise definition" (77.141, 162). Yeats is his companion (*tsure*), and together they confess that they were guilty of insincere attempts to capitalize on *japonisme* and *celticism*. Yeats practices his Irish accent with a *sashi*, singing "made a great Peeeeacock / in the proide ov his oiye" (83.167–68) while Itō dances a slower version of his choreography, *The White Peacock* (1918).[117] The third-category *woman play*, prompted by the sound of "Awoi's hennia . . . in the tent flaps" (77.39), would be modeled on Pound's translation of *Awoi no Uye* (*Aoi no ue*), as was Yeats's *The Only Jealousy of Emer* (1919). Pound would revisit his challenging domestic arrangements during the war when he was living with both wife and mistress. The fourth-category play might feature Mr. Henry Hudson Edwards, the black trainee who covertly constructed a writing table for Pound out of a medical supply box; he would wear the "Baluba mask" and respond to Pound's mix of racism and gratitude (74.319, 81.69). For the fifth-category *demon play*, we might choose to have Pound be possessed by any number of his demons—Mussolini hanged "by the heels at Milano" is a prime candidate (74.5)—and Yeats and Itō would attempt an exorcism holding Pound's "eucalyptus bobble," picked up "for memory" (74.373, 80.14), and chanting from M. E. Speare's *The Pocket Book of Verse* "found on the jo-house seat" (80.663).

These noh-like episodes in *The Pisan Cantos* contain numerous references to the plays Pound was working on thirty years earlier, as many scholars have noticed.[118] Allusions to *Hagoromo*, in particular, unify the moon images repeated throughout the *Pisan* sequence into a trope and establish what I call an *ideogrammic* poetic speaker. Just as Pound, following Fenollosa, believed that Chinese characters created meaning by setting shorthand pictures of things or ideograms in relation to one another, Pound linked a series of mythical, historical, and personal subjects to create his speaker. This ideogrammic speaker is established in the first explicit reference to noh in the initial

poem of *The Pisan Cantos*, when the speaker is visited by the "nymph of Hagoromo . . . as a corona of angels" (74.180). Pound echoes the question he posed
just as he was beginning his cantos: "Whom shall I hang my shimmering garment on; / Who wear my feathery mantle, hagoromo." If that earlier Hakuryō
was searching for a new poetic form in noh, this Hakuryō has lost the magic
robe of inspiration and needs the moon maiden's return, along with a coterie of angels including Artemis and Diana, the Greek and Roman moon
goddesses (74.226); the Sino-Japanese spirit of mercy, Kannon (74.131); and
the love goddesses Aphrodite/Venus/"Cythera, in the moon's barge" (74.190,
80.596). Pound links the Hakuryō of *The Pisan Cantos* to Odysseus, renders the
Greek hero's Cyclops-evading name as OΎ ΤΙΣ (Noman) and lists it as the
caption for the Chinese character *mo* 莫 (no or not) in the *Hagoromo* allusion.
Pound's ideogrammic reading of *mo* 莫 found the character for person (see
the two "legs" of the character) below the radical for sun, providing a figure
for "a man on whom the sun has gone down" (74.178). Moon images unify
the speaking subject as Pound-Hakuryō-Odysseus-OΎ ΤΙΣ- 莫 and illuminate
his dream of redemptive goddesses. If the sun has gone down on him, this
ideogrammic speaker looks to the moon.

The Chinese characters and Greek script in *The Cantos* call attention to the
materiality and foreignness of writing and confuse (even infuriate) readers,
thereby encouraging a self-consciousness about the act of reading that is ag-
gravated by the direct address to "g.r." (gentle reader, 80.239). The full score
for "Le chant des oiseaux" in "Canto LXXV" and other references to music
combine with foreign-language characters to layer visual and auditory elements upon the poetic text, creating a virtual dance and musical composition.[119] Associated with *mo* 莫, the Pound-Hakuryō-Odysseus-OΎ ΤΙΣ speaker
also takes on a material, visual presence in the text, one that can quickly
transform into another character, as does the *shite* in noh. The speaker becomes the soldier and art patron Sigismundo Malatesta (1417–1468) in another moonlit visionary encounter. While standing at a crossing of three paths
(*triedro*), Sigismundo sees the ghosts of three women, including the compas-
sionate lover of the troubadour Sordello, Cunizza da Romano (1198–1270),
and "la scalza," a barefoot country woman fleeing the war's bombs.[120] The lat-
ter is linked to *Hagoromo*'s moon nymph as she speaks one of *The Pisan Cantos*'s
prominent lyrical refrains: "Io la luna" (I am the moon). Just as the Hakuryō-
speaker claims, "The nymph of Hagoromo came to me," the Sigismundo-
speaker insists, "They suddenly stand in my room here" (74.180, 76.11).[121] "La
scalza" and "the corona of angels" return with each repetition of the phrase,

"Io la luna." Such refrains take on the quality of a choral song, just as Pound's Hakuryō-Odysseus-OÝ TIΣ-莫-speaker wears many masks while remaining Pound, "here," in a cage.

The repeated phrases, the presence of "ghosts / patched with histories," and a similar patchwork of speaking voices also contribute to the distinctive time stamp of The Pisan Cantos. Strategies drawn from the ghostly dream vision of noh allow the poem to advance in time yet constrain that progress in a mythic story recounted in the past tense, often a story as familiar to its Japanese audience as the Odyssey would be to Pound's readers. Even if the noh play is not based on a famous tale, its structure produces a feeling of familiarity: An old story is recounted about a famous tree in Takasago or a grave in Nishikigi; then the story is told again in the kyōgen interlude before being performed or relived by the ghost in the second act. Prevailing assumptions of sequential, millennial time are disrupted by this repetition and the capacity of ghosts and spirits to be present to the waki "here" on the stage, both rooted in Sumiyoshi and visiting Takasago. The Pisan Cantos replicates this temporality in its many hauntings: The story of Yeats asking the dying Aubrey Beardsley "why he drew horrors" is recounted in the past, but the response, "Beauty is difficult, Yeats," is given as dialogue in the present. The phrase reappears twice later in the canto without the quotation marks, becoming a refrain that recalls the ghosts of both Beardsley and Yeats (80.611, 617).

These ghosts seem to be there, present in the background of The Pisan Cantos and repeatedly rising to the surface as if without the consent of the poet. Far from being a shōdan design, the sequence often seems to be composed of random, unedited thoughts, coming to the speaker like the birds he counts as they land on wires above his cage. He compares them to musical notes on a staff, an image that inspires the speaker to attempt to remember "what's his name" who developed a new form of musical notation. He recalls "that bastard" Guido d'Arezzo twenty-nine lines later (79.76, 105). These lines call attention to the poem's forward movement in time without the concomitant notion of progress or teleology. And even this random movement is slowed by, for example, the score of "Le chant des oiseaux," which, unlike the birds flitting on and off wires, is all there, instantaneously present in "Canto LXXV" rather than unfolding in time as when music is played on an instrument.

The tension between immediate, instantaneous presence and duration in time resembles another feature of Pound's concept of "ideogrammic" language that he derived from Fenollosa. Pound believed that meaning is layered within juxtaposed shorthand images to provide "the precise definition" without the extraneous material of narrative and grammar, but the sequence of images must continue on forever without end.[122] A similar "ideogrammic" tension exists in Pound's ideas of personhood and subjectivity: The "no man" that is *mo* 莫 is the "everyman" of Pound-Hakuryō-Odysseus-OÝ TIΣ-Sigismundo. These character-figures are usually juxtaposed without comment, which follows Pound's definition of his "ideogrammic" method: "Hang a painting by Carlo Dolci beside a Cosimo Tura. You cannot prevent Mr. Buggins from preferring the former, but you can very seriously impede his setting up a false tradition of teaching on the assumption that Tura never existed."[123] Nonetheless, in the poem's second reference to *Hagoromo*, the speaker does compare his "ideogrammic" sources, distinguishing the fisherman's return of the feathered mantle from the "Greek rascality" of Odysseus's opportunistic attack on Ismarus as he was leaving Troy. Against Greek "vulgarity," Pound celebrates Kumasaka's acknowledgment of the superiority of the warrior who killed him (79.62–63). He continues this didactic stance in his third reference to the moon angel. Her return is prompted by the darkest of the lunar references, when the barefoot woman, *la scalza*, recounts an image left out of the previous visions: her dead son nailed to the ground with arms stretched in the shape of a cross, "Io son' la luna" (80.247–50). This leads to a parody of pretty, romantic moon imagery in an overblown personification: "The moon's arse been chewed off by this time" (80.258). *Hagoromo* returns with the line that shamed Hakuryō: "With us there is no deceit" / said the moon nymph immacolata / Give back my cloak, *hagoromo*" (80.258–62).

Did Pound learn Hakuryō's lesson? Did he echo the response, "I am ashamed. I give you your mantle" (PFNoh, 102)? Did he, like the noh warrior Kumasaka, "tell of his own defeat" and make "reparation for his brigandage by protecting the country"? (PFNoh, 38–39). These questions have been put to *The Pisan Cantos* since its early readers argued whether or not the controversial author, having been determined mentally unfit for trial and imprisoned in St. Elizabeths Hospital should have received the Library of Congress's first (and only) Bollingen Prize.[124] The Congress's press release insisted, "The fellows are aware that objections may be made to awarding a prize to a man situated as is Mr. Pound [in an asylum]. . . . To permit other considerations than that of poetic achievement to sway the decision would destroy the significance of the award and would in principle deny the validity of that objective perception of value on which civilized society must rest."[125]

Objections were made, perhaps most vehemently by the president of the Poetry Society of America, Robert Hillyer. He published his outrage in the

Saturday Review of Literature, arguing that the award had been given to a traitor who had "served the enemy in direct poetical and propaganda activities against the United States" and suggested a link between "an intellectual neo-Fascism and the new estheticism," which he equated with New Criticism.[126] In her most recent statement on the controversy, poetry critic Marjorie Perloff insists that by now, "most critics would agree that, whatever else the sequence was or wasn't, it was certainly the best book of poems published in 1948 and hence well deserved the much disputed prize."[127] Her "one caveat," interestingly enough, returns us to the author, although this is Pound the lover rather than the one "situated" in the asylum. Perloff complains that "men are allowed to be men" in the poem, whereas the "women in Pound's life" are "never mentioned by name."

Much of the debate about the sequence hinges on whether or not Pound is the speaker of the famous "Pull down thy vanity" chant (81.521–22).[128] Pound's "ideogrammic" Noman subjectivity renders this question one of the least answerable of the many invoked by *The Pisan Cantos*. The speaker of the poem is the humbled Hakuryō who has stolen the magical mantle and must return it, and Kumasaka who must do penance, and Odysseus who will attack yet another village on his way home from Troy, and the one on whom the sun has gone down, and Pound himself, turning his incarceration into a gripping story. This is a collaborative subject, and the fact that he does not also imagine himself as the grieving mother "*la scalza*," singing "Io la luna," probably does reflect the gendering of his homosocial collaborations and the relative absence of "named" women. The imagined audience for the "Pull down thy vanity" passage is large and ranges from Pound himself to the military to humankind more generally. It is the kind of lesson a noh play would offer in response to Kumasaka's thought: "What can he do, that young chap, if I ply my secret arts freely? Be he god or devil, I will grasp him and grind him" (PFNoh, 44). This passage is sung by the chorus in Pound's version of *Kumasaka*, and the chorus in noh can speak for and to the *shite* and *waki*, ghosts and the living, or address no person in particular. The "Pull down thy vanity" passage is similarly choric and open in its address.

I read "Pull down thy vanity" as a chant that responds to the many statements of shame, doubt, and arrogance coexisting in *The Pisan Cantos*. The final lines of the sequence mix invocations of natural beauty and pop culture, "out of all this beauty something must come / O moon my pin-up," with fascist celebrations, "Xaire Alessandro / Xaire Fernando, e il Capo" (84.71–78). Pound tries, using his ideogrammic method, to place the sun and moon next to each other as they are in the character *ming* 明, which Pound translates as "the sun and moon, the total light process . . . hence the intelligence" (84.90).[129] He leaves the contradictions in *The Pisan Cantos*, juxtaposed and brightly lit.

CONCLUSION: TEACHING NOH AND FASCISM

> Teach? at Harvard?
> Teach? It cannot be done. (74.302–3)

The first time I assigned *The Pisan Cantos* in a graduate seminar (at Boston University, not Harvard), a student at the end of the period stated, "This should not be taught" and then added, "to undergraduates, I mean." Undoubtedly an indication of my own inadequacy as a teacher, the comment prompted me to ask the class why we were all so uncomfortable with Pound's work (and to keep them way too late). Some students suggested they wished Pound had apologized in his poetry.[130] I asked if they were satisfied by the different ways in which T. S Eliot and Wyndham Lewis had recanted their support for totalitarianism or fascism. Do we wish Pound had deceitfully distanced himself from the regime he supported in the manner of Martin Heidegger, Paul de Man, or Leni Riefenstahl? My class's surprise at this list of important intellectuals and artists who were at least somewhat sympathetic to fascism confirmed that I needed to keep teaching *The Pisan Cantos*. If as undergraduates, they had received a Pound devoid of his well-documented fascism, anti-Semitism, racism, homophobia, and orientalism, then they had received a dangerously sanitized version of modernism—and maybe an overly pious version of the work we do as students and teachers of cultures. Our attempts to distinguish ourselves from the cultures that produced the international fascist and genocidal political transformations of the twentieth century may hinder our understanding of totalitarianism's appeal to a diverse group of artists and intellectuals as well as masses of supporters.[131] Simplistic moralisms and convenient amnesia will prevent us from learning all that these movements might teach us. Pound is "difficult," and not just because his work was often filled with beauty. Indeed, Pound *should* be very difficult.

My intention in this conclusion is not to defend Pound or explain his fascism but to examine how the construction of personhood in noh might contribute to our understanding. The Japanese noh theater and its modernist adaptations in the twentieth century are haunted by totalitarianism. Noh's definition of the person and its divergence from liberal humanism can shed little light on Pound's economic theories, belief in monetary reform, and program for Social Credit, but it may have encouraged his enthusiasm for Mussolini.[132] Noh's emphasis on submission to tradition, authority, and hierarchy, and the pleasures that might accompany such submission exposes illusions and contradictions in humanism's freedom-loving subject—but it also resembles fascism.

Pound's interest in fascism was partly driven by his rejection of liberal democratic capitalism, particularly its mass consumerist culture and concentration of wealth among powerful industrialists.[133] Pound believed that the kinds of mass consumption demanded by capitalism would leave no room for artists or the study, preservation, and translation of the great cultural achievements of the past to which he was so committed: "Fear god and the stupidity of the populace" (74.27). The unequal distribution of wealth in capitalist societies produces the slavery of the masses, as Marxism contends, and fails to sufficiently value artists and intellectuals. Marxism was not appealing, however, because Pound believed that the rule of the masses would destroy high culture just as vehemently as would capitalism.[134] While "the oligarchs manipulated the masses through the mass media," Pound, as one of the "great men of culture," believed that he could influence a dictator and even imagined that "he had the ear of Mussolini."[135] Pound also believed that a new renaissance, like that in fourteenth-century Italy, would be brought about by a fusion of Eastern and Western cultures. In this, he was following Fenollosa's aspirations for the study of Chinese and Japanese art: "Vistas of strange futures unfold for man, of world-embracing cultures half-weaned from Europe, of hitherto undreamed responsibilities for nations and races." Fenollosa compared the achievements of Asian cultures with those of "ancient Mediterranean peoples" and claimed, "We need their best ideals to supplement our own."[136] Pound's passion for "world-embracing" translation and for combining the best of different cultures and times, however biased and inflected through orientalism, made him less enthusiastic about the ideologies of cultural purity that accompanied fascism.

Part of Pound's interest in noh was due to his—not entirely erroneous— belief that it was the product of a time when elite men of culture, warrior-poets, ruled Japan. He celebrated noh as a "recondite" and "subtle" art, created by priests and the court, and performed "only for the few; the nobles; for those trained to catch the allusion" (PFNoh, 4). A theatrical tradition designed for audiences with enough mastery of Japanese and Chinese classical poetry and myth to recognize noh's many references and quotations appealed to the author of the allusion-filled *Cantos*. The connection between Pound's elitism and noh was abundantly evident in his speeches on Rome Radio. In response to accusations of Japanese barbarism following the attack on Pearl Harbor, Pound declared: "Anybody who has read the plays entitled Kumasaka and Kagekiyo, would have avoided the sort of bilge printed in Time and the American press . . . the Awoi no Uye, Kumasaka, Nishikigi, or Funa-Benkei. These are Japanese classical plays, and would convince any man with more sense than a pea hen, of the degree of Japanese civilization."[137] Here, he defines the degree of civilization primarily by a tradition of great art, rather than politics or international military conduct, and he believed that fascism would support such an aesthetic tradition.

In noh plays like *Takasago*, Pound found an emphasis on the combined poetic and religious powers of the emperor, which would have supported the idea that a great "totalitarian" leader would promote art. When Pound mistook the title of the imperially commissioned poetry anthology, *Kokinshū*, for the name of an emperor, he foreshadowed Walter Benjamin's famous claim that fascism "is the introduction of aesthetics into political life."[138] The aestheticization of politics was a crucial part of fascism's appeal for Pound, who wrote, "Take him [Mussolini] as anything save the artist and you will get muddled in contradictions."[139] Pound also believed that the artist might serve as a diplomat within totalitarianism, a delusion bolstered by his success in obtaining an interview with Mussolini on January 30, 1933.[140] He even seriously attempted to persuade the American public that the war with Japan could be concluded to the benefit of all if the United States would "give Guam to the Japanese in return for one set of color and sound films of the 300 best Noh dramas."[141]

Pound's references to Mussolini as "the boss" and celebrations like "Xaire . . . e il Capo" (84.78) suggest the pleasures in submission to authority and the appeal of hierarchy described by Susan Sontag:

> Fascist aesthetics . . . flow from (and justify) a preoccupation with situations of control, submissive behavior, extravagant effort, and the endurance of pain; they endorse two seemingly opposite states, egomania and servitude... The fascist dramaturgy centers on the orgiastic transaction between mighty forces and their puppets, uniformly garbed and shown in ever swelling numbers. Its choreography alternates between ceaseless motion and a congealed, static, "virile" posing. Fascist art glorifies surrender, it exalts mindlessness, it glamorizes death.[142]

In this formulation, fascist aesthetics faintly echoes the submissive behavior and endurance of the pain of kneeling in noh pedagogy; the glorification of a good death in the warrior plays and the "'virile' pose" of gods and demons; the puppet-like gestures of the performers and the ways in which the mask and elaborate costuming turn them into things; the Buddhist-derived suggestion that the individual personality or mind would interfere with immersion in a sacred tradition. Of course, it would be ahistorical to claim that noh is a fascist theater, but elements of noh performance and pedagogy, including submission and surrender, have offered pleasure and beauty in many different cultures and political systems. Sontag connected fascism to sadomasochism, observing that the S/M "fad for Nazi regalia" was "a response to an oppressive freedom of choice in sex (and in other matters), to an unbearable degree of individuality."[143] She recognized that "beauty" is part of the seduction of both sadomasochism and fascism, but she suggested that the principal impetus was the twentieth-century moment when the excesses of freedom had become intolerable. Sontag implied that fascist subjects are duped rather than responding to the appeal of submission and that the continued appeal of fascism reveals the failure of humanism's exaltation of freedom and individualism.

In The Pisan Cantos, Pound maintained that liberal democratic subjects also are duped if they believe the nation ensures freedom: "Free speech without free radio speech is as zero" (74.42). Sontag, like many other critics who are understandably horrified by fascism, may have overlooked the "situations of control" and "endurance of pain" demanded, but rarely acknowledged, in liberal societies. Her discussion of S/M as a response to "freedom of choice in sex" ignored the regulatory mechanisms in all cultures that continue to limit choices about sex and constructions of gender, although liberal cultures tend to make both seem more free. She did not entertain the possibility that S/M might reflect the diversity of desire or, in an interpretation less conducive to liberalism, that S/M might explode normative social relations and temporalities and forge new subjectivities.[144] Pound was not, to my knowledge, a sadomasochist, although his interest in deviant sexualities is evident in his translation of Remy de Gourmont's argument for sexual liberation, The Natural Philosophy of Love (1922). His "Translator's Postscript" connects masculinist sexual and intellectual liberty, presenting the brain as a "great clot of genital fluid" and thought as ejaculation.[145] He also was interested in pedagogical scenes with S/M dynamics. Among the selections Pound published from Fenollosa's diary was an anecdote about the sketchy performance texts handed down from the master actor (*taiyu*) to his sons. Fenollosa reported that when gestures cannot be described, Umewaka wrote "'kuden' (tradition) to show that this is something that can be learned only from a master. Sometimes his teacher used to beat him with a fan when he was learning" (PFNoh, 30). The interest of this scene, for Pound, sheds some light on the appeal of both fascism and noh: They offered a secret tradition gained through severe effort, a great leader or sensei, and the promise that individual pain or achievement would be valued by a vaguely defined community Pound sometimes called "Kulchur."

Pound was most absorbed in noh during the traumatic periods of the two great wars, when submitting to these ancient texts might disrupt the traumas of the present and allow him to reimagine his art in relation to another time and another tradition. Again, I do not intend to encourage sympathy for Pound's beliefs, but his disapproval of the contradictions he found in liberal democratic capitalism, interest in fascism, and bigoted rants are the product of very human desires. They animated nations. I worry that denying them, not teaching any number of "difficult" texts like *The Pisan Cantos*, might lead to other dangerous denials. There is a contradiction in the longing for Pound's apology or hope that he was asking himself to "pull down his [own] vanity," in that it demands something like the postures of humility and submission that many of us find horrifying when he addressed them to Mussolini. We want submission only to the ideologies that are so normal they aren't called ideologies. Liberal democracies sometimes hide their demands for submission under other labels. Pound's submission to Mussolini is troubling for a liberal culture, but he was indicted for treason and forced to submit to the U.S. prison regime because his *subversive speech* on Rome Radio was believed to pose a "clear and present danger" to that liberal state—and then to be judged as crazy by that state's definitions of insanity.[146]

The more lyrical passages of Pound's Rome Radio broadcasts recalled his noh collaborations and the beauty of Kume's dance: "I have never seen anything that could touch the movement of the tennin in the Hagoromo dance that Tami Koumé did for me in his London studio 25 years ago."[147] As late as 1957, the year he was released from his thirteen-year incarceration in St. Elizabeths Hospital, Pound wrote, "Hagoromo is a sacrament."[148] But Pound's *Hagoromo* is not the only story in the angel's transnational tour. The Fenollosa-Hirata-Pound translation launched her into another fertile collaboration, one in which Pound played a minor role while Itō and Yeats took center stage. Yeats's *At the Hawk's Well* (1916) introduced another bird-woman whose dance influenced understandings of nation and freedom during World War I. This conflict sent both *Hagoromo* and *Hawk's Well* across the Atlantic with Itō, to become the first modernist noh plays to be performed in the United States. Later Itō, in a surprising parallel to Pound, was imprisoned by the United States as an enemy spy and transported back to Japan as part of his own devastating journey through World War II.

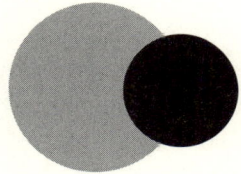

2. THEATER IN THE "DEEP"

W. B. Yeats's *At the Hawk's Well*

I sometimes fence for half-an-hour at the day's end, and when I close my eyes
upon the pillow I see a foil playing before me, the button to my face. We meet
always in the deep of the mind, whatever our work, wherever our reverie carries
us, that other Will.

W. B. Yeats, *Per Amica Silentia Lunae*

THE EVENING FENCING LESSONS THAT POUND GAVE TO YEATS
during their three winters at Stone Cottage (1913–1916) provide more than
insight into their exercise habits and a fun anecdote for the opening of a
chapter. In *Per Amica Silentia Lunae* (1918), Yeats recalled those lessons and described meeting "that other Will" of the daemon or anti-self as if in a fencing
match located in "the deep of the mind." Yeats was fascinated by experiences
involving intense mental and/or physical sparring with, or submission to,
"that other Will," which often figured as a relation between a teacher and a
student, an old man and a young man, or another part of himself. I specu-
late that Pound remembered his matches with Yeats when he exercised with
an imaginary fencing foil in his cage at the U.S. Army Disciplinary Training
Center at Pisa. In *The Pisan Cantos*, Pound recalled scenes from Stone Cottage,
including Yeats chanting "Peeeeacock / in the proide ov his oiye" (83.167–68).
Pound also remembered the "shade" of *Kumasaka*, whom he praised for nobly
admitting that the young apprentice warrior who killed him was the "better

fencer" (74.600). Pound, refusing to be an obedient poetic apprentice to Yeats, ignored the older poet's suggestions for revisions when he published *Kumasaka* and the other noh plays they discussed at Stone Cottage.[1]

In 1916, the year that Yeats premiered the most famous of his noh-inspired plays for dancers, *At the Hawk's Well*,[2] he called for an "unreal theatre" that stages a ghostly fencing match with reality itself: "Now the art I long for is also a battle but it takes place in the depths of the soul, and one of the antagonists does not wear a shape known to the world or speak a mortal tongue. It is the struggle of a dream with the world."[3] This could be a description of noh's haunted theater in which a ghost like Kumasaka reenacts a battle with his young killer onstage but is actually trying to relinquish his own struggle with the world and find peace. Soon after he began to work with Pound on the Fenollosa-Hirata draft translations of noh, Yeats was convinced that he had discovered the dramatic form he had been seeking, one that did not follow realist theatrical conventions but taught audiences to reach into the "deeper" and, for Yeats, more "Irish," parts of the mind.[4] Yeats understood that noh is a didactic and nationalist theater, offering teachers in the form of ghosts of noble warriors and great lovers from Japanese legend and history.[5] He hoped to adapt noh to stage his country's legends and teach Irish audiences to revive what he believed to be their own national art separate from British influence.

Yeats's "deep" theater required a performance technique and form that diverged from the two that dominated British and Irish stages in the early twentieth century: the animated, stylized gestures of popular melodramas and the naturalistic acting in realist plays.[6] In 1915, Pound introduced Yeats to his ideal actor in the *dancer* Itō Michio. Yeats described watching Itō dance in a small studio (probably the noh lesson conducted by Itō and his friends in June or July 1915) and then in a drawing room (probably the "Sword-Dance and Spear-Dance" recital that Pound organized for Itō):

> In the studio and in the drawing-room alone where the lighting was the light we are most accustomed to, did I see him as the tragic image that has stirred my imagination. There where no studied lighting, no stage-picture made an artificial world, he [Itō] was able, as he rose from the floor, where he had been sitting cross-legged or as he threw out an arm, to recede from us into some more powerful life. Because that separation was achieved by human means alone, he receded, but to inhabit as it were the deeps of the mind. (PFNoh, 153)

Without the elaborate lighting of much avant-garde performance or the naturalistic scenery of dramatic realism, but using only "human means," Itō could
dance in "the deeps of the mind" and represent possession, trance, madness,
and other extreme mental states. Yeats's enthusiasm for Itō, like Pound's, can
be partly attributed to his attraction to "exotic" types. Critics have often quite
condescendingly pointed out that Yeats was "stirred" by a performer who was
not an "authentic" noh actor. While Itō never underwent the years of training required by noh (or even the limited amateur lessons that I took), Itō and
Yeats never used the language of authenticity to describe the artistic collaboration that produced Hawk's Well.

Yeats was interested in adapting noh for his own aesthetic and political
purposes rather than attempting an authentic recreation of it. As he claimed,
"With the help of these plays 'translated by Ernest Fenollosa and finished
by Ezra Pound' I have invented a form of drama, distinguished, indirect and
symbolic, and having no need of mob or press to pay its way—an aristocratic
form" (PFNoh, 151). Yeats had been shocked when audiences behaved like
mobs protesting plays produced by the Irish National Theatre Society and
when the press called for censorship and fanned the flames. The "aristocratic
form" of Hawk's Well might appear to turn away from his earlier work for a
national theater and leap into a confused exoticism; some critics even accuse Yeats of committing a "form of cultural colonization" that contradicted
his protest against British rule over Ireland.[7] In debates over Yeats's politics,
simmering since the indictment written by poet W. H. Auden in 1939, Hawk's
Well sometimes appears as evidence of Yeats's shift from being an ambivalent
Irish nationalist to being an elitist reactionary and then becoming an outright fascist.[8] More moderate assessments acknowledge that Yeats occupied
conflicting political positions over his lifetime.[9] Several critics emphasize his
commitment to an individualism that is sometimes misrepresented as a self-
evident antidote to fascism, as in a description of Yeats as a "clear-sighted
individualist rather than a mystical totalitarian."[10]

Yeats's Hawk's Well actually presents a mystical dissolution of a rational or
clear-sighted individual in the "deeps of the mind." A deep theater is not exempt from politics, for the "deeps of the mind" shape any individual's relationship to groupings like nations. Instead, Hawk's Well suggests that national
fervor produces not a "freedom-fighter" but an irrational, easily possessed,
and possessive person who may have access to the "deeps of the mind" but
rarely understands them. If it offers an ambivalent critique of this irrational

nationalism, *Hawk's Well* also refuses the alternative of a nation founded on reason and freedom as it stages battles between a mythic spirit-world, irrational heroism, and everyday pleasures.

YEATS'S IRISH (TRANS)NATIONAL THEATER MOVEMENT

In the series of books I edit for my sister I confine myself to those that have I believe some special value to Ireland, now or in the future. I have asked Mr. Pound for these beautiful plays because I think they will help me to explain a certain possibility of the Irish dramatic movement.

Yeats, *Certain Noble Plays of Japan*

Yeats's interest in noh was not a departure from the national theater movement to which he devoted tremendous effort as a playwright, manager, fundraiser, and more. His desire for a theater that taps the "deeps of the mind" was present in his earliest collaborations with his staunch patron, Lady Augusta Gregory, as well as with Edward Martyn and George Moore, cofounders of the Irish Literary Theatre in 1899.[11] They were committed to the pedagogical power of theater to educate a particular kind of nation. According to Yeats, "Literature is, to my mind, the great teaching power of the world, the ultimate creator of all values, and it is this, not only in the sacred books whose power everybody acknowledges, but by every movement of imagination in song or story or drama" (PC, 57). The "intensity and sincerity" of the drama was to do the teaching, not the propaganda of the plays, although Yeats acknowledged that "we may have to deal with passing issues until we have recreated the imaginative tradition of Ireland" (PC, 58, 11). He viewed the patriotic subjects demanded by the radical national movement and publications such as the *United Irishman* and the *Independent* as "passing issues" compared with the wellspring of Ireland's imaginative tradition, primarily its legendary "saints and heroes."

In 1904, the Irish Literary Theatre was renamed the Irish National Theatre Society, and the group acquired the Abbey Theatre along with the "National" in its title. Yeats wrote with satisfaction after their first season: "An audience with National feeling is alive, at the worst it is alive enough to quarrel with" (PC, 143). The substance of the quarrel was generally about whether "our plays are slanders upon their country" (PC, 149). Yeats wanted two kinds of productions at the Abbey: "plays of peasant life and plays of a romantic and heroic life such as one finds in the folk tales." These would have been poorly received in other countries because of the stranglehold of dramatic realism, which Yeats described as "fifty years of mistake" (PC, 155–58). Ireland's interest in "questions of practical reform" was related less to realism than to its status as a "misgoverned country," which was, for Yeats, the primary "antagonist of imaginative writing" (PC, 158–59). Yeats recognized, long before contemporary postcolonial theorists did, that nations are largely imagined and that empire suppresses the imagination of a people.[12] He believed that his "unreal theater" would struggle with the realities of Ireland's colonial status and that plays of peasant and heroic life could penetrate the deep places of the mind and rekindle a national imagination.

Yeats's nation was an imagined collective shaped by its legends and arts, but it was also, even at the founding of the Irish National Theatre, surprisingly transnational. His nation was partly defined by imaginative work moving across national lines and becoming altered, even deformed, during these travels. He viewed the Abbey Theatre as an Irish enterprise that was part of a national theater movement taking place around the globe, just as he considered the Irish battle for independence in relation to—his imagined version of—India's struggle against the British Empire and Japan's against Western cultural colonization. As early as 1901, when he stated that his primary desire was "to get our heroic age into verse," particularly "dramatic verse," he also stated that all Irish playwrights must "study the dramatic masterpieces of the world" (PC, 9). Four years later, he celebrated plays originally produced at the Abbey that were staged at the Deutsches Theater of Berlin and the National Bohemian Theatre in Prague. Cathleen ni Houlihan (1902), Lady Gregory and Yeats's play about the 1798 United Irishmen rebellion against Britain, was translated into Irish and played at the Oireachtas "before an audience of some thousands" (PC, 140). By 1908, Yeats believed their enterprise served as an example for other national theaters, if sometimes an inaccurate one: "In Japan there are some who believe very erroneously that we are a great success, and even making money, and one of their distinguished critics uses our example to urge upon his countrymen the support of their native drama."[13] As the free use of the Abbey Theater was coming to an end in 1909, the Irish National Theatre Society needed money but was not "ashamed" because, as Yeats claimed, "the celebrated Moscow Art Theater is, after ten years, still carried on at a loss."[14] National theater movements faced common challenges across borders.

The transnational character of Yeats's nationalism was one source of his refusal to make "patriotism," "propaganda," or "passing issues" the basis of the Irish national theater. Glancing back at Cathleen ni Houlihan in 1931, nearly thirty years after the premiere of the popular play, Yeats declared that other nations had used it for different purposes. For Yeats, Cathleen is "Ireland herself."[15] She is transformed from an old crone whose "four beautiful green fields" have been "taken" (VP, 223) into a girl with "the walk of a queen" (VP, 231) when Michael Gillane joins the French soldiers who arrive to help Cathleen put "the strangers out of my house" (VP, 226). Other nations gave her "a different personality": In England she recruited soldiers for World War I, and in India and Ireland Cathleen ni Houlihan was "an anti-English play, while in Poland it figured as anti-Russian."[16] Yeats attributed Cathleen's power to move across national lines to the fact that the play had not been written as "if some external necessity had forced me to write nothing but drama with an obviously patriotic intention" (PC, 56). Yeats's story of the play's composition suggests that its nationalism emerged from "dreams and daily thoughts" (and erased his collaboration with Gregory): "I am a Nationalist, and certain of my intimate friends have made Irish politics the business of their lives, and this made certain thoughts habitual with me, and an accident made these thoughts take fire in such a way that I could give them dramatic expression. I had a very vivid dream one night, and I made Cathleen ni Houlihan out of this dream" (PC, 56). Yeats believed that the dream, not his patriotism, was the primary source of his ability to "write movingly."

Even as Yeats celebrated Cathleen's transnational relevance, he was ambivalent about the play's ability to recruit soldiers to fight for Irish, Indian, and Polish nationalism but also for the empires that would suppress them—and about recruitment more generally. In the late poem "Man and the Echo" (1938), he famously asked: "Did that play of mine send out / Certain men the English shot?" (VP, 632). The answer is probably yes: Cathleen may have sent men to the 1916 Easter Rising when Republicans occupied sites in Dublin for six days before the British suppressed the rebellion and shot the leaders at Kilmainham Gaol. In the play, men are recruited not by logical arguments about the values of Republicanism or the evils of empire but through a kind of enchantment. Michael acknowledges that he does not understand the meaning of Cathleen's song, yet he is so possessed by it and the cheering of the crowd welcoming the French that he can no longer hear his family, finds his weeping fiancée Delia as unrecognizable as a "stranger," and he takes on "the look of a man who has got the touch" (VP, 28–231). Cathleen's visit transforms Michael from a romantic but reasonable man about to be married to a "nice comely girl" into an irrational follower. His mental change precedes Cathleen's inexplicable transformation from an old crone into a beautiful girl. The play suggests that nationalism is driven by enchantment and other "deeps of the mind" that Yeats would later explore with the help of noh's ghosts and scenes of possession.

These "deeps" were a source of great power and danger for Yeats, who worried particularly about irrational crowds.[17] When Michael's enchantment seems to be slipping, he turns back toward his family and bride but is diverted again by "the sound of cheering outside" (VP, 230). The crowd's cheers reinstate the trance and mirror the possibly cheering but sometimes booing audience in the theater. By 1913 when Yeats and Pound began wintering together at Stone Cottage, Yeats had found himself embroiled in his "quarrel" with the "audience with National feeling" that he had helped establish. Dublin audiences rioted against J. M. Synge's The Playboy of the Western World in 1907, and Yeats was forced to face "the mob" and argue for artistic freedom and the value of plays not bound by the standards of realism. The Playboy riots were only the most famous of the debacles that made Yeats doubt the national theater. When he and Pound began working together on noh translations, Yeats believed they had found a theater that refused a "mob" and was never contaminated by the realism representing "the world as we know it," a theater that invited an elite audience to "pass for a few moments into a deep of the mind that had hitherto been too subtle for our habitation. As a deep of the mind can only be approached through what is most human, most delicate, we should distrust bodily distance, mechanism and loud noise. It may be well if we go to school in Asia" (PFNoh, 151–54). In positioning himself as a student of Japanese drama, Yeats celebrated the noh form but also exhibited ethnocentric and exotic assumptions. His "school in Asia" did not include the diversity of theatrical traditions in Japan, much less those of the Asian continent. He assumed that the Japanese, like his ideal native Celts, were spiritual nature lovers, steeped in ancient traditions:

> The adventure [of the play] itself is often the meeting with ghost, god or goddess at some holy place or much-legended tomb; and god, goddess or ghost reminds me at times of our own Irish legends and beliefs, which once it may be differed little from those of the Shinto worshipper. . . . These Japanese poets too feel for tomb and wood the emotion, the sense of awe that our Gaelic speaking country people will sometimes show when you speak to them of Castle Hackett or of some Holy Well. (PFNoh, 159)

Yeats made Japan somewhat more familiar by making the Irish 'country people" more exotic. His celebrations of exoticism certainly erased the particularities of each culture but also point to similar erasures in common presentations of cultural exchange. We tend to assume general power asymmetries by which the West always dominates the East, but the particular histories of Ireland and Japan trouble these assumptions. While Yeats was celebrating Irish and Japanese ghosts and holy wells, Japan was rapidly becoming modernized and militarized. Japan shocked the world by defeating Russia in 1904 and then expanding its dominance farther into China and Manchuria in an attempt to build a Pan-Asian empire. Becoming an industrial and military superpower with astonishing speed, Japan hoped to avoid the patterns of the European colonization of Asia and borrowed arguments that had long been used to justify Western empires. Yeats produced *Hawk's Well* in England in 1916, just weeks before the Easter Rising. His interest in noh as a form of drama free from British influence, one that could help him decolonize the Irish theater, might appear to have little to do with political realities. Yet the irrational, possessed spirits that danced for *Hawk's Well* in London had surprising afterlives in both Japan and Ireland.

NOGUCHI'S LESSONS ON NOH SUBMISSION

Yeats thought of himself as going to school in Asia without the inconvenience of international travel. But he took part in a series of intercultural lessons that included Pound and Itō, who were his primary noh collaborators but not his first teachers. Rather, the bilingual poet and art critic Noguchi Yone (1875–1947) introduced Yeats to noh, which contradicts the common story, one that I myself have told in earlier, erroneous presentations.[18] When Yeats and Noguchi first met in 1903, Noguchi was engaged to the American journalist Ethel Armes, with whom he became acquainted at the home of his lover, the writer Charles Warren Stoddard. Noguchi was also in a romantic relationship with Léonie Gilmour, who, in 1904, gave birth to his son Isamu Noguchi, the famous sculptor (and stage designer for the modern dancer Martha Graham).[19]

Noguchi's descriptions of Yeats suggest a fascination with an older writer that may have resembled his interest in Warren Stoddard. Noguchi described his "unconditional surrender to Yeats" upon their first meeting and the "sudden awakening of Celtic temperament in my Japanese mind."[20] Ireland and Japan shared a "patriotism" that encouraged some to think that *Cathleen ni Houlihan* would be "actable" in Japan, but Noguchi claimed that the play's "symbolism" made it fail there, because (in an unusual reversal of stereotypes about Eastern spirituality) the "Japanese are able to think of patriotism only physically."[21] He also noted that the "poetical characteristics" of Ireland and Japan were similar but that the encroachment of Chinese literature had "ruined" Japan, whereas Ireland had fought off British influence.[22] If he emphasized China's historical influence on noh and other classical arts, Noguchi concealed Japan's efforts to build an Asian empire and Ireland's struggles to battle British influence. Noguchi and Yeats's collaboration, conducted in English rather than the Japanese or Irish languages, reveals the productive erotic and political messes produced by cross-cultural exchange.

As early as 1907, Noguchi associated Yeats and noh in his articles for the *Japan Times*, Tokyo's foremost English-language newspaper (in which Pound later published essays on Yeats and noh). Noguchi wrote of Yeats's desire "to reform and strengthen the Western stage": "I am happy to think that he would find his own ideal in our No performance, if he should see and study it. Our No is sacred, and it is poetry itself."[23] In books and articles aimed at European, American, and Japanese readers, Noguchi fueled the popular interest in Japanese art and culture in the early twentieth century and prepared the ground for modernism's fertile reception of the Fenollosa-Hirata-Pound translations and Yeats's noh-derived plays for dancers—as well as Japan's reception of these works.[24] His personal relationships and collaborations were just as significant as the textual exchanges. A friend of Mary Fenollosa, Noguchi may have influenced her decision to send the Fenollosa-Hirata noh manuscripts to Pound in 1913. Noguchi had dinner with Yeats on January 17, 1914, during his London lecture tour, and the two discussed noh, particularly its ability to combine in one play the "folk" and aristocratic elements Yeats sought to stage at the Abbey. They were joined later in the evening by Pound and the artist Henri Gaudier-Brzeska.[25] Pound appears to have arranged another dinner with Noguchi when he was preparing to publish his versions of the Fenollosa-Hirata translations.[26] Noguchi took little credit, however, for teaching Yeats about noh in a 1917 letter to Hirata, claiming that most of Yeats's imperfect knowledge came from Fenollosa. Noguchi also told Hirata that "the word 'Nō' has spread over the general educated class because of the fact that Yeats adopted the Japanese Nō."[27] Hirata later wrote, "I was happy that my crude, youthful efforts had not entirely been in vain," although Fenollosa and Pound certainly did not sufficiently credit his work on the translations.[28]

These dinners, conversations, and letters reveal a transnational, homosocial network through which artists taught one another and helped secure publishing opportunities. If Noguchi encouraged Yeats and Pound to attempt to write their own original noh, they certainly supported his interest in translating noh plays (he published seventeen between 1916 and 1919) and writing new noh in English. Noguchi's "The Everlasting Sorrow: A Japanese Noh Play" (1917) and then his essay "The Japanese Noh Play" (1918) were published in the *Egoist*, a magazine over which Pound exerted considerable influence.[29] In the same letter to John Quinn from Stone Cottage (February 26, 1916) in which Pound stated, "I have *took up* again with the 'Egoist,'" he also reported:

> Yeats is brrring in the next room. re-doing a lyric for his new playlet. He is doing an introduction for my versions of a few of Fenollosa's japane[se] plays. and I am highly honoured. . . . Also he [Yeats] has a scheme for a Theatre-less stage—very noble & exclusive—his new play and a farce of mine are to be performed before an audience composed exclusively of crowned heads and divorcées in six or eight weeks time.[30]

Yeats's new play, performed without Pound's farce, was *At the Hawk's Well*.

Noguchi's work was one source for the more passive or submissive and less egotistical characters Yeats hoped to create in his plays, an interest reinforced by Yeats's readings on Zen Buddhism. In his copy of Daisetz Teitaro Suzuki's *Essays in Zen Buddhism* (1927), Yeats marked a passage claiming that "spiritually a state of perfect freedom is obtained only when all our egoistic thoughts are not read into life and the world is accepted as it is as a mirror reflects a flower as flower and the moon as moon."[31] At least six years before Yeats marked the passage about freedom from "egoistic thoughts," he wrote to Noguchi, probably the year his *Four Plays for Dancers* was published (1921): "A form of beauty scarcely lasts a generation with us, but it lasts with you for centuries. You no more want to change it than a pious man wants to change the Lord's Prayer, or the Crucifix on the wall [blurred] at least not until we have infected you with our egotism."[32] Yeats associated Europe with an infectious "egotism" that destroyed aesthetic traditions or forms of beauty and even religious traditions (of which he was often quite suspicious).

Noguchi's discussions of noh in *The Spirit of Japanese Poetry* would have confirmed Yeats's desires for reform of the "Western ego" along with the theater, as the chapter emphasized noh's "dignity" and "simple lesson of simplicity" and the actors' "motionlessness of posture."[33] Noguchi insisted that an elite audience must struggle to learn to become noh "appreciators": "Those elected in this particular art, where appreciation is not less, perhaps is greater, than the acting itself, will find their own lives vitalized with the sense of power in Japanese weariness."[34] For Noguchi, an elect audience learns to appreciate noh through a labor that is even greater than the work of "acting." This position would have appealed to Yeats, who famously declared a break from the Abbey Theatre when he wrote, "I want to create for myself an unpopular theatre and an audience like a secret society where admission is by favour and never to many" (PC, 212). This audience, like the members of an occult society (such as Yeats's own Golden Dawn), would submit to the labor of appreciating art but also to the rules, rituals, and traditions of the society. As Noguchi proposed to "Western" poets: "I think it is time for them to live more of the passive side of Life and Nature . . . to value the beauty of inaction so as to emphasise action, to think of Death so as to make Life more attractive."[35] Both the tension between the active and inactive life and the extremely passive state of being possessed by another spirit are central themes in Yeats's *Hawk's Well*.

Although Yeats seemed to have appreciated and understood Noguchi's lessons about "passive" modes of being, he was often a "poor" student of Japanese drama. Like Pound, he found what he was looking for in noh, including ghosts and legends that seemed to resemble those he had collected in the Irish countryside.[36] Yeats wanted noh to confirm his celebration of a cultured aristocracy and a symbolic poetic theater that rejected realism and "naturalistic effect" (PFNoh, 158). These desires encouraged some of his factual errors: He suggested that Zeami, the now celebrated performer, theorist, and author/reviser of many noh plays, was a "small daimio or feudal lord" rather than an actor born into a low-class family who, as a child, became the artistic and sexual protégé of the shogun Ashikaga no Yoshimitsu. Yeats's desire for a nonrealistic, impersonal acting style may be reflected in his claim that noh movement was "copied from the marionette shows of the fourteenth century" (PFNoh, 155). The puppet theater (bunraku), however, actually emerged later and borrowed some techniques from noh.

If Yeats's aesthetic interests contributed to some of his errors, others were drawn from the Fenollosa-Hirata-Pound translations. I am particularly interested in the undoubtedly inaccurate transmissions that occurred during Yeats's collaborations and lessons with other artists. Although these pedagogical scenes are difficult to document, they produced fertile exchanges of performance forms and bodily techniques that were particularly important to Yeats's theater. While performance always involves the potentially volatile contributions of writers, actors, designers, directors, musicians, and audience members, this work is particularly fraught and interesting when it involves artists from different cultural traditions. Noguchi was Yeats's first noh teacher, and Pound played a crucial role in the transmission of noh texts, but Itō was Yeats's principal *performance* collaborator.

REHEARSING WITH ITŌ

My play is made possible by a Japanese dancer . . .
Yeats, *Certain Noble Plays of Japan*

The passive construction, unnamed dancer, and present tense of that sentence make it a strange one, especially for someone so skilled with words. If Yeats did not actively say that Itō made his play possible, he mourned Itō in his "Note on the First Performance of 'At the Hawk's Well'": "Perhaps I shall turn to something else now that our Japanese dancer, Mr. Itow, whose minute intensity of movement in the dance of the hawk so well suited our small room and private art, has been hired by a New York theatre" (PC, 420). After Itō moved to New York, Yeats must have introduced him to Noguchi in February 1920 when both Yeats and Noguchi were on lecture tours in the United States and Noguchi was attempting to arrange a two-year visiting appointment for Yeats at Tokyo Imperial and Keiō Universities. On February 7, 1920, Noguchi wrote two letters on stationery bearing the logo of Itō's new dance school.[37] The Yeats-Itō collaboration was brief but remarkably influential for both. Yeats first saw Itō perform and imagined the possibility of dance plays at the noh recital Pound organized with Itō and his friends Kōri Torahiko and the painter Kume Tamijurō (also known by Tami Koumé and other names) in June or July of 1915.[38] Before that informal and undoubtedly inaccurate recital, Pound and Yeats had studied the Fenollosa-Hirata draft translations together and sought help from Noguchi, Arthur Waley, and other scholars. The books in Yeats's library, including an autographed presentation copy of Noguchi's *The Spirit of Japanese Poetry*, show that he attempted to inform himself as much as possible about noh and Japanese theater more generally. The demonstration by Itō, Kōri, and Kume was Yeats's first opportunity to imagine noh in performance—even the first rehearsal for *Hawk's Well*.

Itō's performance at the noh recital and ability to dance in "the deeps of the mind" won him the role of the Guardian of the Well (PFNoh, 153). While we cannot know exactly what Itō, with the help of Kōri and Kume, performed for Yeats, I believe that Itō relied on his previous training and experiences as a spectator of noh and other Japanese performance forms to create a style that powerfully stirred Yeats's imagination. If so, a precise account of Itō's training before meeting Yeats would help clarify their collaboration. Interestingly, it was Itō's lack of conventional noh training that has led some to dismiss the Yeats-Itō collaboration and cultural exchange. Joseph Lennon claims that "Yeats believed he had found an authentically trained Japanese Noh dancer in Michio Ito, a modern dancer trained in Paris, the irony of his mistake is significant."[39] Itō was not a noh actor, but there is no evidence that he passed himself off as one or that Yeats "believed" he was (Pound certainly knew better). Nor was Itō a "modern dancer trained in Paris," and that mistake indicates how difficult it is to shift our attention from canonical figures and their errors to lesser-known transnational artists. Before leaving Japan in 1912, Itō studied nihon buyō (Japanese classical dance) with Kichitoyo Wakayagi for approximately ten months as well as Western-style opera and probably kabuki, a dance-drama influenced by noh.[40] This training is important because noh, nihon buyō, and kabuki have exchanged "stylistic features, movement vocabulary, musical styles, and story plots" to such an extent that one scholar/artist claims it is difficult to "differentiate one from the other."[41] I disagree, for anyone with a basic knowledge of the forms would recognize the differences in a performance, even though nihon buyō includes dances drawn from the kabuki stage and kabuki adopted plots from noh. But all share similar pedagogical formats and performance philosophies, including the ōmugaeshi (parrot-repetition method) and the focus on direct, teacher-to-student transmission in a hierarchical guild organization.[42]

Perhaps most significant for the dance lessons that Itō gave Yeats are the common bodily styles and movement techniques shared by Japanese traditional performance forms. Noh, nihon buyō, and kabuki all feature the basic bodily posture called kamae or kitachi, in which the pelvis is tipped forward, in opposition to the lift of the chest and head. Both noh and nihon buyō feature gestures with a fan and require that the arms be held in front of the body in a curved position that displays the long sleeves of the kimono. The main locomotor step of all three, and of most Japanese art forms, is the suriashi (sliding step). In fact, so much time in a noh play is spent walking down the hashigakari entrance bridge or across the stage that noh has been dubbed "the art of walking." My training in noh performance taught me that the basic difference between dance techniques lies in the posture of the body (kamae versus ballet's first position) and the walking step (suriashi versus ballet's turned out–pointed toe step with the weight on the ball of the foot) (clips 1 and 4). Most human movements are otherwise quite similar. My noh lessons also reminded me that performers are disciplined by movement techniques, often to such an extent that they do not recognize the ways in which their bodies are declaring their training. My quarter century of ballet and modern dance training interfered with my ability to perform the seemingly simple gestures in noh movement forms (kata). The choreography (katatsuke) for Hagoromo's kiri (closing section) includes beautiful fan work, such as crossing both arms at the wrists in front of the torso and then swinging them open to the sides of the body (clip 3). The gesture is repeated twice while the moon maiden walks diagonally across the stage and the chorus sings of the treasures she bestows on the land. In ballet, an arm swinging up and out to the side (from fifth position en avant with wrists crossed through fifth en haut and opening to second position) while moving diagonally across the stage is frequently accompanied by a tilt of the head and a gaze out at the audience across the front arm (clip 4). Such stylizations are not part of Hagoromo's kata, and the head in noh generally remains centered over the torso, except for some dramatic "cuts" with the mask in warrior pieces or to represent insanity. Although I knew the rules, it was extremely difficult for me to stop tilting my head as I performed the arm movements. I didn't think I was doing it, but my sensei performed an imitation of my tilting head (ōmugaeshi [parrot-repetition] in reverse), to the great amusement of the other students observing my lesson.

One of the premises of this book is that bodily techniques tour with performers and reveal how culturally specific movement practices affect performances—along with ideas about race, ethnicity, and gender. Itō took his dance training and technique with him on his travels, even when he hoped to become a Western and modern performer. He combined his early training in Japanese performance forms with his brief studies in Europe (about a year at the Émile Jaques-Dalcroze Institute of Eurhythmics, which I discuss in chapter 3) to shape the noh lesson he gave Yeats and then his choreography for Hawk's Well. Itō's studies in Japan were certainly not a replacement for the decades of training required of an actor or scholar before they are believed to have any deep understanding of noh (and that is a good reminder of how insufficient my own training must be considered). Nonetheless, Itō's recital was a pedagogical scene of cultural transmission and one from which Yeats learned a good deal; his own description of noh movement is remarkably accurate:

> At the climax . . . there is a dance, a series of positions and movements which may represent a battle, or a marriage, or the pain of a ghost in the

Buddhist Purgatory. I have lately studied certain of these dances, with Japanese players, and I notice that their ideal of beauty, unlike that of Greece and like that of pictures from Japan and China, makes them pause at moments of muscular tension. The interest is not in the human form but in the rhythm to which it moves, and the triumph of their art is to express the rhythm in its intensity. They move from the hip, keeping constantly the upper part of their body still, and seem to associate with every gesture or pose some definite thought. They cross the stage with a sliding movement, and one gets the impression not of undulation but of continuous straight lines. (PFNoh, 158)

Here Yeats is describing the noh standing posture (*kamae*), and with the forward tip of the pelvis and bent knees, movement does seem to be "from the hip." This posture allows the upper body to remain "still," as does *suriashi*, which Yeats calls, accurately enough, "a sliding movement." The bodily oppositions required by *kamae* along with the grounded, sliding step and the often slow pace of the movements on the noh stage create a feeling of "muscular tension," and there are lengthy pauses, as Yeats points out. The precise movement patterns that form noh's dance vocabulary are sometimes coded with meaning, as in the weeping gesture (*shiori*) or the *kata* for sleeping. Others are abstract floor patterns and stamps.

The lesson given by Itō, Kōri, and Kume also introduced noh chanting (*utai*) to Yeats, who believed that it offered an ancient, perfected example of poetic chant that, at the heights of emotion, becomes enflamed nearly into song. Yeats had been searching for a form of musical theater that would allow the human voice to be "freed from this competition [with an orchestra] and find itself among little instruments, only heard at their best perhaps when we are close about them" (PFNoh, 153). Itō also was very interested in the power of the human voice and had even hoped to become a Western opera singer, but he was exposed to traditional Japanese chant in all of the performance forms he studied. Kume had taken noh lessons with Fenollosa's teacher, Umewaka Minoru, as Pound pointed out. Although Pound's further claim that Kume accurately performed *Hagoromo* at the recital is probably an exaggeration, Kume probably knew something about the text and movement and may have demonstrated selections for Yeats and Pound, both of whom were interested in the play. Yeats believed that *Hagoromo* provided evidence of the transnational, universal aspect of myths and legends: "The feather-mantle, for whose lack the moon goddess, (or should we call her fairy?) cannot return to the sky, is the red cap whose theft can keep our [Irish] fairies of the sea upon dry land" (PFNoh, 159). He also offered the play as an example of how poetry and drama can be organized by a repeated image or metaphor: "In 'Hagoromo' the feather-mantle of the fairy woman creates also its rhythm of metaphor. In the beautiful day of opening spring 'the plumage of Heaven drops neither feather nor flame,' 'nor is the rock of earth over-much worn by the brushing of the feathery skirt of the stars'" (PFNoh, 161). Pound had developed his strategy for composing a long imagist poem from the repeated images in noh (sometimes imagined or mistranslated). Yeats believed that noh's "rhythm of metaphor" replaced "character," which seems "essential" to Western dramatists," but the replacement "made possible a hundred lovely intricacies" in noh (PFNoh, 161).

Yeats echoed *Hagoromo* with his own bird-maiden-Guardian who dances her enchantment and possession rather than flies away from the *Hawk's Well*.[43] Yeats had been interested in staging such deep mental states long before he encountered noh (as Michael's possession in *Cathleen ni Houlihan* attests). The spirits that haunted the noh stage provided an ancient model of multilayered possession, and in his first published statement on noh, Yeats celebrated "the exorcism of a ghost which is itself obsessed by an evil spirit" and is "represented by a dancer wearing a 'terrible mask with golden eyes.'"[44] The role he and Itō later created in *Hawk's Well* was that of a mystical dancer "with face made up to resemble a mask" whose possession by another being leads to her dance (PC, 338). Itō played a "solitary girl" who is charged by the Irish spirits called the Sidhe to watch over a well into which flow the "miraculous waters" of immortality sought by the Young Man (PC, 346). This role reinforces common assumptions about Asians in the early twentieth century (and still today), stereotypes that Itō promoted, as did Noguchi, while they were trying to build careers in Europe and the United States. As a Japanese man, Itō was assumed to be less bound to reason, more spiritual, and perhaps therefore more easily possessed. Asian men have long been stereotyped as more effeminate than Europeans, which may explain why the fact that Itō was performing in drag as the Guardian of the Well was, and still is, rarely mentioned.[45] While stereotypes of feminine Japanese men contributed to the drag role, Yeats had been interested in transvestism as a strategy for disrupting stage realism and invoking depths behind the surface of performance as early as 1899 when he cast his lover/collaborator Florence Farr in the role of the male poet Aleel in *The Countess Cathleen*.[46]

Yeats's claim to have found in Itō the "tragic image that has stirred my imagination" cannot be separated from his assumptions about the exotic Japanese, but that does not render their collaboration meaningless or erase the remarkable features of the Guardian role they created (PFNoh, 153). The Guardian seems to have tasted the magical water and gained eternal youth, whereas the Old Man in the play has wasted fifty years of his life waiting for the well to fill. She is "possessed" by "The woman of the Sidhe herself / The mountain witch, the unappeasable shadow" just as the water runs into the well, and the enchantment that leads to her dance puts the Old Man to sleep so that he cannot drink the water (PC, 349). While possessed, she calls with a hawk's voice, and her identity is ambiguous enough to confuse the Young Man, who cries out, "Why do you gaze upon me / with the eyes of a hawk? / I am not afraid of you, bird, woman, or witch" (PC, 352). He is wooed away from the well of immortality and into a life of battle by the Guardian in a dance that, when performed by Itō, suggests the hypnotic power of the cross-dressed "foreign" dancer over the Old Man, the Young, and many other audiences.

AT THE HAWK'S WELL: THE ORIGINAL COLLABORATION

Yeats hoped that Hawk's Well would solve the aesthetic and political problems that had arisen in the Irish National Theater and made him want to abandon drama altogether before 1916. Hawk's Well is part of Yeats's cycle of five plays about the mythic Celtic warrior Cuchulain, telling the story of his initiation into a life of heroic battle. Unlike the other plays, it is not based on any of the legends from the Táin or Lady Gregory's version of the Ulster saga published in 1902 with a preface by Yeats.[47] Instead, it draws loosely from Hagoromo and another play from the Fenollosa-Hirata-Pound translations, Yoro or Sustenance of Age, in which an imperial servant journeys in search of a miraculous spring whose waters are rumored to heal the aging. Many critics have compared Yeats's plays and his noh models, and they commonly point out that his misunderstanding of the form was shaped by his exoticism as well as oddities in the Fenollosa-Hirata translations and performance notes, which were then further reinterpreted by Pound.[48] Of course, I argue that no cross-cultural transmission is completely accurate and that every lesson, regardless of the status of teacher and student, produces some misunderstanding.

Yeats and his collaborators adapted those elements of noh that provide a feeling of ritual and depart from realist stage traditions so as to represent deep states of mind and invoke those states in the audience: All the performers wore masks or makeup that resembled a mask. The stage design was simple and intimate. A small ensemble of musicians played during songs and accentuated the spoken dialogue with drumbeats, as in noh. All the actors used stylized movement, and the climax of the play was a dance scene. The play text alternated between characters speaking to each other in the usual dramatic dialogue and characters or the chorus describing the stage and the actions taking place there, as well as between traditional poetic forms with rhymes and meter and spoken verse that is more free or variable. I will take up *Hawk's Well*'s performance elements in turn, emphasizing how they contribute to a theater "in the deeps" that presented nationalism as an irrational state that can possess characters.

MASKS

The French artist Edmund Dulac, famous for his illustrations of *The Arabian Nights* (1907), designed the masks for *At the Hawk's Well*, and they were crucial to Yeats.[49] He opened his "Introduction to *Certain Noble Plays of Japan*" with the statement: "I am writing these words with my imagination stirred by a visit to the studio of Mr. Dulac. . . . I saw there the mask and headdress to be worn in a play of mine by the player who will speak the part of Cuchulain, and who wearing this noble half-Greek half-Asiatic face will appear perhaps like an image seen in revery [sic] by some Orphic worshipper" (PFNoh, 151) (figure 2.1). Yeats used the phrase "the player who will speak the part of Cuchulain" to describe the relation between character and performer rather than the more common formulations, the actor who will *play* or *be* Cuchulain. He does not want the actor to *become* the character as in realist acting technique, and the mask is one of the "devices to exclude or lessen character" that also immediately invokes the realm of performance and myth.[50] The photograph of the mask for the Young Man/Cuchulain, which Yeats published in *Four Plays for Dancers*, reveals that it is, as in noh, a full face mask carved in wood with mouth and eye details.[51] A helmet with a horn appears to bear two stylized eyes on the forehead, an important design given the many images of eyes in the play, including the eyes of the Guardian described by the Old Man as "not of this world, / Nor moist, nor faltering; they are no girl's eyes," and by the Young Man/Cuchulain as "the eyes of a hawk" (PC, 351).

FIGURE 2.1 British actor Henry Ainsley [Ainley] as Cuchulain in W. B. Yeats's *At the Hawk's Well* (1916). (Photograph © George Eastman House, International Museum of Photography and Film)

The full facial mask also obscures the movements of the mouth, tongue, and face as well as the excesses like saliva and spit that accompany speech. The mask separates language from the physical effort of speech and minimizes movement on the stage, one of Yeats's goals for his theater: "The stage must become still that words might keep all their vividness—and I wanted vivid words."[52] Another advantage of the mask, Yeats claimed, is that it replaced the face of a "commonplace player" with "the fine invention of a sculptor." It also allowed him "to bring the audience close enough to the play to hear every inflection of the voice. A mask never seems but a dirty face, and no matter how close you go is still a work of art" (PFNoh, 155). In his preface to *Four Plays for Dancers* (1920), Yeats returned to Dulac's masks and suggested that Cuchulain's could be used for Dervorgilla in another dance play, *The Dreaming of the Bones*. Yeats called for "a small number of typical masks, each capable of use in several plays" (PC, 334). He imagined writing "plays for certain masks" and claimed that another noh-inspired dance play in his Cuchulain cycle, *The Only Jealousy of Emer*, "was written to find what dramatic effect one could get out of a mask, changed while the player remains upon the stage to suggest a change of personality" (PC, 334). While a noh mask is donned onstage only in the ritual play *Okina*, garments are added and removed by the stage assistants (*koken*) in full view of the audience, as in *Hagoromo* when the angel regains her feathered mantle from the fisherman and prepares to dance. Making such costume changes visible, like the use of masks, calls attention to the fact of the performance and its costumes. At the same time, Yeats hoped it would defamiliarize the play enough to disrupt the audience's habits of reception and encourage them to open "the deeps of the mind."

STAGE DESIGN

Yeats used noh to help him imagine an intimate theater that can be

> played in a room for so little money that forty or fifty readers of poetry can pay the price. There will be no scenery, for three musicians, whose seeming sun-burned faces will I hope suggest that they have wandered from village to village in some country of our dreams, can describe place and weather, and at moments action, and accompany it all by drum and gong or flute and dulcimer. (PFNoh, 151)

The first performance of At the Hawk's Well was held on April 2, 1916, in Lady Emerald Cunard's London drawing room with an invited audience that included Ezra Pound and T. S. Eliot. Queen Alexandria of England attended the second charity performance on April 4 in Lady Islington's larger room at Chesterfield Gardens with, according to Yeats, an audience of "three hundred fashionable people" who made his "muses" only "half welcome" (PC, 419).[53] Although both were private affairs, Yeats preferred the first, more intimate, coterie audience, and he described his delight at turning away a newspaper photographer who promised a "whole page" of publicity that Yeats did not need for his new dramatic form.

Yeats had no interest in expensive or heavy scenery for these drawing room performances, so he and Dulac designed a stage property that was to designate the playing space: A "black cloth" with a stylized hawk design emblazoned in the center (figure 2.2). The Three Musicians in the play, with "faces made up to resemble masks," performed a formal gesture of "folding and unfolding of the cloth" as they sang the opening and closing songs (unless the dance plays are played one after another, in which case "it may seem a needless repetition") (PC, 338–39). Andrew Parkin's carefully annotated collection of manuscript materials for At the Hawk's Well reveals that Yeats, with the help of Dulac and Itō, developed this action during the rehearsal process, changing the songs and increasing the number of musicians to three so that the cloth could be unfolded in a triangular formation.[54] Although not present

FIGURE 2.2 The Three Musicians in Yeats's *At the Hawk's Well* (1916). (Edmund Dulac is in the center with the curtain he designed for the play.) (Photograph © George Eastman House, International Museum of Photography and Film)

in noh, this stage action recalls the importance of cloth in noh, evident in plot details like the stolen feathered robe of *Hagoromo*, the elaborately designed costumes, and the many poetic descriptions of moving cloth and swirling sleeves. While the musicians sing the opening lines of the play and the hawk totem becomes visible, the Guardian of the Well enters behind them and lays down a "square blue cloth representing a well," a further element of the dance play's stylization and refusal of naturalism and a device derived from another Fenollosa-Hirata-Pound draft translation, *Aoi no ue*.

MUSIC AND CHORAL SPEECH

Yeats wanted a musical chorus in his plays for dancers that did not resemble any from conventional forms of musical theater. He knew less about noh music than the masks, scene design, movement, and dramatic texts. He also may have been tone deaf.[55] Having little notion of what the music should sound like, he wanted it mainly to "deepen the emotion of the words" (PC, 418). Yeats had long been searching for a method of verse recitation that was not quite singing, or else singing "as if mere speech had taken fire, when it appears to have passed into song almost imperceptibly" (PFNoh, 152). His experiments with the actress Florence Farr, beginning in 1899, resulted in joint recitals throughout the first decade of the twentieth century, with Farr accompanying her recitation on a psaltery, a stringed instrument built by Arnold Dolmetsch that may have influenced the instruments chosen for *Hawk's Well*.[56]

Edmund Dulac produced the original music for *Hawk's Well* as well as the masks and costumes (with Itō's help) and appears to have studied noh both before and after his collaboration with Yeats and Itō. The score was intended for "simple" and "small" instruments that could be learned by near amateurs (figure 2.3).[57] Dulac stated that the harp could be "tuned to any pentatonic scale that suits the play," and appropriately, both Japanese and Celtic folk melodies tend to be in pentatonic, with five notes in each octave (rather than

FIGURE 2.3 The Three Musicians in Yeats's *At the Hawk's Well* (1916). (Dulac is in the center.) (Photograph © George Eastman House, International Museum of Photography and Film)

the seven notes in the common Western major and minor scales). The most noh-like element of the music was the use of the drum and gong to accentuate "the movements of the players" (PC, 342). Dulac wrote, "The drum and gong must be used at times during the performance to emphasise the spoken word; no definite notation of this can be given, and it is left to the imagination and taste of the musician" (PC, 423). Noh drummers do not improvise, but there is some room for creative spontaneity within the established drum patterns. The intermittent wailing of kakegoe (drum calls and beats) can feel improvisational, particularly in the sections where they are not rhythmically matched to chant and movement.[58] Other noh influences may be evident in the relatively short vocal range compassed by the melody, the repetition of the same rhythmic figures appearing over and over again, and the feeling of unmatched rhythm, particularly in the "Prelude to the Dance." The score feels generically exotic or medieval: The zither plays in parallel fifths, leading to a feeling of stagnation, and there are many grace notes, runs, and trills.[59] Another influence is the syllabic structure of noh utai, in which each chanted syllable gets roughly the same emphasis, a style encouraged by the relatively evenly stressed and open (vowel-ended) syllables of the Japanese language. Hawk's Well's opening song for the "folding and unfolding of the cloth" gives each syllable of the poetry an eighth note, and there are only slight fluctuations in pitch.[60] Yeats composed these opening lines mostly of monosyllabic words, which make the variable stresses and closed (consonant-ended) syllables of English more amenable to a noh-style chant: "I call to the eye of the mind / A well long choked up and dry / And boughs long stripped by the wind" (PC, 340; score, 424) (figure 2.4).

In their opening song, the musicians depict an ancient well and bare branches, creating a mythic setting and legendary time appropriate to the Cuchulain saga. The musicians teach the audience to imagine the scenery in the "eye of the mind" because the stage is bare (PC, 340). While the monosyllables in the opening lines allow for a rhythmically even chant, they also resemble a ballad form consisting of short, rhymed lines, and a repetitive rhythm (mostly iambs and anapests). Yeats believed that verse forms recalled the time period in which they were created and used the ballad and other "traditional metres that have developed with the language" to position readers and audience members in the past.[61] Although he acknowledged that Pound had written "admirable free verse," Yeats required "a complete coincidence between period and stanza." The Irish "Heroic Age" and figures like Cuchulain needed the "ballad metre," and he explained that he "created in dance

FIGURE 2.4 Edmund Dulac, "Music for *At the Hawk's Well*," in W. B. Yeats, *Four Plays for Dancers* (London: Macmillan, 1921).

plays the form that varies blank verse with lyric metres" in order to match period with poetic form.[62]

After the initial song, the Musicians of *Hawk's Well* shift from a ballad-like chant to a description of the actor's onstage actions in spoken verse that is rhythmic but irregular in meter:

FIRST MUSICIAN (speaking)
He has made a little heap of leaves;
He lays the dry sticks on the leaves
And, shivering with cold, he has taken up
The fire-stick and socket from its hole.
He whirls it round to get a flame;
And now the dry sticks take the fire
And now the fire leaps up and shines
Upon the hazels and the empty well. (PC, 343)

Dulac's score indicates that this section of spoken text describing the actor building a fire is performed simultaneously with the song "O wind, O salt wind, O sea wind!" (PC, 343, 427). The concurrent speech and song underscores another overlap between stage action or mimesis and narration or diegesis: Mimesis is actors performing a stage action as if they were really doing it and, in the conventions of realistic acting, ignoring the fact of the audience. Diegesis is storytelling, as when a narrator tells us about what is happening onstage or offstage, and it is generally avoided in realist theater.

When the Old Man performs his first stage action of building a fire, we both watch it happen (mimesis) and hear about it (diegesis) from the musicians. This redundancy would be unusual in Western realism, but in *Hawk's Well*, it emphasizes what theatrical conventions usually ask the audience to overlook: An actor would never actually "whirl" a stick to build a fire on stage, not just because actors would have to be super Girl or Boy Scouts to start a fire in that way, but also because fires in the theater are dangerous. The Old Man's pretense of fire making is very different from the actual act. For Martin Puchner, Yeats's use of mimetic stage action with diegetic narration is a "doubling—or clash" that points to some of Yeats's antitheatrical tendencies.[63]

In noh, a doubling of action and narration is not a "clash" or antitheatrical but the very basis of theatricality. The overlap and fluctuation between narration and action is one of the pleasures of the noh theater. The noh chorus can describe or comment on the action that is simultaneously being presented on the stage, but it can also sing with the characters and even repeat and seem to take over their lines when they are dancing or at emotional extremes. In the Fenollosa-Hirata-Pound version of *Yoro*, the chorus speaks as the Old Man in the first person when describing how he drank from the waters that "console ages": "My sleeves were torn, and the shadow of my hands dipping the water is clearly seen in this mountain well."[64] There is a practical purpose for this description. As in Yeats's *Hawk's Well*, there is no mountain scenery on the noh stage, only the pine tree (*oi matsu*) painted on the back wall, the three pines leading down the bridgeway, and, in this play, the intentionally unrealistic frame of a well called, like all such properties, a *tsukurimono* (built thing), a name emphasizing the nonmimetic quality of all stage objects. In *Yoro*, the Old Man as *shite* would be dressed in a valuable and often ancient costume, with gorgeous long sleeves. The chorus asks the audience to imagine tattered sleeves and a sacred well in the mountains. A dance, as in this example from *Yoro*, often begins with the main performer (*shite*) chanting a line, which the chorus repeats and amplifies with multiple voices. Yet another effect of the chorus chanting lines that could belong to the *shite* is to depersonalize the characters in a manner that critics today associate with the instability of identity, to use terminology that sounds uncomfortably contemporary. It also makes the characters more available for possession and haunting.

Even though Yeats's chorus of Musicians in *Hawk's Well* do not speak as the characters, they do influence how the audience sees and understands the characters. They "call to the eye of the mind" another "deep of the mind," and ask us to accept their descriptions of, for example, the characters' faces, which we cannot see beneath their masks or makeup. The masks conceal yet open at the eyes, allowing the actor to see out and the audience to glimpse the body behind the mask. This opening is emphasized by the plays' repeated references to eyes. The Old Man describes the Guardian's eyes as "dazed and heavy" and asks, "Why do you stare like that? / You had that glassy look about the eyes / Last time it happened"—that is, the last time the well filled and the Guardian was possessed by the Sidhe (PC, 344). The Old Man warns the Young Man/Cuchulain, who described fending off a "great grey hawk" as he climbed to the well, that the bird of prey was actually the "woman of the Sidhe" and that those who look upon her "unmoistened eyes" will be cursed to "mix hatred in the love" or to kill their own children (PC, 348–49). The Young Man who becomes initiated as the mythic warrior in Hawk's Well will suffer both curses in Yeats's cycle of Cuchulain plays.

DANCE

At the climax of the play, the Guardian's body becomes occupied by the Sidhe, first indicated by her "glassy eyes" and then by her "shivering": "the terrible life / Is slipping through her veins. She is possessed" (PC, 350). Yeats uses diegetic description to explain and help the audience understand the possession. He also uses dance, which consistently represents the "deeps of the mind" in Yeats's theater. "Shivering" is the first description of the Guardian's movements while possessed. Then, the stage directions indicate "The Guardian of the Well throws off her cloak and rises. Her dress under the cloak suggests a hawk" (PC, 351). Itō's costume, which he helped Edmund Dulac design, is documented in Alvin Langdon Coburn's production photographs (figure 2.5).[65] The costume adapted the long sleeves of the kimono into hawk-like wings. Photographs indicate that Itō choreographed a display of the sleeves that resembled the sayū, a common kata for concluding a noh dance. Itō held fans or sticks to extend the length of the winglike sleeves, a technique that had famously been used by Loïe Fuller to control her long skirts early in the history of modern dance. In figure 2.6, Itō appears to prepare for a stamp, which is common in noh and nihon buyō. Itō's choreography for the Guardian's dance seems to have been a hybrid of noh-like movement and nihon buyō with modern dance movement.

The performance techniques Itō brought across national borders as an early-twentieth-century migrant and to his role as Guardian and the collaboration

FIGURE 2.5 Itō Michio as the Hawk in Yeats's *At the Hawk's Well* (1916), showing the sleeves of the costume. (Photograph © George Eastman House, International Museum of Photography and Film)

FIGURE 2.6 Itō as the Hawk in Yeats's *At the Hawk's Well* (1916), preparing for a stamp. (Photograph © George Eastman House, International Museum of Photography and Film)

FIGURE 2.7 Ainsley [Ainley] as Cuchulain in Yeats's *At the Hawk's Well* (1916). (Photograph © George Eastman House, International Museum of Photography and Film)

of *Hawk's Well* are bodily forms of cultural mixing or hybridity.[66] Itō appears to have taught movement to the other performers, including Henry Ainley, the famous Shakespearean actor who played the Young Man/Cuchulain (AHW Manu, xxxviii–xxxix) (figure 2.7). In rehearsal typescripts, Alan Wade wrote instructions for his movements as the Old Man with "feet turned in" (AHW Manu, 120–21) (figure 2.8), movements that would have required bent knees and a posture similar to that of noh *kamae*—the posture Yeats described in his "Introduction to Certain Noble Plays of Japan" after seeing Itō's demonstration of noh *shimai*/dance (PFNoh, 158). Yeats was deeply invested in the performers' movements. He complained to Lady Gregory of Ainley's habit of "wav[ing] his arms like a drowning kitten," saying that he was "working out gestures for Ainley," which Dulac would draw, presumably for the purpose of teaching them to the actor (AHW Manu, xxxix).[67] A prompt copy of *At the Hawk's Well* reveals that Dulac did in fact sketch the characters' gestures in the margins (AHW Manu, xv). Having been dissatisfied with the professional Ainley, Yeats celebrated the "amateur." He claims, "I shall not soon forget the rehearsal of *The Hawk's Well*, when Mr. Ezra Pound, who had never acted on any stage, in the absence of our

FIGURE 2.8 British actor Allan Wade as the Old Man in Yeats's *At the Hawk's Well* (1916). (Photograph © George Eastman House, International Museum of Photography and Film)

chief player rehearsed for half an hour" (PC, 214). Pound apparently attended some rehearsals and helped with the production—providing an unforgettable half hour of Pound as Cuchulain.

Yeats was happy with Itō's stage movement and choreography, for as the rehearsals progressed, Yeats revised his poetry to enhance and emphasize the dance expression (AHW Manu, xli).[68] Drafts of the play reveal that after beginning rehearsals, Yeats lengthened the dance and pared away the Musician's descriptions of the movement, cutting lines such as "Keep from the ~~terrible~~ dancing feet & terrible eyes / Two feet that are like quivering blades" (AHW Manu, xxxiv, 93). Early drafts of *At the Hawk's Well*, probably written in late 1915 or January 1916, include the following note: "Chorus. Continues description of dance. How they ~~dan~~ go from rock to rock on the mountain side. Is it hate or is it love. Sometimes she ~~runs~~ leads him near the fountain and then away. The fountain bubbles at this moment the woman wh in her daze breaks from him & runs out" (AHW Manu, 29). The only description of the dance that survived to publication is in the stage directions, "the Girl has begun to dance, moving like a hawk. . . . The dance goes on for some time. . . . The dance goes on" (PC, 352). One rehearsal typescript suggests that it went on for eight min-utes—a long dance for a play lasting no more than a half hour (AHW Manu, xxxix, 143–49). Dulac's score for "The Dance" indicates "it ought to last about 3½ minutes" but that does not include the "Prelude to the Dance," in which the flute and harp are given some of the most orientalist effects in the score, including multiple long trills marked with the older baroque notation of the wavy line (PC, 430). Trills also occur in the music for the dance, but interest-ingly, the majority of those wavy lines are for the drum and gong, instruments that cannot technically trill. The wavy line notation lends a foreign or exotic feeling to the *appearance* of the score as well as the sound, so that both reflect the "shivering" that signals the possession of the Guardian. The flute in the "Prelude" repeats a short, low melody while the harp plays arpeggios that cre-ate a feeling of mounting tension without progression—as if the music were incapable of moving.

The Old Man knows that the Guardian's "shivering," "unmoistened eyes," and dancing are the signs of both her possession and the imminent filling of the well, but as in the past, he "cannot bear" her eyes, covers his head, and sleeps shortly after the "Prelude" begins (PC, 351). The Young Man/Cuchul-ain continues to speak through the "Prelude," claiming that he will not leave the well until he is immortal like the Guardian. He even boasts, "I am not afraid of you, bird, woman, or witch" (PC, 351). The melody slowly rises in the first section of the dance, and the tempo increases, with the drum setting a strong 3/4 meter. The second section becomes progressively faster and more intense, and the meter changes in the third section to a sharp 2/4 drumbeat, with increasing frenzy until the Guardian exits.[69] The Musicians report, "The madness has laid hold" on the Young Man (PC, 352). He brags, "Run where you will, / Grey bird, you shall be perched upon my wrist, / Some were called queens and yet have been perched there" (PC, 352). Although he insists he will not leave the well, his body cannot adhere to what he says, and he follows the Guardian offstage as the Musicians describe the "plash" of the water of immortality flowing into the well. Cuchulain's duet with the Guardian causes Eofe to raise her troop of "fierce women of the hills" against him, and Cuchu-lain leaves the stage "shouldering his spear" to "face them" (PC, 354). This "clash of arms" initiates him into a life of battle, and in the Cuchulain mythol-ogy that Yeats followed, it also leads to his sexual initiation. Eofe becomes the mother of the son Cuchulain will unknowingly kill in *On Baile's Strand*, a filicide that Yeats dramatized in a 1904 play by that title.[70] He depicted the aftermath of the tragedy in the second play for dancers, *The Only Jealousy of Emer* (1919).[71]

By translating the masks, chorus, music, and dance of noh for his Cuchulain cycle, Yeats hoped to turn the actor's entire body into "a mask from whose eyes the disembodied looks" or a container that can be filled by spirits, ghosts, and gods.[72] This possession results in dance and the failure of language to dictate action or to allow the individual to determine his or her actions. Yeats's "individual" in this play is anti-individualistic and submissive, from the possessed Guardian, to the Old Man who falls asleep at the height of the drama, to the Young Man/Cuchulain who is seduced by dance away from a magical immortality and toward a mortal life of heroism. Even in his turn to heroism, Cuchulain seems to submit to the exterior forces of the magical Eofe and is seduced away from the well. In becoming less individualistic, Yeats's individual also becomes capable of entering into various deep, irrational states of mind. The possessed, dancing body served as a model for the trancelike state that Yeats hoped to produce in his small, elite audience of fifty lovers of poetry. The audience was supposed to be seduced and possessed by Itō's dance as well as the other features Yeats found or imagined in noh: "rhythm, balance, pattern, images that remind us of vast passions, the vagueness of past times, all the chimeras that haunt the edge of trance . . . that strange sensation as though the hair of one's head stood up."[73] Many of these features, from music to dance, the diegetic narration and stylized movement, have been associated with antitheatricalism. In the noh tradition and other Japanese performing arts, however, these are simply the tools of the theatricality. Yeats was working against a particular form of Euro-American theater to produce a deep, unreal theater. Our application of the term "antitheatricality" in this instance ignores the diversity of theatrical expression around the world.

THE UNREASON OF NATIONALISM, OR CUCHULAIN, THE BEHEADED NATIONALIST

I disagree with accusations that Yeats abandoned the goals of the Irish national theater and appropriated noh as a form of cultural colonization. These indictments stem from our limited visions of theatrical and intercultural transmission. But Yeats's ritualistic, trance-provoking theater actually is distant from the dominant understandings of nationalism in modern Ireland. A noh-haunted and possessed version of Cuchulain appears to be an odd warrior to enlist for building an Irish national consciousness. For this reason, Edward Said ambivalently celebrated Yeats as a "poet of decolonization" who "joins his people to its history" yet resolves national concerns on a "non-political level"—through "aestheticised histories," "quasi-religious poems," and spiritualism. Said claimed that these were "important" only because they served "as a refuge from the colonial turbulence of his immediate experience."[74] For Said, Yeats predicted the limits of the first violent stages of decolonization and nation building and invoked the question of

> how to reconcile the inevitable violence of the colonial conflict with the everyday politics of an ongoing national struggle, and also with the power of each of the various parties in the colonial conflict, with the *discourse of reason, of persuasion, of organizations*, with the requirements of poetry. Yeats's prophetic perception that at some point violence cannot be enough and that *the strategies of politics and reason* must come into play is, to my knowledge, the first important announcement in the context of decolonization of the need to balance violent force with an exigent political and organizational process.[75]

Yeats was prophetic about the limits of violence and also, as early as 1916, about the inability of teleological narratives of decolonization to accommodate the diversity of postcolonial nations—as if they could all move step by step through the postcolonial experience with reasonable political strategies. He was equally prophetic about the limits of "reason, persuasion, organizations." Just as Yeats used the theatrical strategies of noh to create an "unreal" theater, he used the same strategies to represent the "unreason" of the human being—those qualities that do not adhere to the assumptions of Western liberal humanism, many of which have been incorporated into theories of empire and decolonization. Liberal humanism also promoted the formation of European empires under such slogans as "The White Man's Burden," the idea that Euro-American states should bring "civilization" to non-European countries as a kind of philanthropy or service project.[76] However much I might want to believe that this was an easily exploded late-nineteenth-century perversion of humanism, I cannot ignore the similarity of the twenty-first-century pronouncements of George W. Bush that "the central goal of the terrorists is the brutal oppression of women" and that the U.S. military "liberated city after city in Afghanistan" from the "barbaric" Taliban.[77]

Yeats's "aestheticised histories" and "quasi-religious poems" were certainly political for Yeats. They were the substance of what he termed "the imaginative tradition of Ireland" that Empire had stifled; artists could rebuild that tradition by filling "the popular imagination again with saints and heroes" as their particular and crucial contribution to decolonization (PC, 11). Read in this context, Yeats's *Hawk's Well* does not set violent national struggle against the "reason" of "everyday politics"; instead, it offers several competing visions of the Irish nation: peaceful agrarianism against heroism, the Old Man who waits beside the well for half a century against Cuchulain, who will obtain eternal life not by drinking magical water but by achieving legendary feats in battle. The hero also will be cursed with filicide as foreseen by the Old Man; he will destroy the next generation. In their final ballad, the Musicians give voice to the well and leafless tree that hangs over it, perhaps a technique borrowed from the noh chorus's ability to sing for characters. The well might symbolize the potential of Irish legend, and the bare hazel invokes the tree of knowledge in Celtic mythology.[78] Yet the hazel is "leafless" in this play, without progeny (although theater historians recognize it as a precursor to Samuel Beckett's leafless tree in *Waiting for Godot*).[79] Both well and tree celebrate the peasant who chooses a wife, children, "milch cows," and a "comfortable" house, but if this picture of rural joys is dry and leafless, it has no future (PC, 355–56). None of the models of the nation offered by the play is sufficient. The characters are literally possessed by irrational, ghostly forces that fill human actors with sleepy complacency, erratic violence, and mystic dancing. The play suggests that doing nothing (Old Man), doing battle (Cuchulain), and dancing (Guardian) all are forms of possession.

The Old Man waiting fifty years by the well could be an allegory for a sleepy ex-Fenian hoping for "Home Rule." Precisely fifty years before the first staging of *At the Hawk's Well*, the Fenian risings of 1866 and 1867 were devastating failures.[80] Britain's brutal treatment of the rebels organized nationalist sentiments that led to the Easter Rising half a century later, when members of the Irish Volunteers and Irish Citizen Army took over strategic locations in Dublin, and Patrick Pearse read the Proclamation of the Independence of the Irish Republic from the General Post Office steps. It is tempting to read Cuchulain as a warrior of the Rising that occurred the same month as the premiere of *Hawk's Well*, although Yeats was famously shocked and ambivalent about its "terrible beauty" (VP, 394). He was also taking advantage of wealthy British patronage when he staged Hawk's Well in Lady Cunard's and Lady Islington's drawing rooms that fateful month, and the second performance benefited the British effort in World War I, a war that killed some 35,000 Irish soldiers as well. He was still in England three weeks later when the rebellion gripped Dublin in a battle that hardly resembled Cuchulain's contest with the dancing Guardians and Hawk-like Sidhe. Yeats's comfortable position in England was far from Kilmainham Gaol, the prison where the leaders of the rebellion, including fellow poet Pearse, were held before being executed in May.

By emphasizing the multiple and conflicting visions of nationalism and the ease with which each might be transformed into an irrational, ghostly possession, Yeats predicted some of postcolonial theory's current struggles with the nation: Is a commitment to archaic racial and nationalist ideals, including Celticism and nativism, a necessary stage in decolonization or a dead end? Yeats turned to pre-Christian myth to avoid sectarianism and the conservative nationalism of the Irish Catholic Church with its tendency toward censorship. He celebrated the peasant's authentic Irishness, yet he accepted the patronage of the wealthy "colonizers" who financed his theater. He was a senator in Ireland's first postcolonial government and a cosmopolitan critic of myopic national self-interest, recognizing that nationalism's irrational drives have always animated both imperial conquest and liberationist movements.

Ghosts are figures for the uncertainty of reality, hauntingly present even when we don't believe in them. Yeats suggested that nations are like ghosts, spectral in their infamously "imagined" quality. Like all chilling ghosts, they produce some of our greatest stories. If Yeats seemed, at least in At the Hawk's Well, to be dancing out of step with his nation's moment, dragging the ghosts of Japan into Celtic legends, his Cuchulain had a haunting curtain call. In The Death of Cuchulain, Yeats's last play and one that overtly recalled the noh-inspired plays for dancers (and Salome) with its own climactic dance before the decapitated head of Cuchulain, the singer asks, "What stood in the Post Office / With Pearse and Connolly? [in the Easter Rising] . . . Who thought Cuchulain till it seemed / He stood where they had stood?"[81] The ghost of Cuchulain, that undead end of Yeats's imagination, stayed there in the Post Office, memorialized in the statue by Oliver Sheppard (figure 2.9). Visitors to Dublin are always shown the bullet holes on the façade of the building and the statue of dying Cuchulain, visible through a front window and testimony to the contradictions in nationalism that Yeats foresaw and that we are still far from resolving.

FIGURE 2.9 Oliver Sheppard, *The Dying Cuchulain* (1911–1912). (Courtesy of Howard Goldbaum [voicesfromthedawn.com])

THE AFTERLIFE OF AT THE HAWK'S WELL

Fascism is one of the ghosts haunting Yeats's legacy. His interest in unreal theater and unreason, possession, enchantment, and other "deep" states of mind contributed to his suspicion of liberal democracy, with its supposed emphasis on the rational political individual. Submission to forces outside the self can include submission to the authority of a great leader, a central feature of fascism.[82] Some critics have argued that both Yeats and Pound twisted noh deliberately to fuel their swerves toward political conservatism or "the right," as it allowed them (somewhat ironically, given its "Eastern" origins) to celebrate a European cultural elite and a myth-tinted militarism.[83] I am not interested in recuperating a more savory, less complicated version of Yeats, but I do want to argue that he promoted several versions of nationalism over his lifetime and that when making claims about his politics, we must always identify which Yeats, which texts, and whose interests are at stake. Critics have a tendency to co-opt the great Irish poet-playwright and Nobel laureate for the critical theories we want to promote. Edward Said found Yeats to be a poet of only the first stage of decolonization; other critics view him as a pure republican or imperialist; and he is one of my messy transnational students of noh. Yeats's dynamic and often self-contradictory works can be linked to many theoretical and political positions.

Yeats was at least a fleeting proponent of fascism in the form of the Irish Blueshirt movement, which he hoped could resolve the political strife and violence in posttreaty Ireland. His elitism, frustration with democratic politics, and belief in the need for the discipline and order that could be provided by a great leader contributed to his enthusiasm for fascism. This was not a departure from his aspirations for the Irish nation. Nationalism was a crucial component of twentieth-century fascism, although postcolonial theorists often link nationalism to anticolonialism and present it as a subversive and progressive force. Yeats initially indicated his public support for the Blueshirt movement in "Three Songs to the Same Tune," first published in the *Spectator* on February 23, 1934. The songs demonstrate that Yeats's attraction to fascism was intertwined with his interest in the theater and with his belief in the power of submission to a director, teacher, politician, nation, army, or occult spirit. Yeats first mentioned the songs in a letter to Olivia Shakespear on November 30, 1933, in which he described writing "a new national song . . . to be sung at the Abbey Theatre."[84] About his process of composition he claimed,

"Then I put into a simple song a commendation of the rule of the able and the educated, man's old *delight in submission*; I wrote round the line 'The soldier takes pride in saluting his captain.'"[85] When he republished the songs in the magazine *Poetry*, he included a "Note" dated August 1934: "Because a friend belonging to a political party wherewith I had once some loose associations, told me that it had, or was about to have, or might be persuaded to have, some such aim as mine, I wrote these songs. Finding that it neither would nor could, I increased their fantasy, their extravagance, their obscurity, that no party might sing them" (VP, 837). In the debates about Yeats's fascism, politics, and their relationship to his aesthetic beliefs, the role of submission is often ignored. Yeats's *Hawk's Well* suggests that radical nationalism is a force that demands extreme forms of submission, just as empire does, and can lead to fascist as well as decolonizing politics.

The afterlife of *Hawk's Well* included a revival organized by Yeats at the Abbey Theatre on July 22, 1933. Whereas the premiere was performed during World War I as the Irish battle for independence from Britain was marching toward the Easter Rising, by 1933 both that war and the Irish civil war were over but hardly resolved, and the prelude to World War II was well under way: Adolf Hitler was appointed chancellor of Germany in January of that year; the first German concentration camp was built at Dachau in March; and Japan left the League of Nations over the question of its right to occupy Manchuria. Ninette de Valois re-created the role of the Guardian for the revival, wearing Itō's original costume, and performed several different kinds of drag: An Irish-born woman who had starred in the Ballets Russes and changed her name to sound more Russian took a role and a costume that had famously been created by a Japanese man in drag.[86] Yeats seemed largely to ignore the rapid modernization and militarization of twentieth-century Japan, where fascism emerged in tandem with imperialism and partially in an effort to subvert European desires to colonize Japan. *Hawk's Well* traveled to Japan with Itō before the war and was later revived during the efforts to recover from fascist militarization. The play had a remarkable transnational afterlife, and in subsequent chapters, I describe a century of revivals, translations, and adaptations—including two by Itō, which influenced two others for the so-called traditional noh stage by Yokomichi Mario.

My favorite recent adaptation and revival of *Hawk's Well* was also one of the most memorable and moving moments for me as a teacher. On the last day of the 2013 Mellon School of Theater and Performance Research at Harvard

University (also dubbed "drama nerd camp" and "drama boot camp"), the students in my seminar—Theatrical World Tours: Transnational Exchange, Collaboration, Appropriation—staged a version of Yeats's *At the Hawk's Well*. The performance took place in the grand Thompson Room in Harvard's neo-Georgian Barker Center. In the audience were the faculty and drama nerd campers, exhausted by the strenuous regimen of the summer school; my dissertation adviser Elin Diamond, who had given the lecture for the previous night; my one-month-old son, Callan, and his grandmother, who had been stationed as a nanny in a basement office–turned nursery. Maybe it was my own exhaustion—a compound of the exciting two weeks of teaching and the joys of being a new parent, including wake-ups at three-hour intervals. Maybe it was the fact that this was Callan's first experience in the audience for any performance. In any event, I felt that my students' work captured something of the power of the intense collaboration and transnational fusion of modernist arts behind that original 1916 performance of *At the Hawk's Well*.

Along with the text of the play and some reviews and critical responses, I had shown my students photographs of the costumes and masks and had given them Dulac's score—much of the material that shaped this chapter. I also gave them some basic movement lessons in noh *shimai*; we knelt and felt the pain of *seiza*, practiced the *suriashi* sliding step, and learned the opening *kata* for *Hagoromo*'s closing section, which I performed for them in its entirety. As they did in a brief workshop on Itō Michio's choreography and dance technique that I gave a few days later, the students bravely embraced these, probably unexpected, lessons with their entire bodies. The first step toward performance was when the talented musician, arranger, and historian of musical theater, Brian Valencia, performed some of Dulac's score for us in the seminar, significantly influencing my understanding of the ways the music merges generically "oriental" and "medieval" styles with a self-conscious musical modernism. We soon learned that Gibson Cima (whose mother, Gay Gibson Cima, I discussed, with some nervousness, later in our session on Samuel Beckett) was also a gifted vocalist. Not to mention that Cima had brought a lute to the summer school! Valencia produced a digital arrangement of Dulac's score, and he and Cima could be heard singing in the halls of the Barker Center—just the soundtrack a drama nerd camp should have.

The group seemed to take on their roles naturally: Valencia and Cima were the Musicians and singers for all the musical sections, and Erin K. Moodie and Meg Savlonis provided the Musicians' chant. Marissa Béjar agreed to direct, and Jane Barnette served as the dramaturge. Daniel Smith took the role of the Old Man, and Walter Byongsok Chon played the Young Man/Cuchulain. Both adapted elements of noh shimai for their stylized movements, and Chon made fantastic use of an umbrella spear, adopting poses directly from the photographs of Henry Ainley's movements. Presuming that those gestures had been "worked out" by Yeats and drawn by Dulac before being photographed by Coburn, Chon may have given us some of the original 1916 movements. In any case, Yeats would have appreciated both Chon's and Smith's physical control and tension.

The role of the Guardian of the Well was taken by three dancers, Joanna Dee Das, Takiya Nur Amin, and Stella Kao, who also choreographed their own performances "inspired by Itō Michio," according to the playbill. Itō's system of ten arm gestures, discussed in chapter 3, was evident in the movement of the dancers, as was their own dance training. Joanna Dee Das had studied various techniques in modern dance, as had Takiya Nur Amin, although her work in West African dance traditions was particularly crucial to her. Stella Kao drew on her training in butō, a form of modern Japanese dance that features extreme tension throughout the body and owes something to Itō's influence as well as noh and nihon buyō. Although the three dancers choreographed a general plan for moving together through space and around the cloth folded to represent the well, each moved in a distinct style. It seemed absolutely appropriate that three women from different racial and ethnic backgrounds, bearing the traces of their different dance training and bodily regimens, had combined their efforts to reenact the dance that Itō performed in 1916. It was as if it took all three to bear the weight of the collaborative creation of At the Hawk's Well and its historical reconstructions. The dancers, along with their fellow actors and musicians, opened the doors to the "deeps of the mind." As the Musicians in their closing song praised "a pleasant life, / Among indolent meadows," some of us might have thought of how far Harvard was from those meadows and considered why we had chosen the "bitter life" of "Wisdom" (PC, 355). The tree in the play's final question, "Who but an idiot would praise / A withered tree?" might be a symbol for the play (PC, 355–56). But I would say that it isn't withered; I've seen it alive and well.

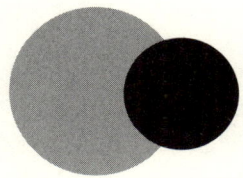

3. ITŌ MICHIO'S *HAWK* TOURS
IN MODERN DANCE AND THEATER

Ito was silent, and then, as though revealing reluctantly a project he had in
mind, said: "You know I told you about the play Yeats wrote for me—what I did
in London. I had a letter flom [sic] him. He is coming to New York to put on play
here. I want you to do it with me. You can design costumes too."
Quoted in Angna Enters, *Silly Girl: A Portrait of Personal Remembrance*

YEATS NEVER SHOWED UP IN NEW YORK TO HELP ITŌ STAGE
At the *Hawk's Well*, and Angna Enters believed that Itō made up the story to
keep her around as a student and dance partner. Yet when Itō left London
in 1916, he carried with him *Hawk's Well* and its message that the pursuit of
immortality, heroism, and even nationhood could lead to irrational states of
possession. For the next thirty years, he periodically mounted performances
of the play around the world. He performed a version with new music by the
Japanese composer Yamada Kosçak in New York in 1918, followed by a brief
East Coast tour.[1] In 1929, Itō staged the play at the Argus Bowl in California,
teaching the Guardian role to the younger dancer Lester Horton, and Itō directed and played the role of the Old Man in a Tokyo performance in 1939.[2]
Itō's *Hawk* tours influenced the Japanese modern theater (*shingeki*), noh, and
late-twentieth-century developments in English noh and fusion theater, all of
which continue to perform versions of *Hawk's Well*.

This archive of a century of *Hawk's Well* performances should serve as an exemplary case study in modernist transnational circuits, and it is particularly exemplary in its paradoxes and contradictions. As this chapter illustrates, Itō built an influential career that included, along with staging *Hawk's Well*, modern solo dances, large ensemble pieces, symphonic dance spectacles, versions of the Fenollosa-Hirata-Pound noh plays, and *kyōgen* in translation. He created the role of the Congo Witch-Doctor in Eugene O'Neill's play *The Emperor Jones* (premiered in 1920) and played the Native Chief in the films *Booloo* and *Spawn of the North* (both Paramount, 1938).[3] Itō also produced spectacular oriental revues to entertain the U.S. occupying forces in Tokyo after World War II, a job that came about through a dramatic twist of fate worthy of its own play. Itō was one of 770 Japanese and Japanese Americans arrested in California as "alien enemies" the day after Japan attacked Pearl Harbor.[4] Itō's own bravado and idealism about uniting East and West may have contributed to his arrest. When his son, Jerry, bragged to a neighbor boy that his father was an important representative of the Japanese government, the boy's mother, Margaret Easley, contacted the FBI.[5] Itō was imprisoned at four different military detention centers over a span of two years before he eventually agreed to be deported to Japan in 1943. His "alien enemy status" seems to have appeared less threatening in Tokyo, where he was hired to direct and choreograph performances at the former Takarazuka Theatre, renamed the Ernie Pyle Theater when it was occupied by American troops. In a remarkable finale to the story, Jerry was sent to Japan while serving in the U.S. Navy and went to the Ernie Pyle Theater, where he was reunited with his father—who helped his son launch his own international acting career.[6]

Itō's deportation, along with the typical marginalization of minorities in histories of dance, led to his current characterization as the "all-but-forgotten pioneer of American modern dance."[7] After long neglect, his choreography began to be reintroduced to the United States in reconstructions beginning in the 1970s, and important critical assessments have followed.[8] Reviews of this so-called rediscovery celebrate Itō as an expressive dance soloist and suggest that his choreography exceeded "ethnic" bounds to achieve "a marriage of East and West."[9] This, however, is a reduction of Itō's career (not to mention his life) that follows trends in dance history; reinforces ideas of the unique, brilliant individual (soloist); and leaves out his multidisciplinary art, consisting of *Hawk* tours, collaborations and networks organized around ideas of "the exotic," versions of noh and *kyōgen* plays, orientalist spectacles, roles as witch doctors and native chiefs, and other work that engages culture and nationality in uncomfortable and not always politically correct ways.

Itō's solos, as opposed to his work in theater, film, and entertainment, are more easily framed as *good* choreographies of "multiculturalism" or "transnationalism" rather than *bad* exoticism or orientalism. The terms "multiculturalism" and "transnationalism" signal our desire to avoid the outdated polarity of East versus West and demonstrate how cultural forms cross borders and span national identities.[10] While it is tempting to suggest that Itō anticipated current models of transnationalism, this claim ignores the ways that his exoticizing choreography and other aspects of his career trouble our pieties about *bad* orientalism and *good* multiculturalism. Like many modern dancers whose "innovations" include choreography that borrows from and misrepresents cultures, Itō did not comply with the current standards of cultural sensitivity. His birth in Japan led audiences to assume he had some privileged access to the "spirit of the orient." Similar assumptions based on an overinvestment in the artist's culture or nation of birth have led some current critics to be embarrassed by Itō's orientalism—even more than Pound's and Yeats's. That is, we expect Itō to teach us accurately about his culture and serve as an authentic representative of his nation, assumptions that have not changed since Itō's time as much as we might wish.[11] I do not intend to provoke shame about our struggles to approach transnational lives and careers; instead, I acknowledge that Itō's work is problematic but important, shaped by misunderstanding and creativity.

Itō's Technique and Pedagogy

One side effect of forcing Itō to be a representative of nation or ethnicity, or even a compound like Asian American identity, is that it tends to direct our attention *away* from his interrelated teaching practices, performance technique, and choreographic method.[12] Hoping to avoid this tendency, I sought out Itō's surviving students in Japan to learn his technique and choreography. On June 4, 2009, I woke up early to take the train out of Tokyo to meet Itō's protégé Ryutani Kyoko and her student, Komine Kumiko. They met me at the train station and took me to a tea ceremony (*chadō*) at the home of their teacher. I initially assumed my *chadō* lesson was a gesture of welcome, and one that would ease our struggle to communicate with my substandard

Japanese. As I wrestled with the small implements and dropped, from a thin piece of *kaishi* paper, the tiny, beautifully decorated *higashi* confectionery I was supposed to eat, I might have preferred the embarrassment of my poor language skills. I rediscovered the pain of *seiza* while kneeling in the circle of tea-drinking students and recognized a variation of the theatrical *suriashi* (sliding step) as they walked into the space of the ceremony. They even held and placed their small folding fans (*sensu*) in a manner that resembled work with the larger noh fan.

Upon arriving at the window-lined dance studio attached to Komine's home, I realized that my lesson in Itō's technique had already begun. The tea ceremony taught me that Itō's movement style is related to the bodily techniques of other Japanese art forms. Ryutani and Komine demonstrated Itō's Ten Gestures and associated them with the arm and hand positions I had botched at the tea ceremony. Itō's two sequences of ten arm gestures were the foundation of his technique. The A, or "masculine," gestural sequence begins with the arms straight down (1), progress up the body to the hips (2), breasts (3), and shoulders (4) and then push forward from the shoulders (5), cross over the chest (6), move to the mouth (7), outside the ears (8) and forehead (9), and extend over the head (10) (clip 5). The gestures of the B, or "feminine," sequence are associated with the same body parts, but the arms are softer or more curved than in the A sequence, in keeping with gendered stereotypes (clip 6).[13] All dancers must master both sequences, so Itō's gendering of the system indicates a form of gestural drag that echoes the "male" and "female" dances of *nihon buyō*; women and men perform both styles in *buyō*. The second-generation Itō dancer Shimazaki Satoru described the importance of these two different qualities of movement as the "masculine side and line, [and] other side, like the Chinese *yo* . . . very graceful like Isadora Duncan." Shimazaki found this diversity of style lacking in "Western" techniques like that of Martha Graham.[14]

The next component of my lesson was to learn Itō's distinctive walking step, which Ryutani associated with *suriashi* and Yeats described as Itō's ability to "cross the stage with a sliding movement" and "move from the hip, keeping constantly the upper part of [his] body still" (PFNoh, 158). In Itō's technique, the dancer first places the ball of the foot on the floor in front and then pushes from the back foot with soft knees to transfer weight without lifting and lowering the body, as in common walking. When moving quickly, the dancer never completely drops the heels to the floor so as to avoid the bouncy quality of running.[15] Itō's technique class involved practicing the Ten Gestures while walking across the floor in Itō's form of *suriashi*: One step with one gesture for every four counts of music (clips 7 and 8). Once the gestures become so comfortable that they can be performed almost automatically, dancers vary the rhythm so that they are stepping and gesturing in patterns such as one half note followed by three quarter notes (half, quarter, quarter, quarter, half . . .). This rhythmic complexity is compounded by the distribution of Itō's Ten Gestures across Western music, which typically contains four or eight measures per phrase. The gestural sequence, therefore, often ends or begins in the middle of a musical phrase to produce an asymmetric quality that is quite uncommon in most dance techniques.[16]

Even more asymmetric (and difficult) is the one-arm lead exercise in which, for example, the right arm begins the sequence a beat before the left so that the right is at A2 when the left hits A1, and so on. Twists of the torso add different torqued shapes to the pattern. The repetition of the arm sequence with variations of rhythm, direction, or lead during a two-hour technique class feels like playing scales on a musical instrument, executing repeated yoga sun salutations, or warming up with a *qi gong* drill in tai chi. For advanced dancers, Itō's technique and form of training can be frustrating because it is not physically taxing yet requires tremendous mental concentration. Shimazaki described the "not just physical power" required as the gestural sequence moves up that body: "Start at zero. . . . Pick up the energy from the earth and bring that energy into sky/heaven: Human being standing between earth and heaven.'[17] The exercise is a practice and a discipline, a submission to a sequence of forms that must be executed without individuality or personal style. Itō's technique class focused on this rhythmic and repetitive movement rather than choreography.

Itō's Ten Gestures appear in his choreography, and Ryutani and Komine even referred to gestures by the A "masculine" or B "feminine" sequence and number when they taught Itō's dances: "Tone Poem II" (to Yamada Kosçak's "Stream of Tone, no. 5" [1928]) is a study in submission to and subversion of an imagined person or force (perhaps a judge, a lover, or a teacher) located downstage right (clip 9).[18] The dancer's shifting attraction and repulsion in relation to that external force is conveyed through a series of arm movements. For example, both arms rise at B10 toward the downstage right corner and fall in submission, and then the right climbs to A10 as the left hits A4 at the shoulder.[19] The final series of arm positions uses the raised gestures at the end of the sequences (left in A6 with right in B8, left B8 and right B9, then B9 and A10), followed by a strong stamp and a deep lunge toward that energized corner with both arms extended in A10 creating a straight line in the body. This concluding pose is ambivalent in relation to the shifting emotions of the dance: Is the dancer's movement pushing that force away with the entire body or offering an energized and complete submission to a demanding, respected, or feared authority?

Itō did not teach choreography by setting movement patterns to counts in the music, a technique Shimazaki describes as a "Western way of counting" that causes the dancer to "lose essence." Shimazaki generalized that in "Japanese dance," you "start with one piece; master dances and student follows."[20] This is another version of the noh ōmugaeshi (parrot-repetition pedagogical method), a way of teaching that emphasizes the teacher's authority and discourages any student's individual interpretation of the repertory. Itō was deeply concerned with teaching and pedagogy, particularly with how to make the experience of training into a work of art. His 1956 autobiography, Utsukushiku naru kyōshitsu, could be translated as To Make a Classroom Beautiful (IAuto, 32–43). He regularly discussed his theories of fusing "East and West," claiming, as a 1917 headline stated, "Eastern Art Spiritual, Western Art Material."[21] The division follows orientalist stereotypes that Itō maintained for his entire career. His autobiography, however, suggests a difference rooted in Japanese submission to training and spiritual as well as physical "discipline": "Western Dance is primarily concerned with body movement, so the beauty of youth is an important prerequisite. Yet, from the Eastern point of view—at least as regards 'spiritual movement'—there are many dances that young men can't do, and in these the dancer's spiritual discipline becomes even more important than the physical" (IAuto, 41). Itō might have been talking about the disciplined training over decades believed to be required to prepare the noh actor to perform certain pieces. He claimed that he was considering returning to the stage in Japan, though no longer as a "young" man. Instead, the more important project for him was to "begin again by setting up a Dance Research Centre to train young people from scratch" (IAuto, 41). As early as 1915, while still in London, Itō wrote to assure his patron, Lady Ottoline Morrell, "I am going to open my dancing school from November. So I beg you will set yourself at easy, that I am still very faithful to my art" [sic].[22] While staging noh and kyōgen in the United States, Itō frequently told the press of his desire to open a school to train performers who could fulfill his broader artistic vision of a troupe that, as noh actors did, studied dance, chant, acting, and music.[23]

First Gestures: Training and Performances
in Japan and Europe

> The first time Pound heard [Japanese chanting], he listened very inattentively,
> but when we started to work through the manuscripts it was my turn to be
> surprised. By that time I was wondering how anything that good could come out
> of Japan! . . . Since then I have been thinking that the ideas of European stage-
> artists of that time such as Gordon Craig and Max Reinhardt were really nothing
> but Noh. (Auto, 35)

Itō's autobiography suggests that Yeats and Pound initiated his interest in noh
but also that they were much less enthusiastic about Japanese art before their
collaboration. Cross-cultural teaching and learning might create an interest
that otherwise would not exist to influence artistic creation. Itō's early training in Japan had already combined both Japanese and foreign performing arts.
While studying traditional Japanese dance, he joined the new theater (shingeki)
group, Toride sha, which was influenced by Gordon Craig and performed modernist works, including Maurice Maeterlinck's Interieur (1895).[24] But Itō originally hoped to become a "Western" opera singer, so he began studying with
the Japanese soprano Tamaki Miura in 1912 to prepare for the entrance exams
for the Tokyo Academy of Music. She introduced him to her nihon buyō teacher,
Wakayagi Kichitoyo, and he studied privately with her for approximately ten
months. Itō's brother Kisaku indicated that he had far more training in buyō
but that claims that Itō earned the advanced natori stage title in any ryū (school
of Japanese dancing) are probably based on stories he told his students to encourage their belief in his "authenticity" as a "Japanese dancer."[25] Still, Itō's
nihon buyō training taught him a bodily technique and pedagogy resembling
that of noh, tea ceremony, and other traditional Japanese arts: He danced in
the kamae posture, used the suriashi step, and learned to perform with a fan.
Itō probably took private lessons and offered his buyō teachers coded gestures
of respect and submission to authority, similar to that in a noh lesson. He
learned a set repertory of buyō choreography while following behind the sensei, as in the ōmugaeshi method.[26] Shimazaki also reveals that Itō continued to
teach choreography that way for the rest of his career.

Itō traveled to Germany at the end of 1912 to study music but shifted
his aspirations to dance after seeing Isadora Duncan perform. He claimed
that he met Duncan, gave her a "present of cloth," and asked her to teach
him, but she was on tour and told him to go to the school run by her sister,

Elizabeth Duncan (IAuto, 33). Instead, he studied eurhythmics at the Émile Jaques-Dalcroze Institute outside Dresden in Hellerau for a year beginning in August 1913. Dalcroze taught gestural "opposition" and "articulation," which Itō combined with the upper body work of *nihon buyō*, among other influences, when he created his sequence of Ten Gestures.[27] Dalcroze's pedagogy was very different from Itō's *nihon buyō* lessons in Tokyo. At Hellerau, Itō was introduced to the ideology of individualism and emphasis on self-expression that suffused early-twentieth-century performance, particularly modern dance.[28] Dalcroze's book *Rhythm, Music and Education* (1920) detailed exercises that would "awaken the student's temperament" and "arouse the personal music of different individualities."[29] Classes based on Dalcrozian eurhythmics continue to emphasize improvisation and individual bodily experiences of musical rhythms rather than a particular technique or repertory. Dalcroze expert Lisa Parker asks her students to "put the rhythm of the music" into their feet or hands and move freely as she plays the piano at different tempos; she directs students to dance "on the beat" and then switch to a syncopated rhythm "off the beat." "The essence of Dalcroze, for me," Parker reports, "is the discovery. Don't tell your students what the time signature is; let them find it."[30]

When Itō began advertising his school in New York in 1919, he promoted the ideas of personal expression through movement that were crucial to the appeal of Euro-American modern dance: "My dance is an expression of my feeling through the medium of the movement of my body. Therefore my dancing is 'Michio Itow's dance' rather than Japanese dance. . . . Every one has his own feeling and his own expression; dance as you feel and as you want—that is a better dance for you than any other kind."[31] It was the idea of "Japanese dance" rather than "Itō's dance" that most appealed to the London artists who helped him launch his career in 1914 after he fled Germany because of the war. These artists believed that modern European culture had a stultifying effect on art and hoped to find new modes of aesthetic expression in the traditions of Asia, the Middle East, and Africa, as well as the "antimodern folk" in Europe (such as Yeats's Celts).[32] Both profiting from and encouraging these interests, Itō began his professional performing career as a soloist in the fashionable salons of London, initially for Lady Ottoline Morrell in November 1914.[33] Before her party, Itō had not been able to afford to eat for two days but refused to dance on the grounds that he had no costume. He reported that Morrell produced "magnificent sheiks' costumes—not the imitations that one wears on stage either—the gold thread glistened brilliantly"

(IAuto, 37). Itō was offered a generically "oriental" costume, in this case one originating from Middle Eastern cultures, and his patrons expected him to provide a generically exotic dance.

Itō internalized the lesson about what audiences expected of an "oriental dancer" at Lady Morrell's party and then a similar affair by Lady Emerald Cunard (IAuto, 37–38).[34] There he danced for Prime Minister Herbert Asquith, according to Itō's autobiography and Ezra Pound's account of the story in The Pisan Cantos, and spoke with Asquith in German, "the language of his enemy" during the war (IAuto, 38). Itō's salon performances made him a "darling" in London society and led to his first professional engagement from May 10 to 22, 1915, at the Coliseum Theatre, a music hall in London. Itō remembered, "Because I was billed as 'The Japanese Dancer' I had to create a 'Japanese' atmosphere. All my dances were original however. I danced a programme based on Shojo and Kitsune and sometimes even wore eboshi and nagabakama [long trousers] as well" (IAuto, 37).[35] Photographs by Alvin Langdon Coburn show Itō in eboshi, a formal Japanese hat (figure 3.1), and nagabakama (figure 3.2), probably created by the stage designer Charles Ricketts and the painter and illustrator Edmund Dulac for Itō's 1915 solo recitals in London.[36] The tension between Itō's "originality" and "Japaneseness" would continue to haunt him and lead him to privilege his "unique" solos very early in his career. In a 1915 letter to Lady Morrell, Itō announced that he would be giving three evenings of performances "alone" at a "theatre studio in Melbury Road in Kensington. The little theatre studio is charming [and] much better than the Coloseum [sic] for my work."[37] As if to further assure her that he had not become a music hall performer, he insisted, "I am still very faithful to my Art." Ezra Pound, whom Itō appears to have met the day before his first appearance at the Coliseum, played a role in arranging these studio performances in 1915, as well as Itō's noh demonstration with Kume Tamijurō and Kōri Torahiko, which inspired Yeats's Hawk's Well.[38]

THE EROTIC "ORIENTAL" NETWORKS OF "SWORD-DANCE AND SPEAR-DANCE"

In early-twentieth-century London, Itō was both marked and marketed as an "oriental" and "exotic dancer" to be "watched" with erotic interest, particularly for his coterie audiences.[39] Itō may have lived with Pound in the summer of 1915, and the poet undoubtedly introduced the dancer into a homosocial

FIGURE 3.1 Itō Michio in *eboshi*. (Photograph © George Eastman House, International Museum of Photography and Film)

network of artists who expressed intimacy partly through their shared interest in foreign, odd, and "oriental" objects and art forms.[40] The network brought together the book and theatrical designer Charles Ricketts (1866–1931), who created several costumes for Itō , including a "daimyo" and a "female demon" dress. Ricketts shared with the painter and lithographer Charles Shannon

FIGURE 3.2 Itō in *nagabakama*. (Photograph © George Eastman House, International Museum of Photography and Film)

(1863–1937) homes or studios in Kennington, Chelsea, Richmond, Kensington, and a country castle retreat at Chilham Keep in Kent. Without ever claiming a gay or an "inverted" identity, the couple expressed their difference from London domesticity by creating museum-like homes organized by aesthetic and exotic interests.[41] Into these semiprivate spaces, they invited Oscar Wilde, for whom Ricketts drew "The Portrait of Mr. W. H."; Wilde's other illustrator, Aubrey Beardsley; the poet lesbian couple known as Michael Field; playwright George Bernard Shaw and his wife; and the classicist and historian of "Greek love" and pederasty, John Addington Symonds; among others. Yeats linked his noh-inspired plays to this network and its gendered exoticism at the end of his *Certain Noble Plays of Japan*: "For though my writings if they be sea-worthy must put to sea, I cannot tell where they may be carried by the wind. Are not the fairy-stories of Oscar Wilde, which were written for Mr. Ricketts and Mr. Shannon and for a few ladies, very popular in Arabia?" (PFNoh, 163).

Wilde died fourteen years before Itō arrived in London, but his old network and Itō's new friends must have acquainted him with Wilde's story. Itō describes becoming a "regular" at the Café Royale, "that 'nest of artists' which Oscar Wilde used to haunt, dressed in velvet and sporting a sunflower in his lapel" (IAuto, 36). Itō continued to think about Wilde throughout his life, and his autobiography claims that he hoped to "do Oscar Wilde's *Salome* as a Noh" late in his career (IAuto, 41). When Itō was part of Ricketts and Shannon's circle, their Friday salon was attended by Yeats, Pound, the French artist Edmund Dulac, and the American photographer Alvin Langdon Coburn, who later captured the costumes and masks that Dulac had designed for *At the Hawk's Well* (see figures 2.1–2.3 and 2.5–2.8).[42] Ricketts painted two costume designs for Itō on a postcard he sent in March 1916 to the Camden Town Group painter Walter Richard Sickert (figure 3.3).[43] Walter's younger brother, Oswald Valentine Sickert, was working in Japan, and between 1916 and 1917, he provided Ricketts with the most detailed information about noh and kabuki performance then available in English, including plot summaries, costume designs, chant, and instrumental rhythms.[44] Walter Sickert was a friend of the Omega Workshops artist Alvara (Chile) Guevara (1894–1951), with whom Itō may have had an erotic relationship.[45] This relationship would have given him access to the Omega artists Roger Fry, Duncan Grant, Vanessa Bell, and perhaps others in the Bloomsbury Group and beyond. Itō's sexuality is never discussed in the existing biographical accounts; heterosexuality is presumed by the fact that he married twice. From 1923 to 1936, he was married to his former student Hazel Wright and then married Itō Tsuyako in 1938.

On October 23, 1915, Ezra Pound wrote to the Irish novelist James Joyce, then living in Zurich, about "awt" in London: "Michio Itow is going to give some performance of Noh dancing, in proper costume, next week. That is all that's on in the 'awtwoild.' Proper japanese *daimyo* dress reconstructed by Du Lac and Ricketts. Etc. very precious. Itow is one of the few interesting japs I

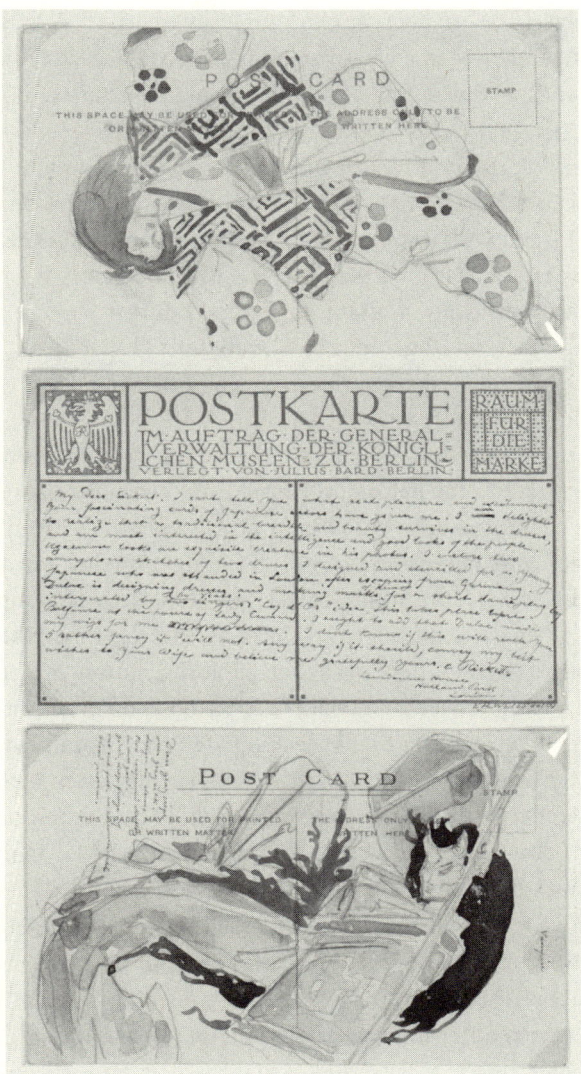

FIGURE 3.3 Postcard from Charles Ricketts (Landsdowne House, Holland Park) to Walter Richard Sickert, undated. (© Victoria and Albert Museum, London)

have ever met. They usually seem lacking in intensity."[46] Pound is referring to three dance-poem recitals featuring Itō, poet/chanter Utchiyama Masirni, and an unidentified flutist "Mr. Minami" at a small theater-studio in Kensington on October 28 and November 2 and 9, 1915. While exhibiting the both dismissive and enchanted racism that Itō encountered even among friends and collaborators, the letter positioned Itō's dance in international modernist networks. This network formed Itō's collaborators and audience for "Sword-Dance and Spear-Dance," and we might use this double casting of collaborators and audiences as a definition of "coterie performance." Pound's letter also invoked concerns of genre, authenticity or "proper"-ness, "intensity," and coterie elitism that characterized this and other important experiments in modernist performance.

Pound provided another audience for the recitals through his published account of the event, in the periodical *Future* (1916), with five classical Japanese poems he had translated with the help of "notes" by Utchiyama Masirni.[47] In this periodical paraperformance, Pound named the intermedial genre as "dance poems," a far more accurate description of the performance than the "noh dancing" he used in his letter to Joyce. Pound described the choreography as a contrast of contained energy and explosive movement reminiscent of his "Vortex": "Itow himself, now rigid in some position of action impending, now in a jagged whirl of motions, slashing with the sword-blade, sweeping the air with the long samurai halberd."[48] These sword-dance poems were, according to Pound, far different from "the splendid and stately dances of the Japanese classical [noh] plays" and "the delicate women's dances and fox-dance, the finer movements of which were lost and almost invisible on the Coliseum stage."[49] Pound must have attended one of Itō's first professional performances at the popular London music hall in May 1915 but preferred the intimate coterie recital "seen by only a few people when [Itō] performed almost privately in a Kensington studio-theatre."[50] Pound also preferred the more masculine movements of the martial-themed dances to the "delicate" drag of Itō's "Japanese Lady with Umbrella and Fan" at the Coliseum. This was not the general response, as the reviewer for *The Era* considered Itō's "Japanese Lady" the "most interesting of the four 'movements' [on that program]. . . . The 'fair one' is evidently a confirmed coquette."[51] In his early *nihon buyō* training, Itō performed both "male dances" (*otoko mai*) and "female dances" (*onna mai*). All dancers must master the different bodily techniques of both genres of *buyō*, performing the large gestures from both an open bowlegged stance in the "male" style and the "female" posture's turned-in feet, bent knees, curved

FIGURE 3.4 Itō Michio. (Photograph © George Eastman House, International Museum of Photography and Film)

spine, and display of the kimono's sleeves, evident in figure 3.4. In *buyō*, as in noh, drag performance is conventional.[52]

The five pieces of "Sword-Dance and Spear-Dance" were based on classical Japanese poems translated by Pound with the help of "notes" by Utchiyama Masirni, who chanted the poems in a "voice booming ominous from behind the curtain" while "Mr. Minami" played a "weird oriental flute."[53] The performance style was adapted from the Japanese sword dance (kenbu), a modern form accompanied by the recitation of classical poems composed in a style called shigin. Kenbu originated during the Meiji Restoration when samurai privilege was disbanded and former samurai developed the performance form to support themselves, drawing on their martial arts training as well as noh, nihon buyō, and kabuki (figure 3.5).[54] All feature similar movement styles and vocal production techniques. It is likely that Itō's training in buyō had also exposed him to kenbu, as well as the "masculine" style of buyō dancing that influenced kenbu. Itō's choreography for "Sword-Dance and Spear-Dance" has not survived, but it may have resembled his 1928 solo "Warrior" (Robert Schumann, Symphonic Etudes), in which the torso is thrust forward with head raised and knees slightly bent to create a low, grounded quality, resembling the standard kamae posture in kenbu, noh, and nihon buyō. The leg movements consist primarily of stamping and a distinctive march, with the toes hitting first and the heel following to create a strong double rhythm.[55] These features of "Warrior" contribute to the impression of a contained energy driving the movement forward, as in Pound's description of an "action impending."

Four of the five dance poems that Itō choreographed were based on classical texts frequently found in kenbu, so at least one of the collaborators had some familiarity with the form.[56] Pound wrote, "Each dance was in itself a drama in miniature, having within the few lines of its text not only the crux of a play but almost the form and structure of a full drama."[57] Pound's translations emphasized or invented related images and themes in each poem that contributed to the feeling of a distilled drama and made the sequence fit his developing theories of unified images as the way to create a long imagist or vorticist poem. "Song for a Foiled Vendetta" was based on a famous sword-dance poem recounting the legendary battle of the Takeda and Uesugi samurai clans at Kawanakajima in 1561.[58] The poem describes how the Uesugi tracked the Takeda (Pound's "Usingi" and "Tagada") through the night, following the "chirring of whips."[59] At dawn, the "foe" looks like a "fang," and Pound added that their "spear-points" are "(Like a tusk on the boar's lip . . .)," an image not present in the original poem. The near miss of the "foiled" attack is underscored by the off rhymes: "whips"-"lip," "ford"-"foe"-"fang," and "star"-"dark." Pound turned the abstract "regret" expressed in the last line of the Japanese text into another concrete and related image as the fang-like foe slithers into a "snake" and escapes.

Given the collaborative nature of the translation, it is impossible to determine who introduced the snake image, but it reappears in later poems

FIGURE 3.5 Itō in warrior costume. (Photograph © George Eastman House, International Museum of Photography and Film)

to establish a continuity or "unity" that appealed to Pound. The speaker of the third dance poem, "In Enemies' Country Just After War," claims, "I start aside from the big snake on the pathway, / Startled I draw my sword, / And slash at the old-pine-tree's shadow."[60] The linked images of "sword" and "snake" become further connected to "the old-pine tree" as the source of a frightening shadow. Pound explained, "The translation might be clearer if one supplied the words, unnecessary in Japanese, 'start aside from what appears to be the snake, and slash at what is really the shadow,' but the essence of Japanese consists in leaving out just this sort of long explanation." The nerve-wracked warrior-speaker could be "The Sole Survivor" of the second dance poem who is traveling home to commit ritual suicide on his "native mountain." The fact that Itō was the solo dancer throughout would suggest that all the poems depict the same character at intense moments in a linked drama. Where the Pound-Utchiyama translations depart from the Japanese texts, they indicate an effort to develop connections through repeated images—the whip, fang, sword, and snake—so that each poem served as a brief, salient scene in a warrior's experience. These experiences were probably interpreted in relation to the ongoing war in Europe, and if so, they provide a negative image of battle, emphasizing "foiled" attacks, the suicidal despair of a lone survivor transforming himself into a "corpse," and the toll of war on the "nerves," which anticipated the shell shock that plagued World War I's returning soldiers.[61] Such images are common in classical Japanese poetry and drama, and their power to expose the suffering of war was reinforced by Itō's dance as a "jagged whirl of motion, slashing with the sword-blade."

Itō continued to develop the technique of offering a "miniature" drama in his later choreography and performed "dance poems" throughout his career, using the term to refer to short solo pieces with pronounced shifts of energy and effort suggestive of intense emotions and an underlying narrative. Itō's choreography for Yamada Kosçak's "Stream of Tone, no. 5" is taught by Itō's students as the story of a "rebel" who "repents before a supreme magistrate" but then grows defiant when he is not forgiven (clip 9).[62] Although such a narrative could not be overtly conveyed in a brief solo dance, the story provides a sequence of emotions to guide the performer and contributes to the concentrated dramatic energy. Itō's later dance poems were undoubtedly influenced by his 1916 collaboration with Pound, and he continued to perform a piece listed as "Sword Dance" or "Kenbu" in his programs in New York, where he moved shortly after his dance in *Hawk's Well*.[63] Itō was offered a contract by the U.S. producer Oliver Morosco, thereby leaving Yeats without a dancer for his dance plays and suspicious of Itō's leap from intimate coterie performance, in which his "minute intensity of movement in the dance of the hawk so well suited our small room and private art" to Broadway (PC, 420). Itō managed to be released from the engagement with Morosco who, he claimed, wanted him to dance in a musical comedy called *So Long Letty* that was way below the artistic standards that had developed in and been applauded by the crucibles of London's intimate modernist networks.[64]

ITŌ'S SOLOS AND MODERN DANCE HISTORY

It is no coincidence that Itō's U.S. career from 1916 to 1943 began to be "recovered" by American historians in the late 1970s, in the aftermath of the civil rights movement that had called attention to the importance of "diversity" and "multiculturalism." Itō can be held up to support arguments that modern dance was multicultural from its first step and that it did not simply steal dances from other cultures. Accordingly, dance historians tend to focus on those aspects of Itō's work that more closely approximate contemporary standards for cultural sensitivity and diversity: His modern dance solos rather than his versions of noh, *kyōgen*, *kenbu*, or other "exotic" forms. They also fit him into the established history of American dance, which describes the first generation of modern dancers as expressive soloists. Jack Anderson's review of Shimazaki's reconstructions of Itō's choreography was titled "Satoru Shimazaki, Soloist."[65] Anderson summarizes the "tradition" of "such choreographic pioneers as Isadora Duncan, Mary Wigman and Michio Itō [who] often presented solo concerts notable for their emotional candor."[66] In standard dance histories, these emotional soloists were followed by a second generation that abandoned "self-expression" to produce systematic training techniques and abstract choreography.[67] Some historians use Itō's system of Ten Gestures to suggest that he was more "advanced" than his generation because he traded emotional expression for modernist technique earlier than others did.[68] But that approach upholds the same master narratives of modern dance history that "forgot" Itō. It also allows us to celebrate Itō as *worthy* of being canonized as an American soloist, *progressive* in that he predicted the next generation's technique, *multicultural* before that was a buzzword, and, most important, *marginalized* by the bigotry of his time rather than ours.[69] I am wary of this comforting story.

Itō was certainly a compelling soloist; racial bigotry was a hallmark of his time; and both contributed to the making and forgetting of his career. Racism can swing toward appreciations of the exotic, as was evident in responses to Itō's signature solo, variously called "Pizzicati," "Shadow Dance," or "Marionette Dance," to a famous section of Léo Delibes's ballet *Sylvia* (figure 3.6). He

FIGURE 3.6 Itō in "Pizzicati" or "Marionette Dance." (Toyo Miyatake Dance Collection owned by Toyo Miyatake Studio. Reproduced by permission of Alan Miyatake)

introduced "Pizzicati" at his first U.S. dance concert in December 1916, and the audience demanded an encore, as did a Pasadena crowd thirteen years later when he performed the piece as the closing number in his "Pageant of Lights at the Rose Bowl." Although the pageant included more than two hundred dancers, the *Pasadena Star News* of September 21, 1929, claimed that the massive ensemble was overshadowed by Itō's ninety-five-second closing solo.[70] One review named "Pizzicati" the "most impressive of his offerings"

and "dramatically gripping" as it celebrated the "broad-minded and generous artistic policy that made possible their [the audience's] enjoyment of that
superb oriental exponent of the dance, Michio Ito."[71] The generosity that was
worthy of such (self-) congratulation in the first half of the twentieth century
is occasionally recycled in today's "broad-minded" ability to enjoy "superb
oriental exponents" of other cultures (clip 10).[72]

"Pizzicati" actually demonstrates few "oriental" characteristics, and a spectator not looking for the advertised "Japaneseness" might have recognized it
as an example of the "music visualizations" common in the period but with
innovations drawn from modernist stage craft.[73] With his feet in a wide second position, Itō's arms and hands thrust diagonally forward and then circle
the body with flicking wrists to the vigorous and playful rhythms of the "pizzi-
cato," or plucked string violin technique. As the music shifts to a more melo-
dious and legato section, the arms sweep across the body and the torso twists
and lifts. Itō's student Ryutani Kyoko pointed out that Itō taught dancers to
imagine a "marionette" moved by strings attached to fingers.[74] The plucked
strings of the music figuratively control the body, which falls as the music
ends, like a puppet when the lines are cut.

Itō's lighting design for "Pizzicati" was crucial to its powerful impact on
audiences: He was lit from the floor so that his shadow fell on a large screen
(40 feet high and 125 feet long) and loomed over the stage like an enormous
puppeteer controlling the body below.[75] The design lent a power to shadow
that emphasized the dancer's body as manipulatable stage material. The
shadow may be reminiscent of the black-clad puppeteers in Japanese bunraku, an association reinforced by Itō's orientalist publicity materials and
signature costume for this piece: a vaguely "Eastern" belted black jacket and
cinched pants. Modernist staging and lighting innovations also were influences, particularly those of Gordon Craig, whose screen designs for Yeats's
plays may have inspired Itō to project his shadow against a huge screen. Itō
was aware of noh's influence on Craig and others, writing that his collaboration with Pound and Yeats taught him "the ideas of European stage-artists of
that time such as Gordon Craig and Max Reinhardt were really nothing but
Noh" (IAuto, 35). One of Itō's early students described his Craig-like lighting design for dance concerts: "He used a large gold folding screen as background for the dances, and on this the stage lighting projected many colors
and reflected multiple shadows, creating theatrical excitement through very
simple means."[76]

The exoticism of Itō's collaborators, even when stereotyped and racist,
created a perspective at variance with his youthful rejection of his nation's

art and taught him how to market himself as a "Japanese dancer," to the great benefit of his career. Itō's first New York concert in December 1916 introduced, along with "Pizzicati," four Japanese-themed solos: "Japanese Fisher Song," "Mai no Hagime: Introduction to Dancing," "Hangia: Female Demon," "Fox Dance," and "Shojyo: The Spirit of Wine, a Symbol of Happiness" (see figure 3.1).[77] Itō had been performing "Fox Dance" and perhaps versions of other pieces since his first professional engagement in London, but material from his collaborations altered the character of the pieces—in the case of "Fox Dance," he literally carried across national borders the fox mask that Edmund Dulac had made for him in London (figure 3.7). The famous dance reviewer H. T. Parker commented on the mask as evidence that Itō was "much cultivated" in London by Dulac and Yeats. He also, somewhat ironically given the mask's origins, claimed it was part of the "one distinctively Japanese number": "Beginning in writhings like the motion of an excited animal it rose to a frenzy of such movement, for the fox of the legend was the Pierrot of beasts, moonstruck into a delirium of the dance until ecstatic death stayed him."[78] Parker's analysis builds on the program notes that Itō provided: "A night of beautiful moonlight. A fox comes out from his den to the hill. He feels so happy and begins to dance. But he does not know how to stop and dances to death."[79] The dance's transnational achievement was intertwined with its combination of art forms, including the "poetized grotesquerie" of the choreography, European masks, Japanese legends of the fox (kitsune), and background screens or "hangings."[80]

Throughout 1916 and 1917, Itō expanded his repertory with Japanese-themed works like "Sword Dance," which featured noh-style chanting by the painter Kawashima Riichirō and recycled Dulac's costumes as well as the choreography from the "Sword-Dance and Spear-Dance" recitals with Pound.[81] Although classified as a solo, "Sword Dance" was a collaboration with other artists and performers. Itō also expanded his exotic offerings with a version of "Golliwog's Cake Walk," a piece that exploited the fascination with African American dancing. Recalling competitions in which slaves mimicked the strutting of their masters for the honor of winning a cake baked in the master's kitchen, a version of "Cake Walk" seems to have been obligatory for any modern dancer using "ethnic" material in the period. Parker combined exoticisms when he described Itō's "playful, fanciful grotesquerie of prancing motion . . . that was quite believable even of a Golliwog à la Japonaise."[82] When Itō explored the same cultural material and fascinations as other choreographers in the period, his dance was still read as "Japanese."

FIGURE 3.7 Itō in a fox mask. (Photograph © George Eastman House, International Museum of Photography and Film)

In the United States, Itō built new artistic networks around celebrations of the exotic, and these networks demonstrate that he was just as interested in diverse theatrical productions as in being a concert dance soloist. In August 1917, he joined Ballet Intime, a company established by former Ballets Russes dancer Adolf Bolm. The company's first performance was presented "for the benefit of the American Ambulance in Russia, and other war charities," a means by which many artistic productions were justified at the time.[83] Ballet Intime featured soloists in "non-Western" and "ethnic dances," all celebrated for their "Mystic Oriental Atmosphere."[84] Demonstrating the flexibility with which the construct could be applied, "Oriental" appeared repeatedly in the promotional material and reviews to identify Bolm as a "Russian," describe Tulle Lindahl as "a Scandinavian dancer," and celebrate the "East Indian dances" of "Roshanara," the daughter of a British official in India's colonial government.[85]

For Ballet Intime, Itō produced dance dramas that recalled At the Hawk's Well and even recycled choreography, costumes, and masks from the period of his London work. Itō's Historical Japanese Sword Dances: a. Kawanakajima (Enemy in the Dawn) and b. Kogun Funto (An Isolated Warrior) Dance recalled the first and second poems that Pound translated for the "Sword-Dance and Spear-Dance" recitals in London, and the poems were usually chanted with the dances.[86] He revised some of his early solos like "Shojyo" (Shōjō) to become duets with Tulle Lindahl. Probably inspired by the noh Shōjō translated by Pound, Fenollosa, and Hirata as an "eclogue" and "god dance" (PFNoh, 46–48), Itō's Shojyo: The Spirit of Wine, a Symbol of Happiness (1916) was described in program notes as a "beautiful boy, who always smiles, invites his friends to drink with him. Soon he becomes drunk and is happy, and finally falls asleep."[87] He added Lindahl to the piece and shifted it toward the romantic tradition of the duet (figure 3.8), including a "vision of a beautiful maiden whom he desires and vainly attempts to ensnare. She escapes him, but his exhilaration continues, until, exhausted, he drops to sleep."[88]

Itō originally choreographed his "Shojyo" to the "Arabian Dance" from Pyotr Ilyich Tchaikovsky's The Nutcracker, indicating again the international fluidity of exotic material.[89] Upon joining Ballet Intime, Itō began collaborating with Charles T. Griffes, a German-trained composer who believed that "modern music tends more and more toward the archaic, especially the archaism of the East."[90] Griffes's "Sho-jo" for Itō developed musical themes from Japanese melodies for a large chamber ensemble, including a Chinese drum, timpani, and tom-toms.[91] Griffes revealed contact with the vogue for

FIGURE 3.8 Itō and his dance partner, Tulle Lindahl. (Photograph © George Eastman House, International Museum of Photography and Film)

Japanese visual arts in his description: "The orchestration is as Japanese as
possible: thin and delicate and the muted string point d'orgue serves as a
neutral-tinted background, like the empty spaces in a Japanese prints [sic]."
The piece captured the attention of the *New Music Review*, indicating that
Griffes's approach to archaic and foreign musical styles was understood in

relation to the "new" of modernist music. Griffes criticized composers who took, for example, "American Indian themes" and "'idealized' rather than developed them in Indian styles" and pointed out that "Japanese music should not be too largely infused with western ideas and procedures; yet Michio Ito . . . believes that it will gain in breath of expression . . . if brought into modified contact with Western art influence."[92]

The fusion of Eastern and Western art was just as important to Itō's American collaborators like Griffes as it was to Yeats, Pound, and Dulac. In interviews, Itō himself repeated a familiar formula: "Eastern art is three-fourths spiritual; Western art is three-fourths material. True art should be one-half spiritual, one-half material."[93] As early as 1916, reviewers credited him with achieving the desired fusion, announcing, "East is East and West is West, but—Kipling notwithstanding—next week the two will meet."[94] The reviewer listed the primitivisms touring American stages with "Hawaiian," "Salomé," "Apache," and "classic dancers" and continued, "Now for the first time we shall see a new Terpsichore, with eyebrows slanted and wearing a kimono." If references to slanted eyebrows wouldn't make it into print today, the persistence of the binary in the first line of Rudyard Kipling's "The Ballad of East and West" (1889) is evident in George Jackson's review of a performance by Dana Tai Soon Burgess's company in 2002 that included four Itō solos: "'Oh, East is West and West is East, and ever the twain shall merge' is how Dana Tai Soon Burgess might rewrite Kipling's much-quoted poem."[95] "Mystique: East Meets West" was the title of Repertory Dance Theatre's 2010 concert. Mary-Jean Cowell, one of the first dance critics to reintroduce Itō to dance history, similarly invoked "East and West in the Work of Michio Ito," suggesting that Itō's goal was to "locate himself and his work in a supranational artists' realm, where he was neither Japanese nor American."[96] The praiseworthy effort to stage a "meeting" also upholds assumptions about the essential differences between the "East" and the "West." As contemporary reviewers, dance companies, and audiences echo Itō's early-twentieth-century context, they demonstrate the prevalence of a thought pattern that carves the world into two polarized halves.

I do not intend to denigrate our attempts to confront the challenge of Itō and other artists who were inspired by their notions of "the exotic" or their desires for cultural fusion. I do want to point out the ways that similar assumptions about "good multiculturalism" continue to shape our desires to remake Itō, his career, and his identity. In 1996, when Dana Tai Soon Burgess became interested in learning what he advertised as "the Michio Ito technique (developed by the first Asian-American choreographer)," he invited Shimazaki to teach and perform with Moving Forward: Asian American Dance Company.[97] Burgess founded the company with the mission of "exploring and expressing Asian American consciousness within the multifaceted American experience."[98] In the 2004/2005 season, Burgess featured "Four Solos by Michio Ito" with his own celebrated "Tracings," a long piece exploring Korean immigration to the United States.[99] At the same time, Burgess was *moving away* from the identity label of an *Asian American* Dance Company, renaming his company after himself: Dana Tai Soon Burgess & Company in 2005 and then Dana Tai Soon Burgess Dance Company in 2013. The increasingly foregrounded name of the choreographer might indicate a reinvestment in American individualism. But it also reflects recent challenges to identity labels like "Asian American," which combines racial, ethnic, and national groups that may be far more diverse than similar.

"The first Asian American choreographer" is an awkward label for Itō, given little evidence to suggest he claimed an Asian American identity or was part of a community organized by that term. Even Los Angeles's *Japanese* American community was suspicious of Itō as an elite artist married to an American woman.[100] Despite this marriage, he never became a citizen of the United States, the country that would deport him as an enemy alien. Moreover, the category "Asian American" may encourage the racist notion that all Asians are alike while ignoring the national identifications (Japanese, Korean) that may be more important to the many that it attempts to include, especially in Itō's period when Japan organized military encroachments into China and Korea in an effort to build a Pan-Asian empire. Nation of origin was the deciding factor when U.S. Executive Order 9066 sent Itō, along with 110,000 Japanese and Japanese Americans to internment camps, regardless of their legal citizenship.[101] Burgess's designation of Itō as "the first Asian American choreographer" reflects his understandable desire to revise dance history and acknowledge overlooked contributions. Dance scholar Yutian Wong also argues that Itō is best understood in the context of an "Asian American history" and that interpretations of him as an "international artist" are premised on naive idealizations of multiculturalism.[102] She makes an important point, but the category of "Asian American" is also shaped by multicultural ideals, ones less relevant to Itō. However "naive," Itō nurtured those reviews of "Michio Ito, Internationally Famous Dancer and Group of Noted Solo Dancers" that celebrated him as both a "cosmopolitan individualist" and "Japan's spiritual ambassador."[103]

Many racial, ethnic, and gendered categories informed Itō's choreography, collaborations, and tours, all of which were enmeshed in orientalist assumptions and aesthetics. Itō cannot be encompassed within an ideally multicultural dance history or a segregated "Asian American history." Even the label "Japanese dancer" ignores the fact that he was a diverse performer/entertainer/choreographer/director in dance, theater, and film. While transnational approaches are essential to discussions of Itō (and dance and modernist studies generally), it would be inaccurate to claim that Itō anticipated our versions of transnationalism or that he was ahead of his time.[104] Itō was very much of a time when exotic and oriental themes would make dance careers, a fact that is part of the same complex of attitudes that brought about his internment. If Itō had refused to capitalize on the fascinations of his period, he more likely would have failed to have a performing career and fallen into obscurity than received more recognition in dance history. To frame his experiences as ironic or exceptional further marginalizes him from an American dance scene that applauded the many shapes and approximations of the "Exotic Oriental."

MODERN AMERICAN NOH AND KYŌGEN

> Michio Itow's Good Deed: The Japanese Dancer Has Introduced Two
> Specimens of the Native "Noh" Drama of Antiquity to This Country
> Solita Solano, headline in the New York Tribune, 1916

Itō's premiere New York performance was not as a solo modern dancer but as a flexible theater practitioner: He staged the Japanese Edo-period play Bushidō, along with dances to chanted poetry, mime plays, and instrumental pieces. Dance history has been quicker than theater history to "remember" Itō, or at least his concert dance solos, but neither field encompasses his career as a performer on low and high stages, film actor, choreographer, designer, and director. The dance scholar Mary-Jean Cowell claimed, "Ito probably considered his film work a financial convenience unrelated to his career as a concert dance artist and teacher."[105] Yet José Limón, Lester Horton, Martha Graham, most of the Denishawn company, and many other modern dancers performed in films and popular theater. Itō may not have aspired to a "career as a concert dance artist and teacher" as we understand it today. He hoped to combine media and modes of performance and train students who could do the same. He told the New York Tribune journalist Solita Solano, among others, that a professional performer, by "the standards of his country," must be able to speak, sing, and dance on stage and that all features of performance would be part of his school, even as he insisted that his art and teachings were "universal" rather than "Japanese."[106]

Itō staged the play Bushidō (billed as written by Takeda Izumo in 1746) with some of his dance pieces for the Washington Square Players in November and December 1916, during the troupe's second season in New York's off-Broadway scene.[107] Itō continued developing collaborations in the little theater movement and presented the Fenollosa-Hirata-Pound version of Tamura from February through April 1918, at the Neighborhood Playhouse, a theater founded in 1915 by the wealthy philanthropist sisters Alice and Irene Lewisohn.[108] Their important enterprise in American modern drama grew out of Lillian Wald's Henry Street Settlement in Manhattan's Lower East Side and its explicit mission of helping assimilate a mostly Jewish immigrant population into American civic life at the turn of the twentieth century.[109] According to Alice Lewisohn Crowley, the settlement cared for the "foreigners" in whom "the unregulated conditions of labor had generated infectious disease of the spirit and body that spread like fire."[110] The Lewisohn sisters were inspired by the festivals and amateur theatricals given by its children's clubs, and their Neighborhood Playhouse was to help produce an integrated community that submitted to aspects of American individualism while supporting progressive ideals concerning suffragism, multiculturalism, and the dignity of labor.[111] Their playhouse was for the people of the neighborhood, not the elite coterie that had surrounded Yeats's work with noh. The playhouse's pedagogical or civic missions and aesthetic ideals were not always aligned, however. The Lewisohns explored the dramatic conventions of foreign theaters, partly to accommodate the immigrant experience of the Neighborhood Playhouse but also to experiment with modernist exoticism.

Irene Lewisohn had visited Japan in March 1910 at the invitation of Takahashi Korekyo and took lessons in noh from a Kongo schoolteacher (probably Kongo Kinnosuke or Kongo Iwao).[112] Irene Lewisohn was one of the first Western women to study noh performance technique and receive training from a noh master. Alice Lewisohn understood noh as a departure from Western-stage individualism: "In a Noh, nothing is left to the individual will of the singer, or dancer, as he is sometimes called. Every step, every gesture, is highly symbolic, prescribed by age-old usage, that the devotional mind may be in accord with the spirit. Through such contemplation, the performer enacts, and yet is acted upon."[113] Just as noh acted on the performer and disrupted notions of the willful individual, the "ritual drama" would also, the Lewisohns hoped, act on audiences. Noh would disrupt audience expectations because it "had nothing about it that could tie it to anything the audience might recognize as familiar."[114] The Japanese form would also address the Neighborhood Playhouse's primary concerns with race, ethnicity, and community through more distant and somewhat safer exoticisms than Jewishness at that early moment of twentieth-century anti-Semitism.[115]

Irene and Alice Lewisohn believed they needed Itō's assistance in staging noh at the Neighborhood Playhouse. They had attended one of his recitals in London and may have even seen Yeats's *At the Hawk's Well*.[116] Shortly after Itō's arrival in the United States, they asked him to help them stage the Fenollosa-Hirata-Pound version of *Tamura*, but as with Pound's request for translation help, he initially resisted the idea. Alice wrote that Itō's "contact with the West, via Dalcroze in Hellerau, had deflected his interest from his native culture. Western art, Western ideals, Western music were firing his imagination."[117] They eventually convinced him to codirect and play the star role of the Cherry Sweeper or the "first apparition, a boy 'dōji'" (temple acolyte) and the "second apparition," the great general Tamura Maro. Irene Lewisohn played the "Waki, a pilgrim priest wandering in front of the Seisui Temple."[118] The physical and vocal performances of each character were split so that Alice Lewisohn "voiced" the *shite*, and Ian Maclaren spoke the lines of the *waki*.[119] The playhouse collaborators knew the terminology for the character types in noh and the basic plot of *Tamura*, which they described in the program:

> The Waki is struck by the spiritual beauty of the boy and asks his name. The boy replies mystically and goes away into the temple.
>
> The Waki watches him disappear and realizes that he has seen a spirit. The old priest prays all night under the cherry blossoms and as a reward for his devotion, the spirit of Tamura reappears as the Warrior. He describes his service to his Emperor in driving out the evil spirits and in bringing peace.[120]

The Lewisohn sisters viewed the play as a comment on the war that the United States had joined the previous year, providing a hopeful message that a great general might achieve peace. *Tamura* was staged on a program along with "Modern and Classic Japanese Pantomimes and Dances," many of which had been performed by Itō and Lindahl for Ballet Intime.[121] There was also an exhibition of Japanese woodblock prints of noh scenes lent by Stewart

Culin, curator for the Brooklyn Museum (listed in the program as "Mr. Stuart Culin"). The event was offered as a multifaceted immersion into Japanese art and culture, and Alice Lewisohn was pleased that the program brought more Japanese immigrants into the playhouse.

Tamura was given again at the Neighborhood Playhouse almost three years later, on January 29 and 30, 1921, so Itō and/or the Lewisohns must have maintained some interest in the play. A review of the production assured audiences that this was "possibly the best approximation to the Japanese 'Noh' dance yet seen in New York" and praised the "gorgeous robes and masks of authentic art."[122] There was a "Musical accompaniment of antique drums, a flute and a masked 'chorus' of chanting narrators," with masks donated by the art collector Howard Mansfield.[123] Itō's Ballet Intime composer, Charles Griffes, praised the production's "most strange and at the same time wonderful effect."[124] A review of the 1921 Tamura stated that "it had been Itow's former intention to give a season of the 'Noh' dance uptown" but did not give a reason for his apparent change of heart.[125] He probably felt he needed to train performers who could dance, sing, and act as the rigorous noh form required. Itō wrote to Pound in December 1920 about his struggles to "find any actors or musician who has suitable training. . . . So, last summer I took twenty-five pupils, and went in a mountain in East Stroudsburgh, PA. and we worked very hard on the Noh drama. Of course, your book 'NOH' I had always in my hand."[126] Itō claimed that their mutual friend Kume was with him and asked Pound if they could use the translations of Shōjō, Kagekiyo, and Hagoromo—and if he would join them in the United States, which he never did.

Without Pound's help, Itō presented the Fenollosa-Hirata-Pound translation of Hagoromo (The Feather Mantle) for the Thursday Evening Club in January 1923, a production that was billed (once again) as a "Japanese Noh Drama, GIVEN FOR THE FIRST TIME OUTSIDE OF JAPAN." Itō played the moon maiden (tennin) whose magical feathered mantle is stolen by the fisherman Hakuryō, played by Kunihiko Nanbu. As with the Neighborhood Playhouse's Tamura, the "chanters" were played by different (probably English-speaking) performers. A chorus of five additional chanters (including Itō's brother Yuji) appeared "courtesy of the Nippos Club." Another character listed as "Guardian of the Play" echoes Yeats's Guardian of the Well and has no corollary in Hagoromo or the Fenollosa-Hirata-Pound version, which the program printed in its entirety. The program also inaccurately described Hagoromo as "one of the earliest" plays in the noh repertory and claimed that it was "produced in substantially the same form and under practically the same conditions that have survived until the present day"—a particularly inaccurate version of this claim, given that Itō used performers who had not undergone the rigorous noh training in a *Hagoromo* produced under "conditions" very different from those of Edo Japan.[127] Still, the production sought to capitalize on noh's tradition of passing on a relatively fixed repertory and performance technique from generation to generation. The myth of the stable tradition seems to have appealed to U.S. audiences in the early twentieth century.

The members of these audiences were not exactly "traditionalists." As in Europe, the U.S. avant-garde and modernist little theater movement was interested in noh, and Itō both benefited from and fueled that interest. Sheldon Cheney, editor of *Theatre Arts Magazine*, used the publication to challenge dramatic realism, encourage modernist experimentation, and nurture audiences who might appreciate forms like noh. He published an enthusiastic review of the Fenollosa-Hirata-Pound *Noh; or Accomplishment* in December 1917, claiming that the noh translations "remind the thinking reader how far we have bound our Western stage to a formula of character and clash; how far we have sacrificed subtlety and lyric beauty for action; and how far we have traveled from that drama which was a ritual and an aesthetic experience for the spectator."[128] Cheney already was critical of realist performance and the related notion that drama should be focused on the development of distinct characters and their conflicts. He promoted progressive theater, foreign drama, eurhythmics, and new dance, always emphasizing the bodily aspects of performance, design elements, and the role of the "artist-director" rather than the actor.[129] He published several installments of Hermann Rosse's "Sketches of Oriental Theatres," including a glowing profile of noh as "a sacristy displayed with measured formality in cadenced motion. A high mass of beauty . . . traditional it may be," Rosse conceded, as if the adjective could rarely be a compliment, "but transportingly beautiful."[130]

If the nontraditionalist avant-garde went for noh, other audiences were less interested and even found noh conventions laughable. Solita Solana, the theater critic who celebrated "Itow's Good Deed" for introducing noh to the United States, also described the audience's limited ability to appreciate Japanese art: "It is painful to record that a representative American audience laughed loudly and continuously during the playing of Japanese instruments."[131] Solana interviewed Itō over lunch "in a Japanese restaurant in Thirty-ninth Street, a place not at all resembling a chop suey headquarters," she claimed in a barbed joke about the Chinese American dish probably not of Chinese origins, which might have been intended to call attention to the prevalent notion that all Asian food (and maybe even all Asian peoples) are the same.

Itō was not totally opposed to jokes, stage comedy, and popular theater, although he tended to emphasize the religious and ritual elements of noh to support his theatrical aspirations. He helped translate and produce some of the first English-language *kyōgen* performances in the United States.[132] Itō's *Hagoromo* at the Thursday Evening Club in 1923 played with the *kyōgen* entitled *Bu su*, which Itō and the poet Louis V. Ledoux translated as *Somebody-Nothing* and published in 1921.[133] Ledoux provided the program notes, emphasizing the continuing (invented) tradition that governs *kyōgen* performance: "In Japan, as in Greece, comedy preceded tragedy. The Kyogen or farce, like the Greek satyr-play, was the primitive form; but later these farces came to be used as comic interludes between the serious and highly developed Noh dramas, the classical language of which they occasionally burlesqued. There is an exact tradition governing every detail of the performance."[134]

In 1923, the year of Itō's *Bu su*, he collaborated with Ledoux on two additional translations of *kyōgen*, *She Who Was Fished* (*Tsuri onna*) and *The Fox's Grave* (*Kitsune zuka*) in *Outlook*.[135] The foreword to the translation of *She Who Was Fished* introduced *kyōgen* as ancient plays "used by the Japanese as comic interludes between their stately and solemn No dramas of lofty moral tone and somewhat obscure meaning."[136] Itō and Ledoux emphasized that in noh, "each step, each posture, each intonation, is prescribed by immemorial tradition" and that the interludes in *kyōgen* "frequently burlesque the matter as well as the manner" of noh. Just as *kyōgen* parodies the "stately" performance style of noh, it often depicts a servant mimicking the "lofty" behavior of the master. The exploration of the relation between servants and masters in *kyōgen* is one aspect of what Itō and Ledoux claimed to be "that unswerving, completely self-sacrificing loyalty, which of all virtues is most dear to the Japanese."[137]

In the *kyōgen* that Itō staged in New York, he played the servant Tarokaja, who appears throughout the repertory with the same name and characteristic: "stupidity that thinks itself cunning." The translation of *The Fox's Grave* in *Outlook* was accompanied by a photograph of Itō as Tarokaja but dressed in an inappropriately master-like costume. In program notes, introductions, and interviews, Itō insisted (however inaccurately) that he performed in submission to a tradition, master, and even the proclaimed "virtues" of his nation of birth. This submission was part of the identity he constructed for himself as a stage artist interested in all aspects of performance, including acting,

directing, stage and costume design, and translation. Along with his emphasis on training and his investment in having a school, which he extolled even
when it did not exist, Itō's career and interests were far more diverse than
those of a "Japanese dancer" or a soloist of expressive modern dance.

WITCH DOCTORS AND HAWK TOURS:
ITŌ AND AMERICAN MODERNIST LITTLE THEATER

Itō's work on noh and *kyōgen* contributed to the confluence of American modernism and Japonisme in the little theater movement. *Bushidō*, Itō's first project with the Washington Square Players (November and December 1916), later
swept through little theaters across the United States on a wave of *Japonisme*.
Bushidō was a term for the austere samurai warrior code in Edo Japan, and the
play was derived from a scene in an eighteenth-century puppet play (bunraku).[138] Despite its roots in pre-Meiji Japan, Itō's *Bushidō* was cited by Elizabeth S. Allen as an example of the most modern techniques of the theater,
including Emile Jaques-Dalcroze's eurhythmics, the "development of bodily
control through rhythm." In 1919, Allen claimed that the American "Little
Theatre movement" was benefiting from the influence of Dalcroze and Isadora Duncan's "natural dance."[139] According to Allen,

> The thread of a rhythmic continuity may unite any group of actors for the
> realization of a dramatic piece. Such was the effect of a remarkable emo-
> tional unity made by the play *Bushido*, as produced by the Washington
> Square Players in 1916. Restraint, formalism, ritual, hiding tender human-
> ity, was the theme of the play, consistently interpreted by the restrained and
> simple movements of the actors. This play was staged by M. Ito, a Japanese,
> and a graduate of the Dalcroze school in Hellerau.[140]

Itō's success with *Bushidō* made him an obvious choice to direct Rita Wellman's *String of the Samisen*, a play inspired by *Bushidō* and produced in 1919 by
the Provincetown Players, perhaps the most famous modernist little theater.
The poet Edna St. Vincent Millay starred (quite improbably) as Tama, a Japanese woman suffering in the Edo period.[141] Unhappily married to a merchant,
Tama takes a lover, who discloses his plot to kill her husband. After promis-
ing to assist in the murder, Tama repents, warns her husband, and takes his
place in bed to be stabbed by her lover. This was the last of Wellman's plays

staged by the Provincetown Players and her only "Japanese piece," but like her other works, it presented the plight of a woman who cannot live with integrity in a patriarchal world. Itō helped create the "authentic" Japanese costumes, along with directing the play and training Millay and other Provincetown Players in eurhythmics-inspired movement.

Itō's next engagement with the Provincetown Players was the following year in the famous production of Eugene O'Neill's The Emperor Jones, first staged at the Provincetown Playhouse on November 1, 1920. Itō choreographed and performed the role of the Congo Witch-Doctor and probably also assisted with the stage movement of other characters. O'Neill's breakthrough play tells the story of an African American Pullman porter, Brutus Jones, who took over an island in the West Indies and then taxed and terrorized the islanders until they prepared to rise up against him. The imminent rebellion is represented by the beating of a tom-tom drum that begins near the end of the first scene "at a rate exactly corresponding to normal pulse-beat—72 to the minute—and continues at a gradually accelerating rate from this point uninterruptedly to the very end of the play."[142] Emperor Jones attempts to escape through the jungle to the coast but is haunted by a series of visions of "Little Formless Fears," including a man he killed, "The Negro Convicts" with whom Jones served a prison sentence, and an "Auctioneer" selling African slaves. Jones's visions culminate in the dance of the Congo Witch-Doctor, which leads directly to Jones's death.

Itō's choreography for the Witch-Doctor has not survived, but the entire scene is composed of stage directions describing the dance. The Witch Doctor emerges from a "sacred tree," "wizened and old, naked except for the fur of some small animal tied about his waist, its bushy tail hanging down in front."[143] The description of this very phallic tail suggests an exaggerated, perhaps even ironic, primitivism that is further accented by red body paint, a head gear of "antelope horns," and a "charm stick with a bunch of white cockatoo feathers tied to the end." Covered in beads and other ornamental objects, "He struts noiselessly with a queer, prancing step," and then gives a "preliminary, summoning stamp of his foot on the earth" and begins dancing and chanting. The "tom-tom" that has been beating throughout the play "grows to a fierce, exultant boom." Jones is "hypnotized" and "joins in the incantation" as the Witch Doctor calls to a River God, who emerges in the shape of the "huge head of a crocodile" and demands that Jones serve as human sacrifice (figure 3.9).[144] "The crocodile heaves more of his enormous hulk onto the land," and Jones fires his last bullet into the puppet-creature's "green

FIGURE 3.9 Itō as the Witch-Doctor in Eugene O'Neill's *The Emperor Jones* (1920). (Courtesy of Jeffrey Kennedy)

eyes." This was the silver bullet he was planning to use on himself before being captured. In the next scene, the audience hears the islanders kill Jones with their own carefully crafted and "charmed" silver bullets before they drag his body onstage.

The Provincetown Players were bewildered by the success of *The Emperor Jones* as audiences flocked to their playhouse and the production eventually moved "uptown" to the Princess Theatre—a move that was somewhat at odds with their little theater commitments. Reviews of the production described the disturbing power of Jones's journey through the jungle haunted by his personal and "racial" past: "As his panic increases the fears become not things in his own life, but old race fears. He sees himself being sold in a slave market and then, most horrible of all, a Congo witch doctor tries to lure him to death in a river where a crocodile god is waiting."[145] Another reviewer declares, "Finally, it is a race memory of old Congo fears which drives him shrieking back through the forest to the very clearing whence he had started and where now his death so complacently awaits him."[146] The play and its reviewers assumed that a common memory and traumatic consciousness was attached to race: An African American man who never lived in the Congo would still be "hypnotized" by a witch doctor and primitive gods, a modern man who was never a slave would be haunted by American slavery. The first assumption—that a black person is linked to (Itō's version of) tribal African dance ritual—presents a chauvinistic view of race as an inescapable biological category. The second—that the slave trade haunts modern blacks—might be part of a liberal recognition of how the legacy of institutionalized slavery, segregation, and other forms of racism continue to shape the lives of African Americans. Even though these two assumptions are associated with divergent perspectives on race, the play's juxtaposition of them as "race fears" implies that they have something in common.

The racism represented in The Emperor Jones is complicated but undeniable and has led some critics to conclude that the play cannot be performed as O'Neill and the Provincetown Players envisioned: "America has long passed the point where a straightforward production of The Emperor Jones, with a black man delivering O'Neill's dialectical speeches as written, could be other than embarrassing."[147] Implying that "America" is no longer conflicted about race in the same way, this critic means that O'Neill's racism is embarrassing but also bad for audiences. Would we say that Shakespeare's racism in Othello, or the bigotry in countless other dramatic texts, makes them both embarrassing and not producible as written? I believe that the racism of The Emperor Jones is actually too close for comfort and that this discomfort is a useful experience for audiences. In the 1920s, reviewers hailed the Provincetown Players' progressive approach to race and celebrated the performance of the black actor Charles Sidney Gilpin in the title role:

> If The Emperor Jones were taken elsewhere we have little doubt that the manager would engage a white man with a piece of burnt cork to play Brutus Jones. They have done better in Macdougal Street [the Provincetown Playhouse]. The Emperor is played by a negro actor named Charles S. Gilpin, who gives the most thrilling performance we have seen any place this season. . . . It is a performance of heroic stature.[148]

The Provincetown Players' original production was distinctive in giving a star role to a black actor at a time when most companies would have cast a white actor in blackface and audiences were racially segregated in New York theaters (albeit illegally.)[149] The issue of cross-racial and cross-gendered casting still framed responses to the Wooster Group's production of *The Emperor Jones* first presented in 1993, with Kate Valk in blackface and drag playing Jones. The white trader Smithers was depicted by Willem Dafoe with face "whitened up" to resemble a kabuki or noh mask.[150] Their performance styles and costumes also adopted and exaggerated Japanese theatrical forms.[151]

Itō as the Congo Witch-Doctor was literally a Japanese performer in blackface. In the 1920s, he could apparently represent the "old race fears" of an African American, even the "most horrible" ones, as his Asian otherness bled into blackness. The generalized racism that undoubtedly shaped the casting decisions of the Provincetown Players takes a different hue in relation to the choices of the Wooster Group's production. Could Itō's performance indicate a radical refusal of racial typecasting or even a self-conscious recognition that his "Japaneseness" served as a malleable and exploitable version of the nonwhite primitive? Might his dance for the Congo Witch-Doctor expose how shades of whiteness, including O'Neill's never-quite-white Irish heritage, and shades of blackness, from Congolese to African American to Asian, are built and torn down in various forms of (drag) performance?[152] If the Wooster Group could pull off such a critique of race for some audiences at the turn of the twenty-first century, the Provincetown Players probably could not in 1920. But again, I am interested in what has not changed: Neither reviewers nor critics from 1920 to the present have commented on Itō's "blackface" performance, even after the Wooster Group invoked noh/kabuki orientalism. *The Emperor Jones* calls attention to racism and primitivism without offering easy, comforting answers. Despite the uneasiness reflected in many reviews and the tense relationship of author, performers, and other collaborators, *The Emperor Jones* was the Provincetown Players' first hit and secured the company's position as a major contributor to modern art theater.

Given the Provincetown Players' attempts to work collaboratively, Itō was probably involved in other aspects of the staging of *The Emperor Jones* in addition to his climactic dance. He may have coached fellow performers in movement, just as he did for the London production of Yeats's *Hawk's Well*. Itō's overlooked performance in *The Emperor Jones* bears some resemblance to his dance as the Guardian in Yeats's noh-inspired play. The comparison suggests that *The Emperor Jones* might actually be considered a dance play accompanied by a drumbeat that resembles the drums in noh's musical ensemble (*hayashi*). Both plays were formative for their writers and other collaborators in the production. Itō went on to perform a cinematic version of his Witch-Doctor role as "the Malayan Sakai Chief" in the Paramount film *Booloo* (1938), for which he choreographed a ritual dance to select the sacrificial maiden.[153] In Paramount's *Spawn of the North* (1938), he was cast as a "Native Chief-dancer" and staged an "Indian ceremonial," although much of this work was cut. In his first film, *Dawn of the East* (1921), he appeared in the nondancing role of "Sotan, the Eurasian villain," but the exotic and deadly spirit of the role was similar to his dancing Witch-Doctors and Native Chiefs as the modernist little theater's problematic engagement with race found another exposure in cinema.

Itō continued to recall his dance with Yeats throughout his career as he staged *At the Hawk's Well* in little theaters around the world. He gave *Hawk's Well* its American premiere and first public performance in New York on July 10, 1918, at the Greenwich Village Theater, along with a short program of Itō's "Japanese" dances and new music by Yamada Kosçak.[154] As with other theatrical productions during the war, the proceeds were devoted to charity, in this case the "Free Milk for France Fund."[155] The American art dealer Martin Birnbaum promoted the production and secured Edmund Dulac's costumes, masks, and screens from the London collaboration to correspond to an exhibition of Dulac's art that included his large portrait of Itō (figure 3.10). Birnbaum had become a "lifelong friend" of Ricketts and Shannon, who, he remembered, "had lived together so long that they were described as Siamese twins." He visited their Friday night salons in Lansdowne House and was their house guest in the Keep at Chilham, describing it as a "unique artistic habitation."[156] At the Lansdowne studio, Ricketts and Shannon introduced Birnbaum to Dulac, Yeats, and Itō, of whom he wrote, "There was something macabre about this thin Oriental. Dulac's full-length portrait caught all his qualities and he was ideally suited, physically and technically, for the role of the sinister bird that guarded the waters of immortality in Yeats's poetical play."[157]

Learning that Itō was in New York, Birnbaum suggested a performance of *Hawk's Well* to grace the opening of his Dulac exhibition. Advance reports of the New York production of *Hawk's Well* indicated a suspicion that was only partially relieved by Yeats's celebrity: "An Irish play done in the ancient-est Japanese manner—that, one might suppose, would be at best an oddity. That William Butler Yeats is sponsor for the combination is reassuring."[158] Birnbaum remembered that Yeats enthusiastically gave him a manuscript copy of his play and left him to make the arrangements. Birnbaum booked the Greenwich Village Theatre, and Yamada composed music with a "simple folk-like style colored with a light Japanese tint," that, unlike Dulac's score, did not

FIGURE 3.10 Edmund Dulac, *Portrait of Itō Michio*. (Copyright © 2009 Bonhams Auctioneers Corp. All rights reserved)

attempt to replicate noh musical structures.[159] Itō, Toshi Komori, and Tulle Lindahl danced and mimed, and the text for the Old Man and Young Man as well as the Musicians was chanted by other performers. Birnbaum claimed that he realized Yeats's words were being "mumbled and distorted" during rehearsals so he memorized the First Musician's lines in two days. With his contribution, he believed, "the play was a huge success."[160] Yeats seems to have had considerable misgivings that the production was not reflected in Birnbaum's account. In a letter to John Quinn, Yeats revealed his continued interest in noh and suggested that his previous collaboration with Itō gave the dancer certain "rights" to Hawk's Well:

> I have finished another "Noh" play, and if you saw the New York perfor-
> mance of my Hawk's Well I would be glad for some news of it. Fate has been
> against me. I meant these "Noh" plays never to be played in a theatre, and
> now one has been done without leave; and circumstances have arisen
> which would make it ungracious to forbid Ito to play The Hawk as he will. I
> had thought to escape the press, and people digesting their dinners, and to
> write for my friends.[161]

Despite his frustration with Itō's digestive theater, Yeats seems to have followed his career, perhaps particularly his staging of noh plays in the United States. The Yeats Library contains a full-page article about Itō from the Boston Post (January 16, 1921): "Noh Dramas, Once Sacred to Shinto Gods, Coming to Boston," with a stamp indicating that Yeats received it from the clipping service "Henry Romeiki, Inc."[162] The article placed Itō's productions of noh in the context of "the Japanese element in the 'Art Theatre' movement," of which Yeats was listed as the Irish "representative" along with "Maeterlinck, Schnitzer, Tschekhoff and Dunsany [sic]" for other countries. From photographs of masks that are not actually for noh to claims that noh masks were made by "the old Buddhist priests of Thibet," where the "sacred dramas" originated, the article is full of misinformation. Its second half includes an interview with Itō, in which he provided a more accurate history of noh as an adaptation of the Chinese comedy Sarugaku. A photograph of Itō in a kyōgen costume with the typical long hakama trousers trailing on the ground—quite different from noh's lavish robes—is captioned, "Michio Itow in one of the unusual costumes of the 'Noh' drama, 'Mai no Hajime.'" A noh play by that title does not exist, although Itō used similar titles for modern dance choreographies with Japanistic flairs. We cannot know exactly how much of the misinformation in the article was provided by Itō or extrapolated by the *Boston Post* journalist, but Itō did provide similarly inaccurate accounts of the history of noh to other journalists.

The noh actor's training is highlighted in the subtitle of the *Boston Post* piece: "Japanese Actors Devote Lives to Perfecting Its Mysteries." The article presented the pedagogical system in which "traditions of performance have been handed down through generations of actor-families, trained in all arts" as "a system which western nations can hardly conceive, although we concede the perfection of the system." Itō declared that because American performers are not sufficiently trained in all the arts, "I have established my own school, and from these I shall choose 15 artists to help me interpret the 'Noh.' . . . I intend eventually to establish a universal art theatre—where art dramas, to which belong the 'Noh,' the Greek, and the art dramas of the moderns, all belong. The "Noh" dramas are but one manifestation of the universal art theatre."

The idea that Japanese actors had extensive training and deep discipline was prevalent in the press, and Yeats was interested in this training. He inserted a four-part profile on Japanese arts published by the *Times* into his issue of Fenollosa-Hirata-Pound's *Noh, or Accomplishment*. The fourth article in the series The Tokyo Stage proclaimed, "While Japan's dramatic genius has not developed along the lines of the purely intellectual drama of the Occident, her actors are the product of the most remarkable stage discipline in the world, and the whole art of the Japanese theatre is done with so much heart that it should be a revelation to the West."[163] Although Itō had not undergone this "stage discipline," he hoped to translate it for "the West," and even took "twenty-five pupils" and "stayed two months in the mountain" to study noh—or so he wrote to Pound.[164] I don't believe Itō set up noh training near a mountain in East Stroudsburg, Pennsylvania (although that location shocked me, given that it is about 75 miles down I-80 from my very first experience with noh training at Bloomsburg, Pennsylvania). Even though Itō had no training, he continued staging *Hawk's Well* and, through that play, teaching modernist noh around the world. Itō moved to California in 1929, and shortly after his arrival, he directed the play at the Argus Bowl. He taught the Guardian role to the younger dancer Lester Horton (1909–1953) who had also just arrived in California and went on to build a remarkable dance career as well as the first little dance theater, modeled on the modernist little theaters that had benefited from Itō's work. Itō's American school probably never met his standards, but he had begun, with Lester Horton's

"Hawk" dance, and other collaborations, to shape the next generation of modern dancers.

DEPORTATION FINALE

In 1940, as his native and adopted countries were about to embark on war, Itō staged Yeats's *Hawk's Well* in Tokyo. He played the Old Man in this production opposite his brother, the famous Brecht-inspired, German-trained actor Senda Koreya as the Young Man. Another brother, Yuji, composed a new Western-style score and designed costumes, and Itō taught the Guardian's dance to Yuji's wife, Teiko. Yet another brother, Itō Kisaku, designed the masks in a family effort that was offered as a gift for their parents' fiftieth wedding anniversary. An announcement of the production included the subtitle "Stresses Need for Fusion of Japan-U.S. Cultures," and Itō told the reporter that he was in Japan to visit his family but that he hoped he might "help in some way to fuse the United States and Japan."[165] He echoed the commonplace that "America is the 'melting pot' of the Occident" and added, "Japan has the culture of the Far East at her elbow and has absorbed much of it." Japan was literally "absorbing" Asia in colonial enterprises, but rather than acknowledging Japan's mobilization for war, he reiterated the orientalist assumption that Japan is rooted in "spiritualism" while the United States is "too topheavy" in "materialism." He stated, "These two great nations, then, have the greatest opportunity and the greatest need for combining their cultures to produce the balance which has been dead since the day of Egypt s power." Itō's family-produced Japanese translation of the great Irish Nobel Prize winner's noh-inspired *Hawk's Well* could not combine cultures in a way that would prevent war. Itō's extended stay in Japan while staging *Hawk's Well* in 1940 fueled the FBI's accusations that he was an "enemy alien" after the Japanese attack on Pearl Harbor a year later. Yet this production and even Itō's deportation influenced the Japanese little theater movement, *shingeki* (new theater), traditional noh theater, and "fusion theater," as it is sometimes called in an echo of Itō's own terminology. While arts lovers tend to appreciate intercultural aesthetic influences, Itō's "fusion" also included introducing the beauty pageant to Japan and entertaining American forces with spectacles on exotic themes.

After treating Itō as an enemy alien, the American authorities must have quickly decided that he was not quite so dangerous. After his deportation, he was hired to direct an entertainment venue for the U.S. occupying forces, which had also occupied the Tōkyō Takarazuka gekijō and renamed it after the famous war correspondent Ernie Pyle. Itō staged spectacular reviews such as *Festival*, "an adaptation of the Buddhist equinoctial festivals of the dead." Promotional materials proclaimed, "You will witness this evening the Ernie Pyle Theatre's Erniettes in their interpretations of the Autumn Festival heightened by the beautiful color of the native scenic settings and costumes all blended in such a manner as to catch the holiday spirit of the festival."[166] *Fantasia Japonica*, *Sakura (Cherry Blossom) Flowers*, and *Dancing Under the Teigo Tree* also were orientalist reviews, but Itō's "Erniettes" provided other versions of "native scenic settings" for the soldiers. *Down South*, performed with blackface makeup and hair kerchiefs, referenced the American South.[167] *Tabasco* was vaguely set in Mexico,[168] while *Jungle Drums* invoked Africa and may have echoed Itō's dance to frenzied tom-toms in O'Neill's *The Emperor Jones*. The primitivist spectacles were staged with state-of-the-art technology at the Ernie Pyle, which was lauded as "the fourth largest stage in the world," with equipment that included "a large turntable, five elevators, a sliding stage and above the stage proper are fifty-eight motor operated pipes, technically known as battens, on which scenery, curtains, and lights are attached." Using this advanced stage technology, Itō's rendition of George Gershwin's *Rhapsody in Blue* sought to capture the spirit of "the entire populace of New York City engaged in their diversed lives." The program also celebrated how the designers "ingeniously" coordinated all aspects of production from choreography to lighting, costuming to scene design to create a "composite art" with "moving figures subordinated into a background and atmosphere of formal beauty."[169]

My first response to Itō's Ernie Pyle work was to feel that Itō had subordinated himself to the American Occupation and the soldiers' presumed desires for primitivism—even to see it as an example of his internalized racism. Displaying all too clearly my embarrassment about Itō's orientalism, I asked Itō's granddaughter Michele Ito if she believed that he had been "unhappy" working at the Ernie Pyle Theater. She pointed out that many people in Tokyo were starving after the air raids and the atomic bombs dropped at the end of World War II, whereas Itō had a paying job and the ability to support Japanese performers and their families who would have suffered without that salary.[170] My question was sanctimonious, to say the least. If not quite to my self-righteous extent, other scholars have been similarly embarrassed by Itō's "Oriental works," claiming that he preserved few after returning to Japan because they "would seem too pseudo-Oriental in his native land."[171] This claim, based only on early modern dance solos, ignores Itō's Ernie Pyle productions and much of his other stage work. Maybe these spectacular productions actually did unite "East and West" better than did much of Itō's work, even better than *Hawk's Well* and other transnational collaborations. Any desire to unite "East and West" is founded on the assumption that these terms are meaningful and that the globe can be divided between them. Itō's productions brought that assumption together with the potentially starving bodies of performers and their better-fed (on military rations) audience of American forces. The power disparity of these two groups was significant, but they shared a theatrical experience around the national, racial, and gendered stereotypes on display at the Ernie Pyle. These same stereotypes contributed to the ways in which World War II was fought and concluded in atomic blasts.

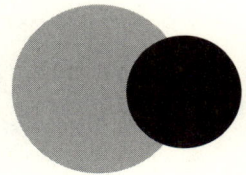

4. PEDAGOGICAL INTERMISSION

A Lesson Plan for Bertolt Brecht's Revisions

The world cf knowledge takes a crazy turn
When teachers themselves are taught to learn.
Bertolt Brecht, *Life of Galileo*

A BOOK CLAIMING TO DEAL WITH PEDAGOGY WOULD SEEM falsely advertised if it did not include a lesson plan. But I risk misrepresenting myself as a teacher by providing one, since I rarely write out lesson plans before class. To avoid failing to include this important pedagogical genre, I have failed to represent myself accurately as a professor. Any approach doomed to fail in one way or another is likely to be a useful approach to Bertolt Brecht's *Lehrstücke* (learning plays) and theories about pedagogical theater. Brecht's *Lehrstücke* failed to convey his vision for a proletarian revolution or even to follow the rules he set for himself in his theories of "epic and didactic theatre."[1] Brecht's failures, therefore, help me teach Brecht—and face my own inadequacies as a teacher and writer, who also will fail in this pedagogical intermission to provide a comprehensive treatment of Brecht's "opera for schools," *Der Jasager* (*He Said Yes*, 1930) and its fascinating score composed by Kurt Weill. My hope is that this pedagogical intermission will wake up readers who might be tired at this middle point of the book, by asking them to try an exercise I use in class to explore the forms of consent and submission Brecht teaches in the noh-derived *Der Jasager*, and particularly in his several revisions of the text.

PROCEDURES

I ask my students to read three different passages aloud: The first, which I dub *Yes* 1 for ease of reference in class, is from *Der Jasager* with Weill's music, which I play in the background throughout the exercise. I tell my students that Brecht's libretto was based on the Japanese noh play *Tanikō*, which tells the story of a student who accompanies his teacher on a pilgrimage through the mountains in order to pray for his sick mother. When the boy falls ill, the teacher tells him that he will contaminate the journey unless he agrees to be thrown to his death. The boy consents to death, but his teacher's grief and the prayers of the other pilgrims lead to his resurrection and a demonstration of Buddha's miraculous power.

Arthur Waley's English translation, *The Valley-Hurling* (1921), which relegated the resurrection to a dismissive footnote, was translated into German by Elisabeth Hauptmann, and this text was the basis for *Der Jasager / Yes* 1, although Brecht did little to acknowledge her contribution (as was common with his female collaborators).[2] Brecht and Weill initially intended *Yes* 1 for Berlin's 1930 Neue Musik festival, a workshop for avant-garde artists concerned with the educational and social aspects of performance as well as the new technologies of radio and film.[3] Neue Musik inspired collaborations by Brecht, Hauptmann, and Weill as well as the composer Paul Hindemith, who was the first to use the term *Lehrstück* in relation to a 1929 Neue Musik festival piece later published by Brecht as the *Baden-Baden Lehrstück vom Einverständnis*. Joining ideas of consent, self-sacrifice, and understanding, *Einverständnis* was central to *Yes* 1 and to Brecht's interpretations of the consent of *Tanikō*'s student. *Yes* 1 was not presented at the Berlin festival but was first performed by students and broadcast on radio on June 23, 1930, followed by between two hundred and three hundred other school performances before Hitler took power in Germany (BCP, 227). In keeping with that tradition, I ask students, mostly nonactors, to read the parts of the Boy and his Teacher on a dangerous "scientific" journey to the mountains. The child, who decided to go on the journey in order to get medicine for his ill mother, becomes sick during the climb and the Teacher tells him:

TEACHER: Listen to me. There's been a law here from ancient times that if anyone's taken sick on such a journey, into the valley's depths he must be hurled—which means instant death. But the same Custom prescribes that the one with the sickness be asked: should we turn back again for that reason? And moreover the Custom says that the sick man must reply: no, you should not turn back.

BOY: I understand.

TEACHER: Do you want us to turn back home for your sake?

BOY: No, you should not turn back.

FREE-WRITING EXERCISE 1

After the performance, I put a prompt on the board and ask my students to follow the directions precisely: Take three minutes to write a paragraph that presents an original claim about whether or not students would benefit from performing this opera. Why or why not? I tell the students I will collect their paragraphs at the end of the writing exercise.

[Dear Reader: Give it a try. Or if you don't feel like writing, sit for a few moments and think about what claim you would make in response to the prompt.]

I collect my students' paragraphs and turn to the second selection, which is from the revision of Yes 1 that Brecht wrote in response to students at the Karl Marx School (Neuköln), who participated in the second performance of the play and then discussed their experience with their teachers and Brecht himself. They performed the revision resulting from these discussions, Yes 2, on May 18, 1931 (BCP, 230). In this version, an epidemic has hit the town, and the Teacher describes the purpose of the journey as "aid" rather than "science." I ask the Teacher and the Boy from Yes 1 to trade roles, invite a new student to read the stage directions aloud, and require that everyone else in the class stand up and read the part of the Three Students. With this casting choice, I hope to demonstrate that authority and submission are distributed to teachers and students as part of their assigned or reassigned roles. The entire class must participate in Yes 2, more closely approximating Brecht's desire for the Lehrstück to be performed by students without an audience.[4]

TEACHER: Because you are ill and can go no further, we must leave you here. But it is right that the one with the sickness be asked: should we turn back again for that reason? [. . . ?]

BOY: I understand.

TEACHER: Do you want us to turn back home for your sake?

BOY: No, you should not turn back.

TEACHER: So are you consenting that you should be left behind?

BOY: I will think it over. *He pauses for thought.* Yes, I am consenting.

The TEACHER *calls from Space 1 to Space 2:* He has answered as necessity demanded.

The FULL CHORUS *and the* THREE STUDENTS *while going down to Space 2:* He has said yes. Go on!

The THREE STUDENTS *remain standing.*

TEACHER: Go on now, no hesitation

On towards our destination.

The THREE STUDENTS *remain standing.*

BOY: Let me say something: I beg you not to leave me lying here, but to throw me down into the valley, for I am frightened to die alone.

THREE STUDENTS: We cannot do that.

BOY: Stop! I demand that you should.

TEACHER: You resolved to go on and leave him there

Deciding his fate is easy

Enacting it is hard.

Are you ready to throw him down into the valley?

THREE STUDENTS: Yes.

FREE-WRITING EXERCISE 2

After the performance, I post a prompt for the second writing exercise: Please take three minutes to write. I tell the students that I will once again ask them to hand in their work.

[Dear Reader: What would you write this time? Please take a few moments to think it over.]

I collect my students' writing, and we turn to the final passage, which is from yet another revision, *Der Neinsager* (*He Said No*), which Brecht published in *Versuche* 4 (1931) with *Yes 2*. Teachers could experiment with different distributions of the roles, but I have the Teacher and the Boy switch again so that they are now performing the same part as they did in *Yes 1*. I ask a new student to read the stage directions, and everyone else stands to perform the Three Students.

> TEACHER: Do you want us to turn back home for your sake? Or do you consent that you should be hurled into the valley as the Custom prescribes?
>
> BOY: *He pauses for thought.* No, I do not consent.
>
> TEACHER *calls from Space 1 to Space 2*: Come on down! He has not replied in accordance with the Custom.
>
> THREE STUDENTS *coming down to Space 1*: He has said no. *To the* BOY: Why have you not replied in accordance with the Custom? Whoever says A must also say B. When you were asked at the start if you would consent to whatever might happen on the journey, you replied yes.
>
> BOY: My answer was wrong, but your question was more so . . . as for the ancient Custom I see no sense in it. What I need far more is a new Great Custom, which we should bring at once, the Custom of thinking things out anew in every situation.

FREE-WRITING EXERCISE 3

I give the students verbal instructions this time: Please take three minutes.
    [Dear Reader: Please take a few moments.]

Discussion

Immediately after the third free-writing exercise, I ask for volunteers to respond to three questions:

1. What claims did you make about whether or not students would derive any benefit from performing the opera?
2. Did your argument change after each of the three pieces?
3. Did the form of your response change with each prompt?

Results

The majority of my students, especially those who volunteered to talk, produced three conventional paragraphs claiming that yes, a group would benefit from performing the Brecht scenes. They cited the benefits of learning about the danger of conformity, engaging in public speaking, and analyzing Brecht's dialogue. After several members of my class shared their thoughts, a rustle of activity became noticeable as students began passing forward their third piece of writing, expecting an evaluation. I feigned an attitude of surprise and asked, "Oh? Do you have something to pass in?"

At which point, I finally acknowledged that my students (and readers) were absolutely justified in their frustration with this belabored exercise, which took fifteen minutes, or even more, of class time. I asked my students to look again at the instructions I posted after the first two readings:

1. Take three minutes to write a paragraph that presents an original claim about whether or not students would benefit from performing this opera. Why or why not?
2. Please take three minutes to write.

I reminded them about the third spoken prompt:

3. Please take three minutes.

The first is a truly horrific prompt, I acknowledged, the kind that might appear on the AP English exam, the ACT college admission test, or another "standardized" writing assessment.[5] The second prompt simply asks students to write for three minutes, so they could have drafted a dramatic scene, an account of their breakfast, or a (legitimate) complaint about the activity. Of course, the pressure of an evaluation encouraged them to apply the explicit instructions from the first prompt to *Yes 2* and to write a paragraph arguing for its pedagogical value. Finally, the third prompt does not even ask students to write, although they tended to produce the same argumentative paragraphs about Brecht's *No*. Accordingly, I renamed the assignment an Unfree-Writing Exercise.

None of the remarkable students in Modernist Exoticisms, my 2014 graduate seminar, saw through my act or overtly questioned my authority. They all appeared to be conscientiously writing their paragraphs, although Paul J. Edwards slyly made fun of the exercise in his writing even as he maintained his typical studious expression. Several others said that they recognized the prompts were atrocious but still wrote the responses they thought would please me. Many students are trained to think that any text a teacher asks them to read is "good," and if they do not find it to be of value, they chalk it up to their own limitations. They also believe all professors wish to be told that their assignments are good. My students wanted to demonstrate mastery of the learning outcomes that they imagined I set for the lesson. A former high school teacher explained to me that she felt compelled to defend the pedagogical value of the exercise, although she could not see why the performance of Brecht's plays would be "good" for students. I had been concerned that I would not be able prevent myself from flagging my performance with some sort of Brechtian self-commentary, but none of my students suspected me of acting. I, along with the entire class, was relieved when I could end this performance and return to my somewhat more subtle role as a professor.

The Brechtian Unfree-Writing Exercise demonstrated to my students how often they submit to the authority of a teacher or "great writer" like Brecht without recognizing that they are being asked to say yes. Most of the students in my seminar had heard of Brecht, and his fame encouraged them to argue for the pedagogical value of his plays. My students also dutifully wrote their paragraphs with claims (even when I didn't ask them to write), because the genre of the paragraph is a "Great Custom," as is the "free-writing exercise," which is anything but free with its prompts, time constraints, and demands that they turn it in, presumably for a grade. Authority and custom regularly determine our actions as well as our supposedly "original claims" and writing styles. (I learned about the conventions and format of the lesson plan in order to write this one, and several middle and high school teachers with whom I spoke suggested that the plans they must submit to their administrators each week are the most detested aspect of their jobs.) A colleague I admire, Julie Townsend, uses similar unfree-writing exercises to teach Michel Foucault's ideas about the disciplinary structures that organize our cultures. Louis Althusser terms these structures "ideological state apparatuses" and describes how they "interpellate" us or, put otherwise, how our lives are compelled by the combined threat of state-sanctioned violence and institutions, like universities, that determine our beliefs.[6] Townsend laudably hopes to inspire her students to recognize these important impositions and fight against them.

My Brechtian unfree-writing exercise taught a very different lesson, one that is more relevant to Brecht, his acting technique, his theories of pedagogical theater, and his use of noh to develop those theories. It should not be surprising that my students attempted to follow my instructions even when they knew the writing prompts were terrible. They are deeply invested in the university system and want to consent to my instructions. They got caught by my "trick" and were unable to follow my instructions because other norms got in the way. Their responses were determined by the conventions of free-writing exercises, paragraphs, the assignments they have done in the past, and especially the consistent demand that they provide "an original claim" about all kinds of materials. The expectation that students be "original" indi-viduals is yet another ideology and a part of various sets of ideas supported by institutions of the state and culture.

Brecht's plays and pedagogical failures have also taught me about my own consent to conventions, including my assumption that a good teacher offers a democratic classroom that avoids hierarchies and encourages individual originality. This pedagogical norm masks the discipline and authority that are part of any educational system and cannot immediately be characterized as dehumanizing or *communist* (heaven forbid). The assumption that we all desire freedom and agency, usually defined as the subversion of tradition, au-thority, or "Great Customs," is built into the liberal arts education and liberal thought more generally, as well as the critical theories we tend to call "radi-cal." Feminist, queer, and postcolonial theories—so crucial to my own train-ing, teaching, and research—all tend to present a model of the individual who subverts norms and traditions. Those who submit—especially if, like Brecht's *Der Jasager*, they appear to have the choice to say yes or no—are condescend-ingly accused of being blind to their own interests, of being dupes of oppres-sive institutions or belief systems. Translated out of critical theory and into our current consumer culture, we are not so far from "Think outside the box" (ad for Apple Computers); "Think outside the bun" (Taco Bell); "Different is good" (Arby's); "Just say no" (the U.S. "War on Drugs"). But say yes to the power to buy your style and "Be your own label" (Zabba Designs). Demands for subversion and demonstrations of individual agency also regularly serve capitalism.

Slogans like "be yourself" shape interpretations of Brecht's *Yes* and *No* plays and other literary texts. Although the operations of authority, Brecht's and mine, influenced my students' claims that the plays should be taught, their unfree-writing revealed that most of them assumed that *Yes* 1 teaches a lesson about the dangers of blindly following a "Great Custom." *Yes* 2 dem-onstrates that under certain dire circumstances, like an epidemic, individu-als should sacrifice themselves for the community, which should then feel guilty. *Der Neinsager/No* crystallizes the lessons learned from the *Yes* versions into a statement that the relative value of the individual and the community can be determined only in a particular situation or context: Individuals should not be pressured to consent to self-sacrifice when it is not warranted (as in Yes 1), but they should agree if the good to a community will outweigh the value of one life, as in Yes 2 when the boy's sacrifice might save an entire town from sickness. Most of my students initially thought that all the plays made the same argument, one that aligns with exaltations of the value of the individual's freedom while demanding sacrifice for the higher good of the community or state.

The very different responses of students who performed Yes 1 at the Karl Marx Schule in 1931 shaped Brecht's revisions. Those students interpreted Yes 1 as praising the Boy's consent (BCP, 230). After all, the chorus's first line states, "Nothing is more important to learn than agreement" (BCP, 47). Most of the German pupils did not like this message. One complained, "The play is inappropriate for our school, because the Teacher is very cold-blooded" (BCP, 224). A precocious ten-year-old recognized that lives have different values (an insight we attribute to much later concepts of biopolitics) and weighed the boy's life against his mother's: "I'd say a young life was worth more than an old one" (BCP, 225).[7] The pupils at Karl Marx Schule found in Yes 1 the message that composer Kurt Weill articulated in a 1930 interview as "the importance of obedience. This message of 'agreement' gives the Lehrstück its political impact—in an elevated sense, not of course in that of party politics" (BCP, 223). Regardless of Weill's and Brecht's intentions, party politics shaped responses to the play. Brecht's liberal friend Frank Warschauer was horrified by the play's support for conformity and blind obedience and undoubtedly feared that it would fuel the rising Nazi Party (BCP, 227). Despite Brecht's support of communism, he did not follow the stylistic recommendations of the second All-Union Congress of Proletarian Writers, which convened in 1928 just as Brecht was writing his first Lehrstück. The congress demanded "realism," but a version of "social realism" that presented the ideal, not exactly real, communist society, so some members of the Communist Party deplored Brecht's ambiguity, ambivalence, and abstraction.[8]

Whether or not Brecht intended to write communist propaganda or an "elevated" lesson on "agreement," the text of Yes 1 was understood to be ambiguous by at least one of the Karl Marx Schule students. As a fourteen-year-old pointed out, "The play could be used to show what damage is done by superstition" (BCP, 226). Brecht appeared to follow this suggestion in Der Neinsager's claim that the "Greatest Custom" would be "thinking things out anew in every situation" (BCP, 59). Yet *Yes* 1 does not critique superstition, and the Boy's consent to being thrown off a mountain in that play can be understood only in relation to Brecht's support for a proletarian or workers' revolution.

My students and I read the plays in a very different context from that in Germany at the end of the 1920s when the Weimar Republic was headed toward political upheaval and a proletarian rather than a fascist takeover seemed possible—at least to Brecht. In his note to *The Lindberghs' Flight*, Brecht wrote, "This exercise is an aid to discipline, which is the basis of freedom. The individual will reach spontaneously for a means to pleasure, but not for an object of instruction that offers him neither profit nor social advantages. Such exercises only serve the individual in so far as they serve the State, and they only serve a State that wishes to serve all men equally" (BOT, 32). Discipline, particularly disciplined service to a socialist state, even one that works to "serve all men equally," seems like an inadequate "basis for freedom" to most liberal societies. Such societies tend to encourage appreciation of notions of freedom *from* discipline, freedom to speak *against* the state (so long as the speech does not threaten "national security"), freedom of choice, and freedom to earn and spend money freely. "Freedom is not free," a slogan engraved on the Korean War Veterans Memorial in Washington, D.C., which was invoked frequently after the terrorist attacks against the United States on September 11, 2001, is usually intended to describe the unfortunate necessity of maintaining a standing military force. Freedom is not free for military members, whom we must pay to defend "liberty and democracy." Liberal societies assume that in the context of military or other such service, sane people do agree to sacrifice their lives for the good of the community, which is, in fact, a form of consent (Einverständnis). If we recognize Einverständnis as a military virtue depicted frequently in the films, theater, and other heroic stories of the "state," it becomes clear that some forms of self-sacrificing consent or submission are idealized in the United States and other liberal cultures.

Many of my students wanted to read *Der Neinsager* as Brecht's final, perfected version of the *Taniko*-derived plays, written after he learned from earlier failures and after he recognized that Einverständnis can be required only when circumstances are very grave (famine, epidemic, war, and so on). They believed that a piece of writing improves with revision, partly because that's what teachers like me have told them. Brecht's unacknowledged collaborator, Elisabeth Hauptmann, and his German editors also treated *Der Neinsager* as his final version, written after *Yes* 2. But the textual and performance record muddies this presumed trajectory. *Der Neinsager* was probably written before *Yes* 2, since it was based on the text of *Yes 1* and did not incorporate *Yes 2*'s epidemic scenario and other revisions. This does not mean, however, that Brecht's final answer was the Boy's consent under the more grave circumstances of *Yes 2*. Brecht's note in *Versuche 4* states, "If possible the two little plays should always be performed together" (BCP, 221). Nonetheless, *Der Neinsager* was not performed with *Yes 2* at the Karl Marx Schule on May 18, 1931. If no were Brecht's final answer, he probably would not have resurrected *Taniko*'s "valley-hurling" plot in *The Decision* (*Die Masnahme*, 1930), which Brecht originally titled *He Said Yes (Rendered Concrete)* (BCP, 236). The first of Brecht's two plays explicitly about Communism, *The Decision* presents four Russian agitators undergoing trial by chorus for throwing their young Chinese comrade into a lime pit after he endangers the cause and agrees that he must die. The Communist Party was no more pleased with this explicit treatment of the value of individual life in a worker's revolution than it was with the vagueness of *Yes* and *No*.

We will never know whether Brecht intended but failed to produce a simple Communist propaganda play with *Yes 1*, or if he recognized his failure and therefore kept trying to rewrite that same plot in *Yes 1, Yes 2, No,* and *The Decision*. Rather than a final answer, or even a revision, each play is, to use a term Brecht appreciated, a performance "experiment" (BOT, 79). "Yes" or "no" never fully answers interesting questions, in spite of that other "great custom," the true or false test. While we tend to think of the *Lehrstück* as a didactic form, a drama with a lesson, Brecht rather self-consciously translated the term as a "learning play" (BOT, 79). The gerund suggests an ongoing process rather than a realized moral. He also defined the *Lehrstück* as "art for the producer, not art for the consumer," and Brecht may have been the "producer" who learned the most from his plays (BOT, 80). Still, my attempts to uphold multiplicity and undecidability founder against the fact that *Yes* was performed between two hundred and three hundred times during Hitler's rise to power, making it Kurt Weill's most successful musical score after *The Threepenny Opera*.[9] Audiences seem to have interpreted the play as praise for the "Prussian military virtues, which were so compatible with the rising Fascist power."[10] In the two years between the first production of *Der Jasager* and Hitler's rise, there is no record that *Der Neinsager* was performed, probably because Weill never wrote music for that revision (BCP, 230). *Yes 1* and its catchy score were part of the Hitler youth's education, regardless of Brecht's and Weill's intentions.

Brecht conceded that his *Lehrstücke* were "full of mistakes with respect to our time" and "unusable for other times."[11] But here Brecht made another error; the Tanikō variants *are* usable in our time, despite being among the least celebrated of Brecht's oeuvre (for good reason). The many valid critiques of these plays are excellent prompts for discussion with students. Accusations of Brecht's orientalism and sense of entitlement to appropriate the art forms of other cultures and other writers (Hauptmann) encourage a number of useful discussions. Classes could interrogate the operations of (male) privilege and the binary of East versus West, including the "East" of communism and the "West" of liberal democracy and the limits of a smorgasbord multiculturalism defined by choosing from the Italian or Mediterranean lines in the college cafeteria. The plays have been read as a series of bad translations: a perfect opportunity to discuss the source text Tanikō and the creative errors written into every translation. And of course, there is the lesson plan that I have described here, with its unfree-writing exercise and exposure of the normative subjects of critical pedagogy.

OUTCOMES

On the last day of "Modernist Exoticisms," Paul J. Edwards, the remarkable graduate student whose subtly written paragraphs made fun of my *Yes* and *No* unfree-writing exercise, cast me in his presentation on Roland Barthes's *Empire of Signs* (1970). I always encourage "performative presentations" in which the form of delivery is integral to the argument or meaning. Edwards's was perfect; it began with a vignette from Brecht's *Der Neinsager*, in which I played the Teacher role opposite his Boy/Graduate Student who could not go on and give his presentation. Brecht's "Great Custom" was replaced by the "Syllabus," which stated that if any student were unable to complete the course, he or she must agree to receive an F and consent to being cast out of the graduate program. As the Teacher, I allowed him to present "what he had," with the warning that he would be "the object of general laughter and disgrace." The presentation, titled "Institution of Signs," went on to subject the University to the semiotic analysis that Barthes applies to the "fictive nation" and sign system he calls Japan in *Empire of Signs*.[12] In an analysis of "academic writing," Edwards concluded that the unique practice of writing about what other writers write, accompanied by pages of citations, constitutes a "performative masochism" comparable to "flagellation." This "academic work" turns the "art of writing" into "writing as a kind of sex act." The Graduate Student, he declared, "loves learning above all else," replaces "meals with espresso," and sighs "in exasperation" in response to questions about the topic of the "dissertation." The "diploma" is a paper filled with empty signs, written in the dead language called Latin that most students cannot read and delivered at the "commencement" each spring, the season apportioned for the "ritual" in the "academic calendar" so that students can leave the "university" to work on their farms.

In the middle of the presentation, Edwards paused to accuse his classmate (the one who had sat next to him around the seminar table all semester, following another unspoken ritual of the "graduate course") of stealing a page of the presentation, which would mean that he would not be able to earn his PhD. The classmate, cast as *Hagoromo*'s Fisherman Hakuryō, who stole the "feathered robe" of a celestial maiden (*tennin*) and wanted to keep it as a "treasure of the realm," declared that having found the presentation of a "doctoral student," he must "secure it as a wonder in this age of the death of the humanities and make it a treasure of the grad lounge." Edwards, now playing the celestial maiden, performed a very (very) slow walk around the seminar table to the very sad music of "Christmas Time Is Here (Instrumental)" by the Vince Guaraldi Trio from *A Charlie Brown Christmas*. Seeing the sadness of the "graduate student," his Hakuryō classmate learned the lesson of sympathy, relented, and allowed the presentation to continue. For Edwards as the celestial maiden Graduate Student, the "pathways of tenure" were now reopened, and he could continue his presentation amid general laughter but little fear of failure.

5. NOH CIRCLES IN TWENTIETH-CENTURY JAPANESE PERFORMANCE

During his 1½ year stay in the United States from 1918, he [Kosaku Yamada] presented his dance-poem piece "At the Hawk's Well" in New York in collaboration with dancer Michio Ito. . . . For "At the Hawk's Well," [Sakiko] Oshima initially used noh steps but eventually got rid of them.

"H. Art Chaos Explores Poetry in Motion," *Japan Times*, June 27, 2004

AFTER THE 1916 DEBUT OF *AT THE HAWK'S WELL* IN A LONDON drawing room, Itō Michio took the play on an American tour during which it shaped modernist conceptions of noh, modern dance, and little theater. The noh-inspired dance play also circled back to Japan, where it has continued to inspire reconstructions and new works like Sakiko Oshima's version, "Buyoshi ga Yomigaeru" (Dance Poems Will Come Back to Life Again), reviewed in the *Japan Times* (2004) with a brief mention of Itō but not Yeats. Itō initially staged *Hawk's Well* in 1940 with his siblings, a production that kept him in Tokyo for a period long enough to ignite the FBI's suspicions. Following his arrest as an enemy alien after the Japanese attack on Pearl Harbor in 1941 and his repatriation to Japan, he mounted performances at the Ernie Pyle Theater for the American occupying forces. In keeping with his eclectic dance, theater, and film work (characteristic of the first generation of modern dancers), Itō's later career in Japan encompassed the *shingeki* (new drama) and traditional theater, dance, and popular entertainment. We have a tendency to draw oversimplified divisions between these genres based on assumptions that noh and other traditional forms remained "independent" of Western influence, whereas shingeki was derivative of Euro-American modern drama. These assumptions contribute to misunderstandings of twentieth-century aesthetic movements in Japan, regardless of whether or not we call them "Japanese modernism." While Itō's activity in modernist performance in Europe and the United States before his career in Japan might seem exceptional, many Japanese-born artists studied abroad and were inspired by traditional Japanese art, local responses to modernity, and international forms of modernism.

Definitions of modernism and its relationship to the world beyond Europe and the United States are continuously debated.[1] In order to skirt the definitional swamp surrounding modernism—and to avoid becoming mired in terrain beyond my knowledge of Japanese art—I have focused on the transnational circuits by which the nonmodernist genre of noh influenced Euro-American modernism. This chapter considers how the complicated, creative, error-ridden products of that exchange returned to Japan in the twentieth century. Despite my efforts to "stay focused," every time I pulled at one proverbial thread of noh's magic robe, I found that I needed to examine modern dance, the modernist little theater movement, and even film, and I ended up with my hands fuller than I expected. The same is true of the influence of modernist noh in Japan, a country that does not fit easily into the most common stories about modernism's impact on the non-Western world. These stories tend to focus on European and American artists who appropriated foreign art forms and asserted that international artists mimicked modernism after a time lag. Yet Japan's so-called opening in 1853, when Commodore Matthew Perry first arrived in Japan, initiated an intense response to modernity. If 1853 is the date for one version of Japanese modernism, it obviously did not lag behind even as it adapted aesthetic techniques, political and economic strategies like empire, and technologies, including film, invented elsewhere. And if engaging the death throes of empire is a crucial element of modernist movements, as it was in Europe, then Japan became a failing empire almost unimaginably fast. After defeating China in the first Sino-Japanese War (1894–1895) and Russia in the first Russo-Japanese War (1904–1905), Japan expanded its dominance over Asia, consolidated holdings during World War I, and found itself sitting among the soon-to-be-fading empires at the Paris Peace Conference in 1919 as one of the "Big Five" (with Great Britain, France, Italy, and the United States).[2]

In the twentieth century, modernist noh returned to Japan many times and in different forms of media. One circle was textual and propelled largely through translations, like the Fenollosa-Hirata-Pound noh plays and Japanese studies of translation. Another circuit involved the performance techniques used by trained performers (or not trained but associated by nation of birth), as when Itō adapted the leftward circling and stamping patterns of noh in his choreography for the Guardian of the Hawk's Well, as pictured in figure 2.6. Itō's interest in noh (sparked by Yeats and Pound) and Japanese pedagogical traditions influenced his work in Europe and the United States, and both modernism and noh shaped his theatrical career in Japan and the school of modern dance, Domonkai, that he established outside Tokyo. The circulation of texts and performance techniques was bound to the international trade in books and (mis)translations, among other objects, immigration practices, the world wars and their technologies of human slaughter and displacement, and the modes of transit that carried artists like Itō to stages and film screens around the world. Cinema is often cited as the quintessential modern art, as its technology of two turning reels that wind and unwind images on film was invented at the outset of aesthetic modernism. Accordingly, this chapter about how modernist noh influenced Japanese modernism also considers the filmmaker Ozu Yasujirō, particularly his depictions of modern life as being intertwined with Japanese tradition and his version of a modernism that intentionally lagged behind others.

From the impact of modernist translation practices on noh scholarship to adaptations of *Hawk's Well* and depictions of noh and kabuki on film, circles of influence wing out from episodes of international collaboration and teaching. Most discussions of Japanese modernism and exchanges between the East and the West overlook these circular patterns and instead imagine a long-distance run toward modernization, in which Japan lagged behind. After its forced "opening," Japan sprinted toward the front of the pack so that by 1895, it had shockingly annexed Taiwan and was leading the race to build an empire in Asia, complete with European-style orientalist claims about civilizing the Taiwanese, Chinese, and Koreans. "Traditionalists" protested this sprint and intentionally lagged behind the race for modernization. In this version of Japanese history, proponents of modernization supposedly imitate Western modernism, but traditionalists are just as derivative because they mimic Japan's own past. Beyond their shared derivativeness, however, traditionalists and modernists are thought to be in separate aesthetic and political relays.

The image of distinct teams racing toward modernity does not characterize the work of Japan's artists in the twentieth century. Nor does it encompass the curvy and error-ridden influence of modernist translations of noh, Itō's complicated (even coerced) tours, and the translations and adaptations of *Hawk's Well*, including *Takahime* (*Hawk Princess*), first staged in 1967 by Yokomichi Mario (1916–2012). Furukawa sensei, my noh teacher in Tokyo, had performed in *Takahime* shortly before I began taking lessons with him in 2009. I watched his recording of the production, and he gave me a copy of the program, which provided a basic introduction to Yeats's interest in noh and his collaboration with Itō. I keep the program in a folder filled with other noh playbills, many with English inserts claiming that noh has not changed for centuries. Noh's invented traditions, including the practice of extolling the value and fixed nature of noh's repertory, produces some fascinating contradictions, like this one in my pile of programs. Noh and kabuki, like Japan's film industry, contributed to the cultural and political projects of militarization and empire during the buildup to World War II, and the same forces and censorship shaped Ozu's depictions of traditional performance on film. Even when artists intend to submit to tradition, they necessarily bring that tradition into their own moment and aesthetic world. *Hawk's Well* has been put to many different uses by postwar theater groups, including NOHO and Theatre Nohgaku, both of which are interested in forms of transnational, intercultural, or fusion theater. These efforts, sometimes associated with "postmodern performance," recall theatrical collaborations that have been traveling with a century of *Hawk's Well* tours.

MISRECOGNIZED IN TRANSLATION

> Nō does possess a unity of imagery, and this has become its most salient characteristic.
>
> Ezra Pound, who discovered this fact, pointed out, however, that this unity of imagery does not exist in all nō but can only be recognized in the "better plays." Pound had no knowledge whatsoever of the authors of nō, but an examination of the "better plays" reveal that almost all of them are plays by Zeami or members of Zeami's group.
>
> Konishi Jin'ichi, A History of Japanese Literature, vol. 3, The High Middle Ages

Konishi Jin'ichi was a famous scholar of literature who wrote the hugely ambitious A *History of Japanese Literature* from the archaic period to the modernism of Mishima Yukio. His history was almost immediately translated into English and has defined the field for many readers.[3] He was exceptional among experts on ancient noh as a speaker of fluent English with an interest in Western modernism. He read and appreciated Pound's translations and analyses of noh plays even as he recognized errors and omissions. In a widely circulated essay of 1962, Konishi introduced Japanese readers to what he called Pound's "discovery" of the "unifying image" (tōitsu imeiji) as a crucial feature of noh.[4] Pound had described what he called a "Unity of Image" or "the intensification of a single Image" in "the better plays," including "the mantle of feathers in the play of that name, Hagoromo" (PFNoh, 27). Konishi pointed out that three of the four "better" noh plays that Pound offered as examples were known to have been written by Zeami: Nishikigi, Takasago, and Sumagenji (but not Hagoromo).[5] Konishi listed "unifying images" in other plays and concluded that Zeami had invented this method of composition. Praising Pound's "poetic sensibility," Konishi believed the American modernist poet had discovered a characteristic of noh that had been overlooked by centuries of Japanese scholars.

Throughout the 1960s and 1970s, Konishi published additional articles using the presence of "unifying images" to determine whether Zeami had written plays in the repertory whose authorship was unknown. Takeuchi Akiko summarized the pitfalls in Konishi's attempt to determine Zeami's authorship based on a noh play's imagery: Konishi did not initially define Zeami's "unifying image," just as Pound never clarified how a "Unity of Image" functioned in noh beyond citing, and occasionally inventing, repeated images related to feathered robes in Hagoromo and snow flurries in Nishikigi, as I described in chapter 2. Konishi's shift in terminology from "Unity" to "unifying" might indicate his slight misreading or desire to make the image more active in shaping the play.[6] In an article in 1970, Konishi finally identified three features of the "unifying image" that he maintained for the rest of his life: The image recurs throughout the play, symbolizes the theme, and was invented by Zeami.[7] He also continued to credit Pound with the discovery of these images, even as he acknowledged that Pound's presentation of the "snow flurry as a unifying image in Nishikigi was based on a mistaken interpretation of the play."[8] A "unifying image" that fulfilled Konishi's first two features could not prove Zeami's authorship, for as Konishi admitted, three of Zeami's known works do not contain such images, although they appear in plays by other authors. Attempting to respond to these problems, Konishi suggested that Zeami adapted the plays of others by adding, in Matsukaze, for example, recurring images of pines and the moon. Konishi also argued that Zeami's three plays without "unifying images" dated from his "middle period" when he was developing the structuring device but when "unity was not yet an aim."[9] This argument is problematic in that Zeami's works often cannot be dated because he continuously adapted and revised his own and others' plays in response to the needs of his troupe, desires of audiences, and changing theatrical fashions.

Konishi's claims about "unifying images" gained wide acceptance in Japan, despite the flaws in the argument. This was partly because he was writing at a moment when noh scholars were fascinated by Zeami. For centuries, there had been little interest in determining the authorship of plays; performance and pedagogical traditions were far more important than authors. In 1909, however, Yoshida Tōgo published the first collection of Zeami's writings on noh, *Zeami jurokubu shu*, and the newly discovered essays revealed that the noh patriarch was also a remarkable theorist of performance, playwriting, and aesthetics. The year after Konishi published his first article citing Pound's "discovery" about noh's imagery, 1963, was Zeami's sexcentennial. Konishi was invited to appear at numerous birthday celebrations at which he discussed his idea of the "unifying image." The idea was also appealing in that it echoed Western aesthetic rubrics like "the three unities" while maintaining noh's distinctiveness at a moment when Japan was renegotiating its position in the world (following the Treaty of Mutual Cooperation and Security [1960]). As Konishi claimed, "Unity is essential to drama, and in the West, there have been many kinds of unity, from the three unities of the neoclassical theater (unity of time, place, and action) to the unity of impression seen in modern theater. None of these various kinds of unity, however, are complete in nō. Nō does possess a unity of imagery, and this has become its most salient characteristic."[10]

The idea that repeated images related to a noh play's theme create a form of unity remains central to noh studies. Although widely accepted as a feature of Zeami's texts, unifying imagery is no longer considered sufficient to determine his authorship. It now seems clear that Konishi wanted to discover a textual feature of noh specific to Zeami, and he believed he had found it in Pound's Image, even as he at least partially recognized its basis in error. Similarly, Pound was hoping to write a long poem that could adhere to his rules for imagism, and he thought he had found the right approach in noh. Both Konishi and Pound found what they hoped to find. But "misrecognition" is a better term for this common experience of finding what you're looking for than "mistake" or "misunderstanding," and like many others operating in cross-cultural transmission, their misrecognitions had remarkably fertile afterlives. Through Konishi's Pound-derived intervention, noh studies developed new methods of textual analysis. Scholars in Japan began offering close readings of plays with analyses of imagery and structure that had generally been reserved for discussions of classical poetry. In modernist studies, the impact of Pound's imagism is widely recognized, but few know of Konishi's admiration and response: "Through Pound, English poets learned of the concept of unified imagery in nō and that it contributed to the development of the Imagism sponsored by Pound and to the aesthetic of W. B. Yeats."[11] Konishi is correct, but he partially mistranslated Pound's "Unity of Image" and, as if following Pound's example, used it to creatively misattribute noh plays.[12]

The Konishi-Pound circuit of misrecognition also reveals current overgeneralizations about Japan and modernism, including the common story that Euro-American artists appropriated "exotic" materials and that Japanese artists were enthralled by and slavishly mimicked the West. Instead, the dynamics of exchange were far more convoluted, involving on all sides misrecognition, error, and mimicry but also serious study and genuine creativity. The Konishi-Pound circuit also complicates the idea that Japan had its modernizers in the shingeki theater, fiction, and, of course, film—which was "modern" to begin with—but those in the traditional arts, including noh, kabuki, and bunraku, among others, universally rejected modernization. Even noh, often assumed to be the oldest and most tradition bound of all, was influenced by interpretive strategies derived from Euro-American modernist factions like Imagism. The modern art of film in Japan, according to Katsumoto Seiichirō's "Characteristics of the Japanese Cinema" (1936), often looked back to traditional performance. Its main function was to "provide images to the story-telling performance of the feudal age and the popular novels of today."[13] For Katsumoto, the "mental position assumed by Japanese poets of the tanka [short poem] and haiku schools since ancient times," elite theater forms, and popular modes of storytelling all coexisted in the cinema. By the 1930s, though, the Euro-American influence on Japanese film, however substantial, was no longer interesting and was a "moot question" for Katsumoto.

More than eighty years later, scholars of modernism are still preoccupied with (tracing, sometimes deploring, sometimes celebrating) the Euro-American influence on Japanese modernism, and vice versa. Konishi's celebration in 1963 of Pound's "discovery" in 1916 might seem to give credence to the idea that Japanese modernity was derivative. This notion of a time lag can serve as the foundation for two well-intentioned and contradictory impulses: One is to suggest that modernism arrived and renovated art in Japan, just as it did in the West, only later. We only need to expand our period bounds for modernism in order to expand our geographical lines and allow Japan and other non-European countries into "the club." This gesture is inclusive but Eurocentric with its hints of a benign imperialist offering the fruits of modernism to other countries. The temporal and geographical expansion of modernist studies can veer too close to the imperial and economic expansionism that prompted Commodore Matthew Perry's "gunboat diplomacy" to open Japan in 1853.[14] The second well-intentioned move by critics follows a similar pattern: When modernism arrived in Japan, some artists were swept up in mimicking the West, and some never passed beyond "the aping of Europe," as Pound put it (PFNoh, 3).[15] For others, modernist mimicry was a passing phase before they returned to their so-called authentic Japanese traditions. Pound and some other Western critics have celebrated their (limited) understanding of Japaneseness and assumed it would have been sullied by Western influence.

The well-intentioned impulse to include or protect Japan from Euro-American modernism still presumes that modernism is of central and unquestioned importance. We give aesthetic movements too much power when we assume that inclusion in modernism could be so beneficial or destructive to Japan. Japanese artists and critics in the period often had a very different take on the relationship between Japan and the world, as evident in Katsumoto's claim that the question of Western influence on Japanese film was "moot." The writer Ryūtanji Yū rejected the "critique that says *modanizumu* is nothing more than the latest display of imported cosmetics" in his essay "Modānizumu bungaku-ron" (1930).[16] William Tyler defines *modanizumu*, a term coined in the 1920s, as "a powerful intellectual idea, mode of artistic expression, and source of popular fashion in Japan from approximately 1910–1940."[17] As a Japanese approximation of the English word "modernism," *modanizumu* is obviously derived from Euro-American modernism and was written in the katakana syllabary used for foreign words. It is not simply a form of mimicry. Ryūtanji's demand for an *atarashii kankan* (new sense-sense) invokes Paris's popular Moulin Rouge dance, the cancan, and exemplifies the playful and worldly character of *modanizumu*, as well as an interest in Western gentlemen's clubs and the erotic displays of women's bodies.[18]

The assumption of Japan's time lag largely comes from our focus on the translation of Euro-American works, aesthetic principles, and artistic techniques. Translations were often produced very quickly: Marinetti's "The

Founding and Manifesto of Futurism" was translated by the novelist Mori Ōgai just three months after it appeared in *Le Figaro* in 1909.[19] Translations of Henrik Ibsen, so crucial to modernist drama around the world, became available in Japan in 1901 with Takayasu Gekkō's *A Doll House* and *Enemy of the People*. Osanai Kaoru (1881–1928) established the Jiyū gekijō (Free Theater) in 1909, modeled on France's Théâtre libre, and produced Ōgai's translation of Ibsen's *John Gabriel Borkman* in its first season.[20] Osanai established another theater with Hijikata Yoshi (1898–1959), the Tsukiji shōgekijō (Tsukiji Little Theater), which had an Ibsen festival in 1928 to mark the centenary of the playwright's birth. Two teams of translators raced to publish James Joyce's *Ulysses* (1922), producing installments between 1930 and 1936. Because of censorship, this prototypical Western modernist novel appeared in Japanese before it was legal to obtain the book in any English-speaking country (the United States was first in 1933).[21]

Japanese artists and scholars speedily and diligently translated far more texts from Western languages into Japanese than ever have been translated from Japanese.[22] They also translated contemporary texts, whereas Euro-American translators such as Pound and Arthur Waley generally chose classical Japanese literature, like noh plays and the epic *The Tale of Genji* (*Genji monogatari*) by Lady Murasaki (ca. 1021).[23] Modernist translation practices contributed to stereotypes of the East as traditional and backward. But Japanese artists and scholars were also interested in representations of their country's artistic past, and they recognized and wrote about error-ridden circuits of translation. The noh scholar and translator Nogami Toyoichirō first published his study "Noh in English Translation" (Eiyakusaretayōkyoku) in 1934, then expanded the piece for the last chapter of his book *The Rebirth of Noh* (*Nōnosaisei*, 1935). He analyzed English versions and developed theories of translation that shaped Japanese understandings of noh and the global circulation of art even before Konishi promoted his Pound-derived "unifying imagery."[24] Nogami had studied English literature at Tokyo Imperial University under the tutelage of the remarkable novelist Sōseki Natsume.[25] Nogami believed that English translations of noh offered the vision of a foreigner, which could help the Japanese understand both noh and the ways in which their country was represented around the world. He examined eight different English translators and fifty-two different translations of forty-two noh plays, of which twenty-six were fourth-category *monoguruimono* (plays about mad people) like *Sumidagawa*.[26] Nogami pointed out that these plays have "the most dramatic shifts and entanglements," which appeal to foreigners who seek plots and conflicts similar to those in Western traditions of theater.[27] But he also extolled the quiet and elegant beauty (*yūgen*) of noh and claimed that foreigners seeking dramatic conflict chose the wrong plays to translate and thereby misrepresented noh.

The aspect of Nogami's translation theory that most appeals to me (as an undeniably amateur lover of the noh theater) is his appreciation for the incomprehension and wonder of the foreign amateur in the audience. This wonder often tips toward simple forms of exoticism, but Nogami suggests that native speakers and experts should watch noh with some of the foreigner's desire for the exotic. Those who attend noh without translation are more likely to grasp what he calls the "essence" of noh than if they follow the chanting (*utai*) in a libretto and try to improve their own recitation or transpose the text into contemporary speech.[28] Noh performance resists the kind of understanding required for translation by, for example, featuring full masks that muffle the words of the chant and preserving archaic pronunciations. Noh texts depart from Western notions of the individual person as represented in the subject of the sentence or act. Translations of *Kumasaka* by Waley and Fenollosa-Hirata-Pound, Nogami revealed, failed to accommodate the indirect, composite, or "elliptical" nature of noh subjectivity. English translators added names and pronouns in an attempt to clarify the "subject" of a passage. That clarification is un-noh-like and unnecessary in the Japanese language: "if Noh song translation is to feel like a Japanese thing, then, for example, thought should be given to contriving the elliptical subject."[29] The relative unimportance of the individual person as represented in the grammar of the *utai* also is evident when the chorus appears to sing for the *shite* or the *waki* and *shite* seem to exchange lines in the dialogue. Further displacing the unique individual are noh's pedagogical practices encouraging mimicry of the teacher's performance, memorization of the repertory, and submission to the authority of the teacher, tradition, and canon.

In the preface to *Translation Theory and Practice* (*Honyakuron: honyaku no riron to jissai*, 1938), Nogami described a "reading circle" that could break down national and linguistic boundaries as it circulates artworks, ideas, political forms like fascism and communism, and other cultural products.[30] Nogami demanded that Japan participate in this reading circle, however complicated and doomed to misrecognition. Rather than return to its former isolationist practices, Japan needed to produce and study translations to enrich the global reading circle as well as control its representation around the world. The empire had invested in earlier projects like the 1919 kabuki initiative in

Korea with similar goals of exporting Japanese culture to its colonies.[31] Japan established the International Cultural Relations Society (Kokusai bunka shinkōkai) to reach beyond Asian colonies, and Nogami wrote the society's first publication in 1935, *Masks of Japan: The Gigaku, Bugaku and Noh Masks*. The Japan Society for the Promotion of Science (Nippon gakujutsu shinkōkai)—which generously funded my research and lessons in Japan—established the Japanese Classics Translation Committee in 1934, and noh was one of its first undertakings. Nogami was appointed to the "Special Noh Committee" to collaborate with other experts on authoritative translations. In 1955, the committee finally published the translation of *Sumidagawa* that William Plomer used as the basis for his libretto for *Curlew River*—which, as I discuss in chapter 6, began yet another fascinating "reading circle."[32]

A Brief Tour of Modern Japanese Theaters

After their 1916 collaboration, Pound continued to follow Itō's career, responding with some suspicion to Itō's efforts to promote noh plays. In 1940, he cited in a letter Itō's lack of the "training" that is so crucial to noh: "I note that Ito is back/ pp/ in *Jap Times* [*Japan Times*] a bit queer. May be O.K. Miscio's strong point was never moral fervor, and he may have a sane desire to popularize. (or not?)"[33] Pound's concern with morality and sanity seems crazy considering his promotion of Mussolini on Rome Radio during the war. His letter responded to the very same trip that Itō took to Japan to stage *Hawk's Well* that the FBI found suspicious and inexplicable, although the *Japan Times* article that Pound read in English included a good deal of information about Itō's theatrical activities during that time. Both Pound and Itō ended up in prison camps run by the U.S. military, which were followed by trials that led to Pound's imprisonment in St. Elizabeths Hospital (originally the Government Hospital for the Insane), where he accepted the Bollingen Prize for *The Pisan Cantos*, and Itō's repatriation to Japan, where he directed productions to entertain the U.S. occupying forces. It is difficult to locate either sanity or morality in relation to these artists and World War II.

Itō's stagings of *Hawk's Well* and modernist noh influenced Japanese *shingeki*, noh, and kabuki, blurring the distinctions usually made between modern and traditional theater. Even though *shingeki* was advertised as the new theater, it was largely modeled on or translated from Western modernism's realist dramas. Noh and kabuki also were changing in response to modernism, as Hawk's Well's Japanese production history reveals. Itō's first Japanese production of Yeats's noh-inspired dance play (the one that provoked the FBI's and Pound's suspicions for very different reasons) was a collaboration with Itō's brothers, who also were active in Japan's modern and little theater movements. They were Itō Kisaku, a stage designer, and Senda Koreya (Itō Kunio), a famous actor and one of Brecht's main proponents in Japan. Through his siblings, Itō became associated with the Shinkyō gekidan, which might be translated as "New Cooperative Theater Company."

The history of the Shinkyō gekidan is exemplary of the financial and political struggles of the modern theater movement in Japan and its battles against censorship. Originally called the "Trunk Players," Shinkyō gekidan actors traveled and performed throughout Japan, carrying their theatrical props in trunks. In 1926, they joined Osanai Kaoru and Hijikata Yoshi's Tsukiji shōgekijō (Tsukiji Little Theater), which often is referred to as "Japan's First Modern Theater," although "firsts" are usually questionable.[34] We might, for example, date the origins of dramatic modernism in Japan to the founding of the "Society for Theatre Reform" in 1886—the year Ibsen wrote Rosmersholm and before his brand of realist drama took hold of London with the 1891 production of A Doll's House. The Tsukiji shōgekijō was built in Tokyo just after the Great Kantō Earthquake and was modeled on European art theaters, opening in June 1924. Both Osanai and Hijikata had studied abroad and were interested in Euro-American modernism.[35] Osanai had been a member of Ayame-kai, an international literary society for the promotion of modernism founded by Noguchi Yone with the help of writers like Yeats and Arthur Symons.[36] Hijikata and Osanai originally refused to stage Japanese shingeki plays, arguing that only by presenting European plays in translation could they build a dramatic art in Japan that was oriented to the "future."[37] In this respect, they initially articulated a very different mission from that of the Abbey and other national theaters, as well as "little" art theaters, which tended to promote native playwrights and theatrical traditions.

After 1926, the Tsukiji shōgekijō began staging contemporary Japanese plays, a change of policy that was encouraged by the Marxist intellectuals and proletarian writers who supported the theater, including members of the Shinkyō gekidan. Numerous left-wing theater troupes and leagues of writers were formed with attachments to the resurrected Communist Party of Japan, which survived from about 1922 to 1934. These groups were committed to "proletarian realism," a dramatic form that used representational strategies based on European realism (far from Japanese theatrical traditions) with the goal of placing "modern" life on the stage and promoting Communist ideals. A realism that depicts life as it is might seem poorly equipped to convey ideals, revolutionary and otherwise. Yet, proletarian realism nearly monopolized the modern drama movement in Japan during this period.[38] Writers who refused to focus on communist politics or use realist methods were excluded from the powerful federations of proletarian writers, including PROT (an abbreviation of the Esperanto name Proletarea Teatoro), which formed in 1929. Like the similar organizations with which Brecht was (albeit ambivalently) associated in Germany, PROT stipulated that its writers all practice proletarian realism and recognize the movement's links to Soviet Russia.

Proletarian realism reached beyond *shingeki* and other modern dramatic movements and into the so-called traditional theaters. Osanai was invited as Japan's most honored director to visit Moscow as the government's guest for the celebration of the Soviet Union's tenth anniversary. Osanai added Rome to his European destinations and, like Ezra Pound, arranged a meeting with Benito Mussolini, who impressed him with his energy and political vision.[39] Upon his return, Osanai wrote the "grand kabuki" play *Mussolini* to feature Ichikawa Sadanji II, a young kabuki actor who had helped him found the Jiyū gekijō (Free Theater) in 1909 for the purpose of staging Western dramas. Osanai directed *Mussolini* at the Meiji Theater in 1928 while he was also working at the Tsukiji and encouraging dramatic techniques very different from those of kabuki. The Mussolini role that Osanai created for Sadanji depicted a great political leader and heroic personality. It is impossible to know if Osanai would have maintained his positive view of Mussolini and fascism through the 1930s, as he died in December 1928, just six months after the closing of *Mussolini*, his last play.

Osanai's work across the genres of kabuki, Western drama, and proletarian theater also combined interests in fascism, communism, and modernism, concerns that he believed could be presented in vastly different theatrical forms such as European realism, *shingeki*, and kabuki. Osanai's *Mussolini* contradicts the common claim that the kabuki repertory was fixed and that new plays were not produced after the end of the Meiji period (1868–1912).[40] The noh repertory is often presented as even more rigid and further removed from contemporary politics than kabuki. Even so, Umewaka Minoru (1828–1909), Ernest Fenollosa's teacher and Pound's hero for preserving noh into the Meiji period, helped create new noh plays with national themes. These include *Mikuni no hikari* (*The Blazing Light of Our Nation*), written by Mōri Motonori (1839–1896) with Umewaka's chant composition (*fushi-zuke*), which premiered in 1896 with Umewaka as the *shite*. The play's closing celebration claimed with nationalistic and militaristic fervor: "More than four hundred countries fear us. All this is due to the Emperor's majestic virtue."[41]

The nationalist and imperialist urges evident in *Mikuni no hikari* persisted in Japanese theater over the next three decades. By 1928, when Osanai and Sadanji presented *Mussolini*, the government had begun attacking leftist thinkers and disbanding Marxist and socialist groups, including the Japan League of Proletarian Arts (Nihon puroretaria geijutsu renmei).[42] In response to increasing governmental suppression of proletarian theater, culminating in a full ban in 1934, the Shinkyō gekidan reorganized and swore off communist politics.[43] The theater then engaged Itō to direct Hideo Nagata's *Daibutsu kaigan* (*The Image of the Great Buddha*) in 1940, during the extended visit that resulted in the first Japanese *Hawk's Well* and the FBI's surveillance. Itō compared the Shinkyō gekidan to the Theater Guild and Washington Square Players of New York in publicity materials, which also emphasized Itō's credentials as an experienced performer in Western little theaters. This publicity seems incongruent with the billing of *Daibutsu kaigan* as a "Play of Olden Japan" with "authentic" costumes from Kyoto and "old court music or Gagaku." Revealing that the little theater movement was likely to be familiar to readers, the *Japan Advertiser* announced, "From the standpoint of little theater stagecraft and production the performance is unusual and outstanding."[44] *Daibutsu kaigan* was certainly unusual for a company like the Shinkyō gekidan, which had performed plays by Euro-American writers such as Maxim Gorki, Clifford Odets, and Eugene O'Neill, for whom Itō had created the role of the Witch-Doctor in the premiere of *The Emperor Jones* (1920).

Yeats and Pound also insisted on promoting "Olden Japan" even when scraps of modern Japan intruded: Yeats's library contains four postcards stamped by "The Tsukiji Shōgekijō Photo Dept.," which feature lavish drawing room sets and actors in modern Western dress. An archivist's note indicates that they may be scenes from Anton Chekhov's *The Seagull* (1896) and *The Cherry Orchard* (1904), yet they are included in two folders of photos and clippings (mis)titled "Japanese Noh Plays," another bad title for my tally of mistakes or misrecognitions.[45] Archivists and scholars are not immune to the appeal of "Olden Japan," it seems. Of the sixty-six images in the folders, only four depict noh scenes: a noh stage and audience from above, a *shite* actor wearing a long black wig, a *koken* (stage assistant) dressing an actor, and a *shite* wearing a goblin mask. Most are images of kabuki, with one clipping of three bunraku puppets. The presence of these images in the Yeats library cannot definitively establish how much Yeats knew about noh, kabuki, and the Tsukiji shōgekijō, but he had some awareness of bunraku, for he incorrectly claimed that noh movement was "copied from the marionette shows of the fourteenth century" (PFNoh, 155).

The Yeats Library contains another scrap of modern Japan inserted into Yeats's copy of Pound and Fenollosa's Noh, or Accomplishment, a pamphlet entitled Japanese Drama and the Shōchiku Dramatic Company.[46] If he read the pamphlet, Yeats would have had some sense of the different Japanese theatrical traditions coexisting at that time. The Shōchiku Company was formed in 1892 and by 1915 had gained almost complete control of the theaters in Kyoto, Osaka, and Tokyo.[47] The undated pamphlet was probably published in the early 1920s because it describes the thirty-year history of the Shōchiku Company's project to "revive the Japanese drama" following the upheaval of the "Reformation" (usually called the Meiji Restoration).[48] Without mentioning noh or the adaptation of performance traditions from China, the pamphlet provides a myth of the origins of the "Japanese drama" in the performances of Okuni, a religious dancer (miko) who, "attired as a nun," danced while beating a drum and reciting Buddhist prayers.[49] Seeking links to "Western drama," the pamphlet claims that "when Okuni established her theater on the bank of the Kamogawa River in 1596, it was just twenty years after the first theatre had been established in London on the bank of the Thames."[50] The pamphlet also describes the "curious contrast" that "actresses" invented Japanese drama and played men, whereas it was the opposite in "the West."

The Shōchiku Company claimed that it embraced all the forms of drama, "all schools and styles," from the kabuki, which it incorrectly identified as the "oldest dramatic art of Japan" to the "Shinko [Shinkyō] gekidan, or newly risen dramatic society."[51] Shōchiku developed its "near monopoly" through intense commercialism, which included creating and casting star actors and offering special group rates to businesses.[52] Shōchiku was part of the governing board of the Tsukiji shōgekijō when it was reorganized and incorporated in 1939 under the leadership of Hideo Nagata. Demonstrating the intertwined "traditional" and "modern" theaters as well as political, popular, and elite performance forms, the Tsukiji's new board was composed of representatives from the Shinkyō gekidan and the Shin Tsukiji (New Tsukiji) groups as well as the enormous Shōchiku and Toho Companies. Along with Shōchiku, Toho eventually controlled most of the larger theaters and film studios in Tokyo and beyond. The strategies that these companies developed to promote the Japanese theater helped them become preeminent film houses as well. Shōchiku introduced the filmmaker Ozu Yasujirō, who adapted noh and kabuki to films during the tumult before and after World War II. Traditional performance influenced Ozu's film scenarios, preferred acting technique, camera work, and even style of collaboration. Kurosawa Akira is more famous for adaptations of noh and Shakespeare in *jidaigeki* (films about samurai of the Edo period), such as *Throne of Blood* and *Ran*.[53] Ozu specialized in films about ordinary people in modern Japan (*shōshimingeki*) and presented noh and kabuki as part of everyday life rather than invoking a distant past and powerful, magical warriors.

OZU YASUJIRŌ'S *A STORY OF FLOATING WEEDS* AND THE ART OF BEING BEHIND

The year that the Japanese government banned proletarian theater and that the Shinkyō gekidan reorganized and abandoned communist politics, Ozu released his silent film *A Story of Floating Weeds* (*Ukigusa monogatari*, 1934).[54] The aging leader of an itinerant kabuki troupe, Kihachi (played by Sakamoto Takeshi), repeatedly scratches his behind when he is distraught, confused, or lying (figure 5.1). This gesture appears to be directed at the viewer's face because of Ozu's famously low camera position, dubbed the "*tatami* shot" by film historians. The name comes from the suggestion that Ozu produced his shot by fixing the camera at the eye level of a person kneeling in *seiza* on the *tatami*-covered floor of a Japanese room.[55] The notion of a "*tatami* shot" implies that Japanese flooring and the practice of kneeling determined Ozu's camera height. To understand how exoticism contributes to this commonplace about Ozu, we might consider the likelihood of an American filmmaker becoming famous for a "linoleum" or "recliner" shot. Ozu's "*tatami* shot" frequently serves as evidence for yet another cliché, that he is "the most Japanese" and "most traditional of Japanese directors."[56] In seeming contradiction, other critics suggest that Ozu's camera work departs from the conventions of popular cinema and makes him "an experimental filmmaker, quite likely the greatest."[57]

Can Ozu's shot be both "traditional" and "experimental"? Absolutely. Like any camera position, it depends on perspective and where we are standing (or kneeling). Ozu's shot seems "traditional" when associated with the prevalence of kneeling in noh, kabuki, and other arts (although actors usually kneel on wood floors rather than the much softer *tatami*). It is "experimental" when compared with Hollywood camerawork. The appeal of the *tatami* shot in film

FIGURE 5.1 Kihachi's scratch in Ozu Yasujirō's *A Story of Floating Weeds* (1934). (Courtesy of Shōchiku eiga, Ozu Yasujirō)

history has led critics to lose sight of Ozu's actual camera position, which was sometimes higher and sometimes lower than *seiza*. This was memorably demonstrated when his trusted cameraman, Atsuta Yuharu, laid rather than knelt on the ground to demonstrate his work behind the camera in Wim Wenders's diary-documentary-tribute to Ozu, *Tokyo Ga* (1985) (figure 5.2). Like most filmmakers around the world, Ozu based his camera height on the scene he was filming rather than the cultural practice of kneeling. He usually set the camera at a height somewhere between the center of the object to be filmed and two-thirds of the way down.[58] While Ozu's camera was lower than that of many directors, proportion determined the height, and the camera position was not fixed. If the object were a person kneeling in *seiza*, as was common in the Japanese homes featured in many Ozu films, the camera would obviously be quite low. If the object were the standing Kihachi in *A Story of Floating Weeds*, the camera would be centered on his rear end when Ozu directed him to scratch, as the director meticulously choreographed his actors' movements. It is tempting to read this scratch as Ozu figuratively turning his behind on the inaccurate and contradictory interpretations of his shot.

FIGURE 5.2 Atsuta Yuharu in Wim Wenders's tribute to Ozu, *Tokyo Ga* (1985). (Courtesy of Chris Sievernich Filmproduktion, Gray City, Westdeutscher Rundfunk [WDR], Wim Wenders Productions, Wim Wenders Stiftung)

Strict distinctions between traditionalism and modernist experimentation are inadequate for both Japanese cinema and theater, as noh and kabuki were adapted for and influenced film and shingeki. Filmmakers and theater artists worked across these forms in twentieth-century Japan and even occupied the same "governing boards" at the Tsukiji Theater.

Although *A Story of Floating Weeds* is a loose adaptation of the American film *The Barker* (1928) by George Fitzmaurice, it usually serves as evidence for Ozu's traditionalism: It is among only five of his fifty-four films not set in modern Tokyo, and aside from some shots of trains and bicycles, it includes few references to modernity. The film is silent at a time when synchronized sound was possible, and its star, Kihachi, is a kabuki player who holds on to his craft (as well as his rear) after audiences have abandoned the show. The title *Ukigusa monogatari* invokes classical, epic Japanese literature (as in Murasaki's *Genji monogatari*). *Ukigusa* (literally, "duckweed") also appears in classical literature as a metaphor for weeds floating aimlessly on the currents of life.[59] Kihachi is floating in many ways, from town to town with his kabuki troupe and from woman to woman and back again—which is the source of the film's central problem. He returns to the mountain village where his former lover, Otsune (Iida Choko) is raising their son, Shinkichi (Mitsui Hideo), to believe that Kihachi is his uncle. To conceal his visits to their home from his current mistress and leading lady, Otaka (Yagumo Reiko), he tells the troupe that he is visiting a patron. Otaka learns of his deceit and his son by a former lover and, in revenge, pays another actress, Otoki (Tsubouchi Yoshiko), to seduce Shinkichi. Kihachi is furious when he discovers the plot, which is as typical as those of his plays, but of course, Shinkichi and Otoki fall in love. Otsune reveals to Shinkichi that Kihachi is his father, yet the actor leaves again with hopes of becoming a great star and making Shinkichi proud to claim him.

In the meantime, Kihachi disbanded his troupe when he drifted into bankruptcy, a regular occurrence for the actor, as memorably portrayed by the moneybag that floats away during an uncle [father]-nephew [son] fishing trip. Kihachi and Shinkichi cast their lines in choreographed unison until the actor drops his wallet in the river, a gag that disrupts the almost sentimental beauty of the scene. Kihachi claims there was money in the bag, but Shinkichi wryly points out, "It's floating, so no coins." Kihachi retorts, "Did you ever think it might be stuffed with bills?" He betrays the lie by scratching his butt (figure 5.3). Kihachi is generally broke, and the final scenes of the film have him reconciling with Otaka and leaving town on a train with plans to start a new troupe, all part of a pattern for actors who float like weeds and empty moneybags on a river.

Kabuki influences the plot of the film and also shapes the performance style of Ozu's actors. Kihachi's signature gestures like scratching his butt and toying with his fan or towel are similar to the codified poses called mie or kimaru that are struck at emotional moments in a kabuki play. Kihachi demonstrates a common mie after the little boy-dog, Tomi-bō, has run off crying during the humorously bad show the troupe gives early in the film. Kabuki, like noh, is composed of kata, movement patterns that appear throughout the repertory in different sequences. Ozu generated kata-like movements for his actors, designating just when and how they were to execute a gesture. Kihachi and Shinkichi perform kata during the fishing scene when they cast precisely together and then bounce their poles exactly three times. The actress Higashiyama Chieko similarly described Ozu's choreography with her teacup in Early Summer (1951): "He was most particular about where the cup should be in relation to each word. . . . If you did just the form [kata] without the spirit, then that was no good either."[60] Ryū Chishū similarly remembers,

FIGURE 5.3 Kihachi's scratch while fishing with Shinkichi in Ozu's *A Story of Floating Weeds* (1934). (Courtesy of Shōchiku eiga, Ozu Yasujirō)

"As to Mr. Ozu's way of direction, he had made up the complete picture in his head before he went on the set, so that all we actors had to do was to follow his directions, from the way we lifted and dropped our arms to the way we blinked our eyes."[61] Ozu ruled over the performance of his actors in the manner of a master of a traditional theater troupe, dictating their physicality and prohibiting personal style. In this sense, Ozu occupied Kihachi's position as troupe master. An authoritarian style of direction and pedagogy is common in Japanese arts, but I have commented on Yeats's similar directing styles and will focus on Beckett's so-called tyrannical direction in chapter 6.

Ozu adapted noh's and kabuki's strict troupe hierarchy and also translated working methods from the theater to cinema. He gathered a group of actors and cast them in similar roles in film after film. Ryū performed many of Ozu's father roles, including those with Hara Setsuko as his daughter Noriko in the *Noriko Trilogy*—so named not for any continuity of plot but because Ryū's and Hara's characters are consistent types across the films.[62] The reappearance of actors and roles emphasizes the theme of repetition in the films and undermines the impact of the individual star actor. In the Kihachi Series, Sakamoto generally plays opposite Iida Choko and depicts a sympathetic drifter who struggles in his relationship with his son.[63] These character types in A Story of Floating Weeds are ironically juxtaposed to the standard kabuki roles: The tateyaku (literally, "standing role" or leading man) was probably played by Kihachi in his troupe's productions, but in the scene from the kabuki play included in the film, he appears to be a drunken swordsman—appropriately enough. Unlike a true tateyaku, Kihachi's daily behavior was not governed by the strict codes of the samurai. He repeatedly succumbs to the worldly attractions of women while shirking his familial responsibilities, and his only battles involve hitting the two women in his troupe, Otaka and Otoki.

Shinkichi defends Otoki from Kihachi's violence by pushing him onto his well-scratched rear. Shinkichi is a more typical nimaime ("second" or good-hearted but flawed romantic character). By falling in love with an actress who is ostensibly beneath him, he causes her pain and damages his future prospects, but he is also repeating the patterns of his parents.[64] Despite the shin (new) implied in his name, Shinkichi is as "fast with the women" as his father was, and like his mother, he fell for an actor. Ozu uses kabuki's stock roles and performance styles as part of a series of repetitions, including Kihachi's two mistresses, actresses with similar names, repetitive gestures, a pattern of bankruptcy, coming and going by train, and a son who repeats the mistakes of his parents.

Ozu's focus on kabuki players in a silent film made just as synchronized sound was transforming cinema around the world recalls the intertwined history of kabuki and Japanese cinema, a context that is overlooked in discussions of A Story of Floating Weeds. The early cameras imported to Japan from the French company Gaumont brought the modern/Western medium of film into contact with Japanese stage arts.[65] Japan's first commercial film in 1898 (just three years after the Lumière brothers screened a film for a paying audience in Paris) was a center shot of three geisha dancing. Cameras focused on the stage for the next decade. There was a brief hiatus from 1904 to 1905 when 80 percent of all films released were documentaries or pseudodocumentaries on the Russo-Japanese War, a phenomenon predicting the Japanese government's insistence that the cinema support the war effort during the 1930s and 1940s.[66] Otherwise, early Japanese films primarily recorded scenes from a kabuki play, which gave rise to a related mixed form called rensageki (chain dramas). These were usually derived from the kabuki repertory but juxtaposed filmed scenes with live performance. The actors would, for example, run backstage as a screen was lowered and appear again onscreen as if they had run directly into the film. The appeal of rensageki was the movement from a live medium to a recorded, technologically mediated one, and the form dominated Japanese film production for twenty-five years. In fact, a poll taken in 1915 showed that a third of Japan's favorite actors worked only in rensageki.[67]

The popularity of rensageki faded after 1920, but another unique and theatrical feature of Japanese cinema still was being celebrated when Ozu made A Story of Floating Weeds: the film narrator called benshi or katsuben.[68] Similar to the chorus of noh and the narrators in kabuki and bunraku, the benshi stood or knelt to the left of the screen in full view of the audience and interpreted the film, reading or improvising dialogue for the actors on screen.[69] Celebrated benshi drew big crowds, sometimes receiving higher billing than the movie stars onscreen.[70] A Story of Floating Weeds would have been screened with a benshi interpreter in 1934, and by refusing synchronous linked sound, Ozu encouraged the benshi's art.[71] Ozu was lagging behind advances in cinematic technology, and the Japanese film industry as a whole was slower to incorporate sound than were industries in Europe and the United States, which were releasing mostly "talkies" by the end of the 1920s.[72] Sound technology arrived in Japan during the Great Depression, so it was difficult for movie theaters to raise the money needed to convert their equipment. The popularity of the benshi also delayed Japan's transition to sound. They resisted with strikes, as cleverly depicted in Takeda Rintarō's translation/adaptation of Bertolt Brecht and Kurt Weill's most famous work as Japan's Three-Penny Opera (Nihon sanmon opera, 1932). Takeda saw George W. Pabst's 1928 film version of The Three Penny Opera in 1931 and then a stage version before creating his "Azuma Abaatamento" slums in which Abaatamento #8 is occupied by a corrupt official in the striking benshi union (replacing Brecht and Weill's Beggar-King).[73]

Both benshi and the mingled cinematic and live form of rensageki are examples of how film used traditional theater for modernist innovation. If modern media like film regularly reposition art forms from the past, the same is true of modern politics. With the rise of an imperialist, promilitarist, totalitarian regime in the 1930s, the Japanese government began to celebrate rural life and theatrical traditions, reimagining popular "low" arts as national treasures and encouraging filmmakers to celebrate "Japaneseness." Kihachi's profession in country kabuki would have been of questionable repute in an earlier cultural moment, but kabuki became celebrated in the 1930s as part of the new "pure Japaneseness." Ozu may have used kabuki to avoid censorship, which intensified after the Regulation for Motion Picture Censorship Act was passed in 1925. Kinugasa Teinosuke's Nichirin (Sun) was suppressed for "blaspheming the national essence," an "unfamiliar charge" in 1926 that became common after the Manchurian and Shanghai incidents of 1931 and 1932.[74] When agrarianist militants assassinated Prime Minister Inukai Tsuyoshi on May 15, 1932, and destroyed banks, power stations, and other signs of urban capitalism in an effort to return to premodern Japan and reveal the true "spirit of the nation," the public responded sympathetically.[75] Along with aggressive militarism, a rediscovery of "Japaneseness" and traditional art forms supported the rise of fascism.

Ozu's A Story of Floating Weeds seems to invoke a village and a theatrical form that had, according to 1930s patriotism, preserved simple, traditional lifestyles. The film gives an early, fleeting nod to militarism when Kihachi points out his son's upcoming eligibility for the draft and confidence that he will be "first class." Any notion of rural purity is undermined, however, by scenes of actors drinking and courting local prostitutes. Ozu's depiction of kabuki, far from celebrating Japanese traditional arts, demonstrates the ironies of the government's newfound appreciation. When Shinkichi wants to see his father perform, Kihachi replies, "Our show isn't for you. You're a student. Your job is to study." If Kihachi's troupe did not perform for the educated, the painfully bad kabuki scene from the film reveals that the village audience is delighted with, for example, the boy-in-a-dog-suit who misses his entrance because he is (tellingly) playing with theatrical devices that mimic the sound of clapping. Ozu's camera dwells less on the show than on the actors in the wings who are scanning the audience for pretty women. The same actors ironically end up in the place of the audience watching the very different show of their theatrical properties being sold. The supposedly exalted "traditional theater" lacks financial support, since the troupe has been forced to disband and sell their props, and Kihachi manages to get barely enough money from the auction to pay his actors' train fares out of town.

A Story of Floating Weeds adopts kabuki acting styles and plot structures in a film about actors cheating on one another and going broke. The film subtly undermines kabuki's new status as a sacrosanct element of Japanese culture without indicating any preference for, or much interest in, Western art forms. A celebration of foreign art would have tipped off the Home Ministry Censorship Division, as would an overt critique of kabuki. At a moment when being a Japanese patriot meant embracing Western military technologies and imperial conquest but celebrating politically driven conscriptions of traditional arts, Ozu engaged the "Western" art of film while refusing to deal with its most recent technological development. His refusal to use cinematic sound suggests a wariness of modernist innovation to match his suspicion of tradition. Just before Ozu received his own marching orders in the military (1937–1939), A Story of Floating Weeds drifts behind the times, pauses to scratch at the new constructions of Japanese traditions and family values, and then turns its back on them along with many celebrations of modernism. His thematic, formal, and technological depictions of *being behind* appear in other films, including his 1959 remake, Floating Weeds, which offered another Kihachi who scratches less frequently but maintains the relevance of this kabuki-derived type in postwar Japan.

OZU'S QUIET SHOT AT THEATER IN LATE SPRING

> The dissolve is not an element of "film grammar" or whatever, but is simply an attribute of the camera.
> Ozu Yasujirō

The main component of Ozu's "film grammar" was a still shot of a single actor facing into a camera set at a relatively low height. Also the most common shot in *rensageki*, it positions the viewer as if in an audience facing a stage. Even as technology enabled more sophisticated camera movements, Ozu's cinematography became more still or quiet. He began to avoid fades after 1930, using only two in A Story of Floating Weeds, and he gave up dissolves at about the same time. Ozu was not stuck in the pre-cinematic aesthetics of Japanese theater, nor did he quiet his camera with the goal of creating a unique modernist style.[76] He claimed, "I always tell people I don't make anything besides *tofu*, and that is because I am strictly a *tofu*-dealer," while making his last film in 1962—just before the rise of international interest in Ozu and in eating tofu to be healthy and save the planet.[77] The staple of Ozu's "film grammar" was the visual composition created on the screen. For Ozu, cinema need not avoid images that recall theatrical effects but should give up shots that depend on the camera as a moving apparatus rather than a tool for creating visual experiences. In fact, filming theater was one means by which Ozu focused attention on the film's image rather than the attributes of cameras.

Perhaps the most famous (and longest) of Ozu's depictions of theater is the 7-minute, 40-second noh segment occupying the middle of Late Spring. Made in 1949 during the U.S. Occupation, Late Spring introduced Noriko (Hara) as the twenty-seven-year-old unmarried daughter of a widowed college professor, Somiya Shukichi (Ryū). Together, they attend a performance

FIGURE 5.4 A scene from *Kakitsubata* in Ozu's *Late Spring* (1949). (Courtesy of Shōchiku eiga, Ozu Yasujirō)

of *Kakitsubata*, a noh play in which the central performer (*shite*) is the ghost of a country girl who loved the aristocrat Narihira but is also the spirit of an iris and of Narihira himself—as a bodhisattva/enlightened teacher of poetry—in one of noh's more remarkable examples of multilayered or ideogrammic characters (figure 5.4).[78] The play's complicated plot (if that's the right word for noh) intersects ambiguously with the film's plot (perhaps not quite the right word for Ozu either), which focuses on the love between father and daughter. In the noh scene, the deep bond between Somiya and Noriko is visually reinforced by their close and parallel body positions as they sit next to each other in *seiza* in the first row of the theater. With obvious delight, Somiya follows the *utaibon* (libretto) in an approach that seems fitting for the professor but, according to Nogami Toyoichirō, runs counter to the trancelike way in which noh should be received (figure 5.5). Somiya looks up and across the audience to see the widowed Miwa Akiko (Miyake Kuniko), whom he intends to marry—or so he has allowed Noriko to believe in order to get her to marry. He correctly thinks that Noriko would not wish to disrupt their lives by leaving him alone. When Miwa, dressed in traditional kimono, meets Somiya's eyes,

FIGURE 5.5 Noriko and Somiya (with *utaibon*) in Ozu's *Late Spring* (1949). (Courtesy of Shōchiku eiga, Ozu Yasujirō)

he bows slightly. Noriko follows her father's gaze, flashes her remarkable smile, and returns his bow. Realization and intense emotion are subtly conveyed through a series of glances, with the music of noh in the background: Noriko looks back at her father, then down, to the woman again, down very deeply (during a long drum call [*kakegoe*]), back to her father, who is watching the play and smiling slightly, back to the woman, and then down once again.

Our understanding of these glances and their emotional content depends on a now familiar assumption about the meaning of film's sequential images: When a shot of Noriko looking at something is followed by a cut to an image of something else, we assume that she is looking at and responding emotionally to that person or object.[79] The noh episode in *Late Spring* juxtaposes these relatively new conventions of film interpretation with theatrical tradition in a way that encourages us to look closely at the visual experiences offered by both. The glances and bows of the film actors echo the famously spare and subtle gestures in noh, and the camera cuts between these gestures and expressions rather than panning across the audience or stage to give a godlike overview. One shot shows Noriko, Somiya, and Miwa seated in a symbolic

FIGURE 5.6 Noriko, Somiya, and Miwa in the audience of *Kakitsubata* in Ozu's *Late Spring* (1949). (Courtesy of Shōchiku eiga, Ozu Yasujirō)

triangle enabled by the configuration of the noh *kensho* (the audience's seating area) on two sides of the stage (figure 5.6). Although the noh theater is the setting for a scene of dramatic looking, the gazes of the film characters are trained on *utaibon* (book of words, lyrics) and fellow audience members as well as the performers on stage. They are, like the noh actors, performing an intense drama. But they also are sitting in an audience, as are the viewers of the film, although the noh audience kneels in a *seiza* position that mirrors the *seiza* of the onstage audience: the *waki*, chorus, and *koken* (stage hands) who kneel for long periods of the play, simply watching (figure 5.7). Ozu calls attention to many forms of looking, which may be quiet but also intensely dramatic. The noh scene suggests that the suffering of living human beings is just as worthy of attention as that of the mythic lovers and warriors depicted onstage. Our lives, like those of Ozu's characters, continue to pass and refuse to pause when we enter the traditional theater or cinema. An intermission in life might be desirable, given the "lateness" in the title of the film and the assumption that Noriko is almost too old to marry.

FIGURE 5.7 The chorus of *Kakitsubata* in Ozu's *Late Spring* (1949). (Courtesy of Shōchiku eiga, Ozu Yasujirō)

The noh play *Kakitsubata* continues in the background of these glances, yet almost eight minutes of the film are patiently given to the entire closing dance (*kiri*) of the play. This scene resonates somewhat ambivalently with the story of jealousy and loss conveyed by Noriko's gazes at Somiya and Miwa. The girl/iris/Narihira *shite* of *Kakitsubata* recalls her lost love, the "iris hedge planted next to our old home," and the "sprig of blue flag" in his hair, matching the blue of the iris.[80] The film might be using the play to suggest that Noriko loves her father with a passion like the *shite*'s, that she feels abandoned by her father, or that the contrived marriage will drive her crazy. The noh chorus describes the break of dawn and the "pale purple clouds in the East" that "herald Amida Buddha's coming" as "the pale purple iris / opens its petals toward enlightenment." The *shite* opens "the folds of her heart" like the iris and accepts the promise "All the earth will be enlightened / even the flowers and trees." If the poetry suggests that Noriko will or should open her heart and accept marriage, worldly attachments are not the ideal of noh's Buddhist ethics. Wrongfully clinging to her beloved is precisely what initially kept *Kakitsubata*'s *shite* from enlightenment. Still, an analogy is enforced in the scene when as the chorus repeats, "All the earth will be enlightened / even the flowers and trees," the camera cuts to a shot of a large tree blowing in the wind. A conventional film technique for providing an image to symbolize Noriko's turbulent feelings, this is a rare shot for Ozu, who avoided such symbolism.[81] The tree also invokes the *oi matsu* (old pine) painted on the back of every noh stage.[82]

As if the real tree has thrust them outside the theater, the next shot shows Noriko and Somiya walking down the sidewalk. He asks if she would like to have a meal with him, but she replies that she has something to do and runs down the street. A relatively rare Ozu tracking shot provides Somiya's perspective of his daughter hurrying away from him. The conclusion to the noh scene in *Late Spring* departs from the many previous still shots of Noriko and Somiya together, often positioned so that their bodies literally establish parallel lines, as when they kneel in the noh audience. They are framed in parallel postures even when it breaks the rule of eye-line matching, which states that the bodies of two people in conversation should be positioned as if they are looking at each other in each shot. When they ride the train to Tokyo together early in the film, their conversation is depicted conventionally with shots of Noriko and "reverse shots" of Somiya. But both their faces are angled to the right in a way that suggests they would actually be looking away from each other while speaking. Ozu was well aware of the "rule" of eye-line matching and claimed that he found "this 'grammar' to be farfetched" because it is clear when characters are engaged in conversation, even if they are not positioned in every close-up as if they were looking at each other.[83] Ozu's statement suggests that he was not seeking to produce a modernist "jolt" of disorientation in the spectator by breaking eye-line matches, as has been suggested by film critics.[84] Instead, he composed each shot so that actors' faces and bodies were angled in the most aesthetically pleasing way, often to parallel each other or create a "'torquing' of the figure," as occurs in the torsos of both Kihachi and Shinkichi in the fishing scene of *A Story of Floating Weeds*.[85] Ozu disturbs some assumptions about film "grammar" and suggests that the camera is more powerful when filmmakers break rules.

The post-noh tracking shot that breaks the parallel positions of Noriko and Somiya as well as Ozu's own quiet film grammar is a turning point in *Late Spring*. Noriko soon agrees to meet and then marry Satake, the man that her father and Aunt Masa have chosen. Somiya assures her that she has the right to refuse Satake (who never appears in the film), so Noriko's submission to the arranged meeting (*omiai*), despite her happiness as a single woman, is tempered by modern assertions of free will. Noriko claims to like Satake and says he looks like the American actor Gary Cooper. *Late Spring* treats both traditional and modern marriage ambivalently. Noriko's friend Aya (Tsukioka Yumeji) is happily divorced, and they enjoy making fun of married school-mates. The film contains many representations of traditional Japanese cul-ture, and as with the noh scene, they are integrated into modern life. Noriko and Somiya attend noh in modern dress, although Miwa wears a kimono. The tea ceremony that opens the film is more a social event than a ritual for Noriko, Miwa, and Aunt Masa. Noriko's and Somiya's visit to Kyoto's ancient temple Kodaiji and the rock gardens of Ryōanji is the setting for Noriko to revise her opinion that remarriage is "filthy" and for Somiya to confess his regret that a father must marry off a daughter but feels "let down" when he succeeds. It is this "rule" that remains intact and that breaks the hearts of father and daughter, even though the daughter might eventually find happi-ness in her marriage. Neither Japanese tradition nor modernity is precisely re-sponsible, but one little family has been torn apart. In the last scene, Somiya is kneeling at home alone, gazing into the distance, and peeling an apple.

Late Spring does not take a side in debates about traditionalism versus modernization or East versus West, and other critics in Ozu's period explic-itly argued that these binary categories needed to be dropped. The literary critic Kobayashi Hideo (1902–1983) claimed in 1933 that unlike the "previous generation, for whom the struggle between East and West figured crucially in their artistic activity," his generation had already lost a feeling for "cultural singularity" and was unable to recognize "Western influence" anymore.[86] Similarly, Katsumoto claimed, in the same year that Ozu made *A Story of Float-ing Weeds* (1936), that the Western influence on Japanese film is a "moot ques-tion" because film creates images for stories from Japanese feudal times and contemporary novels.[87] Katsumoto and Kobayashi focus on the connections between Japan's feudal period and popular modernity, the ways in which the idea of the "everyday" and the "modern" are composed of layers of time.

The past and present, everyday life and traditional art, are intercut in *Late Spring* as Noriko glances at the noh stage, at her father who gazes at an *utaibon*, at her father's presumed love interest, and down as if into her own body. The postwar occupying forces do not seem to be part of the world created by these glances. The film only subtly invokes the ongoing occupation, principally in a famous scene of Noriko and her father's assistant Hattori Shoichi (Usami Jun) biking past an advertisement for Coca-Cola and an English sign, presumably for the military troops, warning that the bridge's weight capacity is thirty tons. Ozu's general silence might be a response to the restrictions placed on the film industry by the U.S. Occupation, just as *A Story of Floating Weeds* quietly sidestepped the censorship of a rapidly militarizing Japan. Film directors were forced to submit screenplays to the U.S. authorities, who scrubbed material that promoted Japanese nationalism and militarization or criticized the Occupation and American culture.[88] Given the restrictions, Noriko's arranged marriage must not have seemed *too arranged*, or the censors might have banned the film for undermining "the importance of the individual," a value they hoped to import to Japan.[89] The censors did cut Noriko's plan to visit her dead mother's grave in Kyoto as an example of dangerous "ancestor worship."[90] They also cut a line about postwar Tokyo being "ruined," and the final script compares "peaceful" Kyoto with "dusty" Tokyo.[91] The detail that Noriko's health was negatively affected by "her work after being conscripted by the [Japanese] Navy during the war" was changed to "forced work during the war."[92] It is impossible to know why "forced work" was more acceptable than "conscription" or why the censors approved of representing wartime suffering as long as the navy was not mentioned. The scene from the noh play *Kakitsubata*, the gorgeous temples and rock gardens of Kyoto, and other references to traditional Japanese life and culture remained in the final version. It may be that the U.S. censors did not understand their significance or the ways in which Japanese traditional arts had been used to support nationalism and militarization in the 1930s.

During my first visit to Japan in 2005, I discovered noh and fell in love with Kyoto. I noticed that Kyoto's ancient temples and gardens like Kodaiji, Kiyomizudera, and Ryōanji (where Noriko and Somiya visit on their last trip before her wedding) had survived, whereas the shrines of Tokyo and other cities were destroyed by the war. The American art historian Langdon Warner is credited with persuading the U.S. military not to bomb Kyoto, owing to the beauty and religious and cultural significance of city's treasures. Toward the end of my two-week tour, when I visited Hiroshima's Peace Memorial Museum near the hypocenter of the nuclear bomb that the United States detonated on August 6, 1945, I read the letters listing Kyoto among the cities removed from the general air-raid list and placed on a list of potential targets for the atomic bomb. The Manhattan Project's "Target Committee" was advised that given the U.S. Air Force's rate of attack, it would "complete strategic bombing of Japan by 1 Jan 46 so availability of future [A-bomb] targets will be a problem."[93] Kyoto was saved from air strikes, not to preserve its cultural treasures, but so that it could later register the full impact of the atomic bomb . . . that fell elsewhere.

AT THE [POSTWAR] HAWK'S WELL

Hawk's Well had a surprising, even conciliatory, postwar turn on the various stages of the old and new Japan that Ozu documented so beautifully in *Late Spring*. Itō's tours with the play introduced *Hawk's Well* to *shingeki* and the little theater movement before the war. After his repatriation, he opened his dance institute, the Domonkai, near Tokyo and taught versions of *Hawk's Well* to dancers at the school. Itō's celebrated student Maki Ryūko became the director of his Domonkai after his death in 1961 and danced the Guardian's role in a 1962 Tokyo production celebrating her teacher's contribution to arts in Japan.[94] *Hawk's Well* also influenced the so-called traditional noh theater. Yokomichi Mario adapted it twice in collaborations with the two most celebrated noh performers of the postwar period, Kita Minoru and Kanze Hisao.

In 1949, the year that Ozu released *Late Spring*, Kita Minoru performed in Yokomichi's first adaptation, *Taka no izumi* (*Hawk's Well*), which generally adhered to noh literary and performance techniques. Still, the production challenged noh institutions, particularly the desired if not exactly accurate tradition that the repertory was fixed during the Edo period (1600–1867) and should not be altered. *Taka no izumi* was also a reparative gesture, given that it adapted an Anglo-Irish text (Ireland was officially neutral during the war but lent significant support to Japan's enemies) for a play staged during the U.S. Occupation as a memorial to Yokomichi's friend who was killed in the war.[95] Yokomichi transformed the Young Man of *Hawk's Well* into Kooburin, who functions like a *waki* in that he is a traveler who encounters the spirit of an Old Man on a remote and mountainous island. To reconstruct the Old Man from Yeats's play as the *shite* (central character), Yokomichi gave him part of the Young Man's original role. The Old Man tells the story of a youthful adventurer who once sought a fountain of eternal youth and then, before he disappears into the mountain, reveals that he himself is the spirit of that young man. In the second act, the *shite* reappears as the Ghost of the Fountain and dances out his pain at being bound to the fountain. The *kyōgen* between the two acts is replaced by the dance of the Hawk Woman, the one fairly unnoh-like aspect of *Taka no izumi*. While Yokomichi was subject to some criticism for this and other choices, his own prestige and the collaboration of Kita

Minoru made the work famous in noh history, although it is not regularly performed today.[96]

Yokomichi significantly reimagined *Taka no izumi* and Yeats's *Hawk's Well* in *Takahime* (*Hawk Princess*), his 1967 readaptation with choreography and music by Kanze Hisao, who also played the Hawk Princess. Cuchulain, as "Kufurin, a young prince of the Land of Persia" (originally performed by Mansaku Nomura), sails a "small sail boat" in search of a "spring" from which "Flows water of eternal life."[97] Yokomichi "Orientalized" the Celtic Cuchulain as a Persian prince and gave him a journey from the Middle to the Far East to find the sacred well. Yeats's Musicians are transformed into a chorus of six Rocks who are given to lamentations ("Oh, pathetic young man. . . . Oh, terror! Oh, woe!") and dance rather than remaining kneeling stage left, as a noh chorus would.[98] They appear in the list of dramatic personae as "the rocks themselves, not their spirits," and the distinction between an object and its spirit is crucial to the play's surprising message about the old myth of the "water of eternal life": Immortality is the torture of being held in thrall to the spirits of things.

The opening of *Takahime* follows Yeats's *Hawk's Well* as the Rock chorus describes the Old Man (originally played by another famous actor, Kanze Hideo) approaching the spring and building a fire: "Look, the Old Man comes climbing up!" Kufurin and the Old Man hear the cry of a hawk, the Maiden begins to quiver, and Kufurin asks if she cries with "the voice of the hawk" (a quote from Yeats's text). The Old Man responds, "This Maiden herself is the hawk. / the princess of hawks is she, / The mountain's very soul." The Hawk Princess's dance is a battle with Kufurin rather than Yeats's dance of possession, and the contest "exhausts [Kufurin's] strength," putting him to sleep. Just as Yeats's Musicians claim that Cuchulain "might have lived at his ease, / An old dog's head on his knees, / Among his children and friends," the Rocks suggest that Kufurin will be punished for seeking to take the sacred well of another land rather than being "content" with a simple mortal life: "Had thou but been content, with friends, / Blissful would thy life have been!"

Takahime's first act reveals Kufurin's desires to conquer and take another people's magic or treasure, and the second act warns of how such pursuits will be punished. The Old Man is dressed in the regalia of the *shite* behind the Hawk Princess's thronelike platform while she fights with Kufurin. At the end of the dance battle, the Hawk Princess leans over the edge of the stage, appears to take the well's magic water into her fan, performs a lively dance, and then carries it offstage. The Old Man is revealed to be the Ghost of one who, like Kufurin, attempted to possess the well and is now suffering "the pain of separation from the hawk's spring." His "soul and body" have been "tied securely" to that "place" until he becomes the "mountain's soul." He is forced to "fight with storms in treetops" and performs these battles with the forces of nature in a "violent" and anxious dance called a *tachimawari*. At the end of the dance, the Old Man/Ghost touches Kufurin with his staff in an initiation ritual that also passes the Old Man's curse to Kufurin, who then takes his place on the Maiden's perch. Kufurin is initiated, not into a life of heroic battle, but into a battle with nature that constitutes a form of purgatorial waiting. In Yeats's play supporting a version of Irish nationalism, Cuchulain becomes a legendary warrior who will eventually die from battle wounds but be commemorated in myth, as well as in Yeats's last play, *The Death of Cuchulain* (1939). Yokomichi's response to Yeats's version of mythic Irish nationalism in postwar and post-Occupation Japan concludes with an eternal deathlessness rather than eternal life. *Takahime* gives *Hawk's Well* a rather dark return to noh, indicating that to become a national myth, like Yeats's Cuchulain, is to face a form of eternal suffering. Even a nationalism rooted in mythic wells and legendary battles is dangerous. *Takahime* is still quite frequently performed in Japan and abroad. Tokyo's *Theatre Year-Book* notes the history of international *Hawk's Well* tours and reports favorably on performances of *Taka no izumi*, *Takahime*, and other adaptations from the 1980s to the present.[99]

The next turn of *Hawk's Well* in Japan is a tangle of noh, modern *shingeki* performance, and English-language theater.[100] Itō Michio's brother Senda Koreya, who had first performed in *Hawk's Well* in 1940 with Itō Michio and other family members, produced yet another version of the play in the mid-1980s in a small Tokyo theater called Studio 200. In the audience was an American student of noh music and performance, Richard Emmert, who was interested in developing what he later called "English noh."[101] Emmert's introduction to noh occurred somewhat improbably when, as a student at Earlham College (Indiana) in 1970, he performed the *shite* role in a noh-inspired play entitled *St. Francis*, written and directed by Arthur Little with music by Leonard Holvik.[102] This production, which still would be unusual in the American Midwest, prompted Emmert's interest in studying noh in Japan (where he subsequently built his career) and in the possibility of performing noh in translation. He served as the musical director of a version of *St. Francis* staged in Tokyo in 1975 but described the composition as an attempt "to suggest nō music rather than follow strictly its traditional melodic and rhythmic structures."[103]

Emmert's first serious effort to compose noh music for an English text came in 1981 when Jonah Salz, the U.S.-born director of NOHO Theatre Group in Kyoto, invited him to compose music for another version of *Hawk's Well*. Salz, currently a professor of comparative theater at Ryūkoku University in Kyoto, was inspired by Leonard Pronko's foundational book *Theatre East and West* (1964) to establish NOHO with Shigeyama Akira, a *kyōgen* actor from the important Shigeyama family in Kyoto. Their goal was to produce a "vital fusion" of "traditional Japanese theatre techniques" and "Western themes and plays."[104] Using Yeats's text, Emmert worked to produce a score that was as noh-like as possible to be performed by professional drummers, who might have balked at completely new drum patterns. Emmert also composed and performed a flute score for the sold-out NOHO performances in Kyoto and Osaka. A revival the following year in Tokyo at the Umewaka Noh Theatre (named for the family of Ernest Fenollosa's teacher) used more traditional noh *kata* for the actors' movements.[105]

Emmert is less interested in the "fusions" of theatrical conventions, performance techniques, and dramatic texts that continue to characterize NOHO's work with, for example, Samuel Beckett's plays, as I describe in chapter 6.[106] Instead, he has committed himself to creating "English noh," which includes translating plays from the noh repertory, but he is most interested in presenting original works in English that follow noh's typical *shodan* (building block) structure. His productions tend to use standard musical patterns and instruments and rely on the choreographic forms (*kata*) and other elements of noh acting technique. To call any production "noh," according to Emmert, it must at the very least use the vocal and physical performance techniques of the noh theater. The "essence" of noh, he claims, lies in "what the actor does with his voice and his body. . . . In a sense, it's the training." In order to reach his goals for English noh, Emmert needed to train English speaking performers in the techniques of *utai* (chant) and *shimai* (dance). He therefore spent the 1990s teaching performers, musicians, and writers, launching the Noh Training Project (NTP) in Tokyo in 1991 and then in Bloomsburg, Pennsylvania, in 1995, as a three-week summer intensive workshop.[107]

Emmert's emphasis on training aligns with the importance of "the lesson" in noh tradition, although he and his collaborators at NTP have adapted the standard pedagogy for their students. The private chant session has been replaced by a group *utai* at the beginning of each day. Whereas students of noh in Japan usually practice movement techniques and *shimai* in the context of learning the repertory, beginners at NTP learn the basic posture, kamae, and common kata such as shikake-hiraki (forward point then opening) in technique classes. After these introductory sessions, NTP follows the repertory driven parrot-repetition (ōmugaeshi) method. Students work one-on-one and follow behind the master teacher, who demonstrates the movements for a particular dance from one of the plays while other students watch the lesson and chant for the chorus. Emmert recognizes that there is no replacement for the noh system's years of intensive training, usually beginning in childhood—or even the intense training he had as a graduate student in Tokyo when he was taking two to four lessons daily and studying all the instruments as well as chanting and dancing.[108] By 2002, Emmert felt that he had a sufficiently well-trained group of students in his workshops to launch a performing company, Theatre Nohgaku. Their first tour featured yet another version of At the Hawk's Well performed in seven different venues.

Theatre Nohgaku's Hawk's Well uses noh movement and vocal techniques, and the score Emmert produced relies on standard drum patterns for the ōtsuzumi, kotsuzumi, and taiko.[109] The nōkan flute blends traditional melodies with innovations, as when it creates the bird cries that Yeats indicated in his stage directions. Theatre Nohgaku does not unfold a cloth with a hawk pattern at the opening and closing of the play, but the setting does include three hanging cloths with plantlike markings designed by Nick Troisi, which invoke the pine tree (oi matsu) painted on the back of the noh stage. The Old Man dances the first shimai with a staff rather than a fan as he describes his experience waiting by the well ("I came like you when young in body and in mind . . ."). The Young Man/Cuchulain dances a second shimai with a long naginata blade after the Hawk's cry prompts him to describe how he drove off a stunning hawk with his sword as he climbed to the well.

The culminating instrumental dance (mai) of the possessed Guardian/Hawk Girl was created and performed by Matsui Akira, a student of Kita Minoru, the famous actor who worked with Yokomichi Mario on Taka no izumi in 1949. Matsui is a traditionally trained shite and full-ranked performer (hokubun) of the Kita school, but he has performed in many nontraditional and experimental productions around the world as he works to disseminate noh and demonstrate its relevance to contemporary performance. He was designated as an "intangible cultural property holder" (mukei bunkazai sōgō shitei) by the Japanese government in 1998.[110] The dance he created for the Guardian uses noh kata, particularly the sliding suriashi step in circular floor patterns, stamping, and ōzayū (zigzag steps displaying the sleeves/wings of the costume). Matsui executed these noh movements while maintaining a kamae posture that was adapted to appear more birdlike, with his arms held behind his back like folded wings. He also choreographed what he calls "new kata," including winglike motions with the arms, deep pliés recalling the perched position of a hawk, and movements with the feet that suggest a bird hopping or dipping a foot into the well.[111] The noh technique gives the birdlike movements a restrained intensity that is appropriately mysterious and haunting. Matsui's choreography for the Guardian of the Well's dance of possession turns the role that Itō Michio originally performed back toward noh, but it also adapts some of the modern dance techniques that Itō introduced to Japan.

Matsui gained an international reputation as a performer yet struggled to make his way into the full hokubun rank of the Kita school, partly because he has been at odds with the iemoto during some phases of his career. Emmert, also part of the Kita school, had more freedom for innovation because he was a foreigner. Both Emmert's flute and taiko teachers had been involved in the original creation of Takahime, and like other masters who had been innovators as young men, they were supportive of Emmert's efforts to develop English noh. One reason that Emmert chose Hawk's Well for the first Theatre Nohgaku performance was that he was interested in the unique transnational history of the play, citing Yeats's original collaboration with Itō, Yokomichi's work, and recent performances of Takahime. For Emmert, "Hawk's Well was and still is the most important play by a non-Japanese playwright to be translated and adapted as a noh play." The production of Takahime by the Tessenkai group of the Kanze school influenced Emmert's Hawk's Well, particularly his decision to make Yeats's Four Musicians into a chorus that moves with noh-style kata rather than kneeling throughout the play as a typical noh chorus would do. Emmert appreciates Hawk's Well but insists that Yeats "didn't know that much about noh" and was mainly "fascinated by the noh as text" rather than performance. Hawk's Well is not structured like a noh play in shōdan sections, nor does it provide precise corollaries for the shite and waki roles. Critics have variously claimed that the Old Man, Young Man, and Guardian are the main characters in Hawk's Well, but Emmert insists it's not useful to argue over role types that Yeats did not understand. Emmert believes he is "correcting some of Yeats's errors," as Theatre Nohgaku produces contemporary plays in English that follow noh forms and conventions more precisely. For that goal, Theatre Nohgaku needs playwrights who understand both noh structure and performance technique, so Writers' Workshops were added to the series of lessons in 2003, followed by Advanced Writers' Workshops, Costume Workshops, and Music Workshops.[112]

I attended the Noh Writers' Workshop in Tokyo in 2010 and the Advanced Writers' Workshop in 2011 at Rogue River Noh Center in Grand Rapids, Michigan, both taught by the former Hōshō school professional and playwright-composer David Crandall.[113] I realized how much I needed the costume workshop when Theatre Nohgaku members Jubilith Moore, Elizabeth Dowd, and Joyce Lim patiently dressed me in the formal Japanese attire called *montsuki* for a lecture-demonstration that Crandall led at Boston University on November 11, 2014. He presented an exciting scene from the noh play *Ama* (*The Diver*) known as *Tama-no-dan* (*Scene of the Jewel*) in Japanese and then in his own English translation and arrangement before dancing the piece a second time in Japanese. *Tama-no-dan* reenacts the story of a woman diver who sacrifices her life to retrieve a jewel from the Dragon King's undersea palace in order to ensure her son's recognition as Lord Tankai's heir. We hoped the sequence of performances in Japanese then English and Japanese again would help our audience think about the translation of languages, performance practices, and ways of knowing or understanding. My graduate students from Modernist Exoticisms reported that although they could understand the dramatic, suicidal story when the scene was performed in English, they also were interested in the emotional valences enabled by their disorientation during the first performance of the piece in Japanese. They experienced what Nogami Toyoichirō celebrated as the wonder and bewilderment of the foreigner in his noh translation theory. This mode of reception is foreclosed by those who, like Ozu's Professor Somiya, follow the *utaibon* during a noh performance. It is undoubtedly the experience of exoticism, valued by Nogami and my students alike, that also contributed to my own initial interest in taking noh lessons. Our desires to experience exotic incomprehension, like submission, are no less powerful for being among the desires we celebrate least.

Our program at the lecture-demonstration also included the Old Man's *shimai* from Theatre Nohgaku's *At the Hawk's Well* and a scene from *Sumidagawa* (*Sumida River*) translated into English by Emmert for a performance with Benjamin Britten and William Plomer's *Curlew River* in November 2015. As I prepared my introduction for the lecture-demonstration, I realized that I was not satisfied with calling aspects of Theatre Nohgaku's work "English noh." That term might suggest that noh, or any theater tradition, could actually be translated to give us English, German, French, or Japanese noh (to name the languages I confronted while writing this book). Nor am I quite satisfied with "fusion" (makes me think of heating, melting, and nuclear technology as well as fusion food), "inter- or trans-national" (too much emphasis on the nation), "inter- or trans-cultural" (is there a between, beyond, or outside culture?), "world" theater (everything is in the world), or any of the other terms commonly used. Whatever we call it, the possibility of a noh-inspired performance art in English, a possibility that inflamed so many modernist theater artists, is still producing work that is interesting and often quite . . . tiring.

Elizabeth Dowd brilliantly introduced the recital at the end of my first Noh Training Project by quoting a phrase her teacher had used—and that I later heard from my own Furukawa sensei when I asked if he was troubled by so many sleeping in the audience at his play: "If they are sleeping, it's going well." If they are sleeping, they are not reading the *utaibon* or even celebrating their wonder or bewilderment. I tend to reject claims of an "essence of noh," particularly when that essence is associated with an exoticism that ignores commonalities and historical change. But I am certain that any noh-inspired performance art must emphasize training, both its exhaustive and exhausting aspects. If I could believe in an essence, perhaps a distinct one created by any individual in his or her particular experience of noh, it could be rooted only in noh lessons and pedagogies. My lessons have changed the way I understand all performance in the world.

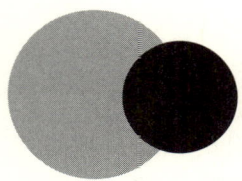

6. TROUBLE WITH TITLES AND DIRECTORS

Benjamin Britten and William Plomer's *Curlew River* and Samuel Beckett's *Footfalls/Pas*

PLOMER TO BRITTEN: I have been brooding over the matter of the title [. . .].
The River is indeed important. I think *The Other Side of the River* a little too
long, & believe a shorter title can be as effective & exact, & easier to remember & to say. I shouldn't like *Across the River*, partly because a bad late novel by
Hemmingway was called *Across the River and Into the Trees*. What do you think
of the possibilities of *Over the River* or *Beyond the River*? Of these I prefer *Over
the River*. . . . seems to me simple euphonious & relevant, though I suppose
it could be thought rather unexciting & impersonal: but then Sumidagawa is
plain & impersonal. (October 26, 1963)

BRITTEN TO PLOMER: I was still very drawn towards the Nō, too close for
comfort [. . .]. Oddly enough, as the work progressed the *Curlew* grew in
significance; & my inclination is to go back to Curlew River as a title!! Colin
(whc is here now) agrees, & Peter not wholly. (February 15, 1964)

Letters in the Britten–Pears Foundation Archives and Library

TITLES ARE TOUGH. WHEN I ARRIVED AT LEARNING TO KNEEL,
it felt like the perfect title but one that would require a very scholarly subtitle.
I brainstormed half a dozen, including the exhausting *Noh, Modernism, and the
Pedagogies of Transnational Performance*. Near the end of revising, I decided to
drop the subtitle altogether. Then my fantastic editor advised me that readers would appreciate some guide to what the book was about and might even
"think it has something to do with religion." So I submitted to another round
of subtitle brainstorming. In this final chapter, I consider two works that
have a lot to do with religion and that underwent multiple revisions based on
the complex relationships of writers, editors, directors, other collaborators,
and theatrical managers. Exploring Britten and Plomer's *Curlew River* alongside Beckett's *Footfalls/Pas* demonstrates the influence of noh-inspired performance and submissive subjects beyond the typical parameters of modernism
and into two later trajectories of performance.

Throughout the eight years of their collaboration on the piece (1956–1964), Benjamin Britten, to some people the most famous British composer of the twentieth century, and the overlooked South African–born writer William Plomer struggled to find a name for the noh-derived church parable they ultimately called *Curlew River*. Their title troubles were linked to their complicated desire for and concerns about gender drag and cultural appropriation: How could they enable Britten's partner, the tenor Sir Peter Pears, to play a tragic female character without the comedic function associated with drag in postwar Britain and still today, or without bursting the open secret of their sexualities? And how "Japanesy" (Britten's term) should they make the production based on the noh play *Sumidagawa*? Noh's influence on the score, libretto, and dramaturgy was both a solution and a problem for the collaborators, who ultimately produced a compromise that drew on elements of the medieval European mystery play as well as noh. The original producer and director of *Curlew River*, Colin Graham, adapted performance conventions from these ancient forms of theater, including stylized gestures and masks that, unlike noh, covered only half the face, in order to allow the vocalists to project their voices.[1] The collaborators—Britten, Plomer, Pears, and Graham—combined ancient performance styles with music that featured a very modernist, semi-improvisational polyphony. Britten, inspired by noh, did away with the conductor and invented a "curlew sign" that allowed vocalists and instrumentalists a flexibility of coordination before bringing them back together at the sign in the score, without the oversight of the conductor.

It might seem surprising that Britten, who famously demanded a good deal of control over productions of his operas and frequently conducted the "definitive" recordings of his own works, would cede so much power to a "curlew sign." Beckett is even more famous for directing the "authoritative" productions of his plays and refusing to allow other directors to depart from his vision, although it's difficult to weigh the multiple albums of the "Britten Conducts Britten" series against the "Beckett Directs Beckett" recording project.[2] In this chapter, I discuss Britten and Plomer's church parable in gender and racial drag alongside Samuel Beckett's *Footfalls*, which he translated somewhat surprisingly as *Pas* (*Step*) in his French version of the play. Along with other late short plays about (old) women, *Footfalls* has been criticized by feminists for not staging inspiring forms of agency for women and for dismissing female power from the stage. This critique is part of a larger indictment of Beckett as a tyrannical director who hurt his women actors and even enjoyed staging the spectacle of female pain. The implication is that the women who performed in Beckett's late plays submitted to the GREAT MAN and his sadism because they failed to recognize they were undermining their own (equated to feminism's) interests, powers, and pleasures.

Learning to Kneel has used the example of noh training to suggest that submission is a crucial aspect of our lives and desires, particularly when that submission is part of the commitment to studying a craft, art form, tradition— basically anything that involves learning anything from a teacher. I read *Footfalls/Pas* as a dance play that, influenced by Yeats's *At the Hawk's Well*, demonstrates how noh-like representational strategies helped dramatists through the end of the century trouble assumptions about agency and individualism. *Footfalls/Pas* stages the operations of bodily and emotional obedience to familial responsibilities, religion, the passage of time, and even a director-figure. Both *Curlew River* and *Footfalls* reveal the tortures, pleasures, and creativity involved in forms of artistic and religious submission.

TITLES ARE A DRAG

Britten, Plomer, and Graham's *Curlew River* brought gender drag into the premiere at Orford Church as it self-consciously appropriated noh and medieval mystery plays to feature Pears as a deranged mother searching for her stolen child. She learns that her son has died and, through the miraculous appearance of his ghost, experiences a very conventional religious renewal that involves submission to divine purpose and prayer. The plot, setting, and title of the piece originally adhered quite closely to the noh play *Sumidagawa* (*Sumida River*) by Motomasa Jurō. Britten and Pears had first seen *Sumidagawa* on February 11 in Tokyo, with the role of the mother performed by Umewaka Takehisa, a *shite* actor from the same school as Ernest Fenollosa's teacher, Umewaka Minoru; they saw *Sumidagawa* again a week later and obtained a tape recording of the music.[3] Britten, Plomer, Graham, and Pears ultimately moved away from *Sumidagawa* and noh conventions to create a form they called "a parable for church performance." It took the collaborators a good deal of compromise and negotiation—with one another and with orientalist, Christian, and modernist ideas—to arrive at *Curlew River*.

Britten claimed in his foreword to the score of *Curlew River* that "there was no question in any case of a pastiche from the ancient Japanese."[4] Plomer similarly wrote that neither they "nor anybody else would want a pastiche of a Nō play, a piece of *japonaiserie*."[5] They actually wondered how much they should follow the "ancient Japanese" *Sumidagawa* and just what would constitute a "pastiche" for years. When Britten and Pears toured Asia in 1956, Plomer recommended that they see noh, which had fascinated Plomer when he lived in Japan from October 1926 until March 1929, a period that also inspired his novel *Sado* (1931). His first publication to address homosexual love, the novel was produced by Leonard and Virginia Woolf's Hogarth Press, the publisher of so many volumes crucial to modernism. In *Sado*, Plomer mentions Mary Stopes, the first translator of *Sumidagawa* into English: "'I do not think that Dr. Stopes is altogether a noble woman,' said Moroi, 'although she has helped to translate some Japanese No plays. But she has a wonderful idea. Perhaps it would have been better if she had been a man, with an idea like that.'"[6]

Thirty-seven years later, Plomer's program note for the church parables described his having been "enchanted" by noh plays and also his many reservations when Britten asked him to develop a libretto for an operetta based on *Sumidagawa*:

> As the original depended entirely upon its *mise en scène*, archaic music, all-male cast and rigidly formal production down to the last detail of masks, costume and movement, it was hardly transferable to the Western operatic stage. What was more, the language and action of the play belonged to an antique Buddhist culture and could only be properly appreciated by highly cultivated Japanese traditionalists. But, like the poets Yeats and Waley (neither of whom ever visited Japan), Britten had been enchanted by the Nō, as I had been enchanted before him, so what was the good of protesting?[7]

Plomer publicly connected his work to that of William Butler Yeats and Arthur Waley, suggesting that he was aware of Yeats's *At the Hawk's Well* and other plays for dancers. He also implied that because they had visited Japan, his and Britten's "enchantment" was somewhat more authentic or justified than that of their predecessors. They had witnessed noh in "formal production," including what he interpreted as rigid stage conventions, perhaps not recognizing the lack of flexibility in much Western opera, including Britten's. Plomer's description of noh's "all-male cast," combined with the reference to Stopes as a noh translator who should have been a man, indicates that Plomer may have been interested in noh's links to an austere, restrained version of masculinity. He privately discussed with Britten the precedent of Marie Stopes's *The Sumida River*, which was used as a libretto for a one-act opera by Clarence Raybould in 1916. Plomer suggested that "the difficulties of translating *utai* [chants] into English verse" had a "tonic effect on her style, which otherwise was apt to err on the side of over-exuberance and lack of restraint" (October 7, 1958, BPFAL).[8]

Even if Japanese *utai* restrained Stopes's (presumably) feminine style, Plomer bypassed her translation and based the first version of the libretto on an English translation by the Japanese Classics Translation Committee and published in 1955 by the Nippon gakujutsu shinkōkai. He described the piece to Britten as "good and recent, & the work of an imposing committee" (July 16, 1957, BPFAL). This "imposing" "Special Noh Committee" included Nogami Toyoichirō, whose *Rebirth of Noh* (1935) had discussed the value of "Noh in English Translation" and the wonder of the amateur twenty years earlier. Plomer secured the noh translation that would have fulfilled Pound's aspirations for a great canon of translation: "Literature belongs to no one man, and translations of great works ought perhaps to be made by a committee."[9]

Plomer's and Britten's early letters referred to their project by the Japanese title *Sumidagawa*, and Plomer listed the advantages of not translating names: "As my mind begins to run on Sumida River, I feel less inclined to shy at Japanese names and place-names. It may be that some of them will be just as useful to you musically as 'Namu Amida' & c." (October 2, 1958, BPFAL). Britten responded, "I am very keen on as many nice evocative Japanese words as possible!" (October 8, 1958, BPFAL). Plomer was concerned that the singers respect the rules for Japanese pronunciation and wrote to Britten, "As you know, in Japanese all goes by syllables, and each syllable is, in theory, of equal weight, so, if Japanese words are to be sung or spoken it is better that they should be rather formally enunciated than slurred or falsely accented. E. g. we ought to have, as nearly as possible: Mi-ya-ko, not Miya'ko" (October 2, 1958, BPFAL). Plomer acknowledged that quickly chanted syllables can feel accented—and that he had read Pound's work on noh—when he wrote, "So *shite*, as Ezra Pound so delicately tells us, can seem to sound like *shtay*" (October 2, 1958, BPFAL).

Britten declared that he was very "excited" by Plomer's first draft with its "evocative Japanese words": "The more I think of it, the more I feel we should stick as far as possible to the original style & look of it—but oh, to find some equivalent to those extraordinary noises the Japanese musicians made!" (October 16, 1958, BPFAL). Britten believed they could approximate the acting style and staging of noh but certainly not the instruments or *utai*, and he was not even convinced he could find "equivalent" musical effects. Five months later, Britten changed his mind about the "style & look." He was concerned that the play would "seem a *pastiche* of a Noh play"—the first use of a word that appeared again when both Britten and Plomer claimed they had never even considered a "pastiche from the ancient Japanese" (April 15, 1959, BPFAL). Britten thought that the libretto and noh performance style might tempt him to write "Japanesy music" and that the mask would be a "colossal problem for the singer." But without the noh setting and style there was, he worried, "no very good reason for Peter to do a female part" (April 15, 1959, BPFAL).

Britten asked Plomer to consider "making it a *Christian* work" and offered the alternative setting "in pre-conquest East Anglia" as a "Mediaeval mystery play" (April 15, 1959, italics in original). Britten suggested that "if we made it Mediaeval, or possibly earlier, it would be accurate that no women should be used; also if the style were kept very artificial, very influenced by the Noh, then it wouldn't seem so odd for a woman to be played by a man, especially if the dresses were very carefully & strongly designed" (April 15, 1959, BPFAL). Britten's interest in "Mediaeval mystery plays" was ignited in part by the success of Noah Greenberg's staging in 1958 of the eleventh-century liturgical drama *The Play of Daniel*, with narration by Britten's former collaborator and friend, the poet W. H. Auden, dressed in monk's garb.[10] This production served as a precedent, perhaps with queer as well as medieval associations, when Britten and Plomer wished to cast Pears as a grieving mother in an all-male cast, though without presenting a humorous or "odd" performance. They debated whether audiences would accept the cross-gender role if Pears were playing a monk depicting a woman, as if in an early modern mystery play, or playing a noh actor in the conventions of the Japanese theater. That is, would gender drag combined with a historical European theatrical form or with that of another culture provide the more "accepted style"? (April 15, 1959, BPFAL).

Plomer agreed that the piece as he had previously conceived it would have turned into a "pasticcio grosso" and resigned himself to, as he put it, "setting fire to your—and indeed my—kimono" (April 7, 1959, BPFAL). He was still worried that "however formalized such a version might be, it might seem odd for the mother to be a man" (April 7, 1959, BPFAL). He agreed to try to rewrite a hybrid form, "Christianizing and Eastanglicizing" the libretto while maintaining the noh "style" of action and the basic plot of *Sumidagawa*. As he worked, he reported, "My own feeling is that the pathos is more intense than before: with your music it might well attain a sort of clarity & intensity of quite a new kind. In working over what I have written, I have found the magic of the situation—or plot, if one can call it that, undiminished" (August 8, 1959, BPFAL).

The collaborators began to use the title "The River" (November 23, 1959), then "Curlew River" (August 4, 1960), "The Woman on the Ferry Boat" (September 7, 1963), "The Other Side of the River" (October 23, 1963), and continued to search for the "right preposition to go with that River" over several letters (November 7, 1963, BPFAL). "Across the River" reminded Plomer of "a bad late novel by Hemmingway," but "Beyond the River" or "Over"? That seemed "simple euphonious & relevant" (November 26, 1963, BPFAL). Britten finally arrived at *Curlew River* or, rather, returned to *Curlew River* (since the title had been mentioned four years earlier) while he was composing the music (February 15, 1964, BPFAL). The subtitle also was a challenge for the collaborators, as Britten replaced his first idea, *The Monk's Play*, with *A Parable for Church Performance* two months later (April 2, 1964, BPFAL). Plomer celebrated the parable as "an earthly story with a heavenly meaning," confirming that there remained not "the least suggestion of false Japonaiserie" (April 5, 1964, BPFAL).

I have belabored Britten's and Plomer's search for titles because it provides evidence of the collaborators' negotiations as they ambivalently and quite self-consciously negotiated with orientalist and Christian attitudes and discourses. In transposing the basic plot of *Sumidagawa* into a medieval church drama, Britten and Plomer avoided a "pastiche" of noh and appeared to be more sensitive to cultural appropriation than had Yeats, Pound, Brecht, and even Itō. Of course, the personal letters tell a slightly different story: Plomer's reference to setting a kimono on fire is a dismissive exoticism probably intended for humor that does not exactly reflect his general respect for Japanese culture. Britten conveys a somewhat flippant Christian commitment when he claims that if they "set it in pre-conquest East Anglia (where there were Shrines galore)," a man could play a woman character (April 15, 1959).[11] Even with the new setting, they worried about the drag through the premiere on June 13, 1964, when a big storm cut the power to the great Orford Church. Keith Grant, the general manager of the English Opera Group (from 1962 to 1973), recalled, 'Ben was very conscious of the fact that he was pushing the boat out in a new direction, and he was worried about the reception that Peter might get in a drag part, so we were all strung up like fiddle-strings. And then suddenly this bathos, when the lights went out."[12] I can imagine the homophobic preaching of divine intervention as a storm threw darkness over a drag performance in a church.

The concerns about drag shared by all of those involved in the original production of *Curlew River* might seem unfounded given the long tradition of cross-dressing in opera, most commonly when a female character dons men's clothing in the "breeches role." Britten and Pears also had previously created a famous countertenor role, in which a man sings in the vocal ranges typically assigned to female contraltos, when they adapted Shakespeare's *Midsummer Night's Dream* in 1960 and cast the famous countertenor Alfred Deller as Oberon the Fairy King.[13] In that sense, *Curlew River* may not have been "pushing the boat out in a new direction," as Grant suggested. Instead, it was staging the Ferryman and his boat in a church, presenting itself as a Christian parable and also potentially airing the open secret by putting Pears in the role of the mother. The music critic for the *Times* all too carefully resisted a homophobic response even as he confessed his "fears" relating to the drag role. He commented that Pears had been "challenged (unfairly, one had expected) to suggest Japanese and medieval English practice by impersonating the distraught mother, and to avoid recalling the much more familiar English pantomime dame." The reviewer judged Pears's performance a success and even confessed that "one felt ashamed at any earlier fears of mirth or embarrassment, since this was clearly a monk playing a, fortuitously female, part in a sacred drama."[14] *Curlew River's* frame as a medieval mystery performed by monks assuaged his embarrassment but, contrary to his assurances, still "recall[ed] the English pantomime dame"—or else he wouldn't have mentioned her.

If drag provoked "fears of mirth or embarrassment" in even a sympathetic reviewer taking pains to suppress his anxieties, Britten and Plomer were right to have been concerned about Pears's drag. They chose an ancient Christian performance form to mediate and contain the drag, but why were they so intent on Pears playing a woman while avoiding the conventions of the "pantomime dame"? In previous presentations on *Curlew River*, I have felt the need to argue, as if by habit, that they were using drag to subvert and protest norms of gender and sexuality. In this tendency, I follow a quarter century of critical thought, beginning with Judith Butler's famous *Gender Trouble: Feminism and the Subversion of Identity* (1990) (absolutely required reading when I was in graduate school). Butler initially presented drag as an example of "subversion," even the model of "gender trouble," as it disrupts the assumed and fervently enforced link between a person's biological sex and gender expression. Not only does drag suggest that a person of any sex can assume any gender but also that there are more than two ways of doing it and no original or correct masculine or feminine model. If so, *any* gender expression is actually a form of drag, a copy or imitation without an original.[15]

In her later work, Butler revisited her idealism and acknowledged that "there is no necessary relation between drag and subversion" because drag can undermine or reinforce gender norms.[16] That is, Pears playing *Curlew River's* mother could promote conventional ideas of femininity and masculinity, including conservative Christian versions of these gender roles. To be sure, Butler insisted that stage drag was different from the drag king or queen in a bus or other public place, but real-world examples often combine everyday and stage drag—and not always in subversive ways.[17] Many queer and gender theorists have built on Butler's drag framework, but Elizabeth Freeman described a form of "temporal drag" relevant to Britten's and Plomer's decision to set their play in medieval England. Noticing that queer drag often imitates and revels in earlier ways of being feminine or masculine (Joan Crawford in the 1945 *Mildred Pierce* or "Mom, circa 1969"), Freeman suggested that queer theory has mistakenly presented queers as "always ahead" of the times and thereby reinforced conventional notions of progress or the assumption that *it's always getting better.*[18] Instead, queers may be "interested in the tail end of things," particularly in "whatever has been declared useless."[19] Freeman defined temporal drag as "a *productive* obstacle to progress" that allows a person to create a gender using the remnants of an earlier version like "Mom, circa 1969" or *Curlew River's* "monk as Mom, circa 1209" (not later, because the pope prohibited clergy from public performances in 1210). The contemporary and the past forms of gender comment on each other, according to Freeman, "using disruptive anachronism to pivot what would otherwise be simple parody into a more earnest montage of publicly intelligible subject-positions lost and gained.'[20] Freeman implied a carefully contained form of "subversion" that is similar to Butler's notion of "an appropriation of dominant culture . . . a making over which is itself a kind of agency."[21] In "making over" "Mom, circa 1969," the drag creates an old costume trunk filled with ways of being gendered, all of which indicate many different and often historically specific ways of doing mom and doing gender.

The temporal drag in Britten and Plomer's *Curlew River* was so "earnest" that it did not function as what Freeman calls a "disruptive anachronism," at least not for the *Times* reviewer in the audience at the premiere. The anachronism made Pears's gender drag *less disruptive* and less like the pantomime dame because he was so "clearly a monk . . . in a sacred drama."[22] Pears's makeover of "monk as Mom, circa 1209" reveals many of the other characteristics of temporal drag that Freeman outlined, including the longing for past ways of being gendered, old theatrical forms like all-male mystery plays, anachronistic drag costumes like monks' robes, and even the timeworn sentimentality invoked by ghosts of dead children, grieving mothers, and miraculous Christian healing. *Curlew River* also drags along the remnants of its inspiration in noh, one of the oldest continuously practiced theaters and one that guards its tradition through the pedagogical practice of handing the repertory from person to person. Britten and Plomer turned to temporal drag in part because it allowed them to curtail the cultural drag or "pastiche from the ancient Japanese." But their "monk's play" (as one of their abandoned subtitles gave it) provided the "accepted style" that allowed Pears to play a woman without seeming "odd" (as in subversive?). *Curlew River* frustrates my desire to find subversion in drag performance or to define a new form of temporal/cultural drag that offers a slightly different "kind of agency." *Curlew River* exposes subversion as my desire, one that it will provoke but not fulfill.

QUEERLY CHRISTIAN SUBMISSION

Curlew River turns back to the past, mixing temporal and cultural drag, archaic theaters, and modes of religious worship, to explore forms of being or subjectivities that to a certain extent, modern culture abandoned. The loss of these ways of being was sufficiently noted by modern culture to have inspired composers like Britten, Noah Greenberg, and others to recover medieval operas, playwrights like Yeats to invoke an ancient, Celtic theater, and "modern dancers" like Itō to present traditional Eastern performance forms as the answer to Western stagnation. The archaic subjectivities they imagined do not adhere to contemporary norms and could be called "queer" following a frequently used definition of the term as "nonnormative." The subjectivities presented by Britten and Plomer also are queer because they are rooted in erotic desire, specifically *submission* to desires that are not considered the "norm," including the desire for a male actor to play a grieving mother in search of her son, another beautiful young boy derived from the noh canon.

What I call the "queerly Christian submission" of *Curlew River* does not easily align with queer or gay theory and activism. This frustrates critics who want Britten, Plomer, and Pears to use drag to challenge the norms of gender and sexuality that not only confined their theater but also threatened them personally. Stage representations of homosexuality were illegal until 1958, and a state license for all stage material was required until 1968, the production year for the last of the Britten-Plomer church parables, *The Prodigal Son*.

When they started working on *Curlew River* in 1956, the British Parliament was beginning to debate sex law reform, spurred by a rise in prosecutions for homosexuality. Among the famous prosecutions was the sentencing of the renowned mathematician and pioneering computer scientist, Alan Turing, to a form of chemical castration for "gross indecency with males." He committed suicide in 1954 by eating an apple laced with cyanide, a story recounted in the film *The Imitation Game* (2014).[23] The Sexual Offenses Act decriminalized most private sex acts between two consenting adults (initially over twenty-one) in 1967, three years after the premiere of *Curlew River*, but the issue of public identities was still at stake.[24] The legislation made private acts exempt from prosecution, but "being a homosexual"—whatever that meant—was still technically illegal, and some critics have argued that the number of prosecutions actually increased after the Sexual Offenses Act was passed.[25] The law shifted its focus from an illegal action to an identity, from a *doing* to a state of *being*, which could be more open to definition (and litigation). Gay rights activists, with a very different goal, have made a similar shift when arguing that gays should be considered a class of persons entitled to special legal protections, rather than a group defined by *doing* illegal sex acts, as they were according to antisodomy laws.[26]

Questions about *doing* and *being* are at the heart of the drag in *Curlew River*, but Britten was not exactly a gay rights activist in his theater or his life. He never publicly declared a sexual identity, spoke against restrictive stage censorship, or fought homophobic laws.[27] His silence has created some consternation at a moment when "coming out" narratives have established their own performance conventions that are still abhorred by a homophobic public, applauded by a gay counterpublic, and demanded by both—and this common demand should also provoke consternation. As Philip Brett acknowledged, "Gay men like myself often have to work through a certain resentment at his [Britten's] exercise of privilege without disclosure; younger radicals presumably have no time for his compromised politics at all."[28] Privileged, compromised, and titled, Sir Benjamin Britten was the first composer to earn the distinction of a life peerage. He was thoroughly parodied, along with Sir Peter Pears, in Dudley Moore's homophobic and hysterical "Little Miss Britten" in *Beyond the Fringe*, a successful stage revue that pioneered British satire in the 1960s.[29] Moore's send-up of Britten's settings of English "folk" songs ("Little Miss Muffet") and Pears's tenor voice and style led directly into a parody of Kurt Weill's and Bertolt Brecht's "The Ballade of Gangster Joe" in the finale performance—staged in the same year as *Curlew River*'s premiere.[30] The parody must have contributed to Britten's concern about Pears's drag mother role in *Curlew River*. Lampooned by *Beyond the Fringe* and interviewed by officers from Scotland Yard during Sir David Maxwell Fyfe's gay hunt (during which the actor Sir Arthur John Gielgud was convicted three months after he was knighted in 1953), Britten was attacked by both the cultural left and establishment reactionaries during his lifetime.[31]

Britten still is subject to attacks from all political directions. Those committed to gay rights feel that he submitted to homophobia with his silence about sexuality and hid behind the protection of his undeniable privilege at the Red House in out-of-the-way Aldeburgh. If Maxwell Fyfe, followed by conservatives today, designated Aldeburgh a sinful hideaway, it was also a location from which Britten could launch the English Opera Group and get his compositions to the stage. Gay activist and homophobic agendas converge when they both presume that he was "in the closet" because of internalized homophobia or to escape the law. Neither side considers that his silence might have been a refusal to confine himself to the gay-straight binary and an attempt to imagine more fluid identities. Philip Brett, one of the first Britten scholars to deal with sexuality, used Eve Sedgwick's "the epistemology of the closet," her powerful idea that all knowledge ("epistemology" refers to theories and methods of knowing) is linked to knowledge about sexuality defined by the binary of homo-/hetero-sexuality.[32] Readings of Britten through the epistemology of the closet have offered substantial insights, but they still tend to look for subversion. Brett suggested that Britten and Plomer's *Curlew River* put both orientalism and gay themes in the closet because "oriental" was always linked to "undesirable" elements in Western culture, which included gays, pederasts, the insane, prostitutes, and women generally.[33] Avoiding association with the first two categories and Scotland Yard's crackdown was, according to Brett, behind Britten and Plomer's transformation of their noh-derived text into a Christian mystery play. This revision, in addition to creating title havoc, allowed Britten "to pay homage to an Eastern tradition by adapting and imitating some of its musical and dramatic procedures without patronizing it, and without using it as a vehicle for the projections of Western fantasies."[34] Brett, Britten, Plomer, and Graham to a certain extent subverted "the colonizing impulse" while engaging and denying the sexual "fantasies" associated with the orient: subversion in and through the closet.[35]

The Japanese influence in *Curlew River* was not, however, closeted for the *Times* reviewer who worried that Pears might play a pantomime dame. The noh inspiration that Britten openly discussed in the program was an indication that the piece was "Britten's *Deo gratias* for musical experience in many different countries of the world."[36] This is a version of the "multiculturalism" that the contemporary conservative philosopher Roger Scruton celebrated in *Curlew River* as part of his 2008 scourge of the English Arts Council's "political correctness" and refusal to fund "anything that might invoke our national greatness": "Our [English] music has reached out to the world in a spirit of inclusion, and if 'multiculturalism' means anything, then *Curlew River* (a 'church parable' in the form of a Noh play) is the quintessential instance of it—and all the more English for that."[37] Such self-aggrandizing multiculturalism would have troubled Britten as a pacifist and conscientious objector. The problem with looking for subversion in the closet is that the door is mirrored and we often find our own political desires reflected back at us.

We tend to find what we're looking for, as this book has repeatedly emphasized, and no approach to other cultures is neutral or correct. *Curlew River* shows me my desire for subversion, which has led to certain norms and habits of interpretation in my work and in a good deal of queer theory. Britten and Plomer's church parable offers a moral about submission to suffering. The timeworn message of Christian redemption through worldly sorrows that will contribute to salvation is voiced by a miraculous ghost:

Go your way in peace, mother.
The dead shall rise again
And in that blessèd day
We shall meet in Heaven.[38]

Like much Christian ideology, the idea of being rewarded for suffering can call up contemporary conservative commands to "pray the gay away" along with other erotic desires.[39] Religion is often depicted in queer theory and activism as an irrational and oppressive force, and for good reason.[40] *Curlew River* indicates some queer possibilities in religious experiences, partly because of their foundation in the irrational and in the longing for immaterial transcendent powers and also for their sensuous, ritualized expressions. The Christian moral about enduring the trials of this life as a preparation for Paradise has the power to encourage submission to worldly injustice as well as to disrupt "normal time" with an apocalyptic explosion of joy that has begun to interest queer theorists.[41] The ghostly boy, the crazed mother, and the noble but dead father suggests that the heteronormative family and its future of inheritance and lineage are not operating.[42]

The dead boy and child actor (kokata) in Sumidagawa certainly contributed to Britten's, Plomer's, and Pears's interest in the play. The letters between the collaborators do not indicate whether they knew that noh pedagogy was both steeply hierarchical and influenced by Japanese shudō (the way of loving youths).[43] Male-male erotics appear in many plays in the noh repertory, and in Sumidagawa, the beautiful young male body served as a locus of desire—motherly, spiritual, aesthetic, and erotic—as it did throughout the arts and popular discourse of Edo and Meiji Japan when audiences were interested in beautiful boys. The nature of Britten's attraction to young men is hotly debated, but he was generously devoted to male students whom he could mentor (or "thin-as-a-board juveniles, i.e. to the sexless and innocent," as his one-time friend and collaborator, the poet W. H. Auden, put it in his famous parting letter, which also accused Britten of "bourgeois convention").[44] It feels obligatory to acknowledge that the thirteen-year-old boy John Newton, who sang the Voice of the Spirit in Curlew River, was one of Britten's favorite and most regular visitors; Britten helped pay for the boy's education and wrote to Pears that the "sweet affectionate child—makes one feel rather what one has missed in not having a child."[45] Britten's yearning parallels the Madwoman's for her son. The boy's beauty and eroticism contained by his death make them all the more haunting.

Moralizing or defensive debates about Britten's Children have their own book and are not particularly useful to me. Instead, I focus more directly on Curlew River's performance of the conventional lesson of Christian renunciation in a charged erotic field that revels in the pleasures of submission and the sensuous religious rituals that teach it. One such ritual opens the Parable as a party of Monks and their Acolytes are dressed or cross-dressed for their roles and are "ceremonially prepared" after processing onstage to the plainsong hymn "Te lucis ante terminum" (CR, 11). Britten's program note indicates that "the whole piece may be said to have grown" from this "wonderful" hymn," sung for the close of the day and to ask God, "Keep far from us all evil dreams and wicked spirits of the night."[46] Curlew River's only "spirit" is that of "a gentle boy, twelve years old maybe, and a Christian," and the parable is set on the anniversary of his death as another ritual is prepared by the "river folk" to commemorate his passing (CR, 25). "A Northman, a foreigner, a big man" brought the boy to the ferry crossing, claiming to have bought him as a slave (CR, 25). The boy was ill, and the Northman beat him and left him to die on the bank of the Curlew River. The boy submitted to this violence and his dying, asked to be buried by the path to a chapel, said a prayer, and spoke "like

a man"—an important phrase in a parable that asks men to play mothers. The
river folk interpreted the boy's precocious or manly submission to death as a
sign of his sainthood and took earth from his grave to heal their illnesses;
some even believed, "His spirit has been seen" (CR, 26).

When the Madwoman hears the story and realizes that her son is dead, she
initially refuses to pray: "Cruel! / Grief is too great, / I cannot pray, / I am struck
down" (CR, 35). The Ferryman and Traveller convince her that a mother's
prayer is "best" and might comfort her son's soul. Her voice brings the spirit of
the boy from the grave to join the monks in the fourth verse of the "Custodes
hominum psallimus Angelos," a hymn sung at vespers for another sensuous
ritual, the feast of the Guardian Angels.[47] But the mother does not become
part of the chorus in a hymn asking for God's grace and the protection of his
Angels, nor does she "pray with the others" in the conventional ways (CR, 36).
Instead, she addresses the "Birds of the Fenland" in a reprise of what I call the
curlew song, a passage that is repeated many times in the church parable and
that, after being introduced by the Madwoman, is sung by all the characters
and monks, although at very different tempi. The curlew song is taken from an
important passage in the noh play Sumidagawa—which quotes a poem from
The Tales of Ise (Ise monogatari), a famous collection of "poem tales" (uta monogatari) dating from the Heian period (794–1185) that influenced many noh plays:

Birds of the Fenland, though you float or fly,	O, birds of Miyako,
Wild birds, I cannot understand your cry.	If you are worthy of
	your name,
Tell me, does the one I love	Tell me, does my love
	still live? (Sumi-
	dagawa, 151–52)

In this world still live? (CR, 20, 37)[48]

The "Curlews of the Fenland" may fill in as understudies for God or his Angels
in this nonprayer, as they prompt the appearance of the boy's ghost, a "sign
of God's grace," according to the Abbot (CR, 40). But they also substitute for
the Miyako birds of Sumidagawa and the Tales of Ise, calling up the very different
ethical worlds of those Buddhist- and Shinto-inflected works. Even in Curlew
River, the Madwoman "cannot understand" their cry. They serve as a sign of
the floating, flying, incomprehensible character of desire. The Madwoman
sings her first address to the "wild birds" after the Ferryman and chorus of
Passengers demand that she "entertain" them by "crazily singing" (CR, 19).

Instead of laughing at her, the Traveller links her erratic tune of mourning for her lost son to an erotic love song. He stands in for the "famous traveler" Ariwara no Narihira who, as recounted in *Sumidagawa*, composed the original poem at the ferry crossing while thinking of his lover. The Traveller and Ferryman repeat the *curlew song* and claim, "Both derive from longing, / Both from love" (CR, 22). Only then does the group feel sorry for making fun of the woman's madness, and the Ferryman agrees to take her aboard (CR, 22). As the *curlew song* gradually gathers the voice of every character and Monk onstage, it suggests that all are connected as crazy searchers and lovers and links madness and diverse sexualities.[49]

UNDER THE CURLEW SIGN

> Each entry of each voice should follow the note indicated by the arrow. After this, the interrelation of the parts in the score is only approximate.
> Benjamin Britten, note introducing the *curlew song* in *Curlew River*

As a universalizing tune of desire, the *curlew song* deviates significantly from the opening and closing plainsong hymns, the only other sections of *Curlew River* that all the characters sing. The hymns are chanted in unison as simple monophonic melodies without accompanying harmony, whereas the *curlew song* is one of the most polyphonic and complex sections in a composition that has no time signatures and assigns unique tempi, pitches, primary instruments, and even harmonic worlds to each character. Britten described the "interrelation of the parts" at the *curlew song* as "approximate." Elsewhere, he included directions such as "Own tempo" or "repeat ad lib," and he used dotted barlines both in "the conventional way as a subsidiary form of solid barline" and, more unusually, as an indication that "there are two different tempi happening simultaneously" (figure 6.1).[50] Britten attempted to approximate the noh theater's conductor-free performances, which are enabled by the years of study and memorization of repertory to which noh performers submit. The ōmugaeshi ("listen to the master and parrot-repeat" method of instruction) aids in memorization while reinforcing the sanctity of the repertory and teaching the noh performer how to listen very closely to the other performers. Noh musicians, actors, and chorus all know their parts in a canonized play like *Sumidagawa* so thoroughly that professionals who have never performed together can mount a performance with little rehearsal. While it might seem that performers are slaves to the repertory, noh

FIGURE 6.1 Example of the curlew sign over musical bars. Designed by Jaho King.
(Courtesy of Jaho King; "Curlew River" Music by Benjamin Britten © 1968 By Faber
Music Ltd., London WCIB3DA Reproduced by permission of the publishers. All
rights reserved)

has built in unique opportunities for flexibility. The syllables of the chant can
be distributed in relation to the drum patterns in different ways in those sections of the play in which chant and drums are matched (au). Each performer
must listen very carefully to the others and recognize where, for example,
a beat of the ōtsuzumi drum falls in relation to the first syllable of a line of
poetry so as to determine how to chant the line. Other passages are rhythmically independent (awazu) and even more variable.[51] Again, this energized
process of listening and adjusting rhythmic relationships occurs without a
conductor.

Britten understood the flexibility and variation in noh music but found it
difficult to replicate the effect without the extensive, repertory-driven training undergone by noh performers. He eventually invented the curlew sign as a
special kind of fermata or "hold" that would allow for a controlled polyphonic
elasticity without a conductor. The curlew sign appropriately looks like the
wings of birds and signals that "an ordinary pause sign is not adequate for
conveying the flexible fitting-in of the different tempi."[52] Britten used ferma-
tas frequently as well, so the curlew sign has a different symbolic value. It
appears over a note, word, or rest to instruct musicians to "listen and wait till
the other performers have reached the next barline, or meeting-point—i.e.,
the note or rest can be longer or shorter than its written value."[53] The score's
flexibility represents a framework in which any of the performers can charge
ahead or lag behind. This "freedom" is controlled by a symbol with an ironically godlike power, in that it gives performers free will to move about their
various musical worlds as long as they follow the rules and arrive at the designated meeting place at the right time. Britten's curlew sign functions like
a diacritical mark to indicate a special way of playing and also like a visual
symbol that "wings" over important moments in both instrumental and vocal
parts.[54] Words and phrases marked with curlew signs include "many a peril
I have faced," "No gleam to show the way," "I see the wild birds fly," "He'll

offer up a prayer for him," "O Curlew river, Cruel Curlew: where all my hope is swept away," and, near the end of the parable, "holy and glorious," "blessed abode," "eternal peacefulness," "angels," "river," "souls." At the miraculous appearance of the boy's spirit, the curlew sign accents the most conventional Christian words and phrases.

The parable's musical characteristics, especially its curlew sign, reinforce its thematic message of Christian submission: At the sign of the curlew, we can find those we seek, those we love in all of love's flighty varieties, but only momentarily. We cannot be with them always. A boy submits to his kidnapping and torture, citing his faith; the Madwoman submits to the death of her son, trusting they will be reunited in Paradise; the Traveller submits to the loss of his beloved, recognizing his longing is like that of a mother for a son and that all are united in their desire and loss. The curlew sign's built-in tension between freedom and restraint work at the level of performance as well: There is independence of musical interpretation and no godlike conductor, but this version of free will requires submission to the authority of the curlew-marked score. That requires a rigorous process of listening to others to detect when they reach the curlew and adjusting one's own tempo accordingly. *Curlew River* might present a noh-derived address to a curlew bird as comparable to conventional prayer, but the parable is bookended by plainsong hymns chanted in unison. A man playing a monk is cross-dressed as a crazy mother, experiencing an unusual freedom of musical range and gender representation, but that liberation is severely circumscribed. Colin Graham, who essentially choreographed the original production, wrote in his detailed production notes, "There should never be any question of female impersonation of the Madwoman's role: one should always be aware that monks are *representing* the characters, just as their movements *represent* and are symbolic of their emotions" (CR Score, 145, italics in original). Even the structure of the play within a play functions to contain potential moments of freedom or subversion.

Graham asked every performer in *Curlew River*, not just the drag Madwoman, to submit to conventions derived from noh and medieval miracle plays, conventions that enabled the drag and bound each performer to stylized stage movement. Graham's production notes dictate every stage action with drawings and numbers appearing at the "exact point in the score where movement should be executed" (CR Score, 145):

> The movement and production details should be as spare and economical
> as possible: the miming which plays an integral part, is symbolic and should

be pared down to its quintessence. Once the spectator becomes geared to the convention his emotions are imperceptibly but passionately involved in a drama doubly distilled by the very economy of its theatrical means. Such involvement can be shattered by a single uncontrolled, weak, or unnecessary gesture. Every movement of the hand or tilt of the head should assume immense meaning and, though formalized, must be designed and executed with the utmost intensity: this requires enormous concentration on the part of the actor, an almost Yoga-like muscular, as well as physical control. The cast of the original production underwent a strenuous course of movement instruction and physical education before rehearsals began and this training was maintained throughout the engagement. (CR Score, 143)

The "Yoga-like muscular" control and "strenuous course of movement instruction" that Graham implemented for the premiere of *Curlew River* might be compared with other forms of dance/movement instruction, learning an instrument, or training to be a classical singer or noh actor. These demands and restraints were placed on actors/vocalists and instrumentalists alike. All represented monks on stage and negotiated scores that allowed for remarkable rhythmic flexibility between curlew signs but also meticulously detailed every movement. Of course, later productions of *Curlew River* have disregarded Graham's production notes as separable from the score and text with which they were published, as Graham seems to have anticipated.[55] In the original production, however, the staging was crucial to the parable's teachings about Christian renunciation as well as submission to foreign or ancient theatrical conventions.

In *Curlew River*'s premiere, every performer's experience was compromised, ambivalent, and disruptive of the usual binaries of freedom and compulsion, much less any typology of sexuality. The queer Christian submission of the church parable went well beyond the specific drag role of the Madwoman to disrupt the "masculine ideal . . . of proud subjectivity" more generally. According to Leo Bersani, this ideal was shared by "men *and* women," the gay liberationist rhetoric of "out of the closets and into the streets," and sex-positive feminists.[56] Despite warnings by Bersani and others, queer theory developed a proud subjectivity and emphasis on resistance, subversion, and masculinist battle cries. This assertive individual is the presumed ideal in most strands of queer theory, as it is in feminism. Britten, Plomer, and Graham's *Curlew River* departs from that norm as it presents an uneven combination of pliable polyphony, freedom and restraint, Christian conservatism, present performance time, the ancient orientalist time of noh, and the medieval miracle play—all compromised by competing, irreconcilable conventions.

The various performers wing off into their own tempos like proud or creative individuals, only to be stopped at the curlew sign and by a universalizing insanity and erotics that unites the mother who loves her dead son madly and any traveler's longing for any lover.

Performing in *Curlew River* was demanding, an experience of ritualized submission, as musicians and actors had to listen to one another as closely as did noh performers. One member of the English Opera Group (EOG), the harpist Brian Wilson, reported that in *Curlew River*, "our parts were full of cues [but] I do remember having to cue the other players when I had finished my 'bit.' . . . Sometimes we were urged to speed things up a bit if we had allowed the dramatic pace to ease off but in the end it all worked very well."[57] There is compromise and danger of (dramatic) failure as the performers listen to and cue one another while trying not to lose themselves in their curlew-marked scores. To quote Wilson again, "The gentle unfolding pace of the work had a magical effect. I always thought that when the Abbot sang 'The moon is risen, the Curlew River is flowing to the sea' that we were all being released from the experience in which we were engaged and being returned to the world from which we had come." Wilson, who knew all the tricks of *Curlew River*'s score, as it allowed for temporary rhythmic unmooring and then reigned him back in, still found the parable "magical." And rather than feeling he had reached an end, Wilson described the experience as both "being released" and "being returned," images of the tension between freedom and restraint that are never resolved in *Curlew River*.

Viewed from another, less magical perspective, the curlews, cues, and pictures of numbered gestures might suggest a maddening musical experiment or a falconer with birds on a string who allows them to fly upward before yanking them back down at the curlew sign. Some critics have characterized Britten as a tyrant who was ruthless in his demands on performers, controlling of his librettists, and unforgiving of anyone who challenged or displeased him. Some of his collaborators reported experiencing seduction alternating with revulsion: "He could make you believe you were the only person in the world"; "he devoured people and spewed out what was left and no use to him."[58] Yet his collaboration with Plomer, Graham, and Pears on *Curlew River* was cordial and productive even as they struggled to find their bearings with gender/cultural/temporal drag, changed directions, scrapped librettos, and endured delays. Of course, Britten established the English Opera Group in 1945 with trusted collaborators and staffed it with friends, in part so that he could have more control over productions of his work. Still, opera and all performances always are collaborative and always are somewhat beyond the control of any one individual on a creative team, which is one reason that performance offers a fascinating vehicle for considering freedom, control, authority, and submission—all of which are central themes in the music, plot, and performance technique of *Curlew River*. Britten, Plomer, Graham, and Pears were interested in using the church parable to explore ways of being that functioned as alternatives to modern subversive individualism. Accusations of artistic tyranny, even political fascism, have been directed at nearly every noh-inspired writer, translator, and performer of the twentieth century, and this was as true of Samuel Beckett as it was of Britten.

TAKING DIRECTION FROM BECKETT

> For me, as for him [Beckett], *Footfalls* was to be an entirely new creative experience. Sometimes I felt as if he were a sculptor and I a piece of clay. . . . Sometimes it felt as if I were modeling for a painter, or working with a musician. The movements started to feel like dance.
> Billie Whitelaw, *Billie Whitelaw . . . Who He?*

Billie Whitelaw, Beckett's favorite English actress, performed the role of May under Beckett's direction for the 1976 premiere of *Footfalls* at the Royal Court Theatre. Dictating her posture, step pattern, arm position, and vocal intonation, he seemed to be a sculptor, painter, musician, and choreographer, as well as director and—some critics have asserted—tyrant. Beckett was also the author, but Whitelaw emphasized his work directly on her body, which exceeded the detailed stage directions that May should pace nine steps back and forth on a dimly lit "strip" "parallel with front" for the entirety of the play.[59] He positioned her arms crossed against her chest, right over left, with each hand clenched near the opposite shoulder; then he moved her "fingers, perhaps no more than half an inch this way or that," leading her to describe herself as a "a piece of marble that he needed to chip away at" (figure 6.2).[60] As the author and director of twenty-three stage and television productions, Beckett often created the kind of detailed choreography that Whitelaw accurately described as a "dance." He and his estate have controversially demanded that all productions of Beckett's work adhere precisely to his stage directions and scene design, but most directors also reconstruct his choreography as documented in production notebooks and recordings as well as stage directions.[61] A Beckett repertory has emerged

FIGURE 6.2 Billie Whitelaw as May in Samuel Beckett's *Footfalls* (1976). (Photograph © John Haynes / Lebrecht Music & Arts)

with detailed production guidelines exceeding any attached to other modern dramatists—and with some surprising affinities to noh's much older repertory of plays and performance traditions. Controversies surrounding Beckett's authority as *master* of this repertory reveal, once again, assumptions about agency and creativity, submission and subversion, which are precisely the central themes of *Footfalls*.

Since the 1960s, critics as illustrious as Gilles Deleuze have tried to position Beckett in relation to noh, but Beckett repeatedly denied any direct influence of the Japanese theater on his work. In 1964, he claimed in a letter, "I am not at all well acquainted with Noh drama or Oriental theater in general and have made no attempt to use such techniques in my plays."[62] When in 1981, his Japanese translator Yasunari Takahashi again asked if noh had influenced his work, he responded a little more ambiguously: "Not consciously."[63] Beckett probably learned more about noh in the intervening years as cultural exchanges made Asian theater forms ever more accessible in Europe.

One of Beckett's first and most important inspirations was Yeats's modernist noh dance plays.[64] Beckett saw *At the Hawk's Well*, among other plays by Yeats at the Abbey Theatre, when he was a student at Trinity College (1923–1926). In *Happy Days* (1961), Beckett's quotation-filled character Winnie recites the opening of *Hawk's Well*: "I call to the eye of the mind" (BCDW, 164). Winnie uses this among other half-forgotten "exquisite lines" to point out the "mercy" of remembering "one's classics" as her lower body is immobilized in a mound of dirt that grows higher as the play progresses (BCDW, 164). If Yeats's *Hawk's Well* is one of those remembered classics, the noh theater that inspired Yeats might be another. Noh also includes quotations from Japanese and Chinese classical poetry (like the "Birds of Miyako" poem from the *Tales of Ise* that became the *curlew song*). Noh also requires long periods of enforced immobility kneeling in *seiza*, which can feel as if the legs have been buried in the stage.

Beckett insisted nonetheless that Winnie's "eye of the mind in *Happy Days* does not refer to Yeats" [or noh] but is among the "bits of pipe I happen to have with me."[65] If so, *Hawk's Well* was a particularly important pipe in his stock. Approached for a tribute on George Bernard Shaw's centenary, Beckett declared his preference for other Irish playwrights, particularly Yeats, J. M. Synge, and Seán O'Casey: "I wouldn't suggest that G.B.S. is not a great playwright. . . . What I would do is give the whole unupsettable applecart for a sup of the Hawk's Well, or the Saint's, or a whiff of Juno, to go no further."[66] Seeming to echo Yeats's "deeps of the mind" (PFNoh 153), Beckett's Reader in

Ohio Impromptu (1981) reads, "Profounds of mind. Buried in who knows what profounds of mind" (BCDW, 448). Yeats wanted his actors to be still if they could not, as he claimed of Itō Michio, rise from the floor and "recede" into "the deeps of the mind." Yeats remembered, "I . . . once asked a dramatic company to let me rehearse them in barrels that they might forget gesture and have their minds free to think of speech for a while. The barrels, I thought, might be on castors, so that I could shove them about with a pole when the action required it" (PC, 20). Nearly sixty years later, Beckett confined his *End-game* (1957) characters Nag and Nell in "ashbins," then buried Winnie in her mound, and positioned all three of the performers of *Play* (1963) kneeling in "grey urns" with "neck held fast in urn's mouth" (BCDW, 307). Learning to kneel in *seiza* for noh lessons introduced me to the pain Beckett ignored in his stage direction, declaring that if the kneeling posture in *Play* was "found impracticable," the actors should stand below stage level on traps; if traps were not available, the urns could be enlarged to standing height, but the actors should never sit (BCDW, 319). Lines such as "all the pain" must emerge differently from the kneeling or even standing immobilized body, especially after the torture of the "repeat" in *Play* (BCDW, 319).

Beckett, like Yeats, was interested in making the stage still and exploring how speech emerges from confined bodies. Actors on Beckett's stage do not merely "forget gesture"; their limbs and entire bodies are often shackled to prohibit gesture. The process of burying an actor in a mound, for example, was one strategy for getting them "buried in who knows what profounds of mind" (BCDW, 448). Another was his exacting choreographic work for *Footfalls*, as May's crossed arms and precise stepping pattern prevent any gesticulation or extraneous movement and urge the actor and audience step by step into the deeps and profounds. Beckett's staging, directing, and insistence that every subsequent production follow his stage directions exactly have led to criticisms that he destroyed the actor's and director's agency and demanded their submission to his tyrannical power. Beckett used his theater to examine the very issues of agency, submission, subversion, and authority that have troubled critics of his directing style—as well as critics of noh's pedagogical practices. I suggest that the similarities between Beckett's theater and noh are due not only to Yeats's influence and some thematic and textual parallels but also to comparable physical performance styles, strategies for teaching these bodily techniques, and the versions of subjectivity they invite director and actor or teacher and student to experience. Beckett's bodily techniques and pedagogies influenced his late theater to such an extent that it came to look and feel like noh, regardless of any direct influence (although I will argue there was some). Noh's designation as "the art of walking" could also be applied to *Footfalls*, and both show how much submission and profundity can be conveyed in a pattern of steps across a stage.

Beckett's approach to directing resembles noh's *ōmugaeshi* (parrot-repetition pedagogy), in that he taught bodily movements and vocal techniques mainly by asking actors to replicate his own demonstrations, just as a noh *sensei* would.[67] Beckett demonstrated May's walk and *kamae*-like, forward-leaning shape with arms crossed over his torso in a Paris bistro when he and Whitelaw met to discuss the play, a meeting she described as the "first rehearsal."[68] Whitelaw, like a noh student, followed him, imitating his speed, technique, and posture, and she claimed that Beckett "reiterated that the main thing was to get the movements right, the changing of the body's posture as the play progressed, as though the character was turning slowly inward."[69] Beckett's stage directions indicate that May should step at a gradually slower tempo back and forth along the strip "with a clearly audible rhythmic tread" (BCDW, 399). So that each step could be heard, sandpaper or emery boards were attached to the bottoms of her shoes when Whitelaw premiered the role.[70] Beckett taught her to slide her feet slightly and to produce a "scratching sound."[71] May's costume, a "worn grey wrap hiding feet," helped produce a gliding effect like that of *suriashi*, so appropriate to the spirits haunting noh plays and to May's ghostly presence (BCDW, 399).

Just as the actors learned choreography by imitating Beckett's bodily technique, they began studying his desired vocal production by listening to him read. An often reprinted photograph shows how Whitelaw and Beckett would face each other reciting the text phrase by phrase, marking the rhythm with their hands, or as Whitelaw claimed, "We 'conducted' each other, eyeball to eyeball" (figure 6.3).[72] James Knowlson's biography offers a similar description: "They would sit facing one another at the theater or in her apartment in Camden Square, reciting the text phrase by phrase, Whitelaw capturing Beckett's every inflection."[73] This aspect of Beckett's direction resembles the parrot-repeat method of the noh chant or *utai* lesson in which teacher and student kneel facing each other as the student attempts to replicate the *sensei's* intonation and rhythm (clip 2). Beckett produced recordings of his voice for many productions, and noh students regularly record the *utai* of their teachers to help them practice.[74] Beckett told Whitelaw and Rose Hill, who played the offstage Voice/Mother, "to drain words of conventional emotion" and to "speak in a monotone" with a rhythmic, chantlike quality.[75] When Hildegard

FIGURE 6.3 Samuel Beckett at the Royal Court Theatre with Billie Whitelaw, London, May 1979. (Photograph © John Haynes / Lebrecht Music & Arts)

Schmahl, a slightly less *sculptable* May than Whitelaw, asked Beckett for explanations of the text and psychological motivations for the West Berlin production of *Footfalls* in 1976, he responded, "The position of the body will help to find the right voice."[76] Schmahl ultimately replicated Whitelaw's posture and arm positions for May, as did Delphine Seyrig, Irena Jun, and the actors playing May after Beckett's death, including Holly Twyford in a New York production in 2012 directed by Joy Zinoman (figure 6.4).[77] Beckett's other plays featuring women also establish movement vocabularies, such as Winnie's studied and repetitive gestures in *Happy Days*; the pattern of entrances, exits, and hand-holding in *Come and Go* (1965); and the rocking motion of *Rockaby* (1980).

Beckett's efforts to choreograph and teach performances featuring stylized gestures that could be replicated in each production established a repertory

FIGURE 6.4 Holly Twyford as May in Beckett's *Footfalls* as a part of "Sounding Beckett." Directed by Joy Zinoman and presented by Cygnus Ensemble (New York, 2012). (Copyright © www.photographme.us and Jeremy Tressler)

comparable to that of noh and also a surprisingly similar acting technique. Beckett insisted that an actor's bodily position determined both the vocal style and emotional valence and that performers should never attempt to put feeling into their speech: "Don't act," he instructed.[78] Western stage realism equates acting with expressing or emoting so that a psychological or emotional inner being is conveyed principally through facial expressions, "natural" gestures, and tones of voice. Beckett demanded that his actors avoid these traditional indicators of emotion and replaced acting with a distinctive and precise sequence of movements and gestures, like noh *kata*. In doing so, he exposed the conventions and norms behind stage realism. The expressions, gestures, and intonations thought to produce a realistic character are, when performed on a stage, as conventional and presentational as *kata*. Noh's *shiori* gesture, in which the movement of the open hand arcing upward toward the eye indicates weeping, is certainly "unrealistic." But so is the Western norm of asking an actor to ignore the fact of a real audience, perhaps recall a previous emotion unrelated to the play, bury one's face in one's hands, and mimic sobbing noises. Such stage gestures are only conventionally linked to a technique associated with "the real." Some directors require that choreography with as much "tyranny" as Beckett exhibited when teaching his distinctive movement patterns. The difference is that the face-in-hands sobbing pattern is more familiar and considered "normal." Beckett sought to defamiliarize the standard stage.

Beckett was well aware that his methods of directing were controversial, and in *Catastrophe* (1984) a godlike "Director" bullies "His Female Assistant" and appears to exploit, even torture, a speechless "Protagonist" (BCDW, 457).[79] The Director demands that the assistant manipulate the Protagonist's body by adjusting and unclenching his hands, repositioning his head, and exposing and whitening his flesh as he shivers on a "pedestal" (BCDW, 459). The short play dedicated to the imprisoned Czech artist, dissident, and future president Vaclav Havel also exposes the apparatus of the stage; lighting design; hierarchical organization of directors, assistants, and designers; and audiences' desire to witness tragedies that will assure them of their humanity and appropriate sympathy. It might seem that *Catastrophe* is more explicit than *Footfalls* in staging the failure of theater to fulfill the audience's desires for something like catharsis or purging and to accomplish the similarly humanistic project of building a sense of agency or undermining tyranny. But even without a despotic director figure, Beckett's stage directions in *Footfalls* might be said to govern the play.

BECKETT'S STAGE DIRECTIONS (AND A FEW OF MINE)

Set apart in italics and brackets, stage directions are often thought to be secondary to the spoken dialogue, mere suggestions rather than full participants (or agents) in the theater, and therefore more likely than dialogue to be ignored by directors and actors.[80] Certainly, Colin Graham's production notes for *Curlew River* have been ignored if not ridiculed outright; Mark Morris described then as "dated," "corny," and "bad" when mounting a production in 2013.[81] The style and function of stage directions have varied in theater history, and in the modernist period, stage directions generally became more descriptive, didactic, poetic, and witty as drama was institutionalized as literature to be read.[82] Beckett's stage directions tend to be brief and unambiguous: "(*Pause. M. resumes pacing. Four lengths*)" (BCDW, 399). They discourage the kind of "creative interpretation" that would allow a director to choose a unique "concept," setting, or casting choice. In a note appended to the program of the controversial American Repertory Theatre (ART) production of *Endgame* in 1984 directed by JoAnne Akalaitis, Beckett famously stated that a production that "ignores my stage directions is completely unacceptable to me."[83] Beckett's program note was part of the out-of-court resolution to the battle over Akalaitis's decision to set the play in a subway station rather than an empty room. A rebuttal insert by Robert Brustein, ART's artistic director, stated that Beckett "makes significant revisions in his own text and stage directions" yet "robs collaborating artists of their interpretive freedom." Brustein suggested that Beckett's insistence "on strict adherence to each parenthesis of the published text" interfered with the freedom of theatrical collaborators.[84] This betrayed freedom is almost always located in particular aspects of Beckett's work: the setting, stage design, and blocking but rarely the spoken dialogue of the play. Directors who might shy away from changing a line of a play nonetheless find the parenthetical stage direction an imposition on their "freedom."

Beckett certainly did revise while directing, and this, combined with his publisher's desires to bump up sales of the plays, led to variations in the published texts. Faber & Faber, wanting to make *Footfalls* available for sale before opening night, published the first edition from a typescript that Beckett later revised.[85] Focusing mostly on the stage directions, he changed the number of May's steps in each pass along the strip from seven to nine, and the 1976 edition of *Ends and Odds* adjusted the stage directions but not Voice/Mother's counting of the steps. This disrupted *Footfall*'s precise matching of walk to word. Grove Press regularized the speech in 1976 but included discrepancies in punctuation, such as the number of dots in the ellipses. Grove also ignored Beckett's revision to the lighting design, the addition of a *"Dim spot on face during halts"* and *"Upstage left, a thin vertical beam (B) 3 meters high"*; this beam remained lit during the first three fade-outs to darken only before the curtain.[86] The lack of an authoritative text of *Footfalls*, along with discrepancies in directions about movement and lighting, seems particularly ironic for a playwright who found any departure from stage directions "unacceptable."

Beckett was far more flexible in his work with directors and actors in Japan, where he also revealed a surprising knowledge of Japanese theatrical practices. He continued to deny any direct influence from noh and kyōgen and acknowledged his "profound respect and emulation of the 'ceremoniousness' of Yeats's noh-inspired plays" to Jonah Salz, the founder, along with kyōgen actor Shigeyama Akira of the Kyoto-based Noho Theater Group.[87] Both Salz and Shigeyama share an interest in Beckett and (what Salz calls) "fusion theater," and their very first production, in September 1981, was a performance of Beckett's *Act Without Words* 1 and 2, followed by Yeats's *At the Hawk's Well*. In its first two decades, the company produced a total of thirteen Beckett plays, including Japanese and world premieres.[88] With Salz directing Beckett's *Act Without Words* 1 and 2, Shigeyama "translated" the physical tasks into kyōgen *kata*, or movement patterns, and when there was no direct translation for a particular *kata*, he invented movement rooted in kyōgen bodily techniques.[89] A translation of Beckett's stage design also was required because *Act Without Words* uses a system of wires and pulleys to manipulate objects: A carafe of water is whisked just out of reach by a wire—an unexplained offstage force— as the thirsty man approaches (BCDW, 205). Beckett's wire system could not be imposed on a traditional noh stage, so Noho adapted kabuki's "man-in-black" (kurogo), a stage assistant who is "invisible" according to Japanese convention, to hold a Japanese water bucket above the actor, as in figure 6.5.[90] As the Man's frustration and desperation grows, he prepares for a suicide attempt that, in Beckett's script, is foiled when the scissors are pulled away just before he can slit his throat (BCDW, 206). They "transformed" the act into a preparation for the ritual death of *seppuku*, with the scissors serving as a knife and the middle cube as a "ceremonial tray" before being carried off by the kurogo.

When Salz showed a photograph of the *seppuku* scene to Beckett, he nodded approvingly and replied, "So you're translating not just the language, but

FIGURE 6.5 Akira Shigeyama in Beckett's *Act Without Words*. Directed by Jonah Salz and presented by Noho Theater Group (Kyoto, 1981). (Courtesy of Noho Theater Group)

the culture?"[91] *Act Without Words* was performed again in Tokyo on a noh stage in May 1982 and then more than a hundred times in the fifteen years after its premiere and, according to Salz, "remains in Noho's repertoire as a successful attempt at interculturalism."[92] Beckett revealed additional knowledge of Japanese theatrical conventions when Salz directed the world premiere of Beckett's *Quad* 1 *and* 2 in August 1985 and found that the television dance-play adapted easily to the square noh stage. Even the physicalization was comfortable for the noh- and *kyōgen*-trained actors, as the walkers in *Quad* carry themselves in a position that resembles noh *kamae* and the posture Beckett taught Billie Whitelaw for *Footfalls*.[93] Salz's major challenge was carrying out entrances and exits on the open thrust stage of the noh theater. Salz initially proposed placing screens at the corners of the stage, but Beckett, borrowing from a common Japanese performance convention, suggested that the dancers kneel with their backs to the audience to indicate they are "off-stage."[94] Beckett's knowledge of the Japanese conventions surrounding stage assistants and kneeling indicates that Japanese theater practices, so important to predecessors like Yeats and Brecht, may also have influenced his dramaturgy and directing style for *Footfalls*. Beckett's response to Noho's *Act Without Words* and *Quad* indicates he was more flexible about productions of his plays when confronting different theatrical traditions and cultural variations in stage practices. He also seemed more willing to help companies and directors realize culturally specific visions.

Beckett's stage directions in *Footfalls* dictate setting, design, and especially the actor's vocal tones and movement on the boards so literally trod by May. While they might also direct a performance in the stage ("profounds" or "deeps") of a reader's mind, they are not poetic, ambiguous, or eloquent as if intended for interpretation. There is little ambiguity in Beckett's "Strip: *downstage, parallel with front, length nine steps, width one metre, a little off centre audience right*" (BCDW, 399). (It's tempting to compare that drift to the right with May's bodily lean to the right and the diagonal italics that describe her in Beckett's stage directions.) To avoid any confusion of the "Strip" and "Pacing," Beckett provided an image of the floor pattern, and similar diagrams illustrate *Act Without Words II* (ca. 1960), *Film* (1965), *Come and Go* (1967), *Ghost Trio* (1975), . . . *but the clouds* . . . (1977), *Quad* (1984), and *What Where* (1984). These diagrams indicate the extent to which Beckett's late theater is choreographed, and they are reminiscent of the floor patterns of noh actors' movements included in some recent chanting texts (*utaibon*) and in collections of dance choreography (*shimai tsuke*).[95]

Although the traditional noh theater has no lighting effects, Beckett's lighting design for the Strip in Footfalls recalls the thirty-three-foot bridge called the hashigakari, along which the noh actor slowly walks to enter and exit the main stage. The hashigakari represents a pathway between the realm of spirits and the temporal world figured by the stage. May's pacing also seems to take place somewhere between a temporal world and another that cannot be represented but calls to her with the voice of a dying or dead mother. Voice/Mother indicates that May walks a strip of floor, laid bare so that the feet can be heard, in the "old home, the same where she—(Pause.) The same where she began" (BCDW, 401). Beckett told performers in rehearsal that Voice/Mother nearly said "'the same where she was born.' But that is wrong. She just began. . . . She was never born."[96] May is present but not fully born, and her strip is refigured in the third episode (with episodes distinguished by lighting fades and chimes) as the equally liminal space of the transept of a church. May tells of a girl, whom she calls Amy, who would go to the church at "nightfall" and pace "up and down, up and down, His poor arm" (BCDW, 402). She refers to the metaphor of cruciform church architecture in which the transept that extends north and south represents Christ's arms nailed to the cross. Beckett capitalized "His poor arm" in the final drafts of the play (although it remains lowercase in some early publications) to underscore the reference to Christ, who also is a liminal figure, both "born" as a human yet divine, forced to experience death yet immortal. The allusion suggests that May's step falls in a place where to say amen or to disappear is not to end because she was not quite there, on a hashigakari between worlds.

In addition to meticulously dictating the lighting, the strip, the "faint single chime" that rings between episodes, and the step matched to particular words—all supplementary to any drama defined by dialogue—Beckett's stage directions indicate how the words are to be spoken: "Mother. (Pause. No louder.) Mother" (BCDW, 399). The direction, no louder, repeated twice in the opening dialogue between May and Voice/Mother, indicates that this exchange has been rehearsed and the answers already are known, so there is no urgency in its reiterations. The most frequently repeated word in the brief play is the stage direction "Pause," which appears 102 times, of which two are long pauses. Four additional notes state, "Pause as echoes die." There are eight dashes and seventeen ellipses of varying lengths, from twenty dots to the more common three, and the number is significant in Beckett's meticulous punctuation. For him, "The spoken text must be not only letter-perfect, but punctuation-perfect; he will stop an actor who elides a comma-pause."[97]

The spoken dialogue and stage directions in Footfalls are so intertwined that it would be difficult for any production to ignore Beckett's choreography and stage image as scripted. Voice/Mother speaks lines that serve as May's stage directions from the third line of the play as she counts her daughter's steps and turn at the end of the strip: "seven eight nine wheel . . . . seven eight nine wheel" (BCDW, 399). The line casts Voice/Mother as the offstage director, a dynamic that is reinforced when May asks her if she should perform a catalog of daughterly ministrations: "Would you like me to inject you . . . change your position. . . . Straighten your pillows? (Pause.)" (BCDW, 400). In the second episode, the dramatic dialogue is replaced by Voice/Mother's monologue, and she describes the setting as "the old home," "the floor here, now bare," and counts May's steps (BCDW, 401). Here Voice/Mother continues to speak May's stage directions but also speaks for May, indicating an imagined change of speaker in her monologue by "reading" the character designations that would appear in a script: "May: Not enough. The Mother: What do you mean, May, not enough, what can you possibly mean, May, not enough?" (BCDW, 401). Voice/Mother writes and rehearses all the roles in her own play in a manner that recalls Beckett's line-readings as author/director. She even instructs the audience on the appropriate decorum and attention, saying (with stage directions included), "But let us watch her move, in silence. (M paces. Towards end of second length.) Watch how feat she wheels" (BCDW, 401). (Note the pun on feet.)[98] Voice/Mother, like the offstage playwright/director she mimics, seeks to govern the audience as well as the performers.

May speaks back to Voice/Mother with her own monologue in the third episode, which she opens with a word indicating that she is self-consciously continuing a previous narrative with some literary aspirations: "Sequel. (M begins pacing, after two lengths halts facing front at R.) Sequel" (BCDW, 402). (Please note the homophone "seek well," which was the pronunciation he gave to Whitelaw in his parrot-repetition reading.)[99] May replaces the "old home" setting announced by Voice/Mother with "the little church" and adds in a lighting effect: "Given the right light. (Pause.) Grey rather than white, a pale shade of grey" (BCDW, 401–2). She echoes many of Voice/Mother's directives, including her instructions to the audience: "Watch it pass" (BCDW, 402). She recasts the play with Old Mrs. Winter and her daughter Amy (anagram of May) and speaks the lines of both: "Amy: No, Mother, I myself did not, to put it mildly. Mrs. W: What do you mean, Amy, to put it mildly, what can you possibly mean, Amy, to put it mildly?" (BCDW, 403). She refers twice to a mysterious "reader" who "will remember" (reminding us that her own speech precedes her in a published script that can be read, remembered, and reread) (BCDW, 402–3). This echo-filled scene in which May assumes the roles of director, designer, and performer first occupied by Voice/Mother might seem to indicate the daughter's rejection of an ill mother's tyrannical theater. May appears to replace the geriatric-mother-care form of submission with the patriarchal authority of the Christian church.

By scripting stage directions into Voice/Mother and May's dialogue and monologues, Beckett makes it impossible for any production to avoid submitting to his choreography, stage design, and acting technique and installs the authority of both spoken and unspoken stage directions. May's repetitive and crucial pacing organizes both the movement and the speech of the play into a unified rhythm.[100] She does not have "freedom of movement" and gesture, but in conventional realism, the gestures we might call "free" have been previously chosen by the actors or directors but performed as if they were spontaneous. This illusion of spontaneity requires that gestures seem to be "natural" and not choreographed, but they appear as such, partly because they follow the conventions of realist acting styles. Beckett demands that actors abandon the illusion of spontaneity and realism when he scripts movement into the text and exposes the compulsion behind the actor's gestures. From this perspective, Beckett's strategies are less an anti- than a hyper-theatricalism (although they are antirealistic) in the manner of noh kata. Beckett's "art of walking" in Footfalls indicates that it is a theatrical convention for an actor to walk on a stage with a "normal" stride, pretending there is no audience watching her, to pace nine steps back and forth on a Strip of light, and also to cross the stage using a suriashi step.

CONCLUSION: THE ACTOR, PAIN, AND AGENCY

> Every damn play of Beckett's that I do involves some sort of physically or
> mentally excruciating experience.
> Billie Whitelaw

> A paralyzed jaw in Not I, a spine injury in Footfalls—there is a price to pay. And
> all the while Beckett remains the supreme "nō master," saying a line in rehearsal,
> then asking the actor to repeat it precisely.
> Gay Gibson Cima, Performing Women

Billie Whitelaw described the pain she endured to perform for Beckett as "a price I have most willingly paid."[101] This might have been a response to the

concerns of the feminist critic Gay Gibson Cima about Beckett's demands—
and those of the noh "master" (meaning teacher?). Cima recognizes that
Beckett's female actors who "submitted to the required discipline" experienced "pleasure in that disciplined mastery," but she attributes their willing-
ness to "suffer unusual physical pain" to a kind of enthrallment with Beckett's fame and authority.[102] Whereas some critics celebrate Beckett's ability
to stage the torturous aspects of the lives of his female characters, Cima argues that his theater does not "promote agency for real women" and even has
the "power to harm actual women."[103] Audiences and actors (Cima's "real"/
"actual women") encounter what she calls "structural properties and production techniques that encourage an acting and directing approach similar to
that found in traditional Japanese nō drama and theatre."[104] Cima's comparison of Beckett's work and noh relies on familiar assumptions about agency in
some Western feminist thought that foster misunderstandings of both. Gender theorists have troubled notions of an autonomous, self-determining individual with ideas of identities that are cultural constructs or (as Judith Butler
argues) "performatively constituted," yet subversion continues to be emphasized as if by habit—a habit I share and that noh forced me to confront. If an
act follows rather than subverts norms, it is often assumed to be coerced. If
the actor, like Whitelaw, claims that she *wanted* to adhere to norms, she might
be accused of false consciousness and internalized oppression or of behaving
contrary to her interests. Acts are not considered "free" or agentive if they
conform to cultural conditions that are dictated by religious faith or submission to an authority or tradition, acts like kneeling to pray or bowing before
a noh lesson. Yet the theater is a place where "real" or "actual" human actors
generally conform their actions to the authority of a script and director, often
accepting some degree of physical discomfort in the process. This is one of
the reasons that theater has been a productive metaphor for theorists seeking
to understand "gender roles" and "performative constructions."

Cima's assumptions about agency and the actor become particularly clear
when she compares Beckett with the noh master who, with no pretense of an
egalitarian classroom, requires submission to a strict training technique, rituals like bowing, and formal, honorific language. The gestures of submission
and claims of authority have little to do with anything like individual tyranny;
in Japan, they are part of a widespread pedagogical form. In a discussion of
bowing, Roland Barthes points out that such politeness is regarded with suspicion in "the Occident" owing to a "mythology of the 'person'" as having a
"false 'outside'" and a "personal authentic 'inside.'"[105] Barthes maintains that

culturally specific values of casualness and informality are comparable to—
and no more authentic than—decorous formality. One culture encourages
subjects to perform the gestures of individualism, and the other encourages
compliance with practices of decorum, but both are coded behaviors. Beckett, the noh master, is offered as self-evidently bad, but Beckett as any kind of
master would probably also seem bad in the writing of a Western critic. My noh
lessons encouraged me to consider the value of decorum in a teacher-student
relationship and the ways it enables learning, as well as the similar if less
overtly acknowledged forms of submission to directors, texts, or the conventions of naturalistic acting demanded by Euro-American theatrical practice.

When comparing Western portrayals of femininity and treatment of
women actors with those of noh, we need to be very cautious about acknowledging the specific histories and traditions of theaters and cultures around
the world. Throughout my study of noh, I have observed how concerns for
cultural authenticity have led to easy, generalizing accusations of cultural appropriation and, accordingly, have shut down conversations. Western critics
have learned to voice respect for other cultural practices, but those practices
can conflict with desires to fight misogyny and other forms of oppression.
This is a familiar problem, but noh training has helped make me aware of a
feature of the problem that has not received much attention: the desire for,
and role of, submission in human cultures. We are not particularly good at
describing, much less understanding, the fact that nonsecular, nonliberal
desires, pursuits, and politics exist throughout the world.[106] We often fail to
recognize the complexity of political and cultural movements as varied as
the Egyptian Muslim Brotherhood and mosque movements; the Palestin-
ian group Hamas (we argue whether it is a democratically elected political
party or a terrorist organization and seem unable to acknowledge that a group
might have characteristics of both); and the much less publicized Christian
anti-balaka (anti-machete) groups involved in ethnic cleansing in the Central
African Republic. (We should ask whether we do not talk about this genocide
because some of the atrocities are committed by Christians and the victims
and perpetrators are African). I have argued that Western feminism and gender theory tend to define agency as the ability to pursue one's desires—as
long as those desires reject conventional authorities and traditions, particularly misogynistic traditions like religions and noh theater.

I am not suggesting that extremist religious and political movements are
equivalent to theatrical traditions or that I support their politics. But I do believe that understanding their complexity might encourage more appropriate

and effective responses. Our myopic definitions of agency and assumptions of universal human desires for a "freedom" that is defined in West-centric terms leads to misunderstandings of many political and cultural phenomena, along with Whitelaw's submission to Beckett, May's participation in Christian vespers, Benjamin Britten's silence regarding sexuality and Christian drag, or my own interest in taking noh lessons with a master teacher. Suggesting that Whitelaw is incapable of realizing her own best interests is both dismissive and infantilizing, even when critics are motivated by desires to promote the welfare of women. I recognize that my "appropriation" of noh is entangled with my privilege as an American academic hoping to learn from a "real" noh master as well as my occasionally uncomfortable experience of noh's misogynistic traditions. My desire to behave with a decorum that honors noh traditions and the authority of my sensei is complicated by all of that but is not merely delusional.

The same assumptions about agency underlying discussions of Beckett's direction are evident in responses to his theatrical portrayals of women like May in *Footfalls*. Cima argues that Beckett's theater presents women (borrowing from *Footfalls*) as "dreadfully un-", "at once erased and exalted in an image" that "masks any potential agency that might be exercised by real females—actors or spectators."[107] Would those included in the category of "real females," however that might be defined, understand agency in the same way all around the world? We cannot generalize the liberal definition of what it means to be an agentive person and assume that all theater should support this mode of being. I certainly do not want to ignore the need to fight global injustice, but the tendency to limit agency to a politics and aesthetics of subversion ignores the diverse desires that animate lives around the globe. Beckett's texts and directing style produce a theater that acknowledges the many aspects of our lives not based in subversion. He teaches his actors representational techniques similar to noh, in which *wakis*/Buddhist monks kneel onstage to witness the suffering of ghostly beings who, unable to relinquish wrongful clinging to their individual lives, describe their stories while performing an "art of walking" in circular or zigzag floor patterns. The noh chorus also kneels in *seiza* during the entire play and chants the lines of the characters, just as Voice/Mother and May frequently speak each other's lines. Beckett indicated some interest in Buddhism, the philosophical center of noh, when he quoted a Buddhist principle of identity in his essay "Henri Hayden; homme peintre" (1955): "Gautama . . . said that one is fooling oneself if one says that the 'I' exists, but in saying it does not exist, one is fooling oneself no less."[108] To be ever fooled about the nature of selfhood provokes questions that resonate in *Footfalls*: How does the I exist if it is never properly born? In what language or by what name or anagram can it speak? What would agency or submission mean to such a being?

Footfalls presents an urge for a state resembling a Buddhist "nonbeing" when May insists, "I was not there," and (*taking Mrs. Winter's voice*) asks, "Will you never have done? (*Pause.*)" (BCDW, 400).[109] She registers the torture of existence when Voice/Mother tells her that she is in her forties and she gasps, "So little?" (BCDW, 400). And that exchange takes place in the first of three acts through which May must continue to walk her narrow path until the final moment when the lights rise again on the strip to reveal her absence, a seeming negation or release from "it all." A Western feminist might see the actor playing May/Amy as being tortured by a dramaturgy that would "purge the theatre of bodies" and by Beckett's demand that "female actors evacuate their bodies in front of our eyes."[110] Yet the kind of bodily evacuation achieved through the practice of learning "emptiness" is a profound achievement in Buddhism, far from indicating either "torture" or a lack of "agency." The repetitive motion of walking back and forth may recall the Book of Job's Satan "going to and fro in the earth."[111] For another audience, it might resemble the ritual purification of a space and the zigzag floor patterns of noh dance, which can appear as either an elegant display of the beautiful long sleeves of the costume or the search for demons in a battle.[112] Audiences bring these and other associations based on their own experiences to their interpretation of May's dance. Beckett may be autocratic in demanding the realization of his stage image, but he cannot impose a single obvious meaning on that image, which opens to a range of interpretations, including the following:

The repetitive pattern of May's nine steps, like noh *shimai*, is a figure for a state of being beyond the requirement that the walker reach a destination, perform a coherent individual self, participate in "real" clock time, or produce effective results. The refusal of a stable identity or simple and obvious form of agency, as May rearranges the letters of her name into Amy and constructs stories about herself as another person, is reflected in the speech of both voices: "Will you never have done?" "I saw nothing, heard nothing. I was not there." But the negative is especially prominent in May's voice: "No, Mother." "No sound." "No, Mother, I did not." "No, Mother, I myself did not, to put it mildly" (BCDW, 402–3). Beckett explores experiences and modes of being that emerge, as if from the deeps or profounds of a mind, while submitting to such constraints as a circumscribed posture, a thirty-three-foot strip, and repeatedly reaching an end and turning back. Versions of agency may be achieved through a willing submission to a performance form and rigorous, even painful, bodily practices and training regimens. Beckett's French translation of *Footfalls* as *Pas* encompasses the tension in a partially or "dreadfully un-" being who insistently walks in a precisely choreographed pattern. *Pas* indicates "step," but it also invites me to hear the particle *ne*, which *pas* redundantly follows in French negation as in the sentence *Je ne vais pas faire un pas* (I will not walk another step). Taking direction from Beckett's clever punning, we might hear *Pas* echoing the homophones in the English "no" and Japanese noh.

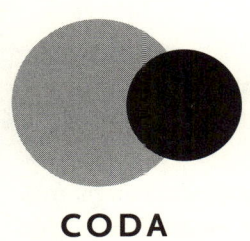

CODA

AT A LATE STAGE OF HIS WORK ON FOOTFALLS, BECKETT HAD
Amy "slip" into the church at the "north" door rather than the "south" (BCDW,
402). While "north" is associated with coldness in the Northern Hemisphere,
the north transept of the church often contains an altar to the Virgin Mary
(*another M name containing all the letters of May and Amy and closely associated with
motherhood*). Benjamin Britten also referred to the cruciform church architecture in an essay entitled "No Ivory Tower" (1969) about the ways in which the
English Opera Group was making music and theater a greater part of the life
of communities:

> The west end of a church is usually suitable for performances. These build-
> ings were the center of local life—rather than the town hall, used for com-
> mittees and assizes. What we are doing has not been done much since the
> Reformation: religious drama with music used to be common before then,
> and little plays were used during the Mass, but this was driven out during

the Reformation. . . . I've learned an enormous amount from the Oriental theater, especially the No drama of Japan.[1]

"No Ivory Tower" is a cool title, but it stands in tension with common assumptions about opera, medieval religious drama, and the noh theater: the major influences on Britten and Plomer's *Curlew River*. Beckett is not usually associated with community theater either, and noh's historical roots in popular entertainment have been carefully scrubbed from current performance contexts.

Today, the "Ivory Tower" usually refers to academia, the institution that allows me to teach, research, and write, a gift for which I am tremendously grateful. I fully recognize the elite and exclusionary practices of the academy that are behind the epithet of the "Ivory Tower" and my privilege within it. Throughout my career, I have submitted to the various rituals (sometimes wearing my academic regalia, a vaguely medieval robe with enormous sleeves), power differentials (often concealed in the seemingly casual relations with chairs and deans who are *never quite not* bosses), and strenuous work regimens ("publish or perish"). To varying degrees, that same submission is true of most of the theorists I have discussed, even those who criticize the pedagogies and celebrate the subversion of everything from gender codes to hierarchies of power to religious and theatrical traditions. Submission is a central experience of our lives, yet it is rarely acknowledged and, unlike subversion, almost never celebrated. There are good reasons for that, but in this book, I have attempted to call attention to the ways that subversion has become a norm so deeply entrenched that we often fail to see its culturally specific manifestations or the ways it, too, can be bound up with privilege.

In *Learning to Kneel*, I tried to discuss elite performance traditions and challenging theories in an accessible writing style that can also incorporate the stories and experiences that brought me to this material. While tracking modernist responses to Japanese noh, I found myself following politically compromised, primarily male artists who, for the most part, are included in the canon of elite or high modernism (which was, at a certain point in the development of this project, surprising and a little troubling to me). I thus offer a more global perspective on these figures by including Japanese collaborators and respondents while avoiding some of the academic conventions of the "Ivory Tower," particularly the habits of evaluation that canonize certain artists and the habits of style that make some of my writing unreadable to many. I made this choice as a way to accommodate *Learning to Kneel*'s particular material and argument, but I acknowledge that some chapters and sections are more successful than others. It is tempting to argue that my failures follow in the great traditions of modernist noh by Ezra Pound, W. B. Yeats, Bertolt Brecht, Benjamin Britten, William Plomer, and Samuel Beckett. Throughout the book, I have also argued against the standards of success and failure as they were applied to these artists, particularly their work with noh. Beckett famously wrote: "No matter. Try again. Fail again. Fail Better."[2] The possibility of being more successful at failing, as this phrase implies, troubles the basic pass/fail binary. For any of the ways I might fail better here, I want to thank, once again, the teachers to whom I dedicate this book.

One of those dear teachers discussed with me the character mu (無, nothingness) as an aesthetic crucial to noh and perhaps the one that the modernists most often failed to approximate. He found mu in the space between gestures, the quiet that must precede music and separate each note, and the blank spaces on a canvas or stage that allow us to see the color elsewhere. In my dancing, writing, performing, and living, I am not very good at making space for nothingness. In fact, I filled that conversation with nonsense by saying that Pound had included the character 無 (mu) in The Pisan Cantos at the moment when he linked the Greek hero of the Odyssey with the fisherman Hakuryō of Hagoromo. I mistakenly claimed that Pound glossed mu with the name Odysseus gave to avoid the Cyclops, ΟΎ ΤΙΣ or Noman, before writing, "the nymph of Hagoromo came to me / as a corona of angels" (74.177–81). I realized my error moments before I almost taught that same mistake to my students. It was the character mo (莫, no, not) that Pound printed with the allusions to the Odyssey and Hagoromo. The desire to make transnational connections and coincidences can lead us to big mistakes. I was only partially consoled that mo, translated as "no," gave me another homonym for noh to add to my list. Then, while doing the research for my sections on Ozu and Japanese modernism, I discovered that the filmmaker's gravestone contains no name, only the character 無 (mu).

NOTES

Preface

1. Edward Said, *Orientalism* (New York: Vintage Books, 1978).

2. *Zeami: Performance Notes*, trans. Thomas Hare (New York: Columbia University Press 2008).

3. I am grateful to Casey Preston and David Crandall for generously helping me create these clips.

Introduction to Noh Lessons

1. The so-called authoritative translation of *Hagoromo* is Royall Tyler, trans. and ed., *Hagoromo* (author and date unknown), in *Japanese Nō Dramas* (London: Penguin, 1992), 96–107. Subsequent references are cited in the text and notes by the abbreviation JND. Clips are available at http://sites.bu.edu/learningtokneel/.

2. I tell the story of my unmasterful training with awareness of Carol Fisher Sorgenfrei's warning that "when scholars of any nation become so proud of their mastery of alien concepts that they forget or suppress their own cultural identity,

they willingly succumb to 'theoretical imperialism'" ("Countering 'Theoretical Imperialism': Some Possibilities from Japan," *Theatre Research International* 32, no. 3 [2007]: 312–24).

3. In addition to studying with Furukawa Mitsuru in 2009 and 2010, I also participated in the Noh Training Project (NTP) directed by Richard Emmert in Tokyo (2009) and Bloomsburg, Pennsylvania (2008, 2010). NTP brings professional noh actors and musicians to Bloomsburg, using a somewhat revised pedagogy for North American, English-speaking students. My lessons with Furukawa sensei also were altered in countless ways as we worked through linguistic and cultural differences.

4. Akiko Miyake, "Ezra Pound and Noh," in *A Guide to Ezra Pound and Ernest Fenollosa's "Classic Noh Theatre of Japan,"* ed. Akiko Miyake, Sanehide Kodama, and Nicholas Teele (Orono, Maine: National Poetry Foundation and Ezra Pound Society of Japan, 1994), xvii–lv.

5. Ezra Pound, *Nishikigi* ("Translated from the Japanese of Motokiyo [Zeami] by Ernest Fenollosa"), *Poetry* 4 (1914): 35–48; Ernest Fenollosa, *Certain Noble Plays of Japan: From the Manuscripts of Ernest Fenollosa, Chosen and Finished by Ezra Pound, with an Introduction by William Butler Yeats* (Churchtown: Cuala, 1916; repr., Shannon: Irish University Press, 1971). In 1917, Knopf published Ezra Pound and Ernest Fenollosa, *"Noh," or, Accomplishment: A Study of the Classical Stage of Japan* in the United States. I will cite from the later edition, *The Classic Noh Theatre of Japan* (New York: New Directions, 1959). Subsequent references are cited in the text by the abbreviation PFNoh.

6. For a compelling argument about the benefits of disrupting the dominance of national rubrics (British drama, American poetry) in literary studies, see Jahan Ramazani, *A Transnational Poetics* (Chicago: University of Chicago Press, 2009).

7. Joseph Lennon's *Irish Orientalism* (Syracuse, N.Y.: Syracuse University Press, 2004), a detailed study of Ireland's interest in the so-called Orient, includes an interesting chapter, "W. B. Yeats's Celtic Orient," that provides only this mention of Itō in a footnote (423–24n.4).

8. Eric C. Rath, *The Ethos of Noh: Actors and Their Art* (Cambridge, Mass.: Harvard University Press, 2004). See also Eric Hobsbawm and Terrence Ranger, eds., *The Invention of Tradition* (Cambridge: Cambridge University Press, 1983). Rath claims that the "drastic narrowing" of the noh canon occurred during the Edo period (*Ethos of Noh*, 201).

9. I am deeply indebted to David Crandall for describing his training as a professional in the Hōshō school of noh performance and for sharing his unpublished account "The Angel" (1978).

10. The other four schools for *shite* actors are Konparu, Hōshō, Kongō, and Kita. The last was founded by Kita Shichidayū in the early seventeenth century (whereas the others had existed for as long as 250 years), and he did not claim a hereditary relation to Zeami.

11. Rath, *Ethos of Noh*, 116–35. Beginning in the mid-seventeenth century, the *bakufu* (shogunate) demanded genealogies in exchange for stipends. Rath details the disputes over noh's traditions, lineages, and repertory that characterized its six-hundred-year history, describing noh from the fourteenth through sixteenth centuries as a "much more inclusive practice" that later became "a closed, male-dominated and largely hereditary profession" (9).

12. Ibid., 235. I observed amateur students who devoted decades of continuous self-cultivation through training, and based on that standard, I can hardly qualify myself as an amateur. For an account of such long-term and rigorous studies of noh, see Katrina Moore and Ruth Campbell, "Mastery with Age: The Appeal of the Traditional Arts to Senior Citizens in Contemporary Japan," *Japanstudien*, October 2009, 223–51.

13. Barbara Geilhorn Trier, "Between Self-Empowerment and Discrimination: Women in nō Today," in *Nō Theatre Transversal*, ed. Stanca Scholz-Cionca and Christopher Balme (Munich: Iudicium, 2008), 108. See also Eric C. Rath, "Challenging the Old Men: A Brief History of Women in Noh Theater," *Women & Performance: A Journal of Feminist Theory* 12, no. 1 (2001): 97–111.

14. Matsumoto Yasushi, "Noh and Kyogen in 2004," in *Theatre Year-Book* (Tokyo: International Theatre Institute, 2005), 47.

15. Rath, *Ethos of Noh*, 230. My interpretation of misogyny in the purification rite is shared by the Shigeyama family of *kyōgen* actors, who refuse to practice it and "consider it a distasteful reminder of feudal sexism" (Jonah Salz, quoted on 229). For interviews with two noh actors who describe their purification practices before performing *Okina*, see William T. Vollman, *Kissing the Mask: Beauty, Understatement and Femininity in Japanese Noh Theater* (New York: HarperCollins, 2010), 41.

16. Crandall points out that the "the text's efficiency as a learning tool is not the primary consideration for those who make and use it" ("Angel," 2).

17. Duncan dancers speak of themselves as part of a third, fourth, or, now, fifth "generation" and trace their lineage (and choreographic heritage) through one of Isadora Duncan's five most famous students and adopted daughters known as the "Isadorables."

18. "In performance practice, neither singers nor instrumentalists count the beats as a means of 'keeping time' but rather rely on the relationship of the drum patterns with the hemistiches and its syllables to assure proper timing" (Richard Emmert,

"Hiranori: A Unique Rhythm Form in Japanese Nō Music," in *Musical Voices of Asia*, ed. Richard Emmert and Yuki Minegishi [Tokyo: Japan Foundation, 1980], 104). My basic understanding of noh music is indebted to Richard Emmert's lessons on the *taiko* drum, classes on music theory at the Noh Training Project (2008 and 2010), and David Crandall's instruction at Advanced Writers' Workshops in Tokyo (2010) and Grand Rapids, Michigan (2011).

19. The Japanese composer Toshio Hosokawa describes his approach to noh tradition when creating his 2011 opera based on Zeami's *Matsukaze*. Quoted in "Haunting Unpredictability," *New York Times*, August 4, 2011, available at http://www.nytimes.com/2011/08/07/arts/music/matsukaze-opera-by-the-japanese-composer-toshio-hosokawa.html (accessed May 18, 2015).

20. Hong Sun, "Pound's Quest for Confucian Ideals: The Chinese History Cantos," in *Ezra Pound and China*, ed. Zhaoming Qian (Ann Arbor: University of Michigan Press, 2006), 96–119; Eric Hayot, *Chinese Dreams: Pound, Brecht, Tel Quel* (Ann Arbor: University of Michigan Press, 2004); Jed Rasula, "Make It New," *Modernism / Modernity* 17, no. 4 (2011): 713–33.

21. Rath describes the efforts of Kanze Sakon, who became the leader of the Kanze school in 1911 just two years before Pound received Fenollosa's noh manuscripts, to regularize the chant books (*utaibon*), standardize the Kanze style by squelching the unique techniques of Kyoto noh families, and categorize all 210 plays in the canon according to the five-category schema: god plays (*waki-nō*), warrior plays (*shura-mono*), woman plays (*kazura-mono*), fourth-category plays (*yonbanme-mono*), and concluding plays (*kiri-nō*) (*Ethos of Noh*, 213–19). This overgeneralized schema remains prevalent in discussions of noh today, although it did not exist in the fifteenth century when the majority of the plays were composed (JND, 13).

22. For a summary of these trends, see Richard Begam and Michael Valdez Moses, introduction to *Modernism and Colonialism: British and Irish Literature, 1899–1939* (Durham, N.C.: Duke University Press, 2007), 1–16.

23. Masaru Sekine and Christopher Murray, *Yeats and the Noh: A Comparative Study* (Savage, Md.: Barnes & Noble, 1990), 1; Okifumi Komesu, "At the Hawk's Well and Taka No Izumi in a 'Creative Circle,'" *Yeats Annual* 5 (1987): 111.

24. Edward Said argues against "indicting" modernism "wholesale," yet he suggests that modernism's response to empire was "ironic" rather than "oppositional"; "cultural texts imported the foreign into Europe" in order to "convey an ironic sense of how vulnerable Europe was" to the colonized other (*Culture and Imperialism* [New York: Vintage Books, 1994], 186–89).

25. For a useful discussion of these assumptions, see Craig Latrell, "After Appropriation," *Drama Review* 44, no. 4 (2000): 44–55.

26. Ian Carruthers, "A Translation of Fifteen Pages of Ito Michio's Autobiography 'Utsukushiku Naru Kyoshitsu,'" *Canadian Journal of Irish Studies* 2, no. 1 (1976): 35.

27. Shinko Kagaya, "Dancing on a Moving Train: Nō Between Two Wars," in *Nō Theatre Transversal*, ed. Scholz-Cionca and Balme, 19–30.

28. Between 1988 and 2008, reviews of ten different performances of At the Hawk's Well and related adaptations were printed in the *Theatre Year-Book*, published annually by the International Theatre Institute of Tokyo.

29. Among the best transnational studies covering the genres that I explore in this book are Susan Leigh Foster, *Worlding Dance* (Basingstoke: Palgrave Macmillan, 2009); Ramazani, *Transnational Poetics*; and Kwame Anthony Appiah, *Cosmopolitanism: Ethics in a World of Strangers* (New York: Norton, 2006).

30. Homi Bhabha offers his famous account of hybridity in *The Location of Culture* (New York: Routledge, 1994).

31. For a recent account of universities as targets of conservatives interested in imposing a different "legitimate culture," see John K. Wilson, *Patriotic Correctness: Academic Freedom and Its Enemies* (Boulder, Colo.: Paradigm, 2008).

32. Bhabha describes a "contest" between pedagogical constructs like "history" and national narratives and the "contentious, performative space of the living" (*Location of Culture*, 225).

33. Performance and performativity are often used somewhat interchangeably. The "performative," taken from linguistic studies like J. L. Austin, *How to Do Things with Words* (Cambridge, Mass.: Harvard University Press, 1962), has been adapted to describe identity categories that are brought into existence through spoken and bodily acts, perhaps most famously by Judith Butler, *Gender Trouble: Feminism and the Subversion of Identity* (New York: Routledge, 1990).

34. Frantz Fanon famously wrote, "The attention devoted to modifying this aspect [of Arab tradition], the emotion the conqueror puts into his pedagogical work, his prayers, his threats, weave a whole universe of resistances around this particular element of the culture" ("Algeria Unveiled," in *The New Left Reader*, ed. Carl Oglesby [New York: Grove Press, 1969], 171, originally published in *L'an cinq de la révolution algérienne* [Paris: Maspero, 1959]).

35. Gayatri Chakravorty Spivak writes, "Imperialism used Woman, 'freeing' her to legitimize itself," in *A Critique of Postcolonial Reason* (Cambridge, Mass.: Harvard University Press, 1999), 244.

36. Bhabha, *Location of Culture*, 89.

37. Drucilla Cornell, "The Secret Behind the Veil: A Reinterpretation of 'Algeria Unveiled,'" *Philosophia Africana* 4, no. 2 (2001): 33.

38. Kim Willsher, "France's Burqa Ban Upheld by Human Rights Court," *Guardian*, July 1, 2014, available at http://www.theguardian.com/world/2014/jul/01/france-burqa-ban-upheld-human-rights-court (accessed May 18, 2015).

39. N. Kawai, H. Miyata, R. Nishimura, and K. Okanoya, "Shadows Alter Facial Expressions of Noh Masks," *PLOS ONE* 8, no. 8 (2013): e71389, available at doi:10.1371/journal.pone.0071389 (accessed September, 29, 2015).

40. Saba Mahmood, *The Politics of Piety: The Islamic Revival and the Feminist Subject* (Princeton, N.J.: Princeton University Press, 2005).

41. Ibid., 8.

42. Ibid., 14.

43. For a classic essay on the marginalization of nonnormative sexual practices in feminist theory, see Gayle Rubin, "Thinking Sex: Notes for a Radical Theory of the Politics of Sexuality," in *Pleasure and Danger: Exploring Female Sexuality*, ed. Carole S. Vance (Boston: Routledge & Kegan Paul, 1984), 267–319. Heather Love edited a special issue, "Thinking Sex," *GLQ* 17, no. 1 (2010), that includes Rubin's "Blood Under the Bridge: Reflections on Thinking Sex," 15–48. See also Gayle Rubin, "The Leather Menace: Comments on Politics and S/M," in *Coming to Power: Writings and Graphics on Lesbian S/M*, ed. Samois (Boston: Alyson Books, 1981), 194–229.

44. For summaries of debates during the so-called sex wars, see Linda LeMoncheck, *Loose Women, Lecherous Men: A Feminist Philosophy of Sex* (New York: Oxford University Press, 1997); and Susan Brownmiller, *In Our Time: Memoir of a Revolution* (New York: Delta Books, 2000). I am grateful to Patricia Stuelke for discussing her research on the neoliberal notions embedded in both sides of the sex wars, and I look forward to her forthcoming publications.

45. In *In an Abusive State: How Neoliberalism Appropriated the Feminist Movement Against Sexual Violence* (Durham, N.C.: Duke University Press, 2008), Kristin Bumiller argues that the radical antiporn position merged with 1980s neoliberalism as it posited a criminalized sphere of sexual activity from which private citizens must be protected.

46. Walter Benn Michaels describes S/M as an "eroticized form of liberalism," in *The Shape of the Signifier: 1967 to the End of History* (Princeton, N.J.: Princeton University Press, 2004), 155. See also Rosemary Hennessy, *Profit and Pleasure: Sexual Identities in Late Capitalism* (New York: Routledge, 2000).

47. Michel Foucault, "Le gai savoir I," *Mec Magazine*, June 1988, 36. See also David M. Halperin, *Saint = Foucault: Towards a Gay Hagiography* (New York: Oxford University

Press, 1995), 94. Gayle Rubin similarly compares S/M with "spiritual disciplines" and points out that "in many cultures the application of carefully chosen physical stress is a method for inducing transcendental mental and emotional states" ("The Catacombs: A Temple of the Butthole," in Leatherfolk: Radical Sex, People, Politics, and Practice, ed. Mark Thompson [Boston: Alyson Books, 1991], 127–28).

48. Halperin, Saint=Foucault, 109. For a very different perspective on Foucault's life as a personal philosophical experiment, see James Miller, The Passion of Michel Foucault (Cambridge, Mass.: Harvard University Press, 1993); and Halperin's critique of Miller (143–52).

49. Eve Kosofsky Sedgwick, Touching Feeling: Affect, Pedagogy, Performativity (Durham, N.C.: Duke University Press, 2003), 160, 166. My thanks to J. Keith Vincent for recommending this book and all that he has taught me about Sedgwick and Japan.

50. Ibid., 169.

51. Ibid.

52. Ibid., 12–13.

53. The play is Izutsu, and the lecture-demonstration featuring my teacher Furukawa Mitsuru; another actor, Shimizu Kanji; Professor Jon Brokering of Hōsei University; and me was held on May 18, 2009.

54. Mary Bryson and Suzanne de Castell, "Queer Pedagogy: Praxis Makes Im/Perfect," Canadian Journal of Education 18, no. 3 (1993): 299.

55. Sedgwick, Touching Feeling, 44.

56. Gregory M. Pflugfelder, Cartographies of Desire: Male-Male Sexuality in Japanese Discourse, 1600–1950 (Berkeley: University of California Press, 1999), 27. See also Gary Leupp, Male Colors: The Construction of Homosexuality in Tokugawa Japan (Berkeley: University of California Press, 1995); and Ihara Saikaku, The Great Mirror of Male Love, trans. Paul Gordon Schalow (Stanford, Calif.: Stanford University Press, 1990).

57. Pflugfelder, Cartographies, 113–14.

58. Zeami: Performance Notes, trans. Thomas Hare (New York: Columbia University Press, 2008), 3–4.

59. Rath, Ethos of Noh, 34–35.

60. William MacDuff may slightly overstate the case when he claims that "the medieval concept of yūgen referred in its simplest form to the aesthetic and sensual charms of beautiful boys" ("Beautiful Boys in Nō Drama: The Idealization of Homoerotic Desire," Asian Theatre Journal 13, no. 2 [1996]: 249). Hare points to the term's origins in classical poetics and suggests that Zeami's use of yūgen "adds a surface romance or even eroticism" but is related mainly to "the abstract

and formal beauty of singing and dance" (*Zeami*, 5). Kenneth Yasuda claims that Zeami associated *yūgen* with "the feminine," quoting from Zeami's *Shikadō* (1420): "What is courtly and graceful in the air of *yūgen* arises from the dynamic aspects of the womanly form" ("The Structure of *Hagoromo*, a Nō," *Harvard Journal of Asiatic Studies* 33 [1973]: 51).

61. *Zeami*, trans. Hare, 27.

62. Ibid., 123–24.

63. Ibid., 428–30.

64. Pflugfelder, *Cartographies*, 74–75; MacDuff, "Beautiful Boys," 250–51. For a historical discussion of Buddhist practice, see Dharmachari Jñanavira, "Homosexuality in the Japanese Buddhist Tradition," *Western Buddhist Review* 3 (2001), available at http://www.westernbuddhistreview.com/vol3/homosexuality.html#_ednref24 (accessed September, 29, 2015).

65. Margaret H. Childs, "Chigo Monogatari: Love Stories or Buddhist Sermons?" *Monumenta Nipponica* 35, no. 2 (1980): 128–29. Sedgwick describes the "greater vehicle" of the bodhisattva's pursuit: "For the bodhisattva, however, the pedagogical imperative of occasioning others' enlightenment takes priority even over one's own spiritual advancement: a bodhisattva defers entering nirvana until after all other sentient beings have learned to do so" (*Touching Feeling*, 160).

66. Pflugfelder, *Cartographies*, 74; MacDuff, "Beautiful Boys," 250. This misogynistic belief contributed to noh's prohibitions against women actors and persists in the (now debated) purification rituals required of the *shikisanban*.

67. Pflugfelder, *Cartographies*, 71.

68. MacDuff, "Beautiful Boys," 252.

69. Ibid., 250.

70. Arthur Waley, *The Nō Plays of Japan* (New York: Knopf, 1922), 167. This is not to say that Waley could have provided a perfect or accurate translation but to emphasize his choice to put half of a play into a couple of footnoted lines.

71. Edward Carpenter, *Intermediate Types Among Primitive Folk: A Study in Social Evolution* (London: George Allen, 1914). Chapter 8 is titled "The Samurai of Japan and Their Ideal." For Waley's relationship with Carpenter, G. Lowes Dickinson, E. M. Forster, and others interested in the homoerotic relationships of the Japanese warrior tradition, see John Walter de Gruchy, *Orienting Arthur Waley: Japonism, Orientalism, and the Creation of Japanese Literature in English* (Honolulu: University of Hawai'i Press, 2003).

72. Carpenter, *Intermediate Types Among Primitive Folk*, 11–12.

73. MacDuff, "Beautiful Boys," 252–53.

74. Ezra Pound, *The Pisan Cantos* (New York: New Directions, 1948), canto 79, l. 63.

1. Ezra Pound as Noh Student

1.   Furukawa Mitsuru, personal communication, April 20, 2009. The so-called authoritative translation of *Hagoromo* is JND, 101.

2.   Zeami writes, "Now, with regard to the Suruga Dance, it has come down to us as a secret piece in this land ever since its inception when a heavenly maiden descended to earth and left it here" (*Zeami: Performance Notes*, trans. Thomas Hare [New York: Columbia University Press, 2008], 101).

3.   Gayatri Chakravorty Spivak asks epistemological questions about how a culture can be known and redefines the "pedagogy of the humanities as the arena of cultural explanations that question the explanations of culture" (*In Other Worlds* [New York: Routledge, 1998], 160). Roland Barthes describes an ontological bind: "Hence Orient and Occident cannot be taken here as 'realities' to be compared and contrasted historically, philosophically, culturally, politically" (*Empire of Signs* [New York: Hill & Wang, 1982], 3)

4.   For additional images and a thorough description of the noh stage as well as many other aspects of noh, see www.the-noh.com.

5.   Kenneth K. Yasuda, "The Structure of *Hagoromo*, a Nō," *Harvard Journal of Asiatic Studies* 33 (1973): 11.

6.   Shōdan are standard subsections that are linked together in different orders but are found throughout the noh canon, and the progression of *shōdan* determines the musical structure of the play. The *waki* often enters singing a *shidai*, a verse rhythmically matched to the drumbeats. Noh has metered and nonmetered passages and songs that are matched and unmatched to the drums, which allows performers to vary the duration and emphasis of their vocalization.

7.   Yasuda, "Structure of *Hagoromo*," 59. The offstage call is termed a *yobikake*.

8.   Ibid., 19. Kita Roppeita performed *Hagoromo* at the Imperial Court on December 8, 1915

9.   *Mondō* is a prose dialogue, and *kakeai* is a recitative sung in an unmatched rhythm.

10.   Bertolt Brecht complained about Western acting and used Chinese and Japanese performance styles to help him develop his ideas of alienated acting, as discussed in "Alienation Effects in Chinese Acting," in *Brecht on Theatre: The Development of an Aesthetic*, ed. and trans. John Willet (New York: Hill & Wang, 1964), 91–99.

11.   Darko Suvin, "Revelation vs. Conflict: A Lesson from Nō Plays for a Comparative Dramaturgy," *Theatre Journal* 46, no. 4 (1994): 534–38.

12.   Ibid., 532.

13.   Zeami, trans. Hare, 429.

14.   Ibid.

15.   Suvin, "Revelation vs. Conflict," 537.

16. Ibid., 538.

17. Eve Kosofsky Sedgwick, *The Weather in Proust*, ed. Jonathan Goldberg (Durham, N.C.: Duke University Press, 2011), 48.

18. For discussion of these contested traditions, see Eric C. Rath, *The Ethos of Noh: Actors and Their Art* (Cambridge, Mass.: Harvard University Press, 2004), 116–35.

19. See the review of the controversial "Picasso and Africa" exhibit in Cape Town, South Africa, by Andrew Meldrum, "Stealing Beauty," *Guardian*, March 14, 2006, available at http://www.guardian.co.uk/artanddesign/2006/mar/15/art (accessed February 15, 2015). Julie McGee criticizes how the exhibit positioned Picasso in relation to "'anonymous' African art" and thereby failed to consider "what agency the 'African art' had aside from aesthetic muteness and artist's muse" ("Primitivism on Trial: The 'Picasso and Africa' Exhibition in South Africa," *Anthropology and Aesthetics* 52 [2007]: 162). To seek "agency" in objects like "African art," even if it is a metaphorical search, is to adopt an almost unintelligible definition of agency. See also Simon Gikandi, "Picasso, Africa, and the Schemata of Difference," *Modernism/Modernity* 10, no. 3 (2003): 455–80.

20. Octavio Paz, "Latin American Poetry" (1973), in *Convergences: Essays on Art and Literature*, trans. Helen Lane (San Diego: Harcourt Brace Jovanovich, 1987), 212.

21. Pound published his series "Provincialism the Enemy" in the *New Age* (1917) just after his work on noh. See Ezra Pound, *Selected Prose, 1909–1965* (New York: New Directions, 1973), 189–203.

22. Ezra Pound, "Three Cantos," *Poetry* 10, nos. 3–5 (1917): 113.

23. Ibid., 117. Ursula Shioji suggests that Hakuryō is a "persona" of Pound in the translations of both *Hagoromo* and *The Pisan Cantos*, in *Ezra Pound's "Pisan Cantos" and the Noh* (Frankfurt am Main: Lang, 1998), 210. See also Keiko Sekiguchi Wells, "Pound's *Hagoromo* as an Imagist Poem," *Ehime daigaku kyōyōbu kiyō* 22 (1989): 25–38.

24. Pound, "Three Cantos," 115.

25. Building on Judith Butler's foundational discussion of drag in *Gender Trouble: Feminism and the Subversion of Identity* (New York: Routledge, 1990), Elizabeth Freeman introduces the idea of "temporal drag" as "a productive obstacle to progress, a usefully distorting pull backward, and a necessary pressure on the present tense" (*Time Binds: Queer Temporalities, Queer Histories* [Durham, N.C.: Duke University Press, 2010], 64).

26. Ce Rosenow discusses some of the collaborations in "Fenollosa's Legacy: The Japanese Network of Ezra Pound," *Philological Quarterly* 85, nos. 3–4 (2006): 371–89.

27. Mary Fenollosa to Ezra Pound, November 25, 1913, in *Ezra Pound and Japan: Letters and Essays*, ed. Sanehide Kodama (Reading Ridge, Conn.: Black Swan, 1987), 8. She selected Pound because he had already declared his interest in Asia in discus-

sions of his haiku-inspired "In a Station of the Metro" (1911) and poems related to China: "After Chu'u Yuan," "Fan-Piece for Her Imperial Lord," and "Liu Ch'e" (1913).

28. Fenollosa to Pound, November 25, 1913, 7; Nick Salvato hears "rich implications" in Mary Fenollosa's "desire for the actors" (*Uncloseting Drama: American Modernism and Queer Performance* [New Haven, Conn.: Yale University Press, 2010], 32–34).

29. Fenollosa to Pound, November 25, 1913, 7.

30. Pound inserted a footnote to Fenollosa's claim that his teachers had praised his "wonderful" progress: "This is in Fenollosa's diary, not in a part of a lecture or in anything he had published, so there is no question of its being an immodest statement" (PFNoh, 28).

31. Tomoji Okada to Ezra Pound, January or August 22, 1959, a response to Okada's earlier letter, informing him of the error, in *Ezra Pound and Japan*, ed. Kodama, 130. See also Tokutarō Shigehisa, "Fenollosa's Ashes and Japan," *Comparative Literature* 2 (1959): 83–84.

32. Fenollosa to Pound, November 25, 1913, 7.

33. Fenollosa was a part-time lecturer in English at the Higher Normal School in Tokyo from 1898 to 1900. See Akiko Miyake, "Ezra Pound and Noh," in *A Guide to Ezra Pound and Ernest Fenollosa's "Classic Noh Theatre of Japan,"* ed. Akiko Miyake, Sanehide Kodama, and Nicholas Teele (Orono, Maine: National Poetry Foundation and Ezra Pound Society of Japan, 1994), xvii–lv.

34. Sachiko Yoshida, *Hagoromo*, in ibid., 171.

35. Ian Carruthers, "A Translation of Fifteen Pages of Ito Michio's Autobiography 'Utsukushiku Naru Kyoshitsu,'" *Canadian Journal of Irish Studies* 2, no. 1 (1976): 39.

36. Midori Takeishi, *Japanese Elements in Michio Ito's Early Period (1915–1924): Meetings of East and West in the Collaborative Works*, ed. and rev. David Pacun (Tokyo: Gendaito-sho, 2006), 20.

37. Ezra Pound, "Study of Noh Continues in the West," *Japan Times and Mail*, December 10, 1939, reprinted as "Study of Noh Continues in the West," in *Ezra Pound and Japan*, ed. Kodama, 156.

38. Ibid.

39. Ezra Pound to Katsue Kitasono, May 24, 1936, in *Ezra Pound and Japan*, ed. Kodama, 27–28.

40. Kume Tamijurō to Ezra Pound, March 22, 1916, in ibid., 9.

41. Kume to Pound, [December?] 13, 1917, in ibid., 13–14.

42. Kume to Pound, July 5, 1918; December 21, 1918; and January 1, 1919, in ibid., 15–17.

43. Kume to Pound, March 10, 1921, in ibid., 20.

44. Ezra Pound, *The Pisan Cantos* (New York: New Directions, 2003), 76.308. Subsequent references are cited in the text and notes by verse and line number. In 1954, Pound wrote in a letter to Wyndham Lewis that "Tami's dream" was "big 10 by 12 feet" and "in low tone buff, yellow and blackish" (*Pound / Lewis: The Letters of Ezra Pound and Wyndham Lewis*, ed. Timothy Materer [New York: New Directions, 1985], 279–80). Pound's daughter, Mary de Rachewiltz, remembers it as

> a gray opaque canvas into which I read nothingness; chaos, the universe or the torso of a giant, crucified. Tami Koume's Super-artificial-growing-creation, whispering: 'We are now standing at the critical moment of humanity. We must be saved by something.' And he was killed in the Tokyo earthquake and his big canvas in Venice torn to pieces during the war. (*Discretions: A Memoir by Ezra Pound's Daughter* [New York: Faber & Faber, 1971], 22)

45. Kume to Pound, March 24, 1923, in *Ezra Pound and Japan*, ed. Kodama, 23.

46. James Longenbach, *Stone Cottage: Pound, Yeats, and Modernism* (New York: Oxford University Press, 1988).

47. Ibid., 54, 39, 193. See also William Pratt, *Ezra Pound and the Making of Modernism* (New York: AMS Press, 2007), 82.

48. Yoko Chiba, "Ezra Pound's Versions of Fenollosa's Noh Manuscripts and Yeats's Unpublished 'Suggestions & Corrections,'" *Yeats Annual* 4 (1986): 136.

49. Although translation is not focused on collaboration, Gayatri Chakravorty Spivak suggests that it is "the most intimate act of reading" and emphasizes the "erotic" aspects of translating over the "ethical," in *Outside in the Teaching Machine* (New York: Routledge, 1993), 183. See also Spivak, "Translating into English," in *Nation, Language, and the Ethics of Translation*, ed. Sandra Bermann and Michael Wood (Princeton, N.J.: Princeton University Press, 2005), 94.

50. Ezra Pound, "Hell," *Criterion*, April 1934, in *Literary Essays of Ezra Pound*, ed. T. S. Eliot (New York: New Directions, 1954), 207.

51. Ezra Pound, "Cavalcanti" (1935), in *Theories of Translation*, ed. Rainer Schulte and John Biguenet (Chicago: University of Chicago Press, 1992), 85 (italics in original).

52. Ibid.

53. Ibid.

54. Ibid., 91–92.

55. Ibid., 92.

56. David L. Eng, Judith Halberstam, and José Esteban Muñoz, eds., "What's Queer About Queer Studies Now?" special issue, *Social Text* 23, nos. 3–4 (2005): 1–17. I hear a hint of "queerer-than-thou competitiveness" in that title, as does Michael Warner, "Queer and Then," *Chronicle of Higher Education*, January 1, 2012, available

at http://chronicle.com/article/QueerThen-/130161/ (accessed February 15, 2015). For me, like many, the power of queer theory is its ability to expose totalizing worldviews that threaten to become entrenched, including an emergent queer liberalism or "homonationalism." See Jasbir K. Puar, *Terrorist Assemblages: Homonationalism in Queer Times* (Durham, N.C.: Duke University Press, 2007).

57. Alan Golding claims, "Crucial to Pound's educational polemics is the connection that he presumes between effective teaching and a limited canon" ("From Pound to Olson: The Avant-Garde Poet as Pedagogue," *Journal of Modern Literature* 34, no. 1 [2010]: 91). The noh canon is usually cited at 200 to 250 plays, and it has been contested and altered throughout the centuries.

58. Roy E. Teele, "A Balance Sheet on Pound's Translations of Noh Plays," *Books Abroad* 39, no. 2 (1965): 168–70. H. L. Joly described Pound's failure to "hug the [source] text," in his early review, "Recent Books on Japan," *Asiatic Review* 12 (1917): 71–80.

59. Miyake defends inaccuracy as originality and celebrates Pound's invention of a cult of love that joins noh to the *Odyssey* and the Eleusinian Mysteries, in "Ezra Pound and Noh," xxix. For similar arguments applied to Pound's *Cathay* (1915), which was based on Fenollosa's manuscript translations of Chinese poetry, see Barry Ahearn, "Cathay: What Sort of Translation?"; and Christine Froula, "The Beauties of Mistranslation: On Pound's English After *Cathay*," in *Ezra Pound and China*, ed. Zhaoming Qian (Ann Arbor: University of Michigan Press, 2003), 31–48, 49–71.

60. Eric Hayot clarifies the trouble with our assumptions about cultural realities in a fascinating reading of Edward Said's ambivalent use of the term "real." Said maintained that "the Orient is an idea" that has "a reality and presence in and for the West" but that there is a "corresponding reality" in Eastern cultures and nations and that "lives, histories, and customs" have a "brute reality." Finally, Said claimed that his study will not deal with the relationship between orientalism and a "'real' Orient"—this time with "real" set off in quotation marks (*Chinese Dreams: Pound, Brecht, Tel Quel* [Ann Arbor: University of Michigan Press, 2004], 5).

61. This contradicts Kodama's claim that Pound ignored "Japanese realities" like modernization and Westernization while imagining "a treasure land for the aesthete" and "the distant mythic country of Hagoromo" (*Ezra Pound and Japan*, xvi). Kevin M. Doak discusses Japanese nationalism in "What Is a Nation and Who Belongs? National Narratives and the Ethnic Imagination in Twentieth-Century Japan," *American Historical Review* 102, no. 2 (1997): 283–309.

62. The foundational study of Japan's influence on Pound is Earl Miner, *The Japanese Tradition in British and American Literature* (Princeton, N.J.: Princeton University Press, 1958). See also Robert Kern, *Orientalism, Modernism, and the American Poem*

(Cambridge: Cambridge University Press, 1996). For a recent study that incorporates the role of visual culture in this transnational exchange, see Rupert Richard Arrowsmith, "The Transcultural Roots of Modernism: Imagist Poetry, Japanese Visual Culture, and the Western Museum System," *Modernism/Modernity* 18, no. 1 (2011): 27–42. For *japonisme*'s reach beyond Euro-American modernism, see Anita Patterson, "*Japonisme* and Modernist Style in Afro-Caribbean Literature: The Art of Derek Walcott," *Review of International American Studies* 2, no. 2 (2007): 19–24.

63. Timothy Materer, "Make It Sell! Ezra Pound Advertises Modernism," in *Marketing Modernisms: Self-Promotion, Canonization, Rereading*, ed. Kevin J. H. Dettmar and Stephen Watt (Ann Arbor: University of Michigan Press, 1996), 17–36.

64. Ezra Pound, "In a Station of the Metro," *Poetry* 2 (1913): 12, and "How I Began," *T. P.'s Weekly*, June 6, 1913, 707. For a detailed summary of Pound's publications involving Japan, see David Ewick's invaluable archive, "Ezra Pound and the Invention of Japan," *Japonisme, Orientalism, and Modernism: A Bibliography* (2003), available at http://themargins.net/bib/B/BK/oobkintro.html (accessed April 1, 2015).

65. Ezra Pound, "Vorticism," *Fortnightly Review*, September 1914, 461–71, reprinted in Ezra Pound, *A Memoir of Gaudier-Brzeska* (New York: New Directions, 1974), 94.

66. Ezra Pound, "The Classical Drama of Japan" ("Edited from Ernest Fenollosa's manuscripts by Ezra Pound"), *Quarterly Review* 221 (1914): 450–77.

67. Ezra Pound, Nishikigi ("Translated from the Japanese of Motokiyo [Zeami] by Ernest Fenollosa"), *Poetry* 4 (1914): 35–48; Ezra Pound to Harriet Monroe, January 31, 1914, in *Selected Letters of Ezra Pound, 1907–1941*, ed. D. D. Paige (New York: New Directions, 1971), 30; Ezra Pound described his work on *Nishikigi*, *Hagoromo*, and *Kinuta* in letters to Dorothy Shakespear, January 6 and 14, 1914, in *Ezra Pound and Dorothy Shakespear: Their Letters, 1909–1914*, ed. Omar Pound and A. Walton Litz (New York: New Directions, 1984), 293–95, 302.

68. The other noh plays Fenellosa ranked highly were *Yōrōboshi* and *Sumidagawa*. According to Umewaka, *Kinuta* "took nearly a life-time, and much prayer and fasting, to learn to sing properly," and *Nishikigi* was "specially loved" by Fenollosa (Fenollosa to Pound, November 25, 1913, 8).

69. Pound treated another play, *Hajitomi*, as an example of a unified image "reinforced by the metric of the Noh speech, by the line of the movements and of the dancing," in an unpublished essay, "Affirmations VI: The Image and the Japanese Classical Stage," which was apparently intended for the Affirmations series he wrote for the *New Age* in 1915 (Ezra Pound Collection on Japanese Drama, Rare Books and Special Collections, Princeton University Library). Akitoshi Nagahata summarized Pound's ideas about "unity of image" in noh but not how they influenced

his translations, in "Pound's Reception of Noh Reconsidered: The Image and the Voice," *Quaderni di palazzo serra* 15 (2008): 113–25.

70. Nobuko Tsukui, *Ezra Pound and Japanese Noh Plays* (Washington D.C.: University Press of America, 1983), 40.

71. *Kefu* is the kind of cloth woven in Michinoku, but it is used as the village name in the play. See Calvin French, trans., *The Brocade Tree (Nishikigi)*, in *Twenty Plays of the Nō Theatre*, ed. Donald Keene (New York: Columbia University Press, 1970), 82–97.

72. The Fenollosa-Hirata draft translation is in Akiko Murakata, "Ernest F. Fenollosa's Studies of No: With Reference to His and Other Unpublished Manuscripts and Ezra Pound's Edition," *Eibungaku hyōron* 51, no. 2 (1986): 1–55.

73. Ernest Fenollosa and Ezra Pound, *The Chinese Written Character as a Medium for Poetry* (1920; repr., San Francisco: City Lights, 1968), 21.

74. French translates the line as "Dyed bright with crimson maple leaves" (*Brocade Tree*, 90).

75. Pound suppressed the Buddhist elements of *Nishikigi* and other noh plays, including the idea that the lovers were suffering because of their "wrongful clinging" to unconsummated passion. See Tsukui, *Ezra Pound*, 43–44.

76. French, *Brocade Tree*, 96. Akiko Takeuchi translates the cliché phrase *yuki wo megurasu mai no sode kana* as "the dancing sleeves whirl the snow around," in "Translation and Creative Misunderstanding: Ezra Pound and Konishi Jin'ichi" (paper presented at the annual convention of the Modern Language Association, Los Angeles, 2011).

77. Murakata, "Ernest F. Fenollosa's Studies of No," 46. See also Scott Johnson, *Nishikigi*, in *Guide*, ed. Miyake, Kodama, and Teele, 89.

78. Fenollosa's draft translation reads, "We have wandered in the darkness of souls which are going out" (quoted in Murakata, "Ernest F. Fenollosa's Studies of No," 46). French translates the passage as "We who dwell in dark delusions / Leave to you who are alive / The question of reality" (*Brocade Tree*, 93).

79. I do not intend to judge the translation in the manner of French, who claims, "Ezra Pound's version of *The Brocade Tree*, based on an unpublished translation by Ernest Fenollosa, is too far from the original to qualify as a translation" (*Brocade Tree*, 83).

80. Ronald Bush points to both the prevalence and uniqueness of controlling symbols and their derivation from noh in "The 'Rhythm of Metaphor': Yeats, Pound, Eliot, and the Unity of Image in Postsymbolist Poetry," in *Allegory, Myth, and Symbol*, ed. Morton W. Bloomfield (Cambridge, Mass.: Harvard University Press, 1981), 371–88. Although Bush's discussion is useful, his definition of noh and supposition of its "unity" are derived entirely from Pound's claims about noh.

81. T. S. Eliot, "Ezra Pound," *Poetry* 68 (1946): 326.

82. T. S. Eliot, "The Noh and the Image," *Egoist*, August 1917, 102–3 (italics in original).

83. Ibid., 103.

84. Ibid.

85. T. S. Eliot to Hallie Flanagan, March 18, 1933, in Hallie Flanagan, *Dynamo* (New York: Duell, Sloan & Pearce, 1943), 83. I learned of this letter to the director of *Sweeney Agonistes* through David Ewick's invaluable web archive: "T. S. Eliot (1888–1965). Verse Drama, 1926–50," *Japonisme, Orientalism, Modernism: A Bibliography of Japan in English-Language Verse of the Early Twentieth Century* (2003), available at http://themargins.net/bibliography.html (accessed April 1, 2015).

86. Pound, "Vorticism," 94.

87. Ezra Pound, *ABC of Reading* (1934; repr., New York: New Directions, 1960), 52, 14.

88. Takeishi claims that Itō lived with Pound, in *Japanese Elements*, 20–21.

89. Ibid., 26.

90. Ezra Pound, "Sword-Dance and Spear-Dance: Texts of the Poems Used with Michio Itow's Dances. By Ezra Pound from Notes of Masirni Utchiyama," *Future* 1, no. 2 (1916): 54–55, reprinted in *Ezra Pound's Poetry and Prose: Contributions to Periodicals*, ed. Lea Baechler, A. Walton Litz, and James Longenbach (New York: Garland, 1991), 2:182–83.

91. Longenbach describes Pound's early imagist poems as "the distilled residue of dramatic narrative" and argues that Pound admired both noh and the dance poems because they "hold dramatic action within the resonant obscurity of the static Image, and . . . showed Pound that his poetry of concision could be extended without reintroducing the 'prose' part of the drama" (*Stone Cottage*, 202–3).

92. Ezra Pound, "Remy de Gourmont [Part I]," *Fortnightly Review*, December 1, 1915, reprinted in Baechler et al., *Contributions to Periodicals*, ed. Baechler, Litz, and Longenbach, 125–32.

93. Ezra Pound, *Tristan and Consolations of Matrimony*, along with two other plays, are in *Plays Modelled on the Noh*, ed. Donald Gallup (1916; repr., Toledo: Friends of the University of Toledo Libraries, 1987). Longenbach offers a more thorough discussion of Pound's writing for and about the theater in his chapter "Theatre Business," in *Stone Cottage*, 197–221. For a discussion of the relation between kyōgen and noh, see Julie A. Iezzi and Jonah Salz, ""Kyōgen Leaps out of Nō's Shadow,"*Asian Theatre Journal* 24, no. 1 (2007): v–ix.

94. Christine Froula, *To Write Paradise: Style and Error in Pound's Cantos* (New Haven, Conn.: Yale University Press, 1984), 56. Froula considers the drafts of "Canto IV"

as crucial documents for Pound's search for a modernist epic form and establishes that the final version of IV is the first finished canto and the "beginning" of his new method (11–13).

95. Ibid., 73.

96. Ezra Pound, *The Letters of Ezra Pound to Alice Corbin Henderson*, ed. Ira B. Nadel (Austin: University of Texas Press, 1993), xxii.

97. Hugh Kenner, *The Pound Era* (Berkeley: University of California Press, 1971), 283–84; Daniel Albright, "Early Cantos: I–XLI," in *The Cambridge Companion to Ezra Pound*, ed. Ira Bruce Nadel (Cambridge: Cambridge University Press, 1999), 59–91, 65.

98. Ezra Pound, "The Classical Stage of Japan: Ernest Fenollosa's Work on the Japanese 'Noh,'" *Drama* 5 (1915): 199–247, reprinted in "Noh," or, *Accomplishment: A Study of the Classical Stage of Japan* (New York: Knopf, 1917) and PFNoh.

99. Ezra Pound to Alice Corbin Henderson, July 7, 1915, in *Letters*, ed. Nadel, 109–17. Because Pound published the other two plays, *Genjo* and *Chorio* (in "Noh," or, *Accomplishment*) that he sent to Henderson, Nadel plausibly imagines that Pound had not kept a copy of *Takasago* (xxiii). The Fenollosa-Hirata draft translation was donated in 1991 to the Princeton University Library with several other unpublished manuscripts. See Earl Miner, "Pound and Fenollosa Papers Relating to Nō," *Princeton University Chronicle* 53, no. 1 (1991): 12–16.

100. Pound to Henderson, July 7, 1915, 110.

101. Rath, *Ethos of Noh*, 107.

102. Pound to Henderson, July 7, 1915, 111.

103. Richard Taylor states in his early assessment of the Fenollosa-Pound transmission that Pound had very little understanding of the "inherent literary structure within individual plays" (*The Drama of W. B. Yeats: Irish Myth and the Japanese Nō* [New Haven, Conn.: Yale University Press, 1976], 38). Pound's comments on *Takasago*, however, indicate otherwise.

104. Pound claims that *Takasago* is entitled "'Shin no issei,' the 'Most Correct,'" but *shin no issei* is a form of entrance music played by the flute and drums that is often used for the entrance of divinities.

105. David Crandall, personal communication, July 4, 2012.

106. For a different perspective, see Daniel Albright, "The Pisan Cantos as a Noh Play," in *Untwisting the Serpent: Modernism in Music, Literature, and Other Arts* (Chicago: University of Chicago Press, 2000), 82–84.

107. Pound to Henderson, July 7, 1915, 113.

108. Ibid., 111.

109. Ibid., 112. For a discussion of the poetry anthologies referenced in Takasago, see JND, 277–79.

110. Pound to Henderson, July 7, 1915, 113. Emperor Shiko is a reference to a Chinese story about the first emperor of the Qin dynasty, who took shelter from the rain under a pine, which then grew taller to protect him (JND, 286).

111. Froula, To Write Paradise, 36.

112. Pound worked on other plays, like Kakitsubata, which were based on the Ise monogatari, tales about the Heian-period poet Ariwara no Narihira (825–880). He echoed "Grow with the pines at Ise" in a later canto (21.99).

113. The speeches are collected in Ezra Pound Speaking: Radio Speeches of World War II, ed. Leonard W. Doob (Westport, Conn.: Greenwood Press, 1978). See also Margaret Fisher, Ezra Pound's Radio Operas: The BBC Experiments, 1931–1933 (Cambridge, Mass.: MIT Press, 2002), 198.

114. Wai-Chee Dimock argues, "Treason is an offense against the state; more than that, it is an offense defined by the state, named as a prosecutable relation to its 'enemies,' and in that naming, the sovereignty of the state is affirmed at the very point of its alleged breach" ("Aesthetics at the Limits of the Nation: Kant, Pound, and the Saturday Review," American Literature 76, no. 3 [2004]: 534). Froula provocatively cites "error" as the crux of both Pound's translations and cantos: his "mistranslation" of Cathay leads to "The Cantos' self-foreignizing English" and a "vanishing subject" that might enable us to "experience something of what it is like to live in a language not one's own" (To Write Paradise, 7).

115. See Richard Sieburth's evocative introduction to The Pisan Cantos (New York: New Directions, 2003), ix–xlii.

116. In this imaginary noh sequence, I cast Pound as a waki, but that is not to claim that his function in The Pisan Cantos is precisely that of the waki role in noh, and in this way, I depart from Albright's notion of Pound as the waki and Yeats as the shite in "Pisan Cantos as a Noh Play," 84. Sanehide Kodama claims that Pound is the shite in Pisa but the waki throughout most of The Pisan Cantos (American Poetry and Japanese Culture [Hamden, Conn.: Archon, 1984], 105).

117. Helen Caldwell, "The Dance Poems of Michio Ito: The White Peacock to Music by Griffes," in Making Music for Modern Dance, ed. Katherine Teck (New York: Oxford University Press, 2011), 18–22. Itō originally performed the piece with the composer Charles Griffes at the piano and later taught the more provocative "Peacock Dance" to Sally Rand.

118. Ursula Shioji maps thirty-five references to noh in The Pisan Cantos and analyzes their layered contexts to conclude that Pound uses noh to establish the Pisan setting as a "Noh landscape, whose representational constituents and symbolic

function can be interpreted in terms of Noh aesthetics" (*Ezra Pound's Pisan Cantos and the Noh* [Frankfurt am Main: Lang, 1998], 299).

119. Albright details the function of the musical notation in "Pisan Cantos as Opera," 84–88.

120. Pound, *Pisan Cantos*, 126nn.445–446.

121. This assertion of presence, "here," recalls Eliot's phrase about noh's particularity: "The method of making the ghost real is different. . . . The ghost is enacted" ("Noh and the Image," 103).

122. Fenollosa and Pound claimed, "But in nature, there is no completeness. . . . All processes in nature are interrelated; and thus there could be no complete sentence . . . save one which it would take all time to pronounce" (*Chinese Written Character as a Medium for Poetry*, 11).

123. Pound, *ABC of Reading*, 26.

124. Dimock points out that since 1949, the Bollingen Prize has been sponsored not by the Library of Congress but by Yale University, in "Aesthetics at the Limits of the Nation," 544–45n.28.

125. Sieberth, introduction, xxxix.

126. Dimock, 'Aesthetics at the Limits of the Nation," 535, 537. Robert Hillyer, "Treason's Strange Fruit: The Case of Ezra Pound and the Bollingen Award," *Saturday Review of Literature*, June 11, 1949; Richard Hillyer, "Poetry's New Priesthood," *Saturday Review of Literature*, June 18, 1949.

127. Marjorie Perloff, "Pound Ascendant," *Boston Review*, April–May 2004, available at http://bostonreview.net/BR29.2/perloff.html (accessed July 7, 2012). See also Perloff, "Fascism, Anti-Semitism, Isolationism: Contextualizing the Case of EP," *Paideuma* 16 (1987): 7–21.

128. Peter D'Epiro summarized the responses to this question and argued that the lesson was meant for his captors, the U.S. military, in "Whose Vanity Must be Pulled Down?" *Paideuma* 29, no. 3 (1984): 248–52.

129. Pound, *Pisan Cantos*, 158n.90.

130. Leon Surette believes that near the end of his life, Pound did offer two convincing retractions of his support for fascism and his anti-Semitism, in an interview with journalist Grazia Livi and in conversations with Michael Reck and Allen Ginsberg, although the retractions' legitimacy has been questioned by supporters and detractors alike, in *Dreams of a Totalitarian Utopia* (Montreal: McGill–Queen's University Press, 2011), 278–79.

131. For a similar view, see Lawrence Rainey, *Ezra Pound and the Monument of Culture: Text, History, and the Malatesta Cantos* (Chicago: University of Chicago Press, 1991). See also Robert Casillo, *The Genealogy of Demons: Anti-Semitism, Fascism, and the*

Myths of Ezra Pound (Evanston, Ill.: Northwestern University Press, 1988); and Vincent Sherry, *Ezra Pound, Wyndham Lewis, and Radical Modernism* (New York: Oxford University Press, 1993).

132. Surette, *Dreams of a Totalitarian Utopia*, esp. 226–29.

133. Ibid., 3–5.

134. Ibid., 9.

135. Ibid., 10–11.

136. Fenollosa and Pound, *Chinese Written Character*, 3–4.

137. Ezra Pound, Radio Broadcast, no. 6, January 29, 1942, in *Ezra Pound Speaking*, ed. Doob, 26.

138. Walter Benjamin, "The Work of Art in the Age of Mechanical Reproduction," in *Illuminations*, trans. Harry Zohn (New York: Schocken Books, 1969), 241.

139. Ezra Pound, *Jefferson and/or Mussolini: L'Idea Statale, Fascism as I Have Seen It* (1935; repr., New York: Liveright, 1970), 34. Joseph Goebbels similarly claimed, "We who shape modern German policy feel ourselves to be artists . . . the task of art and the artist [being] to form, to give shape, to remove the diseased and create freedom for the healthy" (quoted in Susan Sontag, "Fascinating Fascism," in *Under the Sign of Saturn* [New York: Farrar, Straus & Giroux, 1972], 92).

140. Surette, *Dreamsof a Totalitarian Utopia*, 221–24.

141. Ezra Pound, "March Arrivals" (1941), in *Ezra Pound Speaking*, ed. Doob, 384.

142. Sontag, "Fascinating Fascism," 91.

143. Ibid., 104.

144. Freeman considers "sadomasochism as a kind of erotic time machine that offers a fleshly metacommentary on the dual emergence of modernity and its others, on the entangled histories of race, labor, nationhood, and imperialism as well as sexuality"—that is, as a tool for disrupting the march of modern progress and for encountering any number of historical horrors from the slave trade to the concentration camp (*Time Binds*, 138).

145. Remy de Gourmont, *The Natural Philosophy of Love*, trans. Ezra Pound (1903; repr., New York: Boni & Liveright, 1922).

146. Justice Oliver Wendell Holmes used this phrase in the Supreme Court's decision to uphold the conviction in *Schenck v. United States*, a World War I–era First Amendment case tried in 1919.

147. Pound, "March Arrivals," 386.

148. Quoted in *Ezra Pound and Japan*, ed. Kodama, xi.

2. Theater in the "Deep"

1. Yoko Chiba, "Ezra Pound's Versions of Fenollosa's Noh Manuscripts and Yeats's Unpublished 'Suggestions & Corrections,'" *Yeats Annual* 4 (1986): 121–44.

2. First published in *Harper's Bazaar* (March 1917), then with minor variations in *To-Day* (June 1917) and *The Wild Swans at Coole* (1917), and then with more variants and notes in *Four Plays for Dancers* (1921), *Four Plays for Dancers* was reprinted with all the paratextual material in W. B. Yeats, *Plays and Controversies* (New York: Macmillan, 1924), 337–56. Subsequent references are cited in the text and notes by the abbreviation PC.

3. From the unpublished dialogue "The Poet and the Actress," (1916), quoted in Curtis Baker Bradford, *Yeats at Work* (Carbondale: Southern Illinois University Press, 1965), 215.

4. Sylvia Ellis argues that Yeats had been "moving instinctively in the direction of the Noh for some years" (*The Plays of W. B. Yeats: Yeats and the Dancer* [New York: St. Martin's Press, 1995], 87).

5. Although he does not emphasize noh as a pedagogical theater, Marvin Carlson calls it "the most intensely haunted of any of the world's classic dramatic forms" (*The Haunted Stage: The Theatre as Memory Machine* [Ann Arbor: University of Michigan Press, 2001], 20).

6. Yeats appreciated many aspects, including the nationalism, of the dramatic realism initiated by Henrik Ibsen, and he called for "An Irish National Theatre . . . that will reflect the life of Ireland as the Scandinavian theatre reflects the Scandinavian life" (PC, 55). But Yeats lamented the acting style he saw at the London premiere of Ibsen's *Ghosts* at the Independent Theater in 1891: "I could not escape from an illusion unaccountable to me at the time. All the characters seemed to me less than life-size. . . . Little whimpering puppets moved here and there in the middle of that great abyss. Why did they not speak out with louder voices or move with freer gestures?" (PC, 122).

7. Masaru Sekine and Christopher Murray accuse Yeats of having "spent almost twenty years de-colonizing the Irish theatre so as to make it nationalist and truly expressive of individual Irish experience" yet committing the "folly" of "what was virtually another form of cultural colonization" (*Yeats and the Noh: A Comparative Study* [Savage, Md.: Barnes & Noble, 1990], 1). Richard Taylor is less concerned about cultural appropriation but argues that in the context of World War I, the plays must have seemed like "baffling anachronisms": "The real failure of the dance dramas lies in the fact that their subject matter had even less relevance to the lives and sensibilities of his audience than the earlier plays." (The

Drama of W.B. Yeats: Irish Myth and the Japanese Nō [New Haven, Conn.: Yale University Press, 1976], 119).

8. W. H. Auden, "The Public v. the Late Mr. William Butler Yeats" (1939), in *The English Auden*, ed. Edward Mendleson (London: Faber & Faber, 1977), 389–93. In 1965, Conor Cruise O'Brien announced his famous verdict that Yeats was "as near to being a Fascist as the conditions of his country permitted" ("Passion and Cunning: An Essay on the Politics of W. B. Yeats," in *Passion and Cunning: Essays on Nationalism, Terrorism, and Revolution* [New York: Simon & Schuster, 1988], 8–61).

9. Peter Liebregts and Peter van de Kamp, eds., *Tumult of Images: Essays on W. B. Yeats and Politics* (Amsterdam: Rodopi, 1995); Jonathan Allison, ed., *Yeats's Political Identities: Selected Essays* (Ann Arbor: University of Michigan Press, 1996).

10. Elizabeth Cullingford, *Yeats, Ireland and Fascism* (New York: New York University Press, 1981), 157. Marjorie Howes offers a subtle discussion of the relation between Yeats's nationalism and individualism: "This individuality has little to do with the pluralism of liberal political theory. . . . The heightened individual will that Yeats's occult theatre posited as a complement to mystical mental unity demanded less personal individuality than psychic individuation" (*Yeats's Nations: Gender, Class, and Irishness* [Cambridge: Cambridge University Press, 1996], 94). But this paradigm does not describe *Hawk's Well*, which erodes psychic individuation through possession and enchantment.

11. For a concise history, see Joep Leerson, "The Theatre of William Butler Yeats," in *The Cambridge Companion to Twentieth-Century Irish Drama*, ed. Shaun Richards (Cambridge: Cambridge University Press, 2004), 47–61.

12. The classic texts are Benedict Anderson, *Imagined Communities: Reflections on the Origin and Spread of Nationalism* (1986; repr. New York: Verso, 2006); and Frantz Fanon, *The Wretched of the Earth* (1961), trans. Constance Farrington (New York: Grove Press, 1963).

13. British Association Visit, Abbey Theatre, Special Programme, September 1908, manuscript 3001, Yeats Papers, National Library of Ireland, Dublin. Subsequent references are cited in the notes by the abbreviation YPNLI. In the speech, Yeats stated, "Our Patent, for as the laws in Ireland are frequently old-fashioned, we come under the patent system, confines us to plays by Irishmen or upon Irish subjects, or to foreign master-pieces (and among these we may not include anything English)."

14. W. B. Yeats and Lady Augusta Gregory, "The Irish National Theatre: Its Work and Its Needs (1909), YPNLI. The press also positioned the Abbey Theatre in relation to international experiments in drama, performance, and stage design. The *Pall Mall Gazette* compared an exhibition of Robert Gregory's theatrical designs at the

Baillie Gallery with Leon Bakst's designs for the Ballets Russes and pointed out that J. M. Synge's *The Playboy* was being performed in Germany by Max Reinhardt (June 17, 1912, Abbey Theatre Scrapbook, Roll I, 8132, YPNLI).

15. W. B. Yeats, *Cathleen ni Houlihan*, in *The Variorum Edition of the Plays of W. B. Yeats*, ed. Russell K. Alspach and Catherine C. Alspach (New York: Macmillan, 1966), 232. Subsequent references are cited in the text by the abbreviation VP.

16. "W. B. Yeats Talks of Drama and Authors in Isle of Erin," *Springfield Sunday Union & Republican*, November 8, 1931, Abbey Theatre Scrapbook, Roll 8134, YPNLI.

17. Howes recognizes that "Yeats was both fascinated and repelled by crowds" (*Yeats's Nations*, 66).

18. A precise discussion of Yone Noguchi's influence on Yeats is in Edward Marx, "Nō Dancing: Yone Noguchi in Yeats's Japan," in "Influence and Confluence," edited by Warwick Gould, special issue, *Yeats Annual* 17 (2007): 51–94. See also Yoshinobu Hakutani, introduction to *Selected English Writings of Yone Noguchi: Prose* (Cranbury, N.J.: Associated University Presses, 1992), 13.

19. Amy Sueyoshi, *Queer Compulsions: Race, Nation, and Sexuality in the Affairs of Yone Noguchi* (Honolulu: University of Hawai'i Press, 2012).

20. Yone Noguchi, "A Japanese Note on W. B. Yeats" (1911), in *Through the Torii* (London: Elkin Matthews, 1914), 110, 113.

21. Ibid., 117.

22. Ibid., 113.

23. Yone Noguchi, "Mr. Yeats and the No," *Japan Times*, November 3, 1907, 6. This text and "With a Foreign Critic at a No Performance," *Japan Times*, October 27, 1907, which also associated Yeats and noh, were combined with an additional section providing historical information about the drama and reprinted as "The Japanese Mask Play," *Taiyō* 16, no. 10 (1910): 4–9. Marx reprints this version in "Nō Dancing," 88–93.

24. In 1906, Yone Noguchi published a prose version of the noh play *Hagoromo* in *The Summer Cloud: Prose Poems* (Tokyo: Shunyōdō, 1906), 1–4. In January 1912, Noguchi published an essay called "The No Plays," which he then adapted for a lecture at the Royal Asiatic Society in London in March 1914 and for the chapter "No: The Japanese Play of Silence," in *The Spirit of Japanese Poetry* (New York: Dutton, 1914), 54–70. This volume also includes an original noh play in English, "The Morning-Glory (A Dramatic Fragment)," and Noguchi gave Yeats an inscribed presentation copy. For the contents of Yeats's library, see Edward O'Shea, *A Descriptive Catalogue of W. B. Yeats's Library* (New York: Garland, 1985).

25. Yone Noguchi published an account of the dinner in "A Japanese Poet on W. B. Yeats," *Bookman* 43 (1916): 431–33.

26. Both Ellis (*Plays of W. B. Yeats*, 108) and Anthony Cuda ("The Turbulent Lives of Yeats's Painted Horses," in "Influence and Confluence," edited by Warwick Gould, special issue, *Yeats Annual* 17 [2007]: 37) claim that Noguchi visited Yeats and Pound at Stone Cottage in 1913, but Longenbach does not mention the visit or acknowledge Noguchi's considerable influence. I believe that Ellis and Cuda misplaced the 1914 dinners at Stone Cottage.

27. Marx, "Nō Dancing," 69–71. The letter was first published as "Ieitsu to nō" in Yone Noguchi, *Teki wo aise [Love the Enemy]* (Tokyo: Genbunsha, 1922).

28. Quoted in Marx, "Nō Dancing," 71.

29. Ibid., 72; Yone Noguchi, "The Everlasting Sorrow: A Japanese Noh Play," *Egoist* 4, no. 9 (1917): 141–43, and "The Japanese Noh Play," *Egoist* 5, no. 7 (1918): 99.

30. Ezra Pound to John Quinn, February 26, 1916, in *The Selected Letters of Ezra Pound to John Quinn*, ed. Timothy Materer (Durham, N.C.: Duke University Press, 1991), 59–61 (italics in original).

31. Daisetz Teitaro Suzuki, *Essays in Zen Buddhism* (London: Luzac, 1927), 128, YPNLI.

32. W. B. Yeats to Yone Noguchi, June 27, 1921, in Yoshinobu Hakutani, "W. B. Yeats, Modernity, and the Noh Play," in *Modernity in East-West Literary Criticism: New Readings*, ed. Yoshinobu Hakutani (Cranbury, N.J.: Associated University Presses, 2001), 24–25.

33. Yone Noguchi, *The Spirit of Japanese Poetry* (New York: Dutton, 1914), 54, 62, 55.

34. Ibid., 56.

35. Ibid., 24.

36. W. B. Yeats, *Fairy and Folk Tales of the Irish Peasantry* (London: Walter Scott, 1888).

37. Marx, "Nō Dancing," 75.

38. Itō Michio claimed, "Torahiko Gun was there, and Sugano Nijuichi and Kume Taminosuke the painter as well. They were classmates from Gakushuin who practiced Noh chanting, while Kume and his brother had practiced Kyogen" (quoted in Ian Carruthers, "A Translation of Fifteen Pages of Ito Michio's Autobiography 'Utsukushiku naru kyoshitsu,'" *Canadian Journal of Irish Studies* 2, no. 1 [1976]: 35). Subsequent references are cited in the notes by the abbreviation IAuto.

39. Joseph Lennon, *Irish Orientalism* (Syracuse, N.Y.: Syracuse University Press, 2004), 423–24n.4. A similar attitude toward Yeats's work with Itō is evident in John Walter de Gruchy's words:

> Ito knew nothing about the nō, finding it archaic and boring. . . . Nevertheless, Yeats insisted that Ito and only Ito could make his play possible. The attitude toward Ito thus derived from a general Western representational tendency to

treat all things Japanese, including Japanese people, as objects on display, exhibition pieces to satisfy a European taste for the exotic. (*Orienting Arthur Waley: Japonism, Orientalism, and the Creation of Japanese Literature in English* [Honolulu: University of Hawai'i Press, 2003], 96–97)

40. Midori Takeishi, *Japanese Elements in Michio Ito's Early Period (1915–1924): Meetings of East and West in the Collaborative Works,* ed. and rev. David Pacun (Tokyo: Gendaitosho, 2006), 9.

41. Tomie Hahn, *Sensational Knowledge: Embodying Culture Through Japanese Dance* (Middletown, Conn. Wesleyan University Press, 2007), 26–27.

42. Hahn explains *katachi*, the standard posture of *nihon buyō* (ibid., 62), using a description of noh *kamae* in Komparu Kunio, *The Noh Theatre: Principles and Perspectives* (New York: Weatherhill/Tankosha, 1983), 221.

43. Northrop Frye is both dismissive of Yeats's dance plays and imprecise about the Japanese play being compared:

> In another Nō play, *Hagoromo*, a fairy, in order to get back a headdress a priest has stolen from her, teaches him the dance of the phases of the moon. She is a harmless and pretty creature, a Sally Rand who lost her fan, and it is hardly likely that her lessons had anything of the Procrustean pedantry of Yeats's garrulous and opinionated spooks. (*Fables of Identity: Studies in Poetic Mythology* [New York: Harcourt, Brace, 1963], 25)

Surely Frye was not aware that Itō had taught Sally Rand a famous fan piece, "The Peacock Dance," which later was featured in the film *The Sunset Murder Case* (directed by Louis J. Gasnier, 1938). See the newspaper announcements from early 1939, such as "New Dance Created for Sally Rand for Exotic Sunset Murder Case,' *Carteret Press*, March 17, 1939, 5, PCMI.

44. W. B. Yeats, "Swedenborg, Mediums, and the Desolate Places," in *Explorations* (New York: Macmillan, 1962), 38. The essay first appeared in *Visions and Beliefs in the West of Ireland*, ed. Lady Augusta Gregory, 2 vols. (London: Knickerbocker, 1920), but it was dated October 1914 and therefore was written before Yeats's introduction to Ernest Fenollosa and Ezra Pound, *Certain Noble Plays of Japan* (1916; repr., Shannon: Irish University Press, 1971).

45. For a discussion of drag elements in the play, see Katharine Worth, *The Irish Drama of Europe from Yeats to Beckett* (London: Athlone Press, 1978), 39–41.

46. Ibid., 40. See also Ronald Schuchard, "*The Countess Cathleen* and the Revival of the Bardic Arts," *South Carolina Review* 32, no. 1 (1999): 24–37.

47. Lady Augusta Gregory, *Cuchulain of Muirthemne* (London: Murray, 1902).

48. Sekine and Murray compared Yeats's plays and their supposed sources, claiming that *Yoro* was Yeats's model for *Hawk's Well* (overlooking *Hagoromo's* influence), *Nishikigi* for *The Dreaming of the Bones*, and *Aoi no ue* for *The Only Jealousy of Emer*. Even though there was no one-to-one relationship, Sekine and Murray concluded that Yeats failed to make "authentic noh plays" (*Yeats and the Noh*, 1).

49. For a detailed discussion of Yeats's mask theory as it developed from his early work into a technical term in *Per Amica Silentia Lunae* just after he began working with noh, see Warwick Gould, "The Mask Before *The Mask*," in "Yeat's Mask," edited by Margaret Mills Harper and Warwick Gould, special issue, *Yeats Annual* 19 (2013): 3–47.

50. W. B. Yeats, "The Tragic Theatre," in *Essays and Introductions* (New York: Macmillan, 1961), 243.

51. Throughout this chapter, I cite from PC because it, unlike VP, contains Yeats's *Four Plays for Dancers*, with the photographs, designs, and musical score intact. These paratextual features provide a crucial record of the production and Yeats's collaborations.

52. W. B. Yeats, "An Introduction for My Plays," in *Essays and Introductions*, 527.

53. Yeats claimed that the performance was for a "war charity" (PC, 419), but Lawrence Rainey identified the Social Institute's Union for Women and Girls as the beneficiary, in "Introduction to At the Hawk's Well," in *Modernism: An Anthology* (Malden, Mass.: Blackwell, 2005), 35.

54. Andrew Parkin, introduction to *"At the Hawk's Well" and "The Cat and the Moon": Manuscript Materials*, ed. Andrew Parkin (Ithaca, N.Y.: Cornell University Press, 2010), xxvii. Parkin offers a detailed reading of the manuscripts and history of performance. Subsequent references are cited in the text by the abbreviation AHW Manu.

55. For a discussion of Yeats's facility with rhythm but not tone or tune, see Ronald Schuchard, *The Last Minstrels: Yeats and the Revival of the Bardic Arts* (New York: Oxford University Press, 2008), 85–86.

56. Predicting Yeats's description of noh chanting, Florence Farr described her method as "song in speech" in her widely discussed book *The Music of Speech* (London: Elkin Mathews, 1909). Yeats discussed their experiments in "Speaking to the Psaltery" (1907), first published in the *Monthly Review* and reprinted in *Essays and Introductions*. Mark Morrisson details the British "verse-recitation movement," although he does not discuss Yeats's interest in noh, in "Performing the Pure Voice: Elocution, Verse Recitation, and Modernist Poetry in Prewar London," *Modernism / Modernity* 3, no. 3 (1996): 25–50.

57. "Music for 'At the Hawk's Well' by Edmund Dulac," in PC, 422–23.

58. Hiro Ishibashi describes this aspect of noh music: "Freedom is allowed only to players in complete command of the pattern and its divisions; the patterns exist to establish and delimit a freedom and spontaneity which will not mar the unity of beauty and which at the same time will provide a rhythmic power to the performance" (*Yeats and the Noh: Types of Japanese Beauty and Their Reflection in Yeats's Plays*, ed. Anthony Kerrigan, Yeats Centenary Papers 6 [Dublin: Dolment Press, 1966], 14c).

59. My understanding of Dulac's music here and in my discussion of the dance music later is greatly indebted to the digital arrangements produced by Brian Valencia during the Mellon School of Theater and Performance Research at Harvard in June 2013. The performance is described in the conclusion to this chapter.

60. Anthony W. Sheppard claims, "The only suggestion of the influence of Noh on Dulac's music is in the minimal instrumentation and in his instructions for the accompaniment to the dialogue. Dulac composed for a bamboo flute, harp, drum, and gong, and noted that the drum and gong should be 'oriental' in form" (*Revealing Masks: Exotic Influences and Ritualized Performance in Modernist Music Theater* [Berkeley: University of California Press, 2001], 82). Like Takeishi, I find other influences, although she suggests that based on additional research on noh, Edmund Dulac may have revised the score after the performance but before publication. Dulac's eleven pages of detailed notes on Noël Peri's *Le théâtre nō: Études sur le drame lyrique japonais* (Hanoi: Imprimerie d'Extrême-Orient, 1909) and dated June 1917 (after the first performances) are held in the Harry Ransom Center, at the University of Texas at Austin, along with his proofs of the score. Dulac's introduction to the score suggests that it was used in the early productions: "In order to apply to the music the idea of great simplicity of execution underlying the whole spirit of the performance, it was necessary to use instruments that any one with a fair idea of music could learn in a few days" (PC, 422).

61. Yeats, "Introduction for My Plays," 522.

62. Ibid., 523–24.

63. Martin Puchner, *Stage Fright: Modernism, Anti-Theatricality, and Drama* (Baltimore: Johns Hopkins University Press, 2002), esp. chap. 5, "William Butler Yeats: Poetic Voices in Theatrical Space," 131.

64. In Japanese, pronouns do not usually specify a particular subject, but there is little ambiguity in English, so Fenollosa-Hirata-Pound produced a fluid first-person pronoun that could be assumed by the chorus or other characters and

that Yeats developed in *Hawk's Well*. Taylor included the Fenollosa-Hirata-Pound *Yoro* in *Drama of W. B. Yeats*, 125.

65. Itō claims to have helped design the costumes in an interview partially translated by Carruthers (IAuto, 35). Alvin Langdon Coburn was an American photographer who, perhaps influenced by ukiyo-e prints, experimented with mirrors and lenses in his "vortographs" to achieve effects of shadow and light that were championed by Pound as "vorticist" photography. Coburn first photographed Itō in a suit of Japanese armor in 1915 and then documented the costumes and masks used for *At the Hawk's Well*. See *Alvin Langdon Coburn: Photographs, 1900–1924*, ed. Karl Steinorth (Zurich: Stemmle, 1998).

66. I imagine Itō as a hybrid migrant, inspired by Homi Bhabha's discussion of these terms in *The Location of Culture* (New York: Routledge, 1994). The migrants invoked by postcolonial theories often remain imagined figures of intermingling cultures rather than the actual complicated human beings, like Itō and Yeats, who taught, performed, took roles and jobs they disliked, revised their work, toured and traveled, learned from one another . . . and maintained some of the cultural insensitivity common to humans, although usually scrubbed from their critical theories.

67. W. B. Yeats to Lady Gregory, March 26, 1916, in *The Collected Letters of W. B. Yeats*, ed. John Kelly and Eric Domville (New York: Oxford University Press, 1986), 609–10.

68. Helen Caldwell, *Michio Ito: The Dancer and His Dances* (Berkeley: University of California Press, 1977), 48.

69. For an analysis of Dulac's music, see Mary Fleischer, *Embodied Texts: Symbolist Playwright-Dancer Collaborations* (Amsterdam: Rodopi, 2007), 199.

70. The first version of Yeats's *On Baile's Strand* was published in 1903 and then was substantially revised in *On Baile's Strand* (London: Bullen, 1907).

71. W. B. Yeats, *The Only Jealousy of Emer*, *Poetry: A Magazine of Verse* 13, no. 4 (1919): 175–93.

72. Yeats, "Tragic Theatre," 243.

73. Ibid. Yeats similarly defined the "purpose of rhythm" as "to prolong the moment of contemplation . . . by hushing us with alluring monotony, while it holds us waking by variety, to keep us in that state of perhaps real trance, in which the mind liberated from the pressure of the will is unfolded in symbols" ("Symbol as Revelation," in *Essays and Introductions*, 63.

74. Edward Said, *Culture and Imperialism* (New York: Vintage Books, 1994), 237, 227, 238.

75. Ibid., 235 (italics added).

76. Rudyard Kipling, "The White Man's Burden: The United States and the Philippine Islands," *McClure's Magazine*, February 1899.

77. George W. Bush, "Remarks at the Signing Ceremony for Afghan Women and Children Relief Act of 2001" (December 12, 2001), U.S. Department of State Archive: 2001–2009, available at state.gov/p/sca/rls/rm/6816.htm. The president claimed,

> In Afghanistan, America not only fights for our security, but we fight for values we hold dear. We strongly reject the Taliban way. We strongly reject their brutality toward women and children. [Applause] They not only violate basic human rights, they are barbaric in their indefensible meting of justice. It is wrong. Their attitude is wrong for any culture. Their attitude is wrong for any religion.

78. The hazel appears in *The Tain* and prominently in *Macgnimartha Finn* (*The Boyhood Deeds of Finn*). See Paul Rhys Mountfort, *Ogam: The Celtic Oracle of the Trees* (Rochester, Vt.: Destiny, 2000), 95–99.

79. Emily Atkins, " 'Study That Tree': The Iconic Stage in *Purgatory* and *Waiting for Godot*," *South Carolina Review* 40, no. 2 (2008): 66–77; Worth, *Irish Drama of Europe*.

80. I resist the common reading of *At the Hawk's Well* in relation to Yeats's biography that is encouraged by, for example, Richard Ellman's note that Yeats was fifty years old when he wrote the play, in *Yeats: The Man and the Masks* (New York: Macmillan, 1948), 216.

81. W. B. Yeats, "The Death of Cuchulain," in VP, 1063.

82. Submission to authority is one of the traits on the "F scale" or "Fascism scale" set forward by the famous Frankfurt school opus by Theodor W. Adorno, Else Frenkel-Brunswik, Daniel J. Levinson, and R. Nevitt Sanford, *The Authoritarian Personality* (1950; New York: Norton, 1993),

83. de Gruchy claims, "These were not merely the vague misguided sentiments of two disgruntled postwar poets. Pound's avant-garde position was already degenerating toward an extreme conservatism that would become by the 1930's virulent fascism, and Yeats' simmering antidemocratic views would end up in a most unsavory right-wing nationalism" (*Orienting Arthur Waley*, 101).

84. Peter van de Kamp and Peter Liebregts, introduction to *Tumult of Images: Essays on W. B. Yeats and Politics*, ed. Peter Liebreghts and Peter van de Kamp (Amsterdam: Rodopi, 1995), 15.

85. Ibid., 19 (italics added).

86. For a discussion of Yeats's collaboration with Ninette de Valois, see Fleischer, *Embodied Texts*, chap. 5.

3. ITŌ MICHIO'S HAWK TOURS IN MODERN DANCE AND THEATER

1. Yeats apparently viewed the performance with apprehensive interest, but he acknowledged the extent of his collaboration with Itō when he wrote that it would be "ungracious to forbid Ito to play *The Hawk* as he will . . . Ito and his Japanese players should be interesting" (*The Letters of W. B. Yeats*, ed. Allan Wade [London: Rupert Hart-Davis, 1954], 651–52).

2. Shotaro Oshima provides a brief description of the production in "Yeats and Michio Ito," *Yeats Society of Japan Annual Report* 6 (1971): 16. The English-language Japanese press reported on the performance in "Michio Ito to Direct 'Prince Igor' in Tokyo: Will Perform in Yeats' 'Hawk's Well' November: Stresses Need for Fusion of Japan-U.S. Cultures," undated clipping, personal collection of Michele Ito. Subsequent references are cited in the notes by the abbreviation PCMI. I am grateful to Michele for sharing her rich collection of her grandfather's clippings and other materials as well as her informative interviews.

3. Mary-Jean Cowell, "Michio Ito in Hollywood: Modes and Ironies of Ethnicity," *Dance Chronicle* 24, no. 3 (2001): 273.

4. The famous anthropologist Ruth Benedict used the same term "alien enemy" in the opening of her book intended to explain Japan to the United States; she pronounced the Japanese as "the most alien enemy" ever fought by the United States (*The Chrysanthemum and the Sword: Patterns of Japanese Culture* [1946, repr., New York: First Mariner, 2005], 1).

5. Cowell lectured from her forthcoming biography on July 14, 2009, in Salt Lake City. In addition to this citizen's report, Itō made extended visits to Japan in the late 1930s and early 1940s, hired a press agent to improve the popular image of the Japanese in the United States, and was involved in the Pan Pacific Trading and Navigation Company, which was selling oil to Japan and seeking to prevent war through economic means. I am grateful to Kevin Riordan for sharing his forthcoming essay, "Performance in the Wartime Archive: Michio Ito at the Alien Enemy Hearing Board," which is based on extensive research in the FBI files on Itō.

6. Michele Ito, interview with author, Salt Lake City, Utah, July 2, 2009.

7. Anna Kisselgoff, "Michio Ito, an All-but-Forgotten Pioneer of American Modern Dance," *New York Times*, February 26, 1978, D10.

8. Cowell's informative lecture accompanying the Repertory Dance Theatre's performance of Itō's work was titled "Forgotten Pioneer of Modern Dance" (Salt Lake City, July 16, 2009). See also Mary-Jean Cowell and Satoru Shimazaki, "East and West in the Work of Michio Ito," *Dance Research Journal* 26, no. 2 (1994):

11–23. Felicia McCarren treats Itō's work with W. B. Yeats briefly in *Dancing Machines* (Stanford, Calif.: Stanford University Press, 2003), as does Mary Fleischer in *Embodied Texts: Symbolist Playwright-Dancer Collaborations* (Amsterdam: Rodopi, 2007).

9.   Anna Kisselgoff, "Dance: Michio Ito Salute," *New York Times*, October 4, 1979, Michio Itō Clipping File MGZR, New York Public Library for the Performing Arts. Subsequent references are cited in the notes by the abbreviation NYPLPA.

10. Other terms responding to global trade and communication have been proposed, including "international," "global," "cosmopolitan," "postcolonial," "world," and "cross-cultural." No term is sufficient to the range of cultural interaction around the world. See Jahan Ramazani, *A Transnational Poetics* (Chicago: University of Chicago Press, 2009); and Kwame Anthony Appiah, *Cosmopolitanism: Ethics in a World of Strangers* (New York: Norton, 2006). For dance studies, see Susan Leigh Foster, ed., *Worlding Dance* (Basingstoke: Palgrave Macmillan, 2009); and Carrie Noland and Sally Ann Ness, eds., *Migrations of Gesture* (Minneapolis: University of Minnesota Press, 2008). Although dance is notably absent from their bibliography, Douglas Mao and Rebecca L. Walkowitz describe the "transnational turn" in "The New Modernist Studies," *PMLA* 123, no. 3 (2008): 738–48.

11. Here I agree with Ananya Chatterjea, who points out that the contemporary "global stage" is "apparently very inclusive" but identifies trends in "the staging of global and intercultural projects where all too often forms and performers from Asia and Africa are mobilized only to ensure the ascendency of Euro-American aesthetics" ("On the Value of Mistranslations and Contaminations: The Category of 'Contemporary Choreography' in Asian Dance," *Dance Research Journal* 45, no. 1 [2013]: 14).

12. Yutian Wong argues against positioning Itō as an "international artist," in "Artistic Utopias: Michio Ito and the Trope of the International," in *Worlding Dance*, ed. Foster, 144–62. Instead, she considers him a representative of "Asian American history," even though he never claimed this identity and it erases the various national affiliations of Asians living in the United States (159).

13. Pauline Koner began studying with Itō at Carnegie Hall's Studio 61 in the spring of 1928 and described the same set of gestures as "the root of a movement style he was evolving that was unrelated to his neo-ethnic style. This new style relied primarily on the torso and arms" (*Solitary Song* [Durham, N.C.: Duke University Press, 1989], 26–27). Koner does not mention the B, or feminine, sequence.

14. Shimazaki Satoru, "Interview with Billie Mahoney," *Dance On* (June 29, 1989), 28 mins., videocassette, Jerome Robbins Dance Division, NYPLPA.

15. Koner wrote that Itō's

slow walking step had the dancer touch the floor first with the toe, pressing into the ball of the foot, down to the heel, with a slightly bent knee. He said, 'You should feel as though walking in water.' He knew how to cover space with the effortless gliding movement of the Oriental, skimming along the floor without the bouncing and shoulder wagging visible in many dancers. (*Solitary Song*, 27)

Koner later developed Itō's work into a movement technique that she associated with "Kabuki phrasing" and called "point of pulse" or a "surge, an energy curve" (*Elements of Performance: A Guide for Performers in Dance, Theatre and Opera* [1993; repr., New York: Routledge, 2012], 43, 52).

16. Cowell and Shimazaki, "East and West," 15.

17. Shimazaki, "Interview with Billie Mahoney."

18. The reconstruction of "Tone Poem II" was generously provided by the Dana Tai Soon Burgess Dance Company.

19. Ryutani Kyoko and Komine Kumiko, Ito Technique and Repertory Class at Repertory Dance Theatre's Summerdance: Michio Ito, Salt Lake City, Utah, June 29–July 17, 2009.

20. Shimazaki, "Interview with Billie Mahoney."

21. Madeleine Grey, "Eastern Art Spiritual, Western Art Material, Says Michio Itow," *Musical America*, December 8, 1917, 9.

22. Michio Ito to Lady Ottoline Morrell (1915), Harry Ransom Center, University of Texas at Austin.

23. "Noh Dramas, Once Sacred to Shinto Gods, Coming to Boston: Japanese Actors Devote Lives to Perfecting Its Mysteries—Wear Masks Centuries Old Never Before Seen Outside Land of Mikado," *Boston Post*, January 16, 1921, clipping, YPNLI.

24. Midori Takeishi, *Japanese Elements in Michio Ito's Early Period (1915–1924): Meetings of East and West in the Collaborative Works*, ed. and rev. David Pacun (Tokyo: Gendaitosho, 2006), 9.

25. *Natori* is a formal initiation in which a student receives a stage title with the name of the *ryū* (school) as the family name, and it is used across the traditional Japanese arts. Ian Carruthers based his claim that Itō received the Mizuki *natori* on a lecture by Shotaro Oshima, who, in "Yeats and Michio Ito," quoted Itō Kisaku's comment, "I don't remember to what school of dancing my brother belonged, but he was an expert in Japanese dancing" (IAuto, 15). My interview with Mizuki Waka in Tokyo suggested that Itō did not study in the Mizuki school because it was restricted to women pupils at that time. I am grateful to Mizuki Waka, Mizuki Makito, and their students for demonstrating the repertory and technique for me

on May 13, 2009. Itō's American student Helen Caldwell claimed that Itō studied the Hanayagi rather than the Mizuki technique, in *Michio Ito: The Dancer and His Dances* (Berkeley: University of California Press, 1977), 38. Hanayagi Wakana, the wife of Itō's son, Jerry Ito, clarified that Itō's study of *buyō* had been eclectic and sporadic rather than concentrated in a school, although it loomed large in his imagination (Hanayagi Wakana, interview with author, Los Angeles, August 7, 2009). I am grateful to Wakana for her frank discussion of Itō's work and her own performances, which included a version of *Hawk's Well* in 1978 at the University of Toronto.

26. Tomie Hahn quotes from Zeami's treatises to describe the training techniques of *nihon buyō*, in *Sensational Knowledge: Embodying Culture Through Japanese Dance* (Middletown, Conn.: Wesleyan University Press, 2007), 43. She references Zeami's "formal aesthetic technique called jo-ha-kyu (corresponding to 'introduction, scattering, and rushing')" (53).

27. Cowell and Shimazaki's compare Itō's technique with Dalcroze's teachings in "East and West," 15–16.

28. For an analysis of the ideology of individualism in modern dance, its historical sources, and its influence on modernism, see Carrie Preston, *Modernism's Mythic Pose: Gender, Genre, Solo Performance* (New York: Oxford University Press, 2011).

29. Emile Jaques-Dalcroze, *Rhythm, Music and Education*, trans. Harold F. Rubinstein (New York: Putnam, 1921), 130–31.

30. I am grateful to Lisa Parker for allowing me to attend her class on January 31, 2010, in Cambridge, Massachusetts, and for talking with me about Dalcroze's pedagogy.

31. "Michio Itow's School: Season of 1919" (brochure), PCMI.

32. For a summary of these trends in modernist performance, see Elin Diamond, "Deploying/Destroying the Primitivist Body in Hurston and Brecht," in *Against Theatre: Creative Destructions on the Modernist Stage*, ed. Alan L. Ackerman and Martin Puchner (New York: Palgrave Macmillan, 2006), 112–32.

33. Takeishi, *Japanese Elements in Michio Ito's Early Period*, 11.

34. Itō claims that Cunard's event was held the day after Morrell's but also as a birthday party for the British prime minister, Herbert Asquith. Morrell's party was most likely in November, and Asquith was born on September 12, so the dates do not align, and Itō's account of this sequence of events is inconsistent in other ways as well. See bid., 11–12.

35. *Shōjō* is a noh play about the legendary Chinese spirit of wine. Kitsune, a fox figure, appears in Japanese myth and theater, including the *kyōgen* titled *Kitsune zuka*, which Itō Michio and Louis V. Ledoux published in translation as "The

Fox's Grave [*Kitsune zuka*]: An Ancient Japanese Farce," *Outlook*, February 14, 1923, 306–8.

36. Itō may be holding a wine ladle, a prop associated with Shōjō, although other photographs by Coburn show him in this costume dancing with a fan. A similar costume appears in a drawing of Itō as "Sho-jyo," in Marguerite Mooers Marshall, "Woman of 70 Is Not Too Old to Dance, Says New Terpsichore with a Kimono, Symbolizing Emotions of Far East," *Evening World*, December 2, 1916, PCMI.

37. Itō Michio to Lady Ottoline Morrell, undated, Harry Ransom Center. The letter probably was written in the autumn of 1915, just before his performances at the Kensington salon of Charles Ricketts and Charles Shannon.

38. Takeishi, *Japanese Elements in Michio Ito's Early Period*, 13; Itō Michio to Ezra Pound, May 8, 1915, in *Ezra Pound and Japan: Letters and Essays*, ed. Sanehide Kodama (Redding Ridge, Conn.: Black Swan, 1987), 8.

39. Edward Said wrote, "The Orient is watched, since its almost (but never quite) offensive behavior issues out of a reservoir of infinite peculiarity. . . . The Orient becomes a living tableau of queerness" (*Orientalism* [New York: Vintage Books, 1994], 103). This description of the writings of Gustave Flaubert (1821–1880) is focused, as is most of Said's study, on texts about the Middle East, but it could certainly apply to Itō's dances.

40. Takeishi claims that "Ito stayed with Pound" in 1915 and helped him edit the Fenollosa-Hirata draft translation, in *Japanese Elements in Michio Ito's Early Period*, 20–21. Ira B. Nadel states that Itō "rented" Pound's "old apartment at 10 Church Walk" (*The Letters of Ezra Pound to Alice Corbin Henderson*, ed. Ira B. Nadel [Austin: University of Texas Press, 1993], 126n.8). Nadel is not certain if they ever lived there together, however (personal communication).

41. Matt Cook uses the term "queer domesticity" in "Domestic Passions: Unpacking the Homes of Charles Shannon and Charles Ricketts," *Journal of British Studies* 51, no. 3 (2012): 618–40.

42. Takeishi, *Japanese Elements in Michio Ito's Early Period*, 20–23.

43. Takeishi claims that the postcard was sent to Walter Sickert's brother, Oswald, in ibid., 27. But the Victoria and Albert Museum collection indicates that Walter was the recipient.

44. Ibid., 22. Selections of the detailed letters from Oswald Sickert to Charles Ricketts were published in Arthur Waley, *The Nō Plays of Japan* (New York: Knopf, 1922).

45. Emmanuel Cooper, *The Sexual Perspective: Homosexuality and Art in the Last 100 Years in the West*, 2nd ed. (New York: Routledge, 1994), 117. Cooper writes,

> He [Chile] had a sustained relationship with Michio Ito, a Japanese dancer. Because of his masculine manner and powerful body (Guevara had learnt to box

in Chile and he kept up the sport), everyone assumed he was heterosexual and he did little to make his sexual tastes known to anyone but his lovers . . . nor did he approve of the open discussion of buggery that took place in front of women and men at various Bloomsbury social occasions. (117–18)

46. Forrest Read, *Pound-Joyce* (London: Faber & Faber, 1968), 58.

47. Ezra Pound, "Sword-Dance and Spear-Dance: Texts of the Poems Used with Michio Itow's Dances. By Ezra Pound from Notes of Masirni Utchiyama," *Future* 1, no. 2 (1916): 54–55, in *Ezra Pound's Poetry and Prose: Contributions to Periodicals*, ed. Lea Baechler, A. Walton Litz, and James Longenbach (New York: Garland, 1991), 2:182–83.

48. Ibid., 182.

49. Ibid.

50. Ibid.

51. Takeishi quotes from the Coliseum programs and the review in the *Era*, in *Japanese Elements in Michio Ito's Early Period*, 13–14.

52. Mizuki Waka, interview with author, 2009; Hahn, *Sensational Knowledge*, 63–66.

53. Pound, "Sword-Dance and Spear-Dance," 182. Minami has not been identified.

54. Deborah Klens-Bigman, "The Fan and the Sword: Exploring Kenbu," *Journal of Theatrical Combatives*, March 2006, available at http://ejmas.com/jtc/2006jtc/jtcart _klens-bigman_0603.html (accessed March 10, 2015); G. Cameron Hurst, *Armed Martial Arts of Japan: Swordsmanship and Archery* (New Haven, Conn.: Yale University Press, 1998), 153–55.

55. As staged by Ryutani and Komine for Repertory Dance Theatre's Summer Dance: Michio Ito.

56. Takeishi links "Song for a Foiled Vendetta" to "Kawanakajima"; "The Sole Survivor (Kogun funto)," to "Shiroyama"; "In Enemies' Country Just After War" to "Zangetsu"; and "Spear Dance/Honogi," to "Honnoji," in *Japanese Elements in Michio Ito's Early Period*, 27. The fifth piece, "Yamadera," is based, as Pound recognized, on a popular comic song about a Buddhist priest who "[w]ants to play football." Lacking a ball, he "puts a cat in a paper bag" ("Sword-Dance and Spear-Dance," 183). Pound's translation consists mostly of the sounds of the kicking priest and howling cat (*nayon* and *pum*) and, as such, resembles his use of unusual onomatopoeia in noh translations like *Nishikigi*'s "kiri/hatari/cho/chc" (PFNoh, 84).

57. Pound, "Sword-Dance and Spear-Dance," 182.

58. Stephen Turnbull, *Kawanakajima, 1553–1564* (Oxford: Osprey, 2003).

59. Pound, "Sword-Dance and Spear-Dance," 182.

60. Ibid., 183.

61. James Longenbach, one of the few scholars to discuss the dance poems, suggestively describes them as "subtle commentary on the war that raged not so far from Kensington drawing rooms" (*Stone Cottage: Pound, Yeats, and Modernism* [New York: Oxford University Press, 1988], 201).

62. Caldwell, *Michio Ito*, 5. Ryutani Kyoko and Komine Kumiko used a similar narrative in their teaching of the choreography for "Tone Poem II." Clip courtesy of Dana Tai Soon Burgess Dance Company.

63. The New York Library for the Performing Arts has a copy of "Modern and Classic Japanese Pantomimes and Dances" (Neighborhood Playhouse program, April 6, 1918), the performance at which Itō danced the "Sword Dance," along with the Pound-Fenollosa-Hirata translation of the noh play *Tamura* (Itō archives MGZA, NYPLPA). Caldwell indicates that Itō performed the "Sword Dance (*kenbu*) to chant" on April 7, 14, and 21, 1918, at the Greenwich Village Theatre.

64. Takeishi, *Japanese Elements in Michio Ito's Early Period*, 27. Itō identified the play as a "comedy" called *So Long Letty* and claimed, "I couldn't dance as they wanted me to for any amount of money" (IAuto, 27). According to Caldwell, Itō refused to perform in a "sex comedy" about couples swapping partners (*Michio Ito*, 55).

65. Shimazaki began performing Itō's solos in New York in the late 1970s, which influenced subsequent reconstructions, including the five Itō solos included on the American Repertory Dance Company's 1998 Legendary California Choreographers program. The University of Washington's Chamber Dance Company, directed by Hannah Wiley, presented *Five Dance Poems of Michio Ito* in 2001 and 2006, including the solos, "Warrior" (1928, Schumann), "Prelude X" (1927, Scriabin), "Prelude V" (1927, Scriabin), "Prelude VI" (1927, Scriabin), and "Tango" (1927, Albéniz). Kyoko Ryutani and Kumiko Komine set eleven pieces on the Repertory Dance Theater in 2009, and although they staged several as small group pieces, all but one was originally choreographed as a solo. See "Satoru Shimazaki Performing Works of Pioneer Choreographer," at the "Theatre of the Open Eye," October 2–7, 1979, PCMI; and *The Dances of Michio Ito* (film), directed by Hannah C. Wiley (Seattle: University of Washington, Chamber Dance Company Archive, 2001).

66. Jack Anderson, "Satoru Shimazaki, Soloist," *New York Times*, November 20, 1983, available at http://www.nytimes.com/1983/11/20/arts/dance-satoru-shimazaki -soloist.html?scp=1&sq=Satoru+Shimazaki+&st=nyt (accessed March 10, 2015).

67. Mark Franko describes this "modern dance master narrative," which follows common stories about aesthetic modernism, in *Dancing Modernism / Performing Politics* (Bloomington: Indiana University Press, 1995), ix.

68. Cowell and Shimazaki suggest that Itō beat the second generation to a system: "Ito seems to have had a systematic, if eclectic, approach to training before

the development of Graham or Humphrey-Weidman technique" ("East and West," 14).

69. Here I agree with Wong, who argues that the "rehabilitative move" of bringing Itō back into the modern dance canon blames his "exclusion" on the past rather than "the continued practice of writing dance history," a practice that has not interrogated its own "politics of whiteness" ("Artistic Utopias," 156, 149).

70. The reviewer claimed, "Michio Ito's Shadow Dance was the climax of the program." The pageant celebrating the installation of the largest sun arc and its reviews are described in Caldwell, Michio Ito, 88–89. The piece was also listed as "Caprice" and "Marionette Dance" in early concerts, as discussed in Takeishi, Japanese Elements in Michio Ito's Early Period, 37–39.

71. Mae Saunders, "Arts of Music and Dance Provide Rare Treat Here," Bakersfield Californian, December 5, 1933, PCMI.

72. The reconstruction of "Pizzicati" by Dana Tai Soon Burgess was generously provided by the Dana Tai Soon Burgess Dance Company.

73. Ruth St. Denis defined "music visualization" as the "translation into bodily action of the rhythmic, melodic and harmonic structure of a musical composition" ("Dance Visualization" [1925], in Dance as a Theatre Art, 2nd ed., ed. Selma Jeanne Cohen (Princeton, N.J.: Princeton Book, 1992), 130.

74. Ryutani and Komine, Ito Technique and Repertory Class, July 3, 2009.

75. The screen dimensions are given in notebooks in PCMI.

76. Koner describes this backdrop for a 1928 touring company that included Itō's wife, Hazel Wright; Dorothy Wagner; Georgia Graham (Martha Graham's sister); and Koner, in Solitary Song, 29–31.

77. Michio Ito Program File MGZB, NYPLPA. Tulle Lindahl performed in four additional solos, presumably choreographed by Itō. For these early recitals, see Takeishi's analysis of the music in Japanese Elements in Michio Ito's Early Period, 37–39.

78. H. T. Parker, "Roshanara and Ito," December 5, 1917, in Motion Arrested: Dance Reviews of H. T. Parker, ed. Olive Holmes (Middletown, Conn.: Wesleyan University Press, 1982), 258–59.

79. "Michio Itow in Japanese Dances with the Assistance of Tulle Lindahl," Itō Program Notes, Box MGZA, NYPLPA.

80. Parker, "Roshanara and Ito," 258–59.

81. Takeishi, Japanese Elements in Michio Ito's Early Period, 38.

82. Parker, "Roshanara and Ito," 259.

83. "Tour of Resorts for War Charities," New York Times online archive, July 10, 1917.

84. "Orientals Lend Weird Art," Musical America, September 1, 1917, 17.

85. "Ballet Intime," Michio Ito Clipping File MGZB, NYPLPA. Takeishi reprinted the unidentified article in Japanese Elements in Michio Ito's Early Period, 97.

86. Caldwell indicates Itō performed "Sword Dance (*kenbu*) to chant" on April 7, 14, and 21, 1918, at the Greenwich Village Theatre.

87. Parker, "Roshanara and Ito," 258–59.

88. "Manhattan Nights and Exotic Entertainers" (sketches by Frueh of the *World Magazine* staff), NYPLPA.

89. Carol Fisher Sorgenfrei suggests that Itō engaged in "strategic cultural unweaving" rather than "interweaving" by "valorizing the uniqueness and superiority of Japan and the Japanese body" ("Strategic Unweaving: Itō Michio and the Diasporic Dancing Body," in *Politics of Interweaving Performance Cultures: Beyond Postcolonialism*, ed. Erika Fischer-Lichte, Torsten Jost, and Saskya Iris Jain [Florence, Ky.: Taylor & Francis, 2014], 201). The metaphor of "unweaving" ignores Itō's strategic cultural syncretism and strategic orientalism, which he used to promote his work whenever it was helpful.

90. Frederick H. Martens, "Folk-Music in the Ballet Intime," *New Music Review*, October 1917, 762–65, quoted in Takeishi, *Japanese Elements in Michio Ito's Early Period*, 43.

91. Takeishi identifies these melodies (played by the oboe) as "Nen nen korori" and the koto piece as "Chidori no kyoku" and believes that Griffes got them from Itō rather than the soprano Eva Gauthier, as has been widely assumed, in *Japanese Elements in Michio Ito's Early Period*, 43–44.

92. Ibid., 43.

93. "Noh Dramas, Once Sacred to Shinto Gods, Coming to Boston."

94. Marshall, "Woman of 70."

95. George Jackson, "Three Times a Charm: Dana Tai Soon Burgess & Company, Eisenhower Theater, John F. Kennedy Center for the Performing Arts, Washington, D.C., December 7–8, 2001," *Dance Magazine*, April 2002, 76–77, 93.

96. Cowell and Shimazaki, "East and West," 272.

97. Dana Tai Soon Burgess Dance Company, http://dtsbdc.org/69–2/; George Washington Faculty, http://theatredance.gwu.edu/Faculty&Staff/dana.html (accessed March 10, 2015).

98. The solos performed by Shimazaki and Burgess are reviewed in George Jackson, "A Celebration of Michio Ito; or, When Modern was New," *Dance Magazine*, May 1996, 86–87. The mission of Burgess's company was published in the Meyer Foundation's profile of grant winners from 2009 to 2011, available at http://meyer foundation.org/impact/our-grantees/moving-forward%3A-contemporary-asian -american-dance-company (accessed March 10, 2015).

99. The most recent review of Burgess's performances of Itō's choreography is Christopher Correa, "The Change Is Everything: Dana Tai Soon Burgess & Company at the Embassy of Japan, Washington D.C. (April 9, 2005)," *DanceView Times* 3, no. 14

(2005), available at http://danceviewtimes.com/2005/Spring/01/ito.htm (accessed March 10, 2015).

100. Wong, "Artistic Utopias," 157–58.

101. Wong notes that the authorities had very different assumptions about the national affiliations of people of European descent: Italian and German Americans were detained only if they were suspected of direct ties to enemy governments (ibid., 155).

102. Wong writes, "Ito's 'internationalism' becomes historically illegible within a modern dance history premised on neo-liberal understandings of multiculturalism when it comes to the dancing Asian American body" (ibid., 156). Neoliberal assumptions certainly influenced responses to Itō, but Wong does not adequately define neoliberalism or differentiate "neo-liberal understandings of multiculturalism" from the "international" ideals of Itō and others in his period.

103. "Michio Ito, Internationally Famous Dancer and Group of Noted Solo Dancers: Touring the Pacific Coast and Western Canada During October and November 1933," PCMI.

104. Cowell claims that Itō's was "a life in some ways lived before its time" ("Michio Ito in Hollywood," 302).

105. Ibid., 291.

106. Solita Solano, "Michio Itow's Good Deed: The Japanese Dancer Has Introduced Two Specimens of the Native 'Noh' Drama of Antiquity to This Country," New York Tribune (1916), PCMI.

107. "The New Plays," New York Times, November 12, 1916, New York Times online archive.

108. The program "Modern and Classic Japanese Pantomimes and Dances" included Itō's "Sword Dance," along with the Fenollosa-Hirata-Pound translation of Tamura, Itō Program Notes, Box MGZA, NYPLPA.

109. For a discussion of the pedagogical functions of the playhouse in the context of community theater's work to define diverse communities, see Ann Larabee, " 'The Drama of Transformation': Settlement House Idealism and the Neighborhood Playhouse," in Performing America: Cultural Nationalism in American Theater, ed. Jeffrey D. Mason and J. Ellen Gainor (Ann Arbor: University of Michigan Press, 1999), 123–36.

110. Alice Lewisohn Crowley, The Neighborhood Playhouse: Leaves from a Theatre Scrapbook (New York: Theatre Arts, 1959), 7.

111. John P. Harrington, The Life of the Neighborhood Playhouse on Grand Street (Syracuse, N.Y.: Syracuse University Press, 2007), 107.

112. Crowley, Neighborhood Playhouse, 86–87.

113. Ibid., 89.

114. Ibid., 86.

115. Harrington, *Life of the Neighborhood Playhouse*, 108.

116. Crowley, *Neighborhood Playhouse*, 87. Harrington claims that they were at *Hawk's Well*, in *Life of the Neighborhood Playhouse*, 104.

117. Crowley, *Neighborhood Playhouse*, 87–88.

118. "Modern and Classic Japanese Pantomimes and Dances."

119. Crowley, *Neighborhood Playhouse*, 88.

120. "Modern and Classic Japanese Pantomimes and Dances."

121. "Michio Itow in Japanese Dances with the Assistance of Tulle Lindahl, program notes read by Jose Ruben of the Washington Square Players," December 6, 1916, Michio Ito Archives MGZA, NYPLPA.

122. "Give Japanese 'Noh' Dance: Michio Itow in Novelty 'Tamura' at Neighborhood Playhouse," *New York Times*, January 9, 1921, available at http://www.nytimes.com/ref/ membercenter /nytarchive.html (accessed June 18, 2015). The *New York Times* online archive gives the date of the review as January 9, but it probably was published on January 29.

123. *Tamura*, in Neighborhood Playhouse program, January 29 and 30, 1921, Itō Box MGZA, NYPLPA.

124. Quoted in Harrington, *Life of the Neighborhood Playhouse*, 106.

125. "Give Japanese 'Noh' Dance."

126. Itō Michio to Ezra Pound (from "Michio Itow's School"), December 19, 1920, in *Ezra Pound and Japan*, ed. Kodama, 17–18.

127. "Japanese Noh Drama: GIVEN FOR THE FIRST TIME OUTSIDE OF JAPAN," staged by Michio Itow for the Thursday Evening Club, January 18, 1923, program in the NYPLPA.

128. Sheldon Cheney, "New Books: *Noh; or Accomplishment*" (December 1917), in *Sheldon Cheney's Theatre Arts Magazine: Promoting a Modern American Theatre, 1916–1921*, ed. DeAnna M. Toten Beard (Lanham, Md.: Scarecrow Press, 2010), 110.

129. "Sheldon Cheney: A Missionary of Modernism," in ibid., 18.

130. Hermann Rosse, "Sketches of Oriental Theatres I" (May 1918), in ibid., 115–16.

131. Solita Solana later became part of the queer network surrounding Gertrude Stein, Alice B. Toklas, Djuna Barnes, Janet Flanner, and Margaret Anderson.

132. Julie A. Iezzi, "*Kyōgen* in English: A Bibliography," *Asian Theatre Journal* 24, no. 1 (2007): 211–34.

133. Itow Michio and Louis V. Ledoux, "Somebody-nothing," *Asia* 21, no. 12 (1921): 1011–12. The first English translation of *Bussu* [sic] was published by Noguchi Yone in 1917.

134. "Japanese Noh Drama: GIVEN FOR THE FIRST TIME."

135. Itow Michio and Louis V. Ledoux, "*She Who Was Fished [Tsuri onna]*," *Outlook*, January 31, 1923, 218–19, and "*The Fox's Grave*." Noguchi Yone published the first English version of *Kitsune zuka* in 1907. Caldwell claims that Itō performed these *kyōgen* in January 1923, but the location and other details are unknown (*Michio Ito*, 133).

136. Itow and Ledoux, "*She Who Was Fished*," 218.

137. Ibid.

138. The source of *Bushidō* was probably the Terakoya (Temple school) scene in act 4 of *Sugawara denju tenarai kagami* (*Sugawara's Secrets of Calligraphy*), a five-act bunraku play from 1746, according to Caldwell, *Michio Ito*, 166n.3.

139. Elizabeth S. Allen, "Eurhythmics for the Theatre" (January 1919), in *Sheldon Cheney's Theatre Arts Magazine*, ed. Toten Beard, 120.

140. Ibid., 123.

141. Rita Wellman, *The String of the Samisen* (1917), first performed in January 1919 and published in *The Provincetown Plays*, ed. George Cram Cook and Frank Shay (Cincinnati: Stewart & Kidd, 1921), 205–38. For an introduction to Rita Wellman's work with the Provincetown Players, see "Introduction to *The Rib-Person*," in *Women Writers of the Provincetown Players: A Collection of Short Works*, ed. Edith E. Barlow (Albany: State University of New York Press, 2009), 89–93.

142. Eugene O'Neill, *Anna Christie, The Emperor Jones, The Hairy Ape* (New York: Vintage Books, 1972), 20.

143. Ibid., 46.

144. Ibid., 47.

145. Heywood Broun, "Review of *The Emperor Jones*," *New York Tribune*, November 4, 1920), reprinted at eOneill.com: http://www.eoneill.com/artifacts/reviews/ej1 _tribune.htm (accessed March 31, 2015).

146. Alexander Woollcott, "The New O'Neill Play," *New York Times*, November 7, 1920, reprinted at eOneill.com: http://www.eoneill.com/artifacts/reviews/ej1_times .htm (accessed June 28, 2015).

147. Ben Brantley, among other reviewers of the Wooster Group's 1993 reinterpretation of *The Emperor Jones*, suggests that the play is unplayable as written, in "The Emperor Jones," *New York Times*, March 14, 1998, in *The New York Times Theater Reviews, 1997–1998* (New York: Times Books, 2000), 244.

148. Woollcott, "New O'Neill Play."

149. In 1874, New York passed a civil rights law with a statute prohibiting segregation at theaters and other "places of amusement," but the theaters still often required black audience members to sit in the balcony, if they were admitted at all. See Karen Sotiropoulos, *Staging Race: Black Performers in Turn of the Century America* (Cambridge, Mass.: Harvard University Press, 2006), 63.

150. Aoife Monks discusses the Wooster Group's version of *The Emperor Jones* in "'Genuine Negroes and Real Bloodhounds': Cross-Dressing, Eugene O'Neill, the Wooster Group, and *The Emperor Jones*," *Modern Drama* 48, no. 3 (2005): 541.

151. Kate Valk discussed the influence of noh on their adaptation of *The Emperor Jones* in interviews and in *The Wooster Group Work Book*, ed. Andrew Quick (New York: Routledge, 2007). See the Wooster Group's recording of *The Emperor Jones*, directed by Elizabeth LeCompte and Christopher Kondek (2009), DVD.

152. Although Monks never mentions Itō, she considers O'Neill as part of the legacy of "Irish participation in blackface minstrelsy" and argues that Charles Sidney Gilpin and other black actors also crossed into blackface, since they "assumed a hyperbolic blackness in the role of Jones (who himself masquerades as paradoxically white)" ("Genuine Negroes," 548–49). Shannon Steen also claims an autobiographical impulse: "In order to dramatize the problem of whiteness, or at least of Irishness, O'Neill turned to blackness to represent his own crisis of psychic and social alienation" ("Melancholy Bodies: Racial Subjectivity and Whiteness in O'Neill's *The Emperor Jones*," *Theatre Journal* 52, no. 3 [2000]: 356).

153. Cowell, "Michio Ito in Hollywood," 263–305.

154. The London performances were technically private, invitation-only affairs. Takeishi describes Yamada Kosçak's music in *Japanese Elements in Michio Ito's Early Period*, 54–57.

155. "Yeats's Noh Play to Be Seen Here," *New York Times*, July 7, 1918, *New York Times* online archive.

156. Martin Birnbaum, *The Last Romantic: The Story of More Than a Half-Century in the World of Art* (New York: Twayne, 1960), 49. Not widely discussed in modernist, performance, or gay studies, Birnbaum also wrote a sympathetic book of anecdotes about Oscar Wilde that closes with the tribute, "The tragedy of an unfulfilled life was his—a life abounding in pitiful paradoxes, contrasts, and jarring notes of insincerity, from which his finest works are fortunately free. A lasting loveliness is theirs" (*Oscar Wilde: Fragments and Memories* [New York: Drake, 1914], 27–28).

157. Birnbaum, *Last Romantic*, 246.

158. "Yeats's Noh Play to Be Seen Here."

159. Takeishi, *Japanese Elements in Michio Ito's Early Period*, 55–57.

160. Birnbaum, *Last Romantic*, 77.

161. *Letters of W. B. Yeats*, 651–52.

162. Henry Romeike (1855–1903) was a Latvian-born businessman who founded a clipping service in New York in 1887, advertised as "the first established and most complete newspaper cutting bureau in the world" (Archives in the Smithsonian Institution, National Museum of American History [ACNMAH 0338]).

163. YPNLI, 1637, inserts; Ezra Pound and Ernest Fenollosa, "Noh," or, *Accomplishment: A Study of the Classical Stage of Japan* (New York: Knopf, 1917).

164. Itō to Pound, December 19, 1920, in *Ezra Pound and Japan*, ed. Kodama, 18.

165. "Michio Ito to Direct 'Prince Igor' in Tokyo: Will Perform in Yeats' 'Hawk's Well' November: Stresses Need for Fusion of Japan-U.S. Cultures," undated clipping, PCMI.

166. "Review of Eighth Army Special Services Productions that have been presented for your entertainment on the main stage of the Ernie Pyle Theater during the last year and a half," PCMI.

167. An undated program in PCMI reveals that Itō's company performed a piece entitled "Down South" that was choreographed and danced by Itō's first wife, Hazel Wright—meaning that it was probably performed sometime in the 1920s and not later than 1936, when Itō and Wright divorced.

168. Itō toured Mexico in 1934 and may have based *Tabasco* on his experience there. See "Teatro Hidalgo—Michio Ito," *Periodico el mundo*, May 4, 1934, PCMI.

169. "Review of Eighth Army Special Services Productions."

170. Ito interview.

171. Cowell and Shimazaki, "East and West," 19.

4. PEDAGOGICAL INTERMISSION

1. Bertolt Brecht, "Theatre for Pleasure or Theatre for Instruction?" (Vergnügungstheater oder Lehrtheater?), in *Brecht on Theatre: The Development of an Aesthetic*, ed. and trans. John Willet (New York: Hill & Wang, 1964), 76. Subsequent references are cited in the text and notes by the abbreviation BOT.

2. John Fuegi, *Brecht and Co.: Sex, Politics, and the Making of the Modern Drama* (New York: Grove Press, 1994).

3. John Willet describes the genesis of the *Lehrstück* in his introduction to Bertolt Brecht, *Collected Plays*, vol. 3, part 2, "The Mother" and Six *Lehrstücke*, ed. John Willett (London: Methuen, 1997), ix–xix. Subsequent references are cited in the text by the abbreviation BCP.

4. Brecht described any *Lehrstück* performance as "false" if it divided an audience from the performers (BOT, 208). Frederic Jameson famously claimed that Brecht's achievement was not in establishing a "doctrine" but in turning the doctrine into a "method," the actors into the public/audience, and the "teaching of practice" into "practice." For Jameson, "this particular 'sublation' or 'transcendence' is meant not to abolish both sides of the opposition but, rather, to complete both, to intensify what may be called the 'usefulness' of each" (*Brecht and Method* [London: Verso, 1998], 65).

5. The ACT, for those who haven't applied to college in a while (or helped younger applicants), offers aspiring college students the option of writing an essay in thirty minutes based on a prompt that states an issue, gives two perspectives, and asks the writer to take and support a position. The ACT announced that it will be changing this format in 2015.

6. Julie Townsend teaches at the University of Redlands, Johnston Center for Integrative Studies, and is the author of *The Choreography of Modernism: La Danseuse, 1830–1930*, Research Monographs in French Studies (Oxford: Legenda, 2009). See also Michel Foucault, *Discipline and Punish: The Birth of the Prison*, trans. Alan Sheridan (1975; repr., New York: Vintage Books, 1995); and Louis Althusser, "Ideology and Ideological State Apparatuses," in *Lenin and Philosophy and Other Essays*, trans. Ben Brewster (1968; repr., New York: Monthly Review Press, 1971), 85–126.

7. An influential articulation of "biopolitics" can be found in Michel Foucault, *Society Must Be Defended: Lectures at the Collège de France, 1975–1976*, trans. David Macey (New York: Picador, 2003).

8. Andrew E. Doe, "Brecht's Lehrstücke: Propaganda Failures," *Educational Theatre Journal* 14, no. 4 (1962): 293–95.

9. Darko Suvin, *Lessons of Japan: Assayings of Some Intercultural Stances* (Montreal: Ciadest, 1996), 211, n. 10.

10. Doe, "Brecht's Lehrstücke," 294.

11. Roswitha Mueller, "Learning for a New Society: The *Lehrstück*," in *The Cambridge Companion to Brecht*, ed. Peter Thomson and Glendyr Sacks (Cambridge: Cambridge University Press, 2006), 112.

12. Roland Barthes, *Empire of Signs* (New York: Hill & Wang, 1982), 3.

5. Noh Circles in Twentieth-Century Japanese Performance

1. Susan Stanford Friedman summarizes these debates and advocates for a very expansive "planetary approach to modernism" in "Planetarity: Musing Modernist Studies," *Modernism / Modernity* 17. no. 33 (2010): 471–99.

2.   For a discussion of the rise and fall of Japan's empire, see Andrew Gordon, *A Modern History of Japan from Tokugawa Times to the Present* (New York: Oxford University Press, 2003).

3. Konishi Jin'ichi, *Nihon bungeishi* (A History of Japanese Literature), 5 vols. (Tokyo: Kodansha, 1985–1992); Marian Ury, review of *A History of Japanese Literature*, vol. 1, *The Archaic and Ancient Ages*, *Journal of Asian Studies* 44, no. 4 (1985): 842–44.

4. My discussion of Konishi's career and his interpretation of Pound's understanding of noh imagery follows Takeuchi Akiko, "Translation and Creative Mis-

understanding: Ezra Pound and Konishi Jin'ichi" (paper presented at the annual convention of the Modern Language Association, Los Angeles, 2011). See also Takeuchi, "Nō no hon'yaku: bunka no hon'yaku wa ikanishite kanōka," [Fenollosa, Pound, Konishi Jin'ichi: Creative misunderstandings in translations] 21 seiki COE kokusai nihongaku kenkyū sōsho 8 (2007): 129–52.

5. Konishi Jin'ichi, A History of Japanese Literature, vol. 3, The High Middle Ages, ed. Earl Miner, trans. Aileen Gatten and Mark Harbison (Princeton, N.J.: Princeton University Press, 1991), 539–40.

6. Takeuchi translates Pound's unity of image" as imeiji no tōitsu, whereas Konishi's "unifying image" is tōitsu imeiji.

7. Konishi wrote, "Zeami's invention of unifying imagery is another important development in his middle period. In Takasago, for example, the image of pines recurs again and again throughout the play and is symbolic of its theme" (History of Japanese Literature, 3:539).

8. Ibid.

9. Ibid., 540.

10. Ibid., 539.

11. Ibid., 540–41.

12. For a study of Pound's interest in the Chinese characters and his reception in China, see R. John Williams, "Modernist Scandals: Ezra Pound's Translations of 'the' Chinese Poem," in Orient and Orientalisms in US-American Poetry and Poetics, ed. Sabine Sielke and Christian Kloeckner (Frankfurt am Main: Lang, 2009), 145–65.

13. Katsumoto Seiichirō, "Characteristics of the Japanese Cinema," in Japan Film Yearbook (1936), quoted in Noël Burch, To the Distant Observer: Form and Meaning in the Japanese Cinema, rev. Annette Michelson (Berkeley: University of California Press, 1979), 148–49.

14. "Expansion" is a term used by Douglas Mao and Rebecca L. Walkowitz to characterize the spatial and vertical movements of modernism in their important essay "The New Modernist Studies," PMLA 123, no. 3 (2008): 737–48. Max Brzezinski's provocative critique, "The New Modernist Studies: What's Left of Political Formalism?" Minnesota Review 76 (2011): 109–25, expands the meanings of "expansion" to include empires and corporate moves, but he goes too far when he merges the neo in neoliberalism with the new of new modernist studies.

15. This view is evident in one of the earliest studies in English to use the term "modernism" in relation to Japanese literature: Dennis Keene, Yokomitsu Riichi: Modernist (New York: Columbia University Press, 1980), in which he argues that Japanese modernism should be defined as "the most extreme instance of Western

influence upon Japanese literature" (88–90) and that Yokomitsu should be studied "as an example of what the introduction of European modernism into Japan
in the 1920s meant, and . . . what went wrong in that process" (viii).

16. William J. Tyler, introduction to *Modanizumu: Modernist Fiction from Japan, 1913–1938*,
ed. William J. Tyler (Honolulu: University of Hawai'i Press, 2008), 6.

17. Ibid., 19.

18. Only two of the twenty-five works included in Tyler's important anthology of
modanizumu fiction were written by women.

19. Tyler, introduction, 21; F. T. Marinetti, "The Founding and Manifesto of Futurism," in *Marinetti: Selected Writings*, ed. R. W. Flint (New York: Farrar, Straus &
Giroux, 1972), 39–44.

20. Kevin J. Wetmore Jr., "Healing the (Metaphysically) Sick Theatre: The Buddhist
Ibsen in Christian Japan," in *Inexorable Modernity: Japan's Grappling with Modernity in
the Arts*, ed. Hiroshi Nara (Lanham, Md.: Lexington Books, 2007), 188.

21. A group of Hōsei University graduates directed by the novelist Morita Sōhei, a
student of Sōseki Natsume, published the first three volumes of their translation with the distinguished publisher Iwanami in 1932 and the fourth in 1936.
Another team, which included the novelists Itō Sei, Nagamatsu Sadamu, and
Tsujino Hisanori, published installments in a magazine between 1930 and 1931
and then in a two-volume edition with the avant-garde publisher Dai'ichi-shobō
(1931, 1934).

22. For a foundational discussion of Japanese modernism and translation, see Hosea
Hirata, *The Poetry and Poetics of Nishiwaki Junzaburo: Modernism in Translation* (Princeton, N.J.: Princeton University Press, 1994.)

23. Arthur Waley translated Lady Murasaki's *The Tale of Genji* in six very successful
volumes between 1919 and 1933.

24. Beverley Curran, "Nogami Toyoichirō's Noh Translation Theories and the Primacy of Performance," in *Translation in Theatre and Performance*, ed. Silvia Bigliazzi,
Paola Ambrosi, and Peter Kofler (Florence, Ky.: Taylor & Francis, 2013), 211–22.

25. For a discussion of Sōseki and the homoerotics of Japanese modernism, see
J. Keith Vincent, *Two-Timing Modernity: Homosocial Narrative in Modern Japanese Fiction* (Cambridge, Mass.: Harvard University Press, 2012).

26. Curran, "Nogami Toyoichirō's Noh Translation Theories," 215–16.

27. Quoted in ibid., 216.

28. Ibid., 218–19.

29. Quoted in ibid., 220.

30. Ibid., 213.

31. Ibid., 214.

32. Japanese Classics Translation Committee of the Nippon gakujutsu shinkōkai, *The Noh Drama: Ten Plays from the Japanese* (Rutland, Vt.: Tuttle, 1955).

33. Ezra Pound to Kitasono Katue, December 30, 1940, in *Ezra Pound and Japan: Letters and Essays*, ed. Sanehide Kodama (Redding Ridge, Conn.: Black Swan, 1987), 106.

34. Brian Powell, "Japan's First Modern Theater: The Tsukiji Shōgekijō and Its Company, 1924–26," *Monumenta Nipponica* 30, no. 1 (1975): 69–85.

35. Brian Powell, *Japan's Modern Theatre: A Century of Change and Continuity* (Abingdon: Routledge, 2013), 59–61.

36. Edward Marx, "Nō Dancing: Yone Noguchi in Yeats's Japan," in "Influence and Confluence," edited by Warwick Gould, special issue, *Yeats Annual* 17 (2007): 55.

37. Powell, *Japan's Modern Theatre*, 62–63. Osanai visited the Dalcroze school in Vienna during his study tour in Europe (1912–1913) and observed the system of eurhythmics that Itō Michio had studied; he later saw them used in actor training methods at the Moscow Art Theater.

38. Brian Powell, "Communist *Kabuki*: A Contradiction in Terms?" in *A Kabuki Reader: History and Performance*, ed. Samuel L. Leiter (New York: Sharpe, 2001), 173.

39. James R. Brandon, "Mussolini in Kabuki: Notes and Translation," in *Japanese Theatre Transcultural: German and Italian Intertwinings*, ed. Stanca Scholz-Cionca and Andreas Regelsberger (Munich: Iudicium, 2011), 74–75.

40. Ibid., 72.

41. Shinko Kagaya, "Dancing on a Moving Train: Nō Between Two Wars," in *Nō Theatre Transversal*, ed. Stanca Scholz-Cionca and Christopher Balme (Munich: Iudicium, 2008), 24–26.

42. Brandon, "Mussolini in Kabuki," 76.

43. Powell, "Communist *Kabuki*," 173.

44. "Shinkyo Troupe Presents Play of Olden Japan: Modern-School Dramatic Group Has Had Hard Struggle for Its Ideals," *Japan Advertiser*, February 11, 1940, PCMI.

45. YPNLI, manuscript 40, 585–86.

46. YPNLI, 1637, insert 1015: *Japanese Drama and the Shōchiku Dramatic Company* (Tokyo: no date). Three articles from a series about the Japanese theater printed in the *Times* (London), December–January 1918–1919, were inserted with the Shōchiku pamphlet (YPNLI, 1637, inserts 1015, 2143, 2144).

47. Brian Powell, "Communist *Kabuki*," 171–72.

48. YPNLI, 1637, insert 1015, 4.

49. Ibid., 1.

50. Ibid., 2.

51. Ibid., 12.

52. Powell, "Communist *Kabuki*," 153.

53. Keiko I. McDonald, "Noh into Film: Kurosawa's *Throne of Blood*," *Journal of Film and Video* 39, no. 1 (1997): 36–41; Zvika Serper, "The Bloodied Sacred Pine Tree: A Dialectical Depiction of Death in *Throne of Blood* and *Ran*," *Journal of Film and Video* 52, no. 2 (2000): 13–27.

54. *A Story of Floating Weeds* (*Ukigusa monogatari*), directed by Yasujirō Ozu (Tokyo: Shōchiku eiga, 1949), reissued with *Floating Weeds* (*Ukigusa*, 1959) (New York: Criterion, 2004).

55. Vincent Canby, "Film: Yasujirō Ozu, as Director and Subject," *New York Times*, April 1, 1987, available at http://www.nytimes.com/1987/04/01/movies/film-yasu jiro-ozu-as-director-and-subject.html (accessed March 21, 2015).

56. These phrases appear in many discussions of Ozu and in Donald Richie's influential *Ozu* (Berkeley: University of California Press, 1974), xi, 189.

57. David Bordwell, *Ozu and the Poetics of Cinema* (Princeton, N.J.: Princeton University Press, 1988), 6–7. For other formulations of Ozu as a conservative traditionalist, see David Desser, *Eros plus Massacre: An Introduction to the Japanese New Wave Cinema* (Bloomington: Indiana University Press, 1988). Ozu's radical experimentalism and critique of Hollywood were advanced (in somewhat different ways) in Burch, *To the Distant Observer*; and Paul Schrader, *Transcendental Style in Film: Ozu, Bresson, Dryer* (Berkeley: University of California Press, 1972).

58. Bordwell, *Ozu and the Poetics of Cinema*, 76.

59. Donald Richie, "Stories of *Floating Weeds*," Current, The Criterion Collection, available at http://www.criterion.com/current/posts/320-stories-of-floating-weeds (accessed March 21, 2015).

60. Richie, *Ozu*, 144.

61. Ryū Chishū, "Yasujirō Ozu" (1964), in *Yasujirō Ozu: A Critical Anthology*, ed. John Gillett and David Wilson (London: British Film Institute, 1976), 38–39.

62. Ryū Chishū plays Shukichi Somiya in *Late Spring* (*Banshun*, 1949), Koichi in *Early Summer* (*Bakushu*, 1951), and Shukichi Hirayama in *Tokyo Story* (*Tōkyō monogatari*, 1953) opposite Hara in the Noriko Trilogy.

63. The Kihachi Series includes *Passing Fancy* (*Dekigokoro*, 1933), *A Story of Floating Weeds* (*Ukigusa monogatari*, 1934), *An Innocent Maid* (*Hakoiri musume*, 1935), and *Inn in Tokyo* (*Tōkyō no yado*, 1935). Kihachi's son is usually played by Tokkan Kozō, but he plays the boy actor Tomi-bō, and Mitsui Hideo plays the older Shinkichi in *A Story of Floating Weeds*.

64. Tadao Sato, *Currents in Japanese Cinema*, trans. Gregory Barrett (Tokyo: Kodansha, 1982), 15–17.

65. Hiroshi Komatsu, "Some Characteristics of Japanese Cinema Before World War I," trans. Linda C. Ehrlich and Yuko Okutsu, in *Reframing Japanese Cinema:*

Authorship, Genre, History, ed. Arthur Nolletti Jr. and David Desser (Bloomington: Indiana University Press, 1992), 232.

66. Ibid., 239.

67. J. L. Anderson, "Spoken Silents in the Japanese Cinema; or, Talking to Pictures: Essaying the *Katsuben*, Contextualizing the Texts," in *Reframing Japanese Cinema*, ed. Nolletti and Desser, 272.

68. Ibid., 260. *Benshi* means "speaker or orator," whereas the more precise term, *katsuben*, combines *katsudō shashin* (moving photographs) and *benshi*. I use the term *benshi* because it is better known in film studies. Anderson gives the period between 1927 and 1931 as the "golden age" of the *benshi* (279).

69. Ibid., 284.

70. Ibid., 261.

71. Donald Richie describes *benshi* as a "major obstacle to cinematic technique" because of their resemblance to theatrical narrators, in *Japanese Cinema: Film Style and National Character* (New York: Doubleday, 1971]), 6. But there is little evidence suggesting that Ozu resisted the *benshi* and plenty indicating that he resisted sound.

72. The first extant Japanese sound film, Mizoguchi Kenji's *Furusato* (*Hometown*), was produced in 1930, but silent pictures were made for the rest of that decade. See Iwamoto Kenji, "Sound in the Early Japanese Talkies," in *Reframing Japanese Cinema*, ed. Nolletti and Desser, 315. In 1937, one-fifth of Japanese films were still silent and narrated by one of the 3,695 professional *benshi*, whereas by 1931, silent films had virtually disappeared in western Europe and the United States, according to Anderson, "Spoken Silents," 292.

73. Takeda Rintarō, "Japan's Three-Penny Opera," trans. Richard Torrance, in *Modanizumu*, ed. Tyler, 462–81.

74. Peter B. High, *The Imperial Screen: Japanese Film Culture in the Fifteen Years' War (1931–1945)* (Madison: University of Wisconsin Press, 2003), 21. The government, the media, and even the film industry helped orchestrate these incidents to promote rage against the supposed Chinese perpetrators and justify Japanese colonialism in Asia.

75. Ibid., 39–40.

76. Keiko I. McDonald suggests that cinema struggled to disentangle itself from the theater because "theatrical traditions in Japan were so strong that the new art could not at first imagine dramatic conventions as its own. This burden of tradition retarded the formation of a specifically cinematic grammar" (*Reading a Japanese Film: Cinema in Context* [Honolulu: University of Hawai'i Press, 2006], 2).

77. Richie, *Ozu*, 10. In 1972, in *Transcendental Style in Film*, Schrader positioned Ozu alongside experimental European filmmakers. Three years later, William

Shurtleff and Akiko Aoyagi argued that tofu was the most economical and environmentally friendly way to meet the world's protein needs, in *The Book of Tofu* (Brookline, Mass.: Autumn Press, 1975).

78. *Late Spring's* scene from *Kakitsubata* is mistitled "Morikawa" in Bordwell, *Ozu and the Poetics of Cinema* (310) and other works, but a noh play by that title does not exist. Yoshida Kiju correctly identified the play as *Kakitsubata*, in *Ozu's Anti-Cinema*, trans. Daisuke Miyao and Kyoko Hirano (Ann Arbor: University of Michigan Press, 2003), 73.

79. This basic principle in film spectatorship is known as the "Kuleshov effect," so named for the Russian film theorist Lev Kuleshov, who famously intercut the same shot of an actor's face with various objects. Audiences believed that the actor was looking at and responding differently to each object, although the expression was the same. Kuleshov established that each film shot is interpreted in relation to adjacent shots, a feature of cinematic montage.

80. *Late Spring (Banshun)*, directed by Ozu Yasujirō (Tokyo: Shōchiku eiga, 1949; New York Criterion, 2006).

81. Yoshida, *Ozu's Anti-Cinema*, 74.

82. Bordwell, *Ozu and the Poetics of Cinema*, 310.

83. Quoted in *Geijutsu shinchō*, April 1959, quoted in Yoshida, *Ozu's Anti-Cinema*, 65.

84. Burch claims that Ozu attempted to produce a feeling of disorientation with "'bad' eyeline matches," low camera settings, and challenges to cinematic continuity (*To the Distant Observer*, 159).

85. Bordwell, *Ozu and the Poetics of Cinema*, 97.

86. Kobayashi Hideo, "Literature of the Lost Home," in *Literature of the Lost Home: Kobayashi Hideo—Literary Criticism, 1924–1939*, ed. and trans. Paul Anderer (Stanford, Calif.: Stanford University Press, 1995), 52–54.

87. Katsumoto Seiichirō, "Characteristics of the Japanese Cinema" (1936), quoted in Burch, *To the Distant Observer*, 148–49.

88. Lars-Martin Sorensen, *Censorship of Japanese Films During the U.S. Occupation of Japan: The Cases of Yasujirō Ozu and Akira Kurosawa* (Lewiston, N.Y.: Mellen, 2009), 149–50.

89. Kyoko Hirano, *Mr. Smith Goes to Tokyo Under the American Occupation, 1945–1952* (Washington, D.C.: Smithsonian Institution Press, 1992), 70.

90. Sorensen, *Censorship of Japanese Films*, 149.

91. Ibid., 152.

92. Hirano, *Mr. Smith Goes to Tokyo*, 49.

93. Quoted in Barton J. Bernstein, "Atomic Bombings Reconsidered," *Foreign Affairs* 74, no. 2 (1995): 142.

94. Shotaro Oshima, "Yeats and Michio Ito," *Yeats Society of Japan Annual Report* 6 (1971): 17.

95. Richard Doherty, *In the Ranks of Death: The Irish in the Second World War* (Barnsley: Pen & Sword, 2010).

96. Okifumi Komesu describes the Hawk's dance as a "serious violation of Noh convention" and views both Yokomichi and Yeats as "destructive" ("At the Hawk's Well and *Taka No Izumi* in a 'Creative Circle,'" *Yeats Annual* 5 (1987): 103–13.

97. Yokomichi Mario, *The Hawk Princess* (*Takahime*), unpublished translation by Don Kenny. For sharing this text, I am grateful to Kevin Riordan of Nanyang Technological University of Singapore and Richard Emmert, artistic director of Theatre Nohgaku and founding director of the Noh Training Project (NTP).

98. Yokomichi, *Takahime*, staged at Hōshō nōgakudo in Tokyo, on June 30, 1998, and recorded for an NHK BS-1 TV program. The Old Man was played by Kanze Tetsunojō, Takahime by Otsuki Bunzo, and Kufurin by Hosho Kinya. I am grateful to Richard Emmert for sharing the recording.

99. *Theatre Year-Book* (Tokyo: Japan Centre, International Theatre Institute, 1985–2004). Highlights include the international tour of *Takahime* in 1988 (5). At the Yokohama Expo in 1989, Maeda Bibari performed *Takahime* with the noh actor Kanze Tetsunojō and *kyōgen* actor Nomura Takeshi; *Theatre Year-Book* cited the performance as an instance of collaboration between noh and *kyōgen* actors (35). *Takahime* was directed by Umewaka Rokuro in November 2003 (52). Kanze Hideo performed it again at the age of seventy-six in July 2004 (50), and the Nōgaku kanze za staged a performance of *Taka no izumi* starring Tomoeda Akiyo, Kanze Kiyokazu, and Sekine Yoshito on December 25, 2004 (55).

100. Yet another *Hawk's Well* adaptation by the poet Takahashi Mutsurō, *Taka no i*, also merged *shingeki* and noh. *Taka no i* was commissioned by the Hashi no kai and premiered on December 22, 1990, at the Kanze Noh Theatre. The Old Man was played by Shiraishi Kayoko, an actress who was then actively performing *shingeki* theater with the Waseda shōgekijō (Waseda Little Theatre). The Young Man and the Hawk Maiden were double cast and performed by Asami Masakuni of the Kanze school and Tomoeda Akiyo of the Kita school, bringing the two schools together (*Theatre Year-Book*, 28).

101. Richard Emmert, interview with author, July 19, 2008.

102. Richard Emmert, "English nō and Theatre Nohgaku—The How and the Why," in *Nō Theatre Transversal*, ed. Scholz-Cionca and Balme, 144.

103. Ibid.

104. Quoted from NOHO's first program in Jonah Salz, "Leonard's Bastard Son: The Noho Theatre Group's First Two Decades," *Mime Journal* 22 (2002–2003): 135. Salz

is also the director of Traditional Theatre Training in Kyoto, where Shigeyama serves as a primary teacher. I am grateful to Salz for answering my questions about his work and perspectives on "fusion theater" and to Shigeyama for allowing me to attend his introductory *kyōgen* class on April 28, 2009, in Kyoto.

105. Emmert, "English *nō*," 144. NOHO's *At the Hawk's Well* was also performed in August 1984 at the University of Sydney and back in Kyoto in August 1985 and July 1990. The 1990 edition of *Theatre Year-Book* describes Yeats's interest in noh, Salz and Emmert's productions, and another adaptation called *Taka no ido* performed at Main[e] State University.

106. In our interview, Emmert stated regarding his early work with NOHO, "I was not a big fan of the word 'fusion.' I'm still not." According to Salz, "English noh (or English *kyōgen*) is the not-model of what we're after." NOHO does not follow a particular model for intercultural theater, in his view; rather, "each project approaches material in a new way" (e-mail to author, May 18, 2009).

107. I attended the Noh Training Project in Bloomsburg, Pennsylvania, in 2008, in Tokyo in 2009, and again in Bloomsburg in 2010.

108. In our interview, Emmert said that American actors sometimes ask if they are "good or not" after taking one, three-week workshop. He responds, "The training of the noh actor is 5, 6, 7, 8 years before they start to be on stage, and they are still considered young actors. It's when you have been studying 15 years or so that people say you are pretty good or you're getting better. But still, that's compared to people who have been doing it 30 or 40 years. There's a big difference."

109. Theatre Nohgaku's library in Bloomsburg, Pennsylvania, contains several recordings of *Hawk's Well* performances, on which I base my discussion.

110. For a thorough discussion of Matsui's career, see Judy Halebsky and Mariko Anno, "Innovation in Nō: Matsui Akira Continues a Tradition of Change," *Asian Theatre Journal* 31, no. 1 (2014): 126–52.

111. As Emmert pointed out in our interview, certain plays in the traditional noh repertory have unique and specific *kata*.

112. Theatre Nohgaku member John Oglevee originally proposed the idea of a writers' workshop to teach the structure of noh drama in the hopes of inspiring writers to create new English noh plays.

113. David Crandall first wrote, composed, and produced *Crazy Jane*, partly inspired by Yeats's poems about the maddened and wise peasant woman, in Tokyo in 1983, with a Western instrumental ensemble. In 2007, Crandall re-created *Crazy Jane* with an innovative mixture of Western melodies and noh drum patterns performed by the noh ensemble of instruments (*hayashi*). The new *Crazy Jane* toured

Seattle, Tacoma, and Olympia, Washington, in 2007 and was then revived in Bloomsburg, Pennsylvania, in 2010.

6. TROUBLE WITH TITLES AND DIRECTORS

1. Colin Graham's role in the collaboration that produced the original production was so crucial that we should probably call it Britten-Plomer-Graham's *Curlew River*.

2. Decca's several "Britten Conducts Britten" volumes were released between 2004 and 2007. Recordings of plays like *Waiting for Godot, Endgame*, and *Krapp's Last Tape*, marketed as "Beckett Directs Beckett" in the 1990s, are supplemented by the more recent project under that title at the Visual Press of the University of Maryland

3. Mervyn Cooke, "Britten and the Shō," *Musical Times* 129, no. 1743 (1988): 231.

4. Benjamin Britten, *Curlew River: A Parable for Church Performance* (London: Faber & Faber, 1964). Subsequent references are cited in the text and notes by the abbreviation CR Score.

5. William Plomer, program note to a 1968 production, quoted in Mervyn Cooke, *Britten and the Far East* (Woodbridge: Boydell Press, 1998), 141.

6. William Plomer, *Sado* (Oxford: Oxford University Press, 1990), 22.

7. Plomer, program note, quoted in Cooke, *Britten and the Far East*, 141.

8. William Plomer to Benjamin Britten, October 7, 1958, Britten–Pears Foundation Archives and Library, The Red House, Aldeburgh, England. Subsequent references are cited in the text and notes by the abbreviation BPFAL. I enthusiastically recommend a visit to this archive at the Red House in the seaside village of Aldeburgh, England, where Britten and Pears lived from 1957 until they died.

9. Ezra Pound, "Hell," *Criterion*, April 1934, in *Literary Essays of Ezra Pound*, ed. T. S Eliot (New York: New Directions, 1954), 207.

10. I am grateful to Kevin Salfen for reminding me of this production and for generous comments on a draft of this piece. His suggestions shaped the final draft.

11. For a discussion of Britten's complicated Christianity, see Graham Elliott, *Benjamin Britten: The Spiritual Dimension* (Oxford: Oxford University Press, 2006).

12. Humphrey Carpenter, *Benjamin Britten: A Biography* (London: Faber & Faber, 1992), 433.

13. For a discussion of the Britten/Pears Oberon role from one of the most famous countertenors, see James Bowman, "James Bowman on Striking a High Note," *Guardian*, November 26, 2009, available at http://www.theguardian.com/music/2009/nov/26/james-bowman-countertenor-revival (accessed June 29, 2015).

14. William Mann, "East Meets West in New Britten Music Drama," *Times* (London), June 15, 1964, 6, available at http://www.thetimes.co.uk/tto/news/ (accessed June 24, 2014).

15. See, especially, Judith Butler, "Bodily Inscriptions, Performative Subversions," in *Gender Trouble: Feminism and the Subversion of Identity* (New York: Routledge, 1990), chap. 3.

16. Judith Butler, *Bodies That Matter: On the Discursive Limits of Sex* (New York: Routledge, 1993), 125.

17. Butler told the sad story of Venus Xtravaganza, a preoperative Latina transsexual featured in Jennie Livingston's controversial documentary film *Paris Is Burning* (1991) who also performed in New York City drag balls. Venus poignantly described her longing to be "a spoiled rich white girl" with a husband and suburban home. She was murdered in a hotel room before Livingston finished the film. Butler recognized that Venus idealized wealth, whiteness, heterosexuality, and, in her desire for what she called "my sex change," the presumed correlation of biological sex and gender. But Butler still argued that Venus sought a "transubstantiation of gender" (*Bodies That Matter*, 133).

18. Elizabeth Freeman, *Time Binds: Queer Temporalities, Queer Histories* (Durham, N.C.: Duke University Press, 2010), 70, xiii.

19. Ibid., xiii.

20. Ibid., 70 (italics in original).

21. Butler, *Bodies That Matter*, 137.

22. Mann, "East Meets West," 6.

23. *The Imitation Game* (2014), directed by Morten Tyldum, was nominated for Best Picture and awarded writer Graham Moore the Oscar for Best Adapted Screenplay. See Geraldine Bedell, "Coming Out of the Dark Ages," *Guardian*, June 23, 2007, available at http://www.theguardian.com/society/2007/jun/24/communities.gay rights (accessed March 26, 2015).

24. Sexual Offenses Act 1967, National Archives, text available at http://www .legislation.gov.uk/ukpga/1967/60 (accessed March 26, 2015).

25. Peter Tatchell, *Europe in the Pink: Lesbian and Gay Equality in the New Europe* (London: GMP, 1992), 85–87.

26. For a classic discussion of legal definitions of hetero- and homosexuality, see Janet Halley, "The Construction of Heterosexuality," in *Fear of a Queer Planet: Queer Politics and Social Theory*, ed. Michael Warner (Minneapolis: University of Minnesota Press, 1993), 82–102.

27. Philip Brett claims, "Britten himself never mentioned the topic [of his sexuality], and it was only in 1980, after Peter Pears had declared the nature of their relation-

ship in a prime-time Easter Sunday television broadcast [of Tony Palmer's film *A Time There Was*], that others felt fully comfortable alluding to the fact" ("The Britten Era," in *Music and Sexuality in Britten: Selected Essays* [Berkeley: University of California Press, 2006], 208).

28. Ibid., 221.

29. B. W. Young mixes apologetic and reproving tones when characterizing "the personally conservative, perhaps surprisingly conformist, Britten," who was

> out of favour with the *Beyond the Fringe* crowd—remember Dudley Moore's hurtful and arch 'Little Miss Britten' parody, clever, amusing, but undoubtedly homophobic, and produced at exactly the time when David Maxwell Fyfe, a disgracefully re-actionary home secretary, had wanted to make an example of Britten and Pears in his crusade against what he thought of as protective establishment reticence surrounding private homo-sexual relationships. ("'Reading at Intervals': Benjamin Britten's Romantic Poetry," *Essays in Criticism* 62, no. 2 [2012]: 180)

30. The BBC made a TV movie of the farewell performance of *Beyond the Fringe* (1964), featuring Dudley Moore's parodies along with performances by Alan Bennett, Peter Cook, and Jonathan Miller. See the clip of the Britten–Pears spoof at https://www.youtube.com/watch?v=1n7BCUVJkhU&feature=player_embedded (accessed October 16, 2015).

31. Peter Parker, "Britten and the Gang," in *Britten's Century*, ed. Mark Bostridge (London: Bloomsbury, 2013), 49.

32. Eve Kosofsky Sedgwick, *The Epistemology of the Closet* (Berkeley: University of California Press, 1990). Brett's pioneering work on Britten is collected in *Music and Sexuality in Britten*; for Brett's use of Sedgwick, see, especially, "Britten's Dream," 106–28.

33. Philip Brett, ""Eros and Orientalism in Britten's Operas," in *Music and Sexuality in Britten*, 147.

34. Ibid., 148.

35. Ibid., 148–49.

36. Mann, "East Meets West," 6.

37. Roger Scruton, "We Need the English Music That the Arts Council Hates," *Spectator*, April 16, 2008, available at http://www.spectator.co.uk/features/615311/we-need-the-english-music-that-the-arts-council-hates/ (accessed March 26, 2015).

38. William Plomer, *Curlew River: A Parable for Church Performance Set to Music by Benjamin Britten* (London: Faber & Faber, 1964), 39. Subsequent references are cited in the text by the abbreviation CR.

39. "Pray the Gay Away" was associated most strongly with Alan Chambers's Exodus International, which disbanded in 2013, but also with Bachmann & Associates Counseling Centers, owned by the family of Minnesota congresswoman and 2012 presidential candidate Michele Bachmann. "Gay conversion therapy," or "reparative therapy," for minors has been banned in California (2012) and New Jersey (2013), and legislation is pending in other states.

40. Ann Pellegrini pointed out that "when religion has entered into the frame of queer and even feminist academic analyses, it has tended to do so in highly belief-centered terms in which religion gets figured as the expression of irrational superstition, fear, archaic holdover, modernity's remainder" ("Testimonial Sexuality; or, Queer Structures of Religious Feeling: Notes Toward an Investigation," *Journal of Dramatic Theory and Criticism* 20, no. 1 [2005]: 94). She argued, "Because all United States laws regulating homosexuality are, at base, religious in derivation, we contend that religious freedom is a structural condition of sexual freedom" (95).

41. Pellegrini, "Testimonial Sexuality." According to Elizabeth Freeman, "For social change itself enables, and perhaps even requires, that incommensurate temporalities—often most available to us via their corresponding aesthetic forms—rub up against one another, compete, overlap, cross-reference . . . [including] the sacred time of a Christian afterlife" ("Still After," *South Atlantic Quarterly* 106, no. 3 [2007]: 499).

42. Britten's and Plomer's refusal of futurism probably had to do with both sexuality and the threat of nuclear annihilation. See Lee Edelman's controversial polemic, "reproductive futurism," in *No Future: Queer Theory and the Death Drive* (Durham, N.C.: Duke University Press, 2004).

43. Gregory M. Pflugfelder discusses shudō, which he translates as "the way of loving youths," in *Cartographies of Desire: Male-Male Sexuality in Japanese Discourse, 1600–1950* (Berkeley: University of California Press, 1999), 27.

44. W. H. Auden to Benjamin Britten, January 31, 1942, quoted in Neil Powell, *Benjamin Britten: A Life for Music* (New York: Holt, 2013), 206–7. It was sent from Ann Arbor, Michigan, as Britten was leaving the United States to return to England.

45. John Bridcut, *Britten's Children* (London: Faber & Faber, 2006), 271–73.

46. "Te lucis ante terminum / Before the ending of the day," as translated in Britten's "Libretto Drafts," 9100320–23 (BPFAL).

47. "Our Guardian Angels / Custodes Hominum" in *Arundel Hymns*, ed. Henry FitzAlan-Howard and Charles T. Gatty (London: Boosey, 1905), 240–41.

48. The translation that Plomer used was *The Noh Drama: Ten Plays from the Japanese*, trans. Japanese Classics Translation Committee of Nippon gakujutsu shinkōkai (Rutland, Vt.: Tuttle, 1955), 143–60.

49. By universalizing desire, this moment resembles the queer reinterpretation of Michel Foucault's little mad people (*petits foux*) as offering a link among diverse sexualities, unreason, and morality, as suggested in Lynne Huffer, *Mad for Foucault: Rethinking the Foundations of Queer Theory* (New York: Columbia University Press, 2009); and Didier Eribon, *Insult and the Making of the Gay Self*, trans. Michael Lucey (Durham, N.C.: Duke University Press, 2004).

50. Imogene Holst, introduction to CR Score.

51. For a more thorough discussion of the complex rhythmic relationships in noh music, see William P. Malm, *Six Hidden Views of Japanese Music* (Berkeley: University of California Press, 1986), 46–47.

52. Holst, introduction to CR Score.

53. Ibid.

54. I am grateful to my colleague and mentor John T. Matthews for many acts of guidance, including clarifying the function of the "diacritical curlew."

55. Graham requested that productions acknowledge his stage direction if they use it.

56. Leo Bersani, "Is the Rectum a Grave?" *October* 43 (1987): 215–22 (italics in original).

57. Brian Wilson, e-mail to author.

58. Nicholas Spice, "Darkness Audible," *London Review of Books* 15, no. 3 (1993): 3–6. Carpenter's flawed but influential biography, *Benjamin Britten*, emphasizes the tormented and tormenting Britten, while Paul Kildea offers a more balanced account in *Benjamin Britten: A Life in the Twentieth Century* (London: Penguin, 2013).

59. Samuel Beckett, *Footfalls*, in *The Complete Dramatic Works* (London: Faber & Faber, 1989), 399. Subsequent references are cited in the text and notes by the abbreviation BCDW, and all of Beckett's plays will be cited from this source. An excellent version of *Footfalls*, featuring Susan Fitzgerald and directed by Walter Asmus, Beckett's assistant director for the Berlin production, is available on *Beckett on Film*, produced by Michael Colgan and Alan Maloney (Ireland: Blue Angel Films / Tyrone Productions, 2000), DVD.

60. Billie Whitelaw, *Billie Whitelaw . . . Who He?* (St. Martin's Press, New York, 1995), 144–45.

61. The University of Maryland Visual Press videotaped productions under the title "Beckett Directs Beckett." See also *The Theatrical Notebooks of Samuel Beckett*, vol. 1, *Krapp's Last Tape*, ed. James Knowlson (New York: Grove Press, 1990); Samuel Beckett, "Footfalls Notebook," in The Theatrical Notebooks of Samuel Beckett, vol. 4, *The Shorter Plays*, ed. S. E. Gontarski (New York: Grove Press, 1999).

62. Quoted in Leonard Pronko, *Theatre East and West: Perspectives Toward a Total Theatre* (Berkeley: University of California Press, 1967), 106.

63. Yasunari Takahashi, "The Theatre of Mind: Samuel Beckett and the Noh," *Encounter* 58, no. 4 (1982): 68. See also Takahashi, "The Ghost Trio: Beckett, Yeats, and Noh," in *The Empire of Signs*, ed. Yoshihiko Ikegama (Amsterdam: Benjmin, 1991), 257–67; and Minako Okamuro, "Beckett, Yeats, and Noh: . . . but the clouds . . . as Theatre of Evocation," in *Samuel Beckett Today/Aujourd'hui* 21 (2009): 165–77.

64. Gilles Deleuze discussed Beckett's plays for television, noh, and Yeats in "L'Épuisé," in Samuel Beckett, *Quad et Trio du Fantôme, . . . que nuages . . . , Nacht un Träume*, translated from the English by Edith Fournier (Paris: Minuit, 1992), 55–106. For a discussion of Deleuze's essay, see Ronald Bogue, "Deleuze and the Invention of Images: From Beckett's Television Plays to Noh Drama," *Comparatist* 26 (2002): 37–52.

65. Samuel Beckett to James Knowlson, April 11, 1972, quoted in James Knowlson, "Beckett's 'Bits of Pipe,' " in *Samuel Beckett: Humanistic Perspectives*, ed. Morris Beja, S. E. Gontarski, and Pierre Astier (Columbus: Ohio State University Press, 1983), 16 (italics in original).

66. Samuel Beckett to Cyril Cusack, June 1956, quoted by A. J. Leventhal, in James Knowlson, *Samuel Beckett: An Exhibition Held at Reading University Library, May to July 1971* (catalog) (London: Turret Books, 1971), 14.

67. Gay Gibson Cima, *Performing Women: Female Characters, Male Playwrights, and the Modern Stage* (Ithaca, N.Y.: Cornell University Press, 1993), 206–10. See also Jonathan Kalb, "Underground Staging in Perspective," and conversation with Joanne Akalaitis, in *Beckett in Performance* (New York: Cambridge University Press, 1989), 71–94, 165–72; Angela Moorjani, "Directing or In-Directing Beckett: Or What Is Wrong with *Catastrophe*'s Director?" In "Historicizing Beckett/Issues of Performance," special issue, *Samuel Beckett Today/Aujourd'hui* 15 (2005): 187–99; and Thomas Mansell, "Different Music: Beckett's Theatrical Conduct," in "Historicizing Beckett/Issues of Performance," special issue, *Samuel Beckett Today/Aujourd'hui* 15 (2005): 225–39.

68. Whitelaw, *Billie Whitelaw . . . Who He?*, 145, 141.

69. Ibid., 141. Ruby Cohn reports, "He practiced walking with Whitelaw on the strip, establishing the pace, which slows twice" (*Just Play: Beckett's Theater* [Princeton, N.J.: Princeton University Press, 1980], 270).

70. James Knowlson reported that "sandpaper was attached to the soles of Whitelaw's soft ballet slippers" (*Damned to Fame: The Life of Samuel Beckett* [New York: Simon & Schuster, 1996], 551). In her autobiography, Whitelaw claimed that there were "emery boards on the soles of the pumps" to produce the "scratching sound of the feet" (*Billie Whitelaw . . . Who He?*, 144).

71. Whitelaw, *Billie Whitelaw . . . Who He?*, 144.

72. Ibid., 127. Walter Asmus, Beckett's assistant director for most of his productions in Germany, claimed that Beckett commonly gave line readings, which he described as "so fabulous, so inspiring, so true" (quoted in Kalb, *Beckett in Performance*, 176).

73. Knowlson, *Damned to Fame*, 550.

74. Beckett gave Whitelaw a tape of his reading of *Rockaby* and recorded Lucky's monologue before the 1964 Royal Court Production of *Endgame* for Jack MacGowran, according to Knowlson, *Damned to Fame*, 550.

75. Cohn, *Just Play*, 270. "Voice/Mother" is listed as "*Woman's voice (V) from dark upstage*" in the stage directions, but she responds to "Mother" in the first dialogue and is named as such in most discussions of the play.

76. Kalb, *Beckett in Performance*, 64.

77. See the photographs collected in Linda Ben-Zvi, ed., *Women in Beckett: Performance and Critical Perspectives* (Urbana: University of Illinois Press, 1990).

78. Whitelaw, *Billie Whitelaw . . . Who He?*, 120.

79. W. B. Worthen claimed, "In his obsession with the precise stage image, his minute attention to the architecture of the body, his autocratic control of the production, the Director's practice in *Catastrophe* is reminiscent of Beckett's own work as director" (*Modern Drama and the Rhetoric of the Theater* [Berkeley: University of California Press, 1992], 141). Anna McMullan argued, "In the attempt to represent powerlessness, Beckett as director finds himself reproducing the mechanisms of power which subject his characters and actors" (*Theatre on Trial: Samuel Beckett's Later Drama* [New York: Routledge, 1993], 31).

80. For Martin Puchner, Beckett was able to "capitalize on the fact that stage directions are bracketed from (written or printed) dialogue, and he is the first to turn these brackets into a principle for the *mise en scène*" (*Stage Fright: Modernism, Anti-Theatricality, and Drama* [Baltimore: Johns Hopkins University Press, 2002], 168).

81. When preparing for his production of *Curlew River* at the Tanglewood Music Center in Lenox, Massachusetts, Mark Morris ridiculed Graham's production notes: "I just said, wait a minute, first of all, everybody tear that out of your scores" (quoted in Zachery Woolfe, "The Monks Are Asked to Go Natural," *New York Times*, July 30, 2013, available at http://www.nytimes.com/2013/07/31/arts /music/mark-morris-directing-brittens-curlew-river.html?_r=0 [accessed June 29, 2015]).

82. Kevin Jackson described the period between 1870 and 1920 as "the golden age of the stage direction" when it "declined to serve its traditional role as anonymous, self-effacing flunkey of the play's dialogue" ("The Triumph of the Stage Direction," *American Scholar* [1999]: 59). He suggested that Beckett learned his "spare,

scrupulous" style from James Joyce's spoof of extravagant stage directions in the "Circe" chapter of *Ulysses* and from Wagner's "megalomaniacal grandiloquence" (66).

83. Quoted in Kalb, *Beckett in Performance*, 79. In contrast, Colin Graham acknowledged that other productions would abandon his production notes for *Curlew River*.

84. Kalb, *Beckett in Performance*, 79.

85. S. E. Gontarski, "Introduction: De-theatricalizing Theatre: The Post-Play Plays," in *Theatrical Notebooks*, ed. Gontarski, 4:xxv.

86. BCDW does not include the lighting design. Gontarski concluded, "Stagings of *Footfalls* based on any of the published versions of the play . . .will inevitably introduce unnecessary confusion into the production" (ibid.).

87. Salz, "Leonard's Bastard Son," 151n.5.

88. Ibid., 139.

89. Ibid., 140.

90. Ibid., 141.

91. Salz's discussion with Beckett occurred on August 8, 1982, as recorded in Jonah Salz, "Beckett Kyogen Style: Lessons in Intercultural Translation," in *Performer Training: Developments Across Cultures*, ed. Ian Watson (Amsterdam: Harwood, 2001), 146.

92. Ibid.

93. Enoch Brater stated that "each figure [in Quad] holds himself in the same posture Billie Whitelaw used in *Footfalls*, their bodies bent forward as if 'resisting a cold wind'" (*Beyond Minimalism: Beckett's Late Style in the Theater* [New York: Oxford University Press, 1987], 108).

94. Salz, "Leonard's Bastard Son," 145. Mel Gussow reviewed Noho's 1986 performance of *Quad 1 and 2*, *Act Without Words I*, a dance solo derived from Yeats's *At the Hawk's Well* (*Taka no mai*), and the kyōgen *Tied to a Stick* at New York's American Folk Theater. He claimed that Noho's *Quad* "loses some of the hypnotic effectiveness it had on television" and that *Act Without Words I* "loses its Beckettian humor" ("Theater: Beckett, in Japanese Style," *New York Times*, March 12, 1986, available at http://www.nytimes.com/ref/membercenter/nytarchive.html [accessed June 18, 2015]).

95. I am grateful to David Crandall and Takeuchi Akiko for discussing the function of stage directions in noh (personal communications, January 4 and 5, 2011). Along with floor patterns, the Kanze school texts used in *utai* lessons describe the settings and terms for musical direction and vocal delivery.

96. R. Thomas Simone, "Beckett's Other Trilogy: *Not I*, *Footfalls*, and *Rockaby*," in *"Make Sense Who May": Essays on Samuel Beckett's Later Works*, ed. R. J. Davis and L. St. J. Butler (Gerards Cross: Smythe, 1988), 62.

97. Cohn, *Just Play*, 237.

98. Also noted by Brater, *Beyond Minimalism*, 69.

99. Beckett, *Theatrical Notebooks*, 1:285.

100. Puchner considers Beckett's stage directions to be part of "a modernist anti-theatricalism that is primarily directed against the integrity of actors and their freedom of movement," as they helped him rid his stage of gesture (*Stage Fright*, 157).

101. Whitelaw, *Billie Whitelaw . . . Who He?*, 131.

102. Cima, *Performing Women*, 220. Even though I am focusing on Cima's assumptions about agency, my discussion of *Footfalls* and Beckett's directing practice benefited from Cima's discussion.

103. Ibid., 217. Cima referred to Ben-Zvi's argument in *Women in Beckett* that Beckett does not undermine women's liberation but represents the "stultifying gender roles" that confine characters like Winnie in *Happy Days*: "She is the physical embodiment of the condition of being a woman in her society" (x–xiii). See also Elin Diamond, "Speaking Parisian: Beckett and French Feminism," in *Women in Becket*, ed. Ben-Zvi, 208–16. McMullan surveyed responses to *Not I*: "Critics range between an interpretation of the play as a sympathetic portrayal of marginality and dispossession to a voyeuristic exploitation of the feminine as lack" (*Theatre on Trial*, 75).

104. Cima, *Performing Women*, 184.

105. Roland Barthes, *Empire of Signs* (New York: Macmillan, 1982), 63.

106. Talal Asad, Wendy Brown, Judith Butler, and Saba Mahmood examined the secular-liberal justifications for killing in the name of abstract and frequently deceptive concepts such as "freedom and democracy" and their overlooked continuities with religious justifications for killing in the name of "God," in *Is Critique Secular? Blasphemy, Injury, and Free Speech* (Berkeley: University of California Press, 2009), 17.

107. Cima, *Performing Women*, 219. See also Julie Campbell, "The Entrapment of the Female Body in Beckett's Plays in Relation to Jung's Third Tavistock Lecture," in "Historicizing Beckett / Issues of Performance," special issue, *Samuel Beckett Today / Aujourd'hui* 15 (2005): 161–72.

108. Paul Foster, *Beckett and Zen: A Study of Dilemma in the Novels of Samuel Beckett* (London: Wisdom, 1989), 27.

109. Eve Kosofsky Sedgwick, *Touching Feeling: Affect, Pedagogy, Performativity* (Durham, N.C.: Duke University Press, 2003), 169.

110. Cima, *Performing Women*, 221.

111. Cohn, *Just Play*, 136.

112. The zigzag *kata* or *sayū*, according to Monica Bethe and Karen Brazell, "corresponds to the ritual purification of an area by shaking the purifying object to the left and right and front before presenting an offering to the gods" (*Dance in the Nō Theater* [Ithaca, N.Y.: Cornell University Press, 1982], 149). The same *kata* appear in the angel's dance in *Hagoromo* and in the warrior's recounting of a battle in *Tamura*.

CODA

1. Benjamin Britten, "No Ivory Tower" (1969), in *Britten on Music*, ed. Paul Francis Kildea (Oxford: University Press, 2003), 333.

2. Samuel Beckett, *Worstword Ho*, in *Nohow On: Three Novels* (New York: Grove Press, 1996), 87.

GLOSSARY

ai	*Kyōgen* actor who retells the story during the interlude of noh
benshi (katsuben)	Film narrator who stood or knelt to the left of the screen in full view of the audience and interpreted the film
budō	Samurai warrior arts
bunraku	Japanese puppet theater
bushido	Austere code followed by samurai warriors in Edo (or Tokugawa) Japan; title of a play produced by the Washington Square Players in 1916
butō	Modern form of Japanese dance that features extreme bodily tension
chadō	Tea ceremony
chigo	Adolescent acolytes of Buddhist priests
chigo monogatari	Tales of acolytes: literary form that emphasized a monk's spiritual and physical relationship with the *chigo*

daimyo	Japanese feudal lord
doji	Temple acolyte; the first apparition in the noh play *Tamura*
eboshi	Formal Japanese hat
gagaku	Old court music
giri	Ancient codes of honor followed by samurai warriors
hashigakari	Bridgeway that extends roughly twenty-five feet from stage right, used for the entrance of actors
hashira	Pillar at each of the four corners of the square noh stage
hayashi	Noh orchestra
higashi	Decorated confectionery
hiranori	Common noh rhythmic structure in which the (usually) twelve syllables of poetry are distributed over an eight-beat pattern
hokubun	Full-ranked performer of noh
hosonuno	Narrow cloth made of woven feathers that came to symbolize unrequited love
iemoto	Family head of a *ryū*
issei	Ornate verse pattern typically sung by the entering *shite*
jidaigeki	Films about samurai
jiutai	Noh chorus of eight to ten performers who kneel stage left
Jiyū gekijō	Free Theater, founded in 1909 for the purpose of staging western dramas
kagura	Sacred dance that, in *Takasago*, serves as a manifestation of the perfect sovereign
kaishi	Thin paper
kakegoe	Noh drum calls and beats
kakikurasu	Tormented/darkened
kamae (kitachi)	Standard posture of the noh performer: knees slightly bent, pelvis tipped forward, and arms held forward and away from the body
kana	Japanese written characters
kata	Precise movement patterns or gestural sequences in noh
Kawanakajima	Location of the legendary battle of the Takeda and Uesugi samurai clans in 1561
kenbu	Japanese sword dance

kenkin nō	Plays performed to benefit the war effort
kensho	Audience configuration with seating on two sides of the noh stage
kiri	Closing section of a noh play
kitsune	Legendary Japanese fox
kokata	Child actor
koken	Stage assistants who kneel at the back of the noh stage
kokorogake	"Mental attitude" associated with the instruction in budō
kotsuzumi	Shoulder drum in the hayashi
Kuannon	Sino-Japanese spirit of mercy
kuden	Tradition
kurogo	"Man-in-black": stage assistant who is "invisible" by Japanese performance conventions
kyakurai	"The effect of doubling back": term used by Zeami for the enlightened return to the yūgen of boyhood
kyōgen	Comedic plays that are often presented as interludes between noh plays and parody their style
mai	Dance
mie (kimaru)	Codified poses struck at emotional moments during a kabuki play
mo	"No" or "not"
modanizumu	Term derived from "modernism" that signaled a style of artistic expression, a powerful idea about modernity, and a source of popular fashion in Japan from roughly 1910 to 1940
monoguruimono	Fourth-category noh plays about mad people
montsuki	Formal Japanese dress worn during informal noh performances
mugen nō	Dream play
nagabakama	Long trousers
nanori	Naming verse typically used to introduce an actor
natori	"Naming" or formal initiation in which the student usually receives an artistic title with the ryū as the family name
nihon buyō	Classical Japanese dance
Nihon nōgakukai	Japanese Noh Society

nimaime	"Second" or good-hearted but flawed romantic character in kabuki
Nippon gakujutsu shinkōkai	Japan Society for the Promotion of Science
nishikigi	"Brocade trees" or decorated sticks that serve as love charms; title of a noh play
nōkan (fue)	Flute in the hayashi
oi matsu	Large pine tree painted on the back wall of the noh theater
omiai	Arranged meeting or marriage
ōmugaeshi	"Parrot-like repetition": imitative pedagogy of the noh lesson
onna mai	In nihon buyō, dances of women
otoko mai	In nihon buyō, dances of men
ōtsuzumi	Hip drum in the hayashi
ōzayū	Zigzag-stepping kata
rensageki	Chain dramas or popular early Japanese films that juxtaposed live performances of kabuki with filmed scenes
ryū	Schools or guilds dedicated to the study of Japanese arts; there are five such schools in noh
sashi koye (sashi-koe)	"Flow-along tune": a type of sashi sung in a smooth manner
sayū	Common kata for concluding a noh dance
seiza	Kneeling with legs folded underneath the body, buns resting on heels
sensu	Small folding fan
seppuku(o)	Ritual suicide
shigin	Style of reciting classical poems
shikake-hiraki	Common noh kata beginning with a forward step and point, followed by a step back as arms open
shikisanban	"Three rites": plays considered particularly sacred that traditionally require performers to engage in a period of "purification"
shimai	Noh dance
shingeki	Japanese modern theater or "new drama"
Shinkyo gekidan	New Cooperative Theater Company
shiori	Kata for weeping: hand sweeps to the corner of the eye

shite	Central actor or soloist in noh
shōdan	Noh verse pattern or song
shōshimingeki	Films about ordinary people in modern Japan
shudō	"The way of (loving) youths"; not to be misunderstood as a sexual identity
suriashi	"Sliding foot": the noh walking step
taiko	Stick drum in the *hayashi*
taiyu	Master actor
tanka	Similar to a haiku, with two additional lines of seven syllables
tateyaku	"Standing role" or leading man in a kabuki play
tennin	Celestial spirit; in *Hagoromo*, the angel from the palace of the moon
tōitsu imeiji	"Unifying image"
Tokugawa *bakufu*	Rulers during the Edo (or Tokugawa) period (1600–1867)
Tsukiji shōgexijo	Tsukiji Little Theater; often cited as "Japan's First Modern Theater"
tsukizerifu	Noh verse pattern announcing, "We have arrived"
tsukurimono	"Built thing": noh stage properties usually made with wrapped bamboo and little attempt to look real
tsure	Companion role in noh
ukiyo-e	Japanese woodblock prints
utai	Noh chant
utaibon	Books of noh text or libretto
wagashi	Delicate confectionary traditionally served with tea
wakashu	Apprentices of samurai ninja warriors
waki	Witness role in noh, often a traveling monk
wakizure	Companion(s) of the *waki*
yūgen	Profound, mysterious, and elegant beauty associated with noh
zō-onna mask	Mask representing young women and divinities in noh

BIBLIOGRAPHY

Adorno, Theodor W., Else Frenkel-Brunswik, Daniel J. Levinson, and R. Nevitt San-ford. *The Authoritarian Personality*. New York: Norton, 1993.

Ahearn, Barry. "*Cathay*: What Sort of Translation?" In *Ezra Pound and China*, edited by Zhaoming Qian, 31–48. Ann Arbor: University of Michigan Press, 2003.

Albright, Daniel. "Early Cantos: I–XLI." In *The Cambridge Companion to Ezra Pound*, edited by Ira Bruce Nadel, 59–91. Cambridge: Cambridge University Press, 1999.

——. *Untwisting the Serpent: Modernism in Music, Literature, and Other Arts*. Chicago: University of Chicago Press, 2000.

Allen, Elizabeth S. "Eurhythmics for the Theatre." 1919. In *Sheldon Cheney's Theatre Arts Magazine: Promoting a Modern American Theatre, 1916–1921*, edited by DeAnna M. Toten Beard, 120–27. Lanham, Md.: Scarecrow Press, 2010.

Allison, Jonathan, ed. *Yeats's Political Identities: Selected Essays*. Ann Arbor: University of Michigan Press, 1996.

Althusser, Louis. "Ideology and Ideological State Apparatuses." 1968. In *Lenin and Philosophy and Other Essays*, translated by Ben Brewster, 85–126. New York: Monthly Review Press, 1971.

Anderson, Benedict. *Imagined Communities: Reflections on the Origin and Spread of Nationalism*. 1986. Reprint, New York: Verso Books, 2006.

Anderson, Jack. "Satoru Shimazaki, Soloist." *New York Times*, November 20, 1983. Available at http://www.nytimes.com/1983/11/20/arts/dance-satoru-shimazaki-soloist.html?scp=1&sq=Satoru+Shimazaki+&st=nyt. Accessed March 10, 2015.

Anderson, J. L. "Spoken Silents in the Japanese Cinema; or, Talking to Pictures: Essaying the *Katsuben*, Contextualizing the Texts." In *Reframing Japanese Cinema: Authorship, Genre, History*, edited by Arthur Nolletti Jr. and David Desser, 259–311. Bloomington: Indiana University Press, 1992.

Appiah, Kwame Anthony. *Cosmopolitanism: Ethics in a World of Strangers*. New York: Norton, 2006.

Arrowsmith, Rupert Richard. "The Transcultural Roots of Modernism: Imagist Poetry, Japanese Visual Culture, and the Western Museum System." *Modernism/Modernity* 18, no. 1 (2011): 27–42.

Asad, Talal, Wendy Brown, Judith Butler, and Saba Mahmood. *Is Critique Secular? Blasphemy, Injury, and Free Speech*. Berkeley: University of California Press, 2009.

Atkins, Emily. "'Study That Tree': The Iconic Stage in *Purgatory* and *Waiting for Godot*." *South Carolina Review* 40, no. 2 (2008): 66–77.

Auden, W. H. "The Public v. the Late Mr. William Butler Yeats." 1939. In *The English Auden*, edited by Edward Mendleson, 389–93. London: Faber & Faber, 1977.

Austin, J. L. *How to Do Things with Words*. Cambridge, Mass.: Harvard University Press, 1962.

Baechler, Lea, A. Walton Litz, and James Longenbach, eds. *Ezra Pound's Poetry and Prose: Contributions to Periodicals*. Vol. 2. New York: Garland, 1991.

Barlow, Judith E., ed. *Women Writers of the Provincetown Players: A Collection of Short Works*. Albany: State University of New York Press, 2009.

Barthes, Roland. *Empire of Signs*. New York: Hill & Wang, 1982.

Beckett, Samuel. *Footfalls*. 1976. In *The Complete Dramatic Works*, 397–403. London: Faber & Faber, 1989.

——. *Footfalls*. DVD. Directed by Walter Asmus. Performed by Susan Fitzgerald. Produced by Michael Cogan and Alan Maloney. Ireland: Blue Angel Films / Tyrone Productions, 2000.

——. "*Footfalls* Notebook." In *The Theatrical Notebooks of Samuel Beckett*. Vol. 4, *The Shorter Plays*, edited by S. E. Gontarski, 271–351. New York: Grove Press, 1999.

———. *The Theatrical Notebooks of Samuel Beckett.* Vol. 1, *Krapp's Last Tape*, edited by James Knowlson. New York: Grove Press, 1999.

———. *Worstword Ho.* In *Nohow On: Three Novels*, 87–116. New York: Grove Press, 1996.

Bedell, Geraldine. "Coming Out of the Dark Ages." *Guardian*, June 23, 2007. Available at http://www.theguardian.com/society/2007/jun/24/communities.gayrights. Accessed March 26, 2015.

Begam, Richard, and Michael Valdez Moses. Introduction to *Modernism and Colonialism: British and Irish Literature, 1899–1939*, 1–16. Durham, N.C.: Duke University Press, 2007.

Benedict, Ruth. *The Chrysanthemum and the Sword: Patterns of Japanese Culture.* 1946. Reprint, New York: First Mariner Books, 2005.

Benjamin, Walter. "The Work of Art in the Age of Mechanical Reproduction." In *Illuminations*, translated by Harry Zohn, 217–52. New York: Schocken Books, 1969.

Ben-Zvi, Linda, ed. *Women in Beckett: Performance and Critical Perspectives.* Urbana: University of Illinois Press, 1990.

Bernstein, Barton J. "Atomic Bombings Reconsidered." *Foreign Affairs* 74, no. 2 (1995): 135–52.

Bersani, Leo. "Is the Rectum a Grave?" *October* 43 (1987): 197–222.

Bethe, Monica, and Karen Brazell. *Dance in the Nō Theater.* Ithaca, N.Y.: Cornell University Press, 1982.

Beyond the Fringe. Film. Performed by Alan Bennett, Peter Cook, and Jonathan Miller. BBC, 1964.

Bhabha, Homi. *The Location of Culture.* New York: Routledge, 1994.

Birnbaum, Martin. *The Last Romantic: The Story of More Than a Half-Century in the World of Art.* New York: Twayne, 1960.

———. *Oscar Wilde: Fragments and Memories.* New York: Drake, 1914.

Bogue, Ronald. "Deleuze and the Invention of Images: From Beckett's Television Plays to Noh Drama." *Comparatist* 26 (2002): 37–52.

Bordwell, David. *Ozu and the Poetics of Cinema.* Princeton, N.J.: Princeton University Press, 1988.

Bourdieu, Pierre, and Jean Claude Passeron. *Reproduction in Education, Society, and Culture.* London: Sage, 1977.

Bowman, James. "James Bowman on Striking a High Note." *Guardian*, November 26, 2009. Available at http://www.theguardian.com/music/2009/nov/26/james-bowman-countertenor-revival. Accessed June 29, 2015.

Bradford, Curtis Baker. *Yeats at Work.* Carbondale: Southern Illinois University Press, 1965.

Brandon, James R. "Mussolini in Kabuki: Notes and Translation." In *Japanese Theatre Transcultural: German and Italian Intertwinings*, edited by Stanca Scholz-Cionca and Andreas Regelsberger, 71–94. Munich: Iudicium, 2011.

Brantley, Ben. "The Emperor Jones." 1998. In *New York Times Theater Reviews, 1997–1998*, 244–45. New York: Times Books, 2000.

Brater, Enoch. *Beyond Minimalism: Beckett's Late Style in the Theater*. New York: Oxford University Press, 1987.

Brecht, Bertolt. *Brecht on Theatre: The Development of an Aesthetic*. Edited and translated by John Willet. New York: Hill & Wang, 1964.

——. *Collected Plays*. Vol. 3, part 2, "*The Mother*" *and Six Lehrstücke*. Edited by John Willett. London: Methuen, 1997.

Brett, Philip. *Music and Sexuality in Britten: Selected Essays*. Berkeley: University of California Press, 2006.

Bridcut, John. *Britten's Children*. London: Faber & Faber, 2006.

Britten, Benjamin. *Curlew River*. Directed by Mark Morris. Tanglewood Music Center, Lenox, Mass., July 30, 2013.

——. *Curlew River: A Parable for Church Performance*. London: Faber & Faber, 1964.

——. "No Ivory Tower." 1969. In *Britten on Music*, edited by Paul Francis Kildea, 330–34. Oxford: Oxford University Press, 2003.

Broun, Heywood. "Review of *The Emperor Jones*." *New York Tribune*, November 4, 1920. Reprint, http://www.eoneill.com/artifacts/reviews/ej1_tribune.htm. Accessed March 31, 2015.

Brownmiller, Susan. *In Our Time: Memoir of a Revolution*. New York: Delta Books, 2000.

Bryson, Mary, and Suzanne de Castell. "Queer Pedagogy: Praxis Makes Im/Perfect." *Canadian Journal of Education* 18, no. 3 (1993): 285–305.

Brzezinski, Max. "The New Modernist Studies: What's Left of Political Formalism?" *Minnesota Review* 76 (2011): 109–25.

Bumiller, Kristin. *In an Abusive State: How Neoliberalism Appropriated the Feminist Movement Against Sexual Violence*. Durham, N.C.: Duke University Press, 2008.

Burch, Nöel. *To the Distant Observer: Form and Meaning in the Japanese Cinema*. Revised by Annette Michelson. Berkeley: University of California Press, 1979.

Bush, George W. "Remarks at the Signing Ceremony for Afghan Women and Children Relief Act of 2001." U.S. Department of State Archive: 2001–2009, December 12, 2001. Available at www.state.gov/p/sca/rls/rm/6816.htm. Accessed March 31, 2015.

Bush, Ronald. "The 'Rhythm of Metaphor': Yeats, Pound, Eliot, and the Unity of Image in Postsymbolist Poetry." In *Allegory, Myth, and Symbol*, edited by Morton W. Bloomfield, 371–88. Cambridge, Mass.: Harvard University Press, 1981.

Butler, Judith. *Bodies That Matter: On the Discursive Limits of Sex.* New York: Routledge, 1993.

——. *Gender Trouble: Feminism and the Subversion of Identity.* New York: Routledge, 1990.

Caldwell, Helen. "The Dance Poems of Michio Ito: *The White Peacock* to Music by Griffes." In *Making Music for Modern Dance*, edited by Katherine Teck, 18–22. New York: Oxford University Press, 2011.

——. *Michio Ito: The Dancer and His Dances.* Berkeley: University of California Press, 1977.

Campbell, Julie. "The Entrapment of the Female Body in Beckett's Plays in Relation to Jung's Third Tavistock Lecture." In "Historicizing Beckett / Issues of Performance." Special issue, *Samuel Beckett Today / Aujourd'hui* 15 (2005): 161–72.

Canby, Vincent. "Film: Yasujiro Ozu, as Director and Subject." *New York Times*, April 1, 1987. Available at http://www.nytimes.com/1987/04/01/movies/film-yasujiro-ozu-as-director-and-subject.html. Accessed March 21, 2015.

Carlson, Marvin. *The Haunted Stage: The Theatre as Memory Machine.* Ann Arbor: University of Michigan Press, 2001.

Carpenter, Edward. *Intermediate Types Among Primitive Folk: A Study in Social Evolution.* London: George Allen, 1914.

Carpenter, Humphrey. *Benjamin Britten: A Biography.* London: Faber & Faber, 1992.

——. *A Serious Character: The Life of Ezra Pound.* Boston: Houghton Mifflin, 1988.

Carruthers, Ian. "A Translation of Fifteen Pages of Ito Michio's Autobiography 'Utsukushiku naru kyoshitsu.'" *Canadian Journal of Irish Studies* 2, no. 1 (1976): 32–43.

Casillo, Robert. *The Genealogy of Demons: Anti-Semitism, Fascism, and the Myths of Ezra Pound.* Evanston, Ill.: Northwestern University Press, 1988.

Chatterjea, Ananya. "On the Value of Mistranslations and Contaminations: The Category of 'Contemporary Choreography' in Asian Dance." *Dance Research Journal* 45, no. 1 (2013): 4–21.

Cheney, Sheldon. "New Books: Noh; or Accomplishment." 1917. In *Sheldon Cheney's Theatre Arts Magazine: Promoting a Modern American Theatre, 1916–1921*, edited by DeAnna M. Toten Beard, 110. Lanham, Md.: Scarecrow Press, 2010.

Chiba, Yoko. "Ezra Pound's Versions of Fenollosa's Noh Manuscripts and Yeats's Unpublished 'Suggestions & Corrections.'" *Yeats Annual* 4 (1986): 121–44.

Childs, Margaret H. "Chigo Monogatari: Love Stories or Buddhist Sermons?" *Monumenta Nipponica* 35, no. 2 (1980): 127–51.

Cima, Gay Gibson. *Performing Women: Female Characters, Male Playwrights, and the Modern Stage.* Ithaca, N.Y.: Cornell University Press, 1993.

Coburn, Alvin Langdon. *Alvin Langdon Coburn: Photographs, 1900–1924.* Edited by Karl Steinorth. Zurich: Stemmle, 1998.

Cohn, Ruby. *Just Play: Beckett's Theater.* Princeton, N.J.: Princeton University Press, 1980.

Cook, Matt. "Domestic Passions: Unpacking the Homes of Charles Shannon and Charles Ricketts." *Journal of British Studies* 51, no. 3 (2012): 618–40.

Cooke, Mervyn. *Britten and the Far East*. Woodbridge: Boydell Press, 1998.

——. "Britten and the Shō." *Musical Times* 129, no. 1743 (1988): 231–33.

Cooper, Emmanuel. *The Sexual Perspective: Homosexuality and Art in the Last 100 Years in the West*. 2nd ed. New York: Routledge, 1994.

Cornell, Drucilla. "The Secret Behind the Veil: A Reinterpretation of 'Algeria Unveiled.' " *Philosophia Africana* 4, no. 2 (2001): 27–35.

Correa, Christopher. "The Change Is Everything: Dana Tai Soon Burgess & Company at the Embassy of Japan, Washington D.C. (April 9, 2005)." *DanceView Times* 3, no. 14 (2005). Available at http://danceviewtimes.com/2005/Spring/01/ito.htm. Accessed March 10, 2015.

Cowell, Mary-Jean. "Forgotten Pioneer of Modern Dance." Lectures presented in Salt Lake City, July 14 and 16, 2009.

——. "Michio Ito in Hollywood: Modes and Ironies of Ethnicity." *Dance Chronicle* 24, no. 3 (2001): 263–305.

Cowell, Mary-Jean, and Satoru Shimazaki. "East and West in the Work of Michio Ito." *Dance Research Journal* 26, no. 2 (1994): 11–23.

Crandall, David. "The Angel." Manuscript, 1982.

——. *Noh Writers' Workshop*. Tokyo, 2010. Grand Rapids, Mich., 2011.

Crowley, Alice Lewisohn. *The Neighborhood Playhouse: Leaves from a Theatre Scrapbook*. New York: Theatre Arts Books, 1959.

Cuda, Anthony. "The Turbulent Lives of Yeats's Painted Horses." In "Influence and Confluence," edited by Warwick Gould. Special issue, *Yeats Annual* 17 (2007): 37–50.

Cullingford, Elizabeth. *Yeats, Ireland and Fascism*. New York: New York University Press, 1981.

Curran, Beverley. "Nogami Toyoichirō's Noh Translation Theories and the Primacy of Performance." In *Translation in Theatre and Performance*, edited by Silvia Bigliazzi, Paola Ambrosi, and Peter Kofler, 211–22. Florence, Ky.: Taylor & Francis, 2013.

"Dana Tai Soon Burgess." Dana Tai Soon Burgess Dance Company. Available at http://dtsbdc.org/69–2/. Last modified 2015. Accessed March 10, 2015.

"Dana Tai Soon Burgess." George Washington University. Available at http://theatredance.gwu.edu/Faculty&Staff/dana.html. Accessed March 10, 2015.

The Dances of Michio Ito. Film. Directed by Hannah C. Wiley. Seattle: University of Washington, Chamber Dance Company Archive, 2001.

de Gourmont, Remy. *The Natural Philosophy of Love*. 1903. Translated by Ezra Pound. New York: Boni & Liveright Press, 1922.

de Gruchy, John Walter. *Orienting Arthur Waley: Japonism, Orientalism, and the Creation of Japanese Literature in English*. Honolulu: University of Hawai'i Press, 2003.

Deleuze, Gilles. "L'Épuisé." In *Samuel Beckett, Quad et Trio du Fantôme,. . . que nuages . . . , Nacht un Träume*. Translated from the English by Edith Fournier, 55–106. Paris: Minuit, 1992.

D'Epiro, Peter. "Whose Vanity Must Be Pulled Down?" *Paideuma* 29, no. 3 (1984): 248–52.

de Rachewiltz, Mary. *Discretions: A Memoir by Ezra Pound's Daughter*. New York: Faber & Faber, 1971.

Desser, David. *Eros plus Massacre: An Introduction to the Japanese New Wave Cinema*. Bloomington: Indiana University Press, 1988.

Diamond, Elin. "Deploying/Destroying the Primitivist Body in Hurston and Brecht." In *Against Theatre: Creative Destructions on the Modernist Stage*, edited by Alan L. Ackerman and Martin Puchner, 112–32. New York: Palgrave Macmillan, 2006.

——. "Speaking Parisian: Beckett and French Feminism." In *Women in Beckett: Performance and Critical Perspectives*, edited by Linda Ben-Zvi, 208–16. Urbana: University of Illinois Press, 1990.

Dimock, Wai-Chee. "Aesthetics at the Limits of the Nation: Kant, Pound, and the *Saturday Review*." *American Literature* 76, no. 3 (2004): 525–47.

Doak, Kevin M. "What Is a Nation and Who Belongs? National Narratives and the Ethnic Imagination in Twentieth-Century Japan." *American Historical Review* 102, no. 2 (1997): 283–309.

Doe, Andrew E. "Brecht's Lehrstücke: Propaganda Failures." *Educational Theatre Journal* 14, no. 4 (1962): 289–96.

Doherty, Richard. *In the Ranks of Death: The Irish in the Second World War*. Barnsley: Pen & Sword Books, 2010.

Edelman, Lee. *No Future: Queer Theory and the Death Drive*. Durham, N.C.: Duke University Press, 2004.

Eliot, T. S. 'Ezra Pound." *Poetry* 68 (1946): 326–39.

——. "The Noh and the Image." *Egoist*, August 1917, 102–3.

Elliott, Graham. *Benjamin Britten: The Spiritual Dimension*. Oxford: Oxford University Press, 2006.

Ellis, Sylvia. *The Plays of W. B. Yeats: Yeats and the Dancer*. New York: St. Martin's Press, 1995.

Ellman, Richard. *Yeats: The Man and the Masks*. New York: Macmillan, 1948.

Emmert, Richard. "English nō and Theatre Nohgaku—The How and the Why." In *Nō Theatre Transversal*, edited by Stanca Scholz-Cionca and Christopher Balme, 141–53. Munich: Iudicium, 2008.

———. "Hiranori: A Unique Rhythm Form in Japanese nō Music." In *Musical Voices of Asia*, edited by Richard Emmert and Yuki Minegishi, 100–107. Tokyo: Japan Foundation, 1980.

Emmert, Richard, and Yuki Minegishi, eds. *Musical Voices of Asia*. Tokyo: Japan Foundation, 1980.

Eng, David L., Judith Halberstam, and José Esteban Muñoz, eds. "What's Queer About Queer Studies Now?" Special issue, *Social Text* 23, nos. 3–4 (2005): 1–17.

Enters, Angna. *Silly Girl: A Portrait of Personal Remembrance*. New York: Houghton Mifflin, 1944.

eOneill.com: An Electronic Eugene O'Neill Archive (1999–2014). Available at http://www.eoneill.com/index.htm. Accessed June 28, 2015.

Eribon, Didier. *Insult and the Making of the Gay Self*. Translated by Michael Lucey. Durham, N.C.: Duke University Press, 2004.

Ewick, David. *Japonisme, Orientalism, and Modernism: A Bibliography*. Available at http://themargins.net/ bibliography.html. Last modified 2003. Accessed April 1, 2015.

Fanon, Frantz. "Algeria Unveiled." 1959. In *The New Left Reader*, edited by Carl Oglesby, 161–85. New York: Grove Press, 1969.

———. *The Wretched of the Earth*. 1961. Translated by Constance Farrington. New York: Grove Press, 1963.

Farr, Florence. *The Music of Speech*. London: Elkin Mathews, 1909.

Fenollosa, Ernest. *Certain Noble Plays of Japan: From the Manuscripts of Ernest Fenollosa, Chosen and Finished by Ezra Pound, with an Introduction by William Butler Yeats*. Churchtown: Cuala, 1916. Reprint, Shannon: Irish University Press, 1971.

Fenollosa, Ernest, and Ezra Pound. *The Chinese Written Character as a Medium for Poetry*. 1920. Reprint, San Francisco: City Lights, 1968.

———. "Noh," or, *Accomplishment: A Study of the Classical Stage of Japan*. New York: Knopf, 1917.

Fisher, Margaret. *Ezra Pound's Radio Operas: The BBC Experiments, 1931–1933*. Cambridge, Mass.: MIT Press, 2002.

FitzAlan-Howard, Henry, and Charles T. Gatty, eds. "Our Guardian Angels / Custodes Hominum." In *Arundel Hymns*, 240–41. London: Boosey, 1905.

Flanagan, Hallie. *Dynamo*. New York: Duell, Sloan & Pearce, 1943.

Fleischer, Mary. *Embodied Texts: Symbolist Playwright-Dancer Collaborations*. Amsterdam: Rodopi, 2007.

Foster, Paul. *Beckett and Zen: A Study of Dilemma in the Novels of Samuel Beckett*. London: Wisdom, 1989.

Foster, Susan Leigh, ed. *Worlding Dance*. Basingstoke: Palgrave Macmillan, 2009.

Foucault, Michel. *Discipline and Punish: The Birth of the Prison*. 1975. Translated by Alan Sheridan. New York: Vintage Books, 1995.

——. "Le Gai savoir I." *Mec Magazine*, June 1988, 32–36.

——. *Society Must Be Defended: Lectures at the Collège de France, 1975–1976*. Translated by David Macey. New York: Picador, 2003.

Franko, Mark. *Dancing Modernism / Performing Politics*. Bloomington: Indiana University Press, 1995.

Freeman, Elizabeth. "Still After." *South Atlantic Quarterly* 106, no. 3 (2007): 495–500.

——. *Time Binds: Queer Temporalities, Queer Histories*. Durham, N.C.: Duke University Press, 2010.

French, Calvin, trans. *The Brocade Tree* [Nishikigi]. In *Twenty Plays of the Nō Theatre*, edited by Donald Keene, 82–97. New York: Columbia University Press, 1970.

Friedman, Susan Stanford. "Planetarity: Musing Modernist Studies." *Modernism / Modernity* 17, no. 3 (2010): 471–99.

Froula, Christine. "The Beauties of Mistranslation: On Pound's English After *Cathay*." In *Ezra Pound and China*, edited by Zhaoming Qian, 49–71. Ann Arbor: University of Michigan Press, 2003.

——. *To Write Paradise: Style and Error in Pound's "Cantos."* New Haven, Conn.: Yale University Press, 1984.

Frye, Northrop. *Fables of Identity: Studies in Poetic Mythology*. New York: Harcourt, Brace, 1963.

Fuegi, John. *Brecht and Co.: Sex, Politics, and the Making of the Modern Drama*. New York: Grove Press, 1994.

Gikandi, Simon. "Picasso, Africa, and the Schemata of Difference." *Modernism / Modernity* 10, no. 3 (2003): 455–80.

"Give Japanese 'Noh' Dance: Michio Itow in Novelty 'Tamura' at Neighborhood Playhouse." *New York Times*, January 9, 1921. Available at http://www.nytimes.com/ref/membercenter /nytarchive.html. Accessed June 18, 2015.

Golding, Alan. "From Pound to Olson: The Avant-Garde Poet as Pedagogue." *Journal of Modern Literature* 34, no. 1 (2010): 86–106.

Gordon, Andrew. *A Modern History of Japan from Tokugawa Times to the Present*. New York: Oxford University Press, 2003.

Gould, Warwick. "The Mask Before *The Mask*." In "Yeat's Mask," edited by Margaret Mills Harper and Warwick Gould. Special issue, *Yeats Annual* 19 (2013): 3–47.

Gregory, Lady Augusta. *Cuchulain of Muirthemne*. London: Murray, 1902.

——, ed. *Visions and Beliefs in the West of Ireland*. 2 vols. London: Knickerbocker, 1920.

Grey, Madeleine. "Eastern Art Spiritual, Western Art Material, Says Michio Itow." *Musical America*, December 8, 1917, 9.

Gussow, Mel. "Theater: Beckett, in Japanese Style." *New York Times*, March 12, 1986. Available at http://www.nytimes.com/ref/membercenter/nytarchive.html. Accessed June 18, 2015.

Hagoromo. Directed by Kita Roppeita. Performance at the Imperial Court, Kyoto, December 8, 1915.

Hahn, Tomie. *Sensational Knowledge: Embodying Culture Through Japanese Dance*. Middletown, Conn.: Wesleyan University Press, 2007.

Hakutani, Yoshinobu. Introduction to *Selected English Writings of Yone Noguchi: Prose*. Cranbury, N.J.: Associated University Presses, 1992.

——. "W. B. Yeats, Modernity, and the Noh Play." In *Modernity in East-West Literary Criticism: New Readings*, edited by Yoshinobu Hakutani, 23–40. Cranbury, N.J.: Associated University Presses, 2001.

Halebsky, Judy, and Mariko Anno. "Innovation in Nō: Matsui Akira Continues a Tradition of Change." *Asian Theatre Journal* 31, no. 1 (2014): 126–52.

Halley, Janet. "The Construction of Heterosexuality." In *Fear of a Queer Planet: Queer Politics and Social Theory*, edited by Michael Warner, 82–102. Minneapolis: University of Minnesota Press, 1993.

Halley, Janet, and Andrew Parker. *After Sex? On Writing Since Queer Theory*. Durham, N.C.: Duke University Press, 2011.

Halperin, David M. *Saint = Foucault: Towards a Gay Hagiography*. New York: Oxford University Press, 1995.

Harrington, John P. *The Life of the Neighborhood Playhouse on Grand Street*. Syracuse, N.Y.: Syracuse University Press, 2007.

Hayot, Eric. *Chinese Dreams: Pound, Brecht, Tel Quel*. Ann Arbor: University of Michigan Press, 2004.

Hennessy, Rosemary. *Profit and Pleasure: Sexual Identities in Late Capitalism*. New York: Routledge, 2000.

High, Peter B. *The Imperial Screen: Japanese Film Culture in the Fifteen Years' War (1931–1945)*. Madison: University of Wisconsin Press, 2003.

Hillyer, Robert. "Poetry's New Priesthood." *Saturday Review of Literature*, June 18, 1949.

——. "Treason's Strange Fruit: The Case of Ezra Pound and the Bollingen Award." *Saturday Review of Literature*, June 11, 1949.

Hirano, Kyoko. *Mr. Smith Goes to Tokyo Under the American Occupation, 1945–1952*. Washington, D.C.: Smithsonian Institution Press, 1992.

Hirata, Hosea. *The Poetry and Poetics of Nishiwaki Junzaburo: Modernism in Translation*. Princeton, N.J.: Princeton University Press, 1994.

Hobsbawm, Eric, and Terrence Ranger, eds. *The Invention of Tradition*. Cambridge: Cambridge University Press, 1983.

Holst, Imogen. Introduction to Benjamin Britten, *Curlew River: A Parable for Church Performance*. London: Faber & Faber, 1964.

Howes, Marjorie. *Yeats's Nations: Gender, Class, and Irishness*. Cambridge: Cambridge University Press, 1996.

Huffer, Lynne. *Mad for Foucault: Rethinking the Foundations of Queer Theory*. New York: Columbia University Press, 2009.

Hurst, G. Cameron. *Armed Martial Arts of Japan: Swordsmanship and Archery*. New Haven, Conn.: Yale University Press, 1998.

Iezzi, Julie A. "Kyōgen in English: A Bibliography." *Asian Theatre Journal* 24, no. 1 (2007): 211–34.

Iezzi, Julie A., and Jonah Salz. "Kyōgen Leaps out of Nō's Shadow." *Asian Theatre Journal* 24, no. 1 (2007): v–ix.

The Imitation Game. Film. Directed by Morten Tyldum. New York: Weinstein Company, 2014.

"An Interview by Timothy Cowart with Director Bonnie Oda Homsey on Her Film *Michio Ito: Pioneering Dancer-Choreographer*." Dance Films Association. Available at http://www.dancefilms.org/2013/01/ 23/interview-with-director-bonnie-oda-homsey/. Last modified October 27, 2012. Accessed March 10, 2015.

Ishibashi, Hiro. *Yeats and the Noh: Types of Japanese Beauty and Their Reflection in Yeats's Plays*. Edited by Anthony Kerrigan. Yeats Centenary Papers 6. Dublin: Dolment Press, 1965.

Itow [Itō], Michio, and Louis V. Ledoux. "The Fox's Grave [Kitsune zuka]: An Ancient Japanese Farce." *Outlook*, February 14, 1923, 306–8.

——. "She Who Was Fished [Tsuri onna]." *Outlook*, January 31, 1923, 218–19.

——. "Somebody-Nothing [Bussu]." *Asia* 21, no. 12 (1921): 1011–12.

Iwamoto, Kenji. "Sound in the Early Japanese Talkies." In *Reframing Japanese Cinema: Authorship, Genre, History*, edited by Arthur Nolletti Jr. and David Desser, 311–26. Bloomington: Indiana University Press, 1992.

Jackson, George. "A Celebration of Michio Ito; or, When Modern Was New." *Dance Magazine*, May 1996, 86–87.

——. "Three Times a Charm: Dana Tai Soon Burgess & Company." *Dance Magazine*, April 2002, 76–77.

Jackson, Kevin. "The Triumph of the Stage Direction." *American Scholar* (1999): 59–67.

Jameson, Frederic. *Brecht and Method*. London: Verso, 1998.

Japanese Classics Translation Committee of Nippon gakujutsu shinkōkai. *The Noh Drama: Ten Plays from the Japanese*. Rutland, Vt.: Tuttle, 1955.

"Japanese Noh Drama: GIVEN FOR THE FIRST TIME OUTSIDE OF JAPAN." Staged by Michio Itow for the Thursday Evening Club, January 18, 1923. Program. New York Public Library for the Performing Arts.

Jaques-Dalcroze, Emile. *Rhythm, Music and Education*. Translated by Harold F. Rubinstein. New York: Putnam, 1921.

Jñanavira, Dharmachari. "Homosexuality in the Japanese Buddhist Tradition." *Western Buddhist Review* 3 (2001). Available at http://www.westernbuddhistreview.com/vol3/homosexuality.html#_ednref24. Accessed February 15, 2015.

Johnson, Scott. Nishikigi. In *A Guide to Ezra Pound and Ernest Fenollosa's "Classic Noh Theatre of Japan,"* edited by Akiko Miyake, Sanehide Kodama and Nicholas Teele, 89–127. Orono: National Poetry Foundation and Ezra Pound Society of Japan, 1994.

Joly, H. L. "Recent Books on Japan." *Asiatic Review* 12 (1917): 71–80.

Kagaya, Shinko. "Dancing on a Moving Train: Nō Between Two Wars." In *Nō Theatre Transversal*, edited by Stanca Scholz-Cionca and Christopher Balme, 19–30. Munich: Iudicium, 2008.

Kalb, Jonathan. *Beckett in Performance*. New York: Cambridge University Press, 1989.

Kawai, N., H. Miyata, R Nishimura, and K. Okanoya. "Shadows Alter Facial Expressions of Noh Masks." *PLOS ONE* 8, no. 8 (2013): e71389. Available at doi:10.1371/journal.pone.0071389. Accessed February 15, 2015.

Keene, Dennis. *Yokomitsu Riichi: Modernist*. New York: Columbia University Press, 1980.

Keene, Donald, ed. *Twenty Plays of the Nō Theatre*. New York: Columbia University Press, 1970.

Kenner, Hugh. *The Pound Era*. Berkeley: University of California Press, 1971.

Kern, Robert. *Orientalism, Modernism, and the American Poem*. Cambridge: Cambridge University Press, 1996.

Kildea, Paul. *Benjamin Britten: A Life in the Twentieth Century*. London: Penguin, 2013.

Kipling, Rudyard. "The White Man's Burden: The United States and the Philippine Islands." *McClure's Magazine*, February 1899.

Kisselgoff, Anna. "Dance: Michio Ito Salute." *New York Times*, October 4, 1979. Michio Ito Clipping File, New York Public Library for the Performing Arts.

———. "Michio Ito, an All-but-Forgotten Pioneer of American Modern Dance." *New York Times*. February 26, 1978. Available at http://www.nytimes.com/ ref/membercenter/nytarchive.html. Accessed June 18, 2015.

Klens-Bigman, Deborah. "The Fan and the Sword: Exploring Kenbu." *Journal of Theatrical Combatives*, March 2006. Available at http://ejmas.com/jtc/2006jtc/jtcart_klens Modernism/Modernity -bigman_0603.html. Accessed March 10, 2015.

Knowlson, James. "Beckett's 'Bits of Pipe.'" In *Samuel Beckett: Humanistic Perspectives*, edited by Morris Beja, S. E. Gontarski, and Pierre Astier, 16–25. Columbus: Ohio State University Press, 1983.

———. *Damned to Fame: The Life of Samuel Beckett*. New York: Simon & Schuster, 1996.

———. *Samuel Beckett: An Exhibition Held at Reading University Library, May to July 1971*. Catalog. London: Turret Books, 1971.

Kobayashi, Hideo. "Literature of the Lost Home." In *Literature of the Lost Home: Kobayashi Hideo—Literary Criticism, 1924–1939*, edited and translated by Paul Anderer, 52–54. Stanford, Calif.: Stanford University Press, 1995.

Kodama, Sanehide. *American Poetry and Japanese Culture*. Hamden, Conn.: Archon, 1984.

Komatsu, Hiroshi. "Some Characteristics of Japanese Cinema Before World War I." Translated by Linda C. Ehrlich and Yuko Okutsu. In *Reframing Japanese Cinema: Authorship, Genre, History*, edited by Arthur Nolletti Jr. and David Desser, 229–58. Bloomington: Indiana University Press, 1992.

Komesu, Okifumi. "*At the Hawk's Well* and *Taka no Izumi* in a 'Creative Circle.' " *Yeats Annual* 5 (1987): 103–13.

Komparu, Kunio. *The Noh Theatre: Principles and Perspectives*. New York: Weatherhill/Tankosha, 1983.

Koner, Pauline. *Elements of Performance: A Guide for Performers in Dance, Theatre and Opera*. New York: Routledge, 2012.

———. *Solitary Song*. Durham, N.C.: Duke University Press, 1989.

Konishi Jin'ichi. *Nihon bungeishi* [A History of Japanese Literature]. Vol. 3, *The High Middle Ages*, edited by Earl Miner, translated by Aileen Gatten and Mark Harbison. Princeton, N.J.: Princeton University Press, 1991.

Larabee, Ann. "'The Drama of Transformation': Settlement House Idealism and the Neighborhood Playhouse." In *Performing America: Cultural Nationalism in American Theater*, edited by Jeffrey D. Mason and J. Ellen Gainor, 123–36. Ann Arbor: University of Michigan Press, 1999.

Latrell, Craig. "After Appropriation." *Drama Review* 44, no. 4 (2000): 44–55.

Leerson, Joep. "The Theatre of William Butler Yeats." In *The Cambridge Companion to Twentieth-Century Irish Drama*, edited by Shaun Richards, 47–61. Cambridge: Cambridge University Press, 2004.

LeMoncheck, Linda. *Loose Women, Lecherous Men: A Feminist Philosophy of Sex*. New York: Oxford University Press, 1997.

Lennon, Joseph. *Irish Orientalism*. Syracuse, N.Y.: Syracuse University Press, 2004.

Leupp, Gary. *Male Colors: The Construction of Homosexuality in Tokugawa Japan*. Berkeley: University of California Press, 1995.

Liebregts, Peter, and Peter van de Kamp, eds. *Tumult of Images: Essays on W. B. Yeats and Politics*. Amsterdam: Rodopi, 1995.

Longenbach, James. *Stone Cottage: Pound, Yeats, and Modernism*. New York: Oxford University Press, 1988.

MacDuff, William. "Beautiful Boys in Nō Drama: The Idealization of Homoerotic Desire." *Asian Theatre Journal* 13, no. 2 (1996): 248–58.

Mahmood, Saba. *The Politics of Piety: The Islamic Revival and the Feminist Subject*. Princeton, N.J.: Princeton University Press, 2005.

Malm, William P. *Six Hidden Views of Japanese Music*. Berkeley: University of California Press, 1986.

"Manhattan Nights and Exotic Entertainers." Sketches by Frueh of the *World Magazine* staff. New York Public Library for the Performing Arts.

Mann, William. "East Meets West in New Britten Music Drama." *Times* (London), June 15, 1964, 6. Available at http://www.thetimes.co.uk/tto/news/. Accessed June 24, 2014.

Mansell, Thomas. "Different Music: Beckett's Theatrical Conduct." *Historicizing Beckett / Issues of Performance, Samuel Beckett Toda / Aujourd'hui* 15 (2005): 225–39.

Mao, Douglas, and Rebecca L. Walkowitz. "The New Modernist Studies." *PMLA* 123, no. 3 (2008): 737–48.

Marinetti, F. T. "The Founding and Manifesto of Futurism." In *Marinetti: Selected Writings*, edited by R. W. Flint, 39–44. New York: Farrar, Straus & Giroux, 1971.

Marshall, Marguerite Mooers. "Woman of 70 Is Not Too Old to Dance, Says New Terpsichore with a Kimono, Symbolizing Emotions of Far East." *Evening World*, December 2, 1916. Personal Collection of Michelle Ito.

Martens, Frederick H. "Folk-Music in the Ballet Intime." *New Music Review* 16, no. 191 (1917): 762–65.

Marx, Edward. "Nō Dancing: Yone Noguchi in Yeats's Japan." In "Influence and Confluence," edited by Warwick Gould. Special issue, *Yeats Annual* 17 (2007): 51–94.

Materer, Timothy. "Make It Sell! Ezra Pound Advertises Modernism." In *Marketing Modernisms: Self-Promotion, Canonization, Rereading*, edited by Kevin J. H. Dettmar and Stephen Watt, 17–36. Ann Arbor: University of Michigan Press, 1996.

Matsumoto, Yasushi. "Noh and Kyōgen in 2004." In *Theatre Year-Book*, 47–56. Tokyo: International Theatre Institute, 2005.

McAteer, Michael. *Yeats and European Drama*. Cambridge: Cambridge University Press, 2010.

McCarren, Felicia. *Dancing Machines*. Stanford, Calif.: Stanford University Press, 2003.

McDonald, Keiko I. "Noh into Film: Kurosawa's *Throne of Blood*." *Journal of Film and Video* 39, no. 1 (1997): 36–41.

——. *Reading a Japanese Film: Cinema in Context*. Honolulu: University of Hawai'i Press, 2006.

McGee, Julie. "Primitivism on Trial: The 'Picasso and Africa' Exhibition in South Africa." *Anthropology and Aesthetics* 52 (2007): 161–67.

McMullan, Anna. *Theatre on Trial: Samuel Beckett's Later Drama*. New York: Routledge, 1993.

Meldrum, Andrew. "Stealing Beauty." *Guardian*, March 14, 2006. Available at http:// www.guardian.co.uk/artanddesign/2006/mar/15/art. Accessed February 15, 2015.

Michaels, Walter Benn. *The Shape of the Signifier: 1967 to the End of History*. Princeton, N.J.: Princeton University Press, 2004.

"Michio Ito, Internationally Famous Dancer and Group of Noted Solo Dancers: Touring the Pacific Coast and Western Canada During October and November 1933." Personal Collection of Michelle Ito.

Michio Ito Pioneering Dancer-Choreographer. DVD. Directed by Bonnie Oda Homsey. Produced by John Flynn. Los Angeles Dance Foundation, 2013.

"Michio Itow in Japanese Dances with the Assistance of Tulle Lindahl." Program notes read by Jose Ruben of the Washington Square Players. December 6 [1916]. Michio Ito Archives, New York Public Library for the Performing Arts.

Miller, James. *The Passion of Michel Foucault*. Cambridge, Mass.: Harvard University Press, 1993.

Miner, Earl. *The Japanese Tradition in British and American Literature*. Princeton, N.J.: Princeton University Press, 1958.

——. "Pound and Fenollosa Papers Relating to Nō." *Princeton University Chronicle* 53, no. 1 (1991): 12–16.

Miyake, Akiko. "Ezra Pound and Noh." In *A Guide to Ezra Pound and Ernest Fenollosa's "Classic Noh Theatre of Japan,"* edited by Akiko Miyake, Sanehide Kodama, and Nicholas Teele, xvii–lv. Orono, Maine: National Poetry Foundation and Ezra Pound Society of Japan, 1994.

Miyake, Akiko, Sanehide Kodama, and Nicholas Teele, eds. *A Guide to Ezra Pound and Ernest Fenollosa's "Classic Noh Theatre of Japan."* Orono, Maine: National Poetry Foundation and Ezra Pound Society of Japan, 1994.

"Modern and Classic Japanese Pantomimes and Dances." Neighborhood Playhouse Program, April 6, 1918. Michio Ito Archives, New York Public Library for the Performing Arts.

Monks, Aoife. "'Genuine Negroes and Real Bloodhounds': Cross-Dressing, Eugene O'Neill, the Wooster Group, and *The Emperor Jones*." *Modern Drama* 48, no. 3 (2005): 540–64.

Moore, Katrina, and Ruth Campbell. "Mastery with Age: The Appeal of the Traditional Arts to Senior Citizens in Contemporary Japan." *Japanstudien*, October 2009, 223–51.

Moorjani, Angela. "Directing or In-Directing Beckett: Or What Is Wrong with *Catastrophe*'s Director?" In "Historicizing Beckett / Issues of Performance." Special issue, *Samuel Beckett Today / Aujourd'hui* 15 (2005): 187–99.

Morrisson, Mark. "Performing the Pure Voice: Elocution, Verse Recitation, and Modernist Poetry in Prewar London." *Modernism / Modernity* 3, no. 3 (1996): 25–50.

Mountfort, Paul Rhys. *Ogam: The Celtic Oracle of the Trees.* Rochester, Vt.: Destiny, 2000.

Mueller, Roswitha. "Learning for a New Society: The *Lehrstück*." In *The Cambridge Companion to Brecht*, edited by Peter Thomson and Glendyr Sacks, 101–17. Cambridge: Cambridge University Press, 2006.

Murakata, Akiko. "Ernest F. Fenollosa's Studies of Nō: With Reference to His and Other Unpublished Manuscripts and Ezra Pound's Edition." *Eibungaku hyōron* 51, no. 2 (1986): 1–55.

Nagahata, Akitoshi. "Pound's Reception of Noh Reconsidered: The Image and the Voice." *Quaderni di palazzo serra* 15 (2008): 113–25.

"The New Plays." *New York Times*, November 12, 1916. Available at http://www.nytimes.com/ref /membercenter/nytarchive.html. Accessed June 21, 2015.

Noguchi, Yone. "The Everlasting Sorrow: A Japanese Noh Play." *Egoist* 4, no. 9 (1917): 141–43.

——. *Hagoromo.* In *The Summer Cloud: Prose Poems*, 1–4. Tokyo: Shunyōdō, 1906.

——. "The Japanese Mask Play." *Taiyō* 16, no. 10 (1910): 4–9.

——. "The Japanese Noh Play." *Egoist* 5, no. 7 (1918): 99.

——. "A Japanese Note on Yeats." 1911. In *Through the Torii*, 110–17. London: Elkin Mathews, 1914.

——. "A Japanese Poet on W. B. Yeats." *Bookman* 43 (1916): 431–33.

——. "Mr. Yeats and the No." *Japan Times*, November 3, 1907.

——. "No: The Japanese Play of Silence." In *The Spirit of Japanese Poetry*, 54–70. New York: Dutton, 1914.

——. "Ieitsu to nō." *Teki wo aise* [*Love the Enemy*]. Tokyo: Genbunsha, 1922.

——. *The Spirit of Japanese Poetry.* New York: Dutton, 1914.

——. "With a Foreign Critic at a No Performance." *Japan Times*, October 27, 1907.

"the-Noh.com." Available at www.the-noh.com. Last modified 2015. Accessed June 23, 2015.

"Noh Dramas, Once Sacred to Shinto Gods, Coming to Boston: Japanese Actors Devote Lives to Perfecting Its Mysteries—Wear Masks Centuries Old Never Before Seen Outside Land of Mikado." *Boston Post*, January 16, 1921. Clipping in Yeats Papers, National Library of Ireland, Dublin.

Noland, Carrie, and Sally Ann Ness, eds. *Migrations of Gesture.* Minneapolis: University of Minnesota Press, 2008.

O'Brien, Conor Cruise. "Passion and Cunning: An Essay on the Politics of W. B. Yeats." In *Passion and Cunning: Essays on Nationalism, Terrorism, and Revolution*, 8–61. New York: Simon & Schuster, 1988.

Okamuro, Minako. "Beckett, Yeats, and Noh: . . . but the clouds . . . as Theatre of Evocation." *Samuel Beckett Today / Aujourd'hui* 21 (2009): 165–77.

Olsen, Flemming. *Between Postivism and T. S. Eliot: Imagism and T. E. Hulme*. Odense: University Press of Southern Denmark, 2008.

O'Neill, Eugene. *Anna Christie, The Emperor Jones, The Hairy Ape*. New York: Vintage Books, 1972.

"Orientals Lend Weird Art." *Musical America*, September 1, 1917, 17.

O'Shea, Edward. *A Descriptive Catalogue of W. B. Yeats's Library*. New York: Garland, 1985.

Oshima, Shotaro. "Yeats and Michio Ito." *Yeats Society of Japan Annual Report* 6 (1971): 15–20.

Ozu, Yasujirō, director. *Late Spring* [Banshun]. Shōchiku eiga, Tokyo, 1949. Reissue, Criterion, New York, 2006.

——. *A Story of Floating Weeds* [Ukigusa monogatari]. Produced by Shōchiku eiga, Tokyo, 1934. Reissued with *Floating Weeds* [Ukigusa, 1959], Criterion, New York, 2004.

Parker, H. T. "Roshanara and Ito." 1917. In *Motion Arrested: Dance Reviews of H. T. Parker*, edited by Olive Holmes, 258–59. Middletown, Conn.: Wesleyan University Press, 1982.

Parker, Peter. "Britten and the Gang." In *Britten's Century*, edited by Mark Bostridge, 48–62. London: Bloomsbury, 2013.

Patterson, Anita. "Japonisme and Modernist Style in Afro-Caribbean Literature: The Art of Derek Walcott." *Review of International American Studies* 2, no. 2 (2007): 19–24.

Paz, Octavio. "Latin American Poetry." 1973. In *Convergences: Essays on Art and Literature*. Translated by Helen Lane, 201–16. San Diego: Harcourt Brace Jovanovich, 1987.

"The Peacock Dance." In *The Sunset Murder Case*. Film. Directed by Louis J. Gasnier. Performed by Sally Rand. Grand National Pictures, 1938.

Pellegrini, Ann. "Testimonial Sexuality; or, Queer Structures of Religious Feeling: Notes Toward an Investigation." *Journal of Dramatic Theory and Criticism* 20, no. 1 (2005): 93–102.

Peri, Noël. *Le Théâtre nô: Études sur le drame lyrique japonais*. Hanoi: Imprimerie d'Extrême-Orient, 1909.

Perloff, Marjorie. "Fascism, Anti-Semitism, Isolationism: Contextualizing the Case of EP." *Paideuma* 16 (1987): 7–21.

——. "Pound Ascendant." *Boston Review*, April–May 2004. Available at http://boston review.net/BR29.2/perloff.html. Accessed July 7, 2012.

Pflugfelder, Gregory M. *Cartographies of Desire: Male-Male Sexuality in Japanese Discourse, 1600–1950.* Berkeley: University of California Press, 1999.

Plomer, William. *Curlew River: A Parable for Church Performance Set to Music by Benjamin Britten.* London: Faber & Faber, 1964.

——. *Sado.* Oxford: Oxford University Press, 1990.

Pound, Ezra. *ABC of Reading.* 1934. Reprint, New York: New Directions, 1960.

——. "Affirmations VI: The Image and the Japanese Classical Stage." Unpublished essay. Ezra Pound Collection on Japanese Drama, Rare Books and Special Collections, Princeton University Library, Princeton, N.J.

——. "Cavalcanti." 1935. In *Theories of Translation,* edited by Rainer Schulte and John Biguenet, 83–92. Chicago: University of Chicago Press, 1992.

——. "The Classical Drama of Japan" ("Edited from Ernest Fenollosa's Manuscripts by Ezra Pound"). *Quarterly Review* 221 (1914): 450–77.

——. "The Classical Stage of Japan: Ernest Fenollosa's Work on the Japanese 'Noh.' " *Drama* 5 (1915): 199–247.

——. *Ezra Pound and Dorothy Shakespear: Their Letters, 1909–1914.* Edited by Omar Pound and A. Walton Litz. New York: New Directions, 1984.

——. *Ezra Pound and Japan: Letters and Essays.* Edited by Sanehide Kodama. Redding Ridge, Conn.: Black Swan, 1987.

——. *Ezra Pound Speaking: Radio Speeches of World War II.* Edited by Leonard W. Doob. Westport, Conn.: Greenwood Press, 1978.

——. "Hell." *Criterion,* April 1934. In *Literary Essays of Ezra Pound.* Edited and with an introduction by T. S. Eliot, 201–13. New York: New Directions, 1954.

——. "How I Began." *T. P.'s Weekly,* June 6, 1913, 707.

——. "In a Station of the Metro." *Poetry* 2 (1913): 12.

——. *Jefferson and/or Mussolini: L'Idea Statale, Fascism as I Have Seen It.* 1935. Reprint, New York: Liveright, 1970.

——. *The Letters of Ezra Pound to Alice Corbin Henderson.* Edited by Ira B. Nadel. Austin: University of Texas Press, 1993.

——. *A Memoir of Gaudier-Brzeska.* New York: New Directions, 1974.

——. *Nishikigi* ("Translated from the Japanese of Motokiyo [Zeami] by Ernest Fenollosa"). *Poetry* 4 (1914): 35–48.

——. *The Pisan Cantos.* New York: New Directions, 1948.

——. *Pound / Lewis: The Letters of Ezra Pound and Wyndham Lewis.* Edited by Timothy Materer. New York: New Directions, 1985.

——. "Provincialism the Enemy." 1917. In *Ezra Pound: Selected Prose, 1909–1965,* 189–203. New York: New Directions, 1973.

——. "Remy de Gourmont [Part I]." *Fortnightly Review*, December 1, 1915. In *Ezra Pound's Poetry and Prose: Contributions to Periodicals*, edited by Lea Baechler, A. Walton Litz, and James Longenbach, 2:125–32. New York: Garland, 1991.

——. *Selected Letters of Ezra Pound, 1907–1941*. Edited by D. D. Paige. New York: New Directions, 1971.

——. *The Selected Letters of Ezra Pound to John Quinn*. Edited by Timothy Materer. Durham, N.C.: Duke University Press, 1991.

——. *Selected Prose, 1909–1965*. New York: New Directions, 1973.

——. "Study of Noh Continues in the West." 1939. In *Ezra Pound in Japan*, by Sanehide Kodama, 154–57. Redding Ridge, Conn.: Black Swan, 1987.

——. "Sword-Dance and Spear-Dance: Texts of the Poems Used with Michio Itow's Dances. By Ezra Pound from Notes of Masirni Utchiyama." *Future* 1, no. 2 (1916): 54–55. In *Ezra Pound's Poetry and Prose: Contributions to Periodicals*, edited by Lea Baechler, A. Walton Litz, and James Longenbach, 2:182–83. New York: Garland, 1991.

——. "Three Cantos." *Poetry* 10, nos. 3–5 (1917).

——. *Tristan and Consolations of Matrimony*. 1916. In *Plays Modelled on the Noh*, edited by Donald Gallup. Toledo: Friends of the University of Toledo Libraries, 1987.

——. "Vorticism." *Fortnightly Review*, September 1914, 461–71. In *A Memoir of Gaudier-Brzeska*, 81–94. New York: New Directions, 1974.

Pound, Ezra, and Ernest Fenollosa. *The Classic Noh Theatre of Japan*. 1917. Reprint, New York: New Directions, 1959.

——. "Noh," or, *Accomplishment: A Study of the Classical Stage of Japan*. New York: Knopf, 1917.

Powell, Brian. "Communist *Kabuki*: A Contradiction in Terms?" In *A Kabuki Reader: History and Performance*, edited by Samuel L. Leiter, 167–85. New York: Sharpe, 2001.

——. "Japan's First Modern Theater: The Tsukiji Shōgekijō and Its Company, 1924–26." *Monumenta Nipponica* 30, no. 1 (1975): 69–85.

——. *Japan's Modern Theatre: A Century of Change and Continuity*. Abingdon: Routledge, 2013.

Powell, Neil. *Benjamin Britten: A Life for Music*. New York: Holt, 2013.

Pratt, William. *Ezra Pound and the Making of Modernism*. New York: AMS Press, 2007.

Preston, Carrie J. *Modernism's Mythic Pose: Gender, Genre, Solo Performance*. New York: Oxford University Press, 2011.

Pronko, Leonard. *Theatre East and West: Perspectives Toward a Total Theatre*. Berkeley: University of California Press, 1967.

Puar, Jasbir K. *Terrorist Assemblages: Homonationalism in Queer Times*. Durham, N.C.: Duke University Press, 2007.

Puchner, Martin. *Stage Fright: Modernism, Anti-Theatricality, and Drama*. Baltimore: Johns Hopkins University Press, 2002.

Qian, Zhaoming, ed. *Ezra Pound and China*. Ann Arbor: University of Michigan Press, 2006.

Rainey, Lawrence. *Ezra Pound and the Monument of Culture: Text, History, and the Malatesta Cantos*. Chicago: University of Chicago Press, 1991.

——. "Introduction to *At the Hawk's Well*." In *Modernism: An Anthology*, edited by Lawrence Rainey, 351–52. Malden, Mass.: Blackwell, 2005.

Ramazani, Jahan. *A Transnational Poetics*. Chicago: University of Chicago Press, 2009.

Ramos-Burkhart, M., ed. "American Repertory Dance Company." Los Angeles Dance Foundation. Available at http://www.ladancefoundation.org/#!thematic-concerts -listings/carf. Last modified 2012. Accessed March 10, 2015.

Rasula, Jed. "Make It New." *Modernism/Modernity* 17, no. 4 (2011): 713–33.

Rath, Eric C. "Challenging the Old Men: A Brief History of Women in Noh Theater." *Women & Performance: A Journal of Feminist Theory* 12, no. 1 (2001): 97–111.

——. *The Ethos of Noh: Actors and Their Art*. Cambridge, Mass.: Harvard University Press, 2004.

Read, Forrest. *Pound-Joyce*. London: Faber & Faber, 1968.

Richie, Donald. *Japanese Cinema: Film Style and National Character*. New York: Doubleday, 1971.

——. *Ozu*. Berkeley: University of California Press, 1974.

——. "Stories of *Floating Weeds*." Current, The Criterion Collection. Available at http: //www.criterion.com/current/posts/320-stories-of-floating-weeds. Last modified April 19, 2004. Accessed March 21, 2015.

Riordan, Kevin. "Performance in the Wartime Archive: Michio Ito at the Alien Enemy Hearing Board." Unpublished essay. Date unknown.

Robin, William. "Haunting Unpredictability." *New York Times*, August 4, 2011. Available at http://www.nytimes.com/2011/08/07/arts/music/matsukaze-opera-by-the -japanese-composer-toshio-hosokawa.html. Accessed May 18, 2015.

Rosenow, Ce. "Fenollosa's Legacy: The Japanese Network of Ezra Pound." *Philological Quarterly* 85, nos. 3–4 (2006): 371–89.

Rosse, Hermann. "Sketches of Oriental Theatres I." 1918. In *Sheldon Cheney's TheatreArts Magazine: Promoting a Modern American Theatre, 1916–1921*, edited by DeAnna M. Toten Beard, 115–16. Lanham, Md.: Scarecrow Press, 2010.

Rubin, Gayle. "Blood Under the Bridge: Reflections on Thinking Sex." In "Thinking Sex," edited by Heather Love. Special issue, *GLQ* 17, no. 1 (2010): 15–48.

——. "The Catacombs: A Temple of the Butthole." In *Leatherfolk: Radical Sex, People, Politics, and Practice*, edited by Mark Thompson, 119–41. Boston: Alyson Books, 1991.

——. "The Leather Menace: Comments on Politics and S/M." In *Coming to Power: Writings and Graphics on Lesbian S/M*, edited by Samois, 194–229. Boston: Alyson Books, 1981.

——. "Thinking Sex: Notes for a Radical Theory of the Politics of Sexuality." In *Pleasure and Danger: Exploring Female Sexuality*, edited by Carole S. Vance, 267–319. Boston: Routledge & Kegan Paul, 1984.

Ryu, Chishu. "Yasujiro Ozu." 1964. In *Yasujiro Ozu: A Critical Anthology*, edited by John Gillett and David Wilson, 38–39. London: British Film Institute, 1976.

Ryutani, Kyoko, and Kumiko Komine. Ito Technique and Repertory Class at Repertory Dance Theatre's Summerdance: Michio Ito. Salt Lake City, June 29–July 17, 2009.

Said, Edward. *Culture and Imperialism*. New York: Vintage Books, 1994.

——. *Orientalism*. New York: Vintage Books, 1978.

Saikaku Ihara. *The Great Mirror of Male Love*. Translated by Paul Gordon Schalow. Stanford, Calif.: Stanford University Press, 1990.

Salvato, Nick. *Uncloseting Drama: American Modernism and Queer Performance*. New Haven, Conn.: Yale University Press. 2010.

Salz, Jonah. "Beckett Kyogen Style: Lessons in Intercultural Translation." In *Performer Training: Developments Across Cultures*, edited by Ian Watson, 133–52. Amsterdam: Harwood, 2001.

——. "Leonard's Bastard Son: The Noho Theatre Group's First Two Decades." *Mime Journal* 22 (2002–2003): 135–53.

Samois, ed. *Coming to Power: Writings and Graphics on Lesbian S/M*. Boston: Alyson Books, 1981.

Sato, Tadao. *Currents in Japanese Cinema*. Translated by Gregory Barrett. Tokyo: Kodansha, 1982.

"Satoru Shimazaki Performing Works of Pioneer Choreographer." At the "Theatre of The Open Eye," October 2–7, 1979. Personal Collection of Michelle Ito.

Saunders, Mae. "Arts of Music and Dance Provide Rare Treat Here." *Bakersfield Californian*, December 5, 1933. Personal Collection of Michelle Ito.

Scholz-Cionca, Stanca, and Christopher Balme, eds. *Nō Theatre Transversal*. Munich: Iudicium, 2008.

Schrader, Paul. *Transcendental Style in Film: Ozu, Bresson, Dryer*. Berkeley: University of California Press, 1972.

Schuchard, Ronald. "The Countess Cathleen and the Revival of the Bardic Arts." *South Carolina Review* 32, no. 1 (1999): 24–37.

——. *The Last Minstrels: Yeats and the Revival of the Bardic Arts*. New York: Oxford University Press, 2008.

Scruton, Roger. "We Need the English Music That the Arts Council Hates." *Spectator*, April 16, 2008. Available at http://www.spectator.co.uk/features/615311/we-need -the-english-music-that-the-arts-council-hates/. Accessed March 26, 2015.

Sedgwick, Eve Kosofsky. *The Epistemology of the Closet*. Berkeley: University of California Press, 1990.

———. *Tendencies*. Durham, N.C.: Duke University Press, 1993.

———. *Touching Feeling: Affect, Pedagogy, Performativity*. Durham, N.C.: Duke University Press, 2003.

———. *The Weather in Proust*. Edited by Jonathan Goldberg. Durham, N.C.: Duke University Press, 2011.

Sekine, Masaru, and Christopher Murray. *Yeats and the Noh: A Comparative Study*. Savage, Md.: Barnes & Noble, 1990.

Serper, Zvika. "The Bloodied Sacred Pine Tree: A Dialectical Depiction of Death in *Throne of Blood* and *Ran*." *Journal of Film and Video* 52, no. 2 (2000): 13–27.

Sexual Offenses Act of 1967. National Archives. Text available at http://www.legislation .gov.uk/ukpga/1967/60. Accessed March 26, 2015.

Shepart, Todd D. "FORUM: On the Political Implications of Using the Term 'Queer,' as in 'Queer Politics,' 'QueerStudies,' and 'Queer Pedagogy.'" *Radical Teacher* 45 (1994): 52–57.

Sheppard, Anthony W. *Revealing Masks: Exotic Influences and Ritualized Performance in Modernist Music Theater*. Berkeley: University of California Press, 2001.

Sherry, Vincent. *Ezra Pound, Wyndham Lewis, and Radical Modernism*. New York: Oxford University Press, 1993.

Shigehisa Tokutarō. "Fenollosa's Ashes and Japan." *Comparative Literature* 2 (1959): 83–84.

Shigeyama, Akira. Introductory Kyōgen Class. Kyoto, Japan, April 28, 2009.

Shimazaki, Satoru. "Interview with Billie Mahoney." *Dance On*. Videocassette, 28 minutes. June 29, 1989. Jerome Robbins Dance Division, New York Public Library for the Performing Arts.

Shioji, Ursula. *Ezra Pound's "Pisan Cantos" and the Noh*. Frankfurt am Main: Lang, 1998.

Shurtleff, William, and Akiko Aoyagi. *The Book of Tofu*. Brookline, Mass.: Autumn Press, 1975.

Sieburth, Richard. Introduction to Ezra Pound, *The Pisan Cantos*, ix–xlii. New York: New Directions, 2003.

Simone, R. Thomas. "Beckett's Other Trilogy: *Not I, Footfalls, and Rockaby*." In *"Make Sense Who May": Essays on Samuel Beckett's Later Works*, edited by R. J. Davis and L. St. J. Butler, 56–65. Gerards Cross: Smythe, 1988.

Solano, Solita. "Michio Itow's Good Deed: The Japanese Dancer Has Introduced Two Specimens of the Native 'Noh' Drama of Antiquity to This Country." *New York Tribune*, 1916. Personal Collection of Michelle Ito.

Sontag, Susan. "Fascinating Fascism." In *Under the Sign of Saturn*, 73–108. New York: Farrar, Straus & Giroux, 1972.

Sorensen, Lars-Martin. *Censorship of Japanese Films During the U.S. Occupation of Japan: The Cases of Yasujiro Ozu and Akira Kurosawa*. Lewiston, N.Y.: Mellen, 2009.

Sorgenfrei, Carol Fisher. "Countering 'Theoretical Imperialism': Some Possibilities from Japan." *Theatre Research International* 32, no. 3 (2007): 312–24.

——. "Strategic Unweaving: Itō Michio and the Diasporic Dancing Body." In *Politics of Interweaving Performance Cultures: Beyond Postcolonialism*, edited by Erika Fischer-Lichte, Torsten Jost, and Saskya Iris Jain, 201–22. Florence, Ky.: Taylor & Francis, 2014.

Sotiropoulos, Karen. *Staging Race: Black Performers in Turn of the Century America*. Cambridge, Mass.: Harvard University Press, 2006.

"Specimens of the Native 'Noh' Drama of Antiquity to This Country." *New York Tribune*, 1916. Personal Collection of Michelle Ito.

Spice, Nicholas. "Darkness Audible." *London Review of Books* 15, no. 3 (1993): 3–6.

Spivak, Gayatri Chakravorty. *A Critique of Postcolonial Reason*. Cambridge, Mass.: Harvard University Press, 1999.

——. *In Other Worlds*. New York: Routledge, 1998.

——. *Outside in the Teaching Machine*. New York: Routledge, 1993.

——. "Translating into English." In *Nation, Language, and the Ethics of Translation*, edited by Sandra Bermann and Michael Wood, 93–110. Princeton, N.J.: Princeton University Press, 2005.

St. Denis, Ruth. "Music Visualization." 1925. In *Dance as a Theatre Art*, 2nd ed., edited by Selma Jeanne Cohen, 128–33. Princeton, N.J.: Princeton Book, 1992.

Steen, Shannon. "Melancholy Bodies: Racial Subjectivity and Whiteness in O'Neill's *The Emperor Jones*." *Theatre Journal* 52, no. 3 (2000): 339–59.

Sueyoshi, Amy. *Queer Compulsions: Race, Nation, and Sexuality in the Affairs of Yone Noguchi*. Honolulu: University of Hawai'i Press, 2012.

Sun, Hong. "Pound's Quest for Confucian Ideals: The Chinese History Cantos." In *Ezra Pound and China*, edited by Zhaoming Qian, 96–119. Ann Arbor: University of Michigan Press, 2006.

Surette, Leon. *Dreams of a Totalitarian Utopia*. Montreal: McGill–Queen's University Press, 2011.

Suvin, Darko. *Lessons of Japan: Assayings of Some Intercultural Stances*. Montreal: Ciadest, 1996.

——. "Revelation vs. Conflict: A Lesson from Nō Plays for a Comparative Dramaturgy." *Theatre Journal* 46, no. 4 (1994): 534–38.

Suzuki, Daisetz Teitaro. *Essays in Zen Buddhism*. London: Luzac, 1927. Yeats Papers, National Library of Ireland, Dublin.

Takahashi, Mutsurō. *Taka no I*. Kanze Noh Theatre, Tokyo, December 22, 1990.

Takahashi, Yasunari. "The Ghost Trio: Beckett, Yeats, and Noh." In *The Empire of Signs*, edited by Yoshihiko Ikegama, 257–67. Amsterdam: Benjamin, 1991.

——. "The Theatre of Mind: Samuel Beckett and the Noh." *Encounter* 58, no. 4 (1982): 66–73.

Takahime. Film. Written by Mario Yokomichi. Produced by NHK. Tokyo, Japan, June 30, 1998.

Takeishi, Midori. *Japanese Elements in Michio Ito's Early Period (1915–1924): Meetings of East and West in the Collaborative Works*. Edited and revised by David Pacun. Tokyo: Gendaitosho, 2006.

Takeuchi, Akiko. "Nō no hon'yaku: bunka no hon'yaku wa ikanishite kanōka [Fenollosa, Pound, Konishi Jin'ichi: Creative misunderstandings in translations]." 21 seiki COE kokusai nihongaku kenkyū sōsho 8 (2007): 129–52.

——. "Translation and Creative Misunderstanding: Ezra Pound and Konishi Jin'ichi." Paper presented at the annual convention of the Modern Language Association, Los Angeles, 2011.

Tamura. Neighborhood Playhouse Program, January 29 and 30, 1921. Michio Ito Archives, box MGZA, New York Public Library for the Performing Arts.

Tatchell, Peter. *Europe in the Pink: Lesbian and Gay Equality in the New Europe*. London: GMP, 1992.

Taylor, Richard. *The Drama of W. B. Yeats: Irish Myth and the Japanese Nō*. New Haven, Conn.: Yale University Press, 1976.

"Teatro Hidalgo—Michio Ito." *Periodico el mundo*, May 4, 1934. Personal Collection of Michelle Ito.

Teele, Roy E. "A Balance Sheet on Pound's Translations of Noh Plays." *Books Abroad* 39, no. 2 (1965): 168–70.

Theatre Year-Book. Tokyo: Japan Centre, International Theatre Institute, 1989–2007.

Thompson, Mark, ed. *Leatherfolk: Radical Sex, People, Politics, and Practice*. Boston: Alyson Books, 1991.

"Tour of Resorts for War Charities." *New York Times*, July 10, 1917. *New York Times* online archives. Accessed March 10, 2015.

Townsend, Julie. *The Choreography of Modernism: La Danseuse, 1830–1930*. Oxford: Legenda, 2009.

Trier, Barbara Geilhorn. "Between Self-Empowerment and Discrimination: Women in Nō Today." In Nō Theatre Transversal, edited by Stanca Scholz-Cionca and Christopher Balme, 106–20. Munich: Iudicium, 2008.

Tsukui, Nobuko. Ezra Pound and Japanese Noh Plays. Washington, D.C.: University Press of America, 1983.

Turnbull, Stephen. Kawanakajima, 1553–1564. Oxford: Osprey, 2003.

Tyler, Royall, trans. and ed. Japanese Nō Dramas. London: Penguin, 1992.

Tyler, William J., ed. Modanizumu: Modernist Fiction from Japan, 1913–1938. Honolulu: University of Hawai'i Press, 2008.

Ury, Marian. Review of A History of Japanese Literature, by Konishi Jin'ichi. Vol. 1. Journal of Asian Studies 44, no. 4 (1985): 842–44.

Vance, Carole S., ed. Pleasure and Danger: Exploring Female Sexuality. Boston: Routledge & Kegan Paul, 1984.

Vincent, J. Keith. Two-Timing Modernity: Homosocial Narrative in Modern Japanese Fiction. Cambridge, Mass.: Harvard University Press, 2012.

Vollman, William T. Kissing the Mask: Beauty, Understatement and Femininity in Japanese Noh Theater. New York: HarperCollins, 2010.

Waley, Arthur. The Nō Plays of Japan. New York: Knopf, 1922.

Wellman, Rita. The String of the Samisen. 1917. In The Provincetown Plays, edited by George Cram Cook and Frank Shay, 205–38. Cincinnati: Stewart & Kidd, 1921.

Wells, Keiko Sekiguchi. "Pound's Hagoromo as an Imagist Poem." Ehime daigaku kyōyōbu kiyō 22 (1989): 25–38.

Wetmore, Kevin J., Jr. "Healing the (Metaphysically) Sick Theatre: The Buddhist Ibsen in Christian Japan." In Inexorable Modernity: Japan's Grappling with Modernity in the Arts, edited by Hiroshi Nara, 183–97. Lanham, Md.: Lexington Books, 2007.

Whitelaw, Billie. Billie Whitelaw . . . Who He? New York: St. Martin's Press, 1995.

Williams, R. John. "Modernist Scandals: Ezra Pound's Translations of 'the' Chinese Poem." In Orient and Orientalisms in US-American Poetry and Poetics, edited by Sabine Sielke and Christian Kloeckner, 145–65. Frankfurt am Main: Lang, 2009.

Willsher, Kim. "France's Burqa Ban Upheld by Human Rights Court." Guardian, July 1, 2014. Available at http://www.theguardian.com/world/2014/jul/01/france-burqa-ban-upheld-human-rights-court. Accessed May 18, 2015.

Wilson, John K. Patriotic Correctness: Academic Freedom and Its Enemies. Boulder, Colo.: Paradigm, 2008.

Wong, Yutian. "Artistic Utopias: Michio Ito and the Trope of the International." In Worlding Dance, edited by Susan Leigh Foster, 144–62. Basingstoke: Palgrave Macmillan, 2009.

Woolfe, Zachary. "The Monks Are Asked to Go Natural." *New York Times*, July 30, 2015. Available at http://www.nytimes.com/2013/07/31/arts/music/mark-morris-directing -brittens-curlew-river.html. Accessed June 29, 2015.

Woollcott, Alexander. "The New O'Neill Play." *New York Times*, November 7, 1920. Available at http://www.eoneill.com/artifacts/reviews/ej1_times.htm. Accessed June 28, 2015.

The Wooster Group. *The Emperor Jones*. Directed by Elizabeth LeCompte and Christopher Kondek. 2009. DVD.

The Wooster Group Work Book. Edited by Andrew Quick. New York: Routledge, 2007.

Worth, Katharine. *The Irish Drama of Europe from Yeats to Beckett*. London: Athlone Press, 1978.

Worthen, W. B. *Modern Drama and the Rhetoric of the Theater*. Berkeley: University of California Press, 1992.

Yasuda, Kenneth K. "The Structure of Hagoromo, a Nō." *Harvard Journal of Asiatic Studies* 33 (1973): 5–89.

"Yeats's Noh Play to Be Seen Here." *New York Times*, July 7, 1918. Available at http://www .nytimes.com/ref/membercenter/nytarchive.html. Accessed June 21, 2015.

Yeats, W. B. At the Hawk's Well. 1917. In *Plays and Controversies*, 337–56. New York: Macmillan, 1924.

——. *"At the Hawk's Well" and "The Cat and the Moon": Manuscript Materials*. Edited by Andrew Parkin. Ithaca, N.Y.: Cornell University Press, 2010.

——. *The Collected Letters of W. B. Yeats*. Vol. 1, *1865–1895*, edited by John Kelly and Eric Domville. Oxford: Oxford University Press, 1986.

——. "The Death of Cuchulain." In *The Variorum Edition of the Plays of W. B. Yeats*, edited by Russell K. Alspach and Catherine C. Alspach, 1051–63. New York: Macmillan, 1966.

——. *Essays and Introductions*. New York: Macmillan, 1961.

——. *Fairy and Folk Tales of the Irish Peasantry*. London: Scott, 1888.

——. *Four Plays for Dancers*. In *Plays and Controversies*, 331–74. London: Macmillan, 1921.

——. "Instead of a Theatre." *To-Day* 1, no. 3 (1917).

——. *The Letters of W. B. Yeats*. Edited by Allan Wade. London: Rupert Hart-Davis, 1954.

——. *On Baile's Strand*. 1903. London: Bullen, 1907.

——. "The Only Jealousy of Emer." *Poetry: A Magazine of Verse* 13, no. 4 (1919): 175–93.

——. *Per Amica Silentia Lunae*. 1917. In *Mythologies*, 317–42. New York: Macmillan, 1959.

——. *Plays and Controversies*. New York: Macmillan, 1924.

——. "Swedenborg, Mediums, and the Desolate Places." 1914. In *Explorations*, 30–70. New York: Macmillan, 1962.

——. *The Variorum Edition of the Plays of W. B. Yeats*. Edited by Russell K. Alspach and Catherine C. Alspach. London: Macmillan, 1966.

Yeats, W. B., and Lady Augusta Gregory. *The Irish National Theatre: Its Work and Its Needs*. 1909. Yeats Papers, National Library of Ireland, Dublin.

Yokomichi Mario. *The Hawk Princess* [*Takahime*]. Unpublished translation by Don Kenny. Date unknown.

Yoshida, Kiju. *Ozu's Anti-Cinema*. Translated by Daisuke Miyao and Kyoko Hirano. Ann Arbor: University of Michigan Press, 2003.

Young, B. W. "'Reading at Intervals': Benjamin Britten's Romantic Poetry." *Essays in Criticism* 62, no. 2 (2012): 178–97.

Zeami. *Zeami: Performance Notes*. Translated by Thomas Hare. New York: Columbia University Press, 2008.

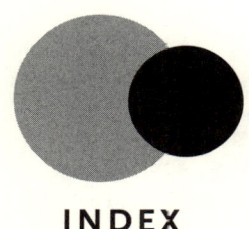

INDEX

Numbers in italics refer to pages on which illustrations appear.